THE ARAB NAHDA AS POPULAR ENTERTAINMENT

THE ARAB NAHDA AS POPULAR ENTERTAINMENT

Mass Culture and Modernity in the Middle East

Edited by
Hala Auji, Raphael Cormack, Alaaeldin Mahmoud

I.B. TAURIS
LONDON • NEW YORK • OXFORD • NEW DELHI • SYDNEY

BLOOMSBURY ACADEMIC
Bloomsbury Publishing Plc, 50 Bedford Square, London, WC1B 3DP, UK
Bloomsbury Publishing Inc, 1385 Broadway, New York, NY 10018, USA
Bloomsbury Publishing Ireland, 29 Earlsfort Terrace, Dublin 2, D02 AY28, Ireland

BLOOMSBURY, I.B. TAURIS and the I.B. Tauris logo are trademarks
of Bloomsbury Publishing Plc

First published in Great Britain 2024
This paperback edition published in 2025

Copyright © Hala Auji, Raphael Cormack, and Alaaeldin Mahmoud, 2024

Hala Auji, Raphael Cormack, and Alaaeldin Mahmoud have asserted their
rights under the Copyright, Designs and Patents Act, 1988, to be identified as
Editors of this work.

Copyright Individual Chapters © 2024 Diana Abbani, Hala Auji, Raphael Cormack,
Till Grallert, Walid El Khachab, Alaaeldin Mahmoud, Elizabeth Matsushita,
Pelle Valentin Olsen, Thana Al-Shakhs.

For legal purposes the Acknowledgments on p. viii constitute
an extension of this copyright page.

Series design by Adriana Brioso
Cover image: Fatma Rouchdi in Images, 1929. (© Centre d'Études Alexandrines)

All rights reserved. No part of this publication may be: i) reproduced or transmitted
in any form, electronic or mechanical, including photocopying, recording or by means
of any information storage or retrieval system without prior permission in writing
from the publishers; or ii) used or reproduced in any way for the training, development
or operation of artificial intelligence (AI) technologies, including generative AI technologies.
The rights holders expressly reserve this publication from the text and data mining
exception as per Article 4(3) of the Digital Single Market Directive (EU) 2019/790.

Bloomsbury Publishing Inc does not have any control over, or responsibility for,
any third-party websites referred to or in this book. All internet addresses given
in this book were correct at the time of going to press. The author and publisher
regret any inconvenience caused if addresses have changed or sites have
ceased to exist, but can accept no responsibility for any such changes.

A catalogue record for this book is available from the British Library.

Library of Congress Cataloging-in-Publication Data
Names: Auji, Hala, editor. | Cormack, Raph, editor. | Mahmoud, Alaaeldin, editor.
Title: The Arab nahda as popular entertainment : mass culture and modernity
in the Middle East / edited by Hala Auji, Raphael Cormack, Alaaeldin Mahmoud.
Description: 1st Edition. | New Yorkn NY : I.B Tauris, an imprint of
Bloomsbury Publishing, 2023. | Includes bibliographical references and index.
Identifiers: LCCN 2023020528 (print) | LCCN 2023020529 (ebook) |
ISBN 9780755647408 (hardback) | ISBN 9780755647446 (paperback) | ISBN
9780755647415 (pdf) | ISBN 9780755647422 (epub) | ISBN 9780755647439
Subjects: LCSH: Civilization, Arab–Western influences. | Civilization, Arab–20th century.
| Middle East–Social life and customs–20th century. | Arab countries–Intellectual
life–20th century.
Classification: LCC DS57 .A73 2023 (print) | LCC DS57 (ebook) |
DDC 909.0974927083–dc23/eng/20230829
LC record available at https://lccn.loc.gov/2023020528
LC ebook record available at https://lccn.loc.gov/2023020529

ISBN: HB: 978-0-7556-4740-8
PB: 978-0-7556-4744-6
ePDF: 978-0-7556-4741-5
eBook: 978-0-7556-4742-2

Typeset by Deanta Global Publishing Services, Chennai, India

For product safety related questions contact productsafety@bloomsbury.com.

To find out more about our authors and books visit www.bloomsbury.com
and sign up for our newsletters.

CONTENTS

List of Figures   vii
Acknowledgments   viii
Notes on Transliteration and Translation   ix

INTRODUCTION: THE NAHDA AND POPULAR ENTERTAINMENT   1
    Hala Auji, Raphael Cormack, and Alaaeldin Mahmoud

PART ONE
LEISURE & MORALITY

Chapter 1
PROPER FUN? STRUGGLES OVER POPULAR ENTERTAINMENT IN
LATE OTTOMAN DAMASCUS (1875–1914)   17
    Till Grallert

Chapter 2
IMMORAL ENLIGHTENMENT: MEDIA AND MORAL ANXIETY IN THE
LATE NAHDA   39
    Walid El Khachab

Chapter 3
NOCTURNAL BAGHDAD: NIGHTCLUBS AND POPULAR ENTERTAINMENT   53
    Pelle Valentin Olsen

PART TWO
PERFORMANCE & SPECTACLE

Chapter 4
FEMALE PERFORMERS IN BEIRUT (1900–1930s): AGENTS AND
METAPHORS OF SOCIAL CHANGE   69
    Diana Abbani

Chapter 5
ANDALUSI MUSIC AS CULTURAL RENAISSANCE IN TWENTIETH-
CENTURY NORTH AFRICA   82
    Liz Matsushita

Chapter 6
ON THE ROAD: SULAYMAN AL-QARDAHI AND THE TRAVELING
THEATRICAL TROUPES OF THE NAHDA   100
    Raphael Cormack

PART THREE
MEDIA & THE IMAGINARY

Chapter 7
INCREDIBLE PRINTS: THE INTERSECTION OF KNOWLEDGE AND
ENTERTAINMENT IN JOURNAL ILLUSTRATIONS   117
    Hala Auji

Chapter 8
EGYPTOMANIAC EGYPTIANS? ANCIENT EGYPT IN THE POPULAR
LITERARY IMAGINARY IN TWENTIETH CENTURY EGYPT   144
    Alaaeldin Mahmoud

Chapter 9
THE EARLY EGYPTIAN FILM INDUSTRY AND THE FORMATION OF
NATIONALITY: STUDYING MUHAMMAD KARIM'S *ZAYNAB* AS A
VISION OF MODERN STANDARDS   157
    Thana al-Shakhs

List of Contributors   177
Notes   180
Bibliography   215
Index   233

FIGURES

1.1	Crowded riverbanks with the municipal garden to the right	18
1.2	Darwishiyya Street south of the future entrance to Suq al-Hamidiyya after remodeling according to the "new style" in the mid-1880s. Note the sign for "Cazino Munchie" on the left and the newly stratified traffic	20
1.3	View of Suq 'Ali Pasha with men sitting around a low table next to a water basin. Behind the basin, men sit in front of a café, Damascus, 1909	21
1.4	The new municipal café during remodeling, May 1894	26
1.5	Suq al-Khayl, Damascus (Bain News Service)	30
1.6	Midan Road south of Suq al-Sinaniyya, Damascus	32
1.7	Female spectators crowding the rooftops along Midan Road watching the Hajj caravan's departure, Damascus	33
1.8	Detail from Figure 1.7	34
1.9	Woman wearing a *mandil* on Darwishiyya Street, Damascus. Detail from *An Oriental Bazaar*, American Colony, Jerusalem, 1900	35
7.1	Engraving of "the Lofty Tower" picturing the world fair at Antwerp in 1894	118
7.2	Portrait of Ali Pasha Mubarak	125
7.3	Celestial diagram of Earth's orbit around the sun	128
7.4	Diagram of telegraphic equipment	129
7.5	Page from an article featuring a diagram of different bacteria as seen via a microscope	130
7.6	Photoengraving of electric sparks	131
7.7	Diagram of "Mars" from three distances	133
7.8	Image of "Earth from the moon"	134
7.9	"Image of Millie Christine while she dances"	136
7.10	"Image of Millie Christine from her back"	137
7.11	Engraving of a group of people accompanying an article on Egyptians	138
7.12	Engraving of three figures accompanying an article on Egyptians	139
7.13	Engraving of a North African figure accompanying an article on Egyptians	140
7.14	Engraving of Madame De Staël	141
9.1	*Zaynab*'s film advertisement, *Ruz al-Yusuf*, March 11, 1930	166

ACKNOWLEDGMENTS

We, as editors of this volume, are very grateful to the people who have helped us in various ways, including providing comments on the work text. The germ of this book emerged as a panel organized by Alaaeldin Mahmoud at the MESA 2020 54th Annual Meeting, which took place virtually on October 5–17, 2020, under the title "Global and Local Popular Entertainments of the Nahdah: An Interdisciplinary Approach." In this panel, we received many insightful comments from both established and emerging scholars. Since then, it has evolved in various ways and we are grateful to all who helped us along the way. We would like to thank the editors at I. B. Tauris/Bloomsbury Rory Gormley and Yasmin Garcha as well as the anonymous reviewers who provided positive feedback at various stages of this manuscript's journey.

Hala Auji would like to thank the staff members of the Archives and Special Collections department, particularly Ms. Samar Mikati and Ms. Shaden Dada, at the American University of Beirut's Jafet Library for their assistance with procuring images and accessing research materials. Auji would also like to thank the Universitätsbibliothek Tübingen, the Universitäts- und Landesbibliothek Bonn, and the Bayerischen Staatsbibliothek München for granting her permission to reproduce images from their collections.

Raphael Cormack would like to thank Adam Mestyan, Pamela Takefman, and Elijah Takefman.

Alaaeldin Mahmoud would like to thank Maguid Mustafa Al-Saʿidy, Karam Youssef, and the librarians and staff at Al-Babtain Library for Arabic Poetry in Kuwait for their assistance in locating and accessing rare Arabic periodicals such as *Ruz al-Yusuf*, *al-Sabah*, and *al-Masrah*, as well as granting permission to reproduce images when needed.

NOTES ON TRANSLITERATION AND TRANSLATION

This volume uses the simplified version of the *International Journal of Middle East Studies* (IJMES) transliteration guidelines for Arabic and Ottoman Turkish words. We do not use diacritics except in cases where the ʿayn or *hamza* need to be preserved. Foreign language words have been transliterated into English and italicized. The exception is when foreign terms have a commonly used equivalent in English or appear in the *Merriam-Webster*. In those cases, we used the spellings given in that dictionary.

Spellings of Arabic proper names were standardized throughout the volume. However, slight variations will expectedly exist. For example, we opted for using the *j* in spelling names such as Hijazi and Najib; variants like Higazy and Naguib might occur. The final *i* as in Wahbi and Rushdi might appear as *y* (Wahby, Rushdy). The long *i* as in Salima and Sabiha will be used instead of the *ee*. Proper names starting with ʿ*Abd* will be spelled as ʿAbd al-Wahhab, rather than ʿAbdel-Wahhab or ʿAbdul-Wahhab. With proper names such as Husayn and Haykal, we opted for using *ay* rather than *ai* as in Husain and Haikal.

As a general rule, we opted for the most common spelling of Arabic proper names in the case of existing variants such as Nazim (instead of Nadhim or Nathem). With names that have different variants in colloquial and Modern Standard Arabic (MSA), we selected the MSA version, such as Yusuf, in preference to Youssef, Yousef, or Yusif.

INTRODUCTION

THE NAHDA AND POPULAR ENTERTAINMENT

Hala Auji, Raphael Cormack, and Alaaeldin Mahmoud

In 1877, during the *mawlid* of al-Sayyid al-Badawi (a Sufi festival) in Tanta (Egypt), a young ʿAbd Allah al-Nadim (1845–96), the Alexandria-born novice littérateur who would soon become one of Egypt's notable journalists and orators, was strolling the streets of the Nile Delta city. While al-Nadim was seated in al-Sabbagh coffee shop in the company of a cohort of literati such as Shaykh ʿAli Abu'l Nasr and Shaykh Ahmad Abu'l Faraj al-Damanhuri, he cast his eyes on a *zajal* event, a public literary contest. Overhearing some commentary from al-Nadim's cohort, one of the contestants came up to the group and proceeded to panegyrize each of them. When he got to al-Nadim, he addressed the latter with:

> Gimme your cash, Soldier [*Enʿim bi ershak ya gindi*] /
> Or else some clothing Mister [*walla eksina ummal ya afandi*]
> Cos I have, I swear, been [*Walla wi hyatak ʿandi*] /
> for two months sufferin' hunger [*baʿa li shahrin tul giʿan*]

To that, al-Nadim replied jokingly:

> As for money, I ain't submit [*Amma el fulus ana maddishi*] /
> And you say ya aint' let [*wenta teʾulli mamshishi*]
> My high head, I must admit [*Yetlaʿ ʿalaya hashishi*] /
> tells I should show my anger [*aaʾum amallaslak li-wdan*]¹

The mirthful exchange between the two figures captures the boisterous spirit of *zajal* exchanges and its often-tongue-in-cheek playfulness with quotidian colloquialisms and class distinctions. In his journal *al-Ustaz* (The Master), al-Nadim recounted this happenstance, a public encounter, over a full ten pages. Through a detailed retelling of the various verse exchanges between him and his literary rival, al-Nadim was able to convey to his journal readers the sense of mass amusement and excitement that was in the air that evening. Serendipitously, the spontaneous *zajal* contest between the two men, which quickly drew a crowd and morphed into a major spectacle, was attended by the community's highest dignitaries such as Shahin Kanj Pasha, the inspector general for Lower Egypt. As a fan of literary entertainment, Kanj Pasha moved the contest between al-Nadim and the *udabati* (his minstrels) to the vicinity of his house in Tanta so that it would be a spectacle viewed by "thousands of people." To heighten the excitement and stakes, the Pasha also played the role of contest judge. He even set rules for the "game": if the *udabatiyya* (minstrels) could out-perform al-Nadim, they would each be awarded 1,000 piasters (ten Egyptian pounds). However, if al-Nadim was undefeated, the *udabatiyya* would each be flagellated twenty times with a whip. As is typical of these hyperbolical tales, al-Nadim was declared the victor, yet the purportedly kind-hearted Pasha changed his mind about whipping the minstrels and tipped them each five Egyptian pounds instead of the promised flagellations.

Despite it being a likely overdramatized retelling of this entertaining encounter, al-Nadim's story remains one of few extant (purportedly) first-hand accounts describing the happenings of a *zajal* competition, or Arabic minstrelsy, as it unfolded on the streets of Tanta in late Ottoman Egypt. As a key figure of the eventual ʿUrabi Revolt (1881–2) that would unfold only a few years after this incident and a prominent voice among the scholarship of the Arab Nahda, al-Nadim's emphasis on this public event in his literary journal exemplifies the spirit of the age that saw myriad intersections between the revivalist culture of the elite intelligentsia and the populist interests of general audiences. As a pivotal intellectual movement in modern, Arabic cultural history, the Nahda (roughly translated as "Arab Renaissance") of the long nineteenth century has primarily been seen as belonging to and concerned with the literary elite of key metropoles like Cairo, Alexandria, and Beirut, with a list of Nahdawi scholars who have been seen as central protagonists of and contributors to this moment.

While the Nahda first emerged from literary-scientific associations, publishing circles, and other exclusive realms of the educated elite, its audiences and impact were certainly not limited to this small coterie of readers. Rather, what encounters like the one retold by al-Nadim demonstrate is how Nahdawis, their works, and their concerns came together in unplanned and expansive ways that went beyond, and even blurred, the professedly closed-off nature of elite cultural practices at this time. Through the *zajal* competition, the playful improvised exchanges, and the publication in which this event is retold, the example from al-Nadim's *al-Ustaz* brings together orality, performance, spectacle, publishing, and mass audiences. With contributions that discuss similar intersections between these cultural vectors, this collection of essays endeavors to imagine a framework for the Nahda as a *popular* movement that took on an alternative existence in the streets among everyday masses. In essence, the book's chapters explore possible answers to the question: What would the Arab Nahda look like when taken from the perspective of popular culture or "ordinary people"?

Scholarship has shown that the Nahda, as a product of the age of modernization and reforms, engaged various, often opposing, views on politics and society, as well as language, literature, and culture writ large. These perspectives, which were promoted, negotiated, and debated in a wide range of mediums and forums, from literary journals to theatrical performances, were accessed by members of various social strata—educated and illiterate alike—as well as various spheres of contact and exchange, as part of the "lived experiences of modernity."[2] Recent studies on the

Nahda have evidenced the multivalent nature of Nahdawi thinking, scholarship, and sociopolitical projects/commitments. A bilingual anthology of texts, edited by Tarek El-Ariss, has shown the breadth of intellectual production at the time, including extracts taken from poems, plays, novels, articles, and other genres on a range of topics including feminism, religious tolerance, politics, censorship, and literary theory.[3] Scholarly work on the Nahda has expanded this movement's focus by taking on various new approaches and topics, from translation to literary studies, political theory, intellectual history, psychoanalysis, and more.[4] At the risk of falling into cliché, the idea that there was not just one Nahda but many different Nahdas is now far more prevalent.

Through contributions spanning the late nineteenth to the mid-twentieth century across the Arab world, including Iraq, Egypt, Lebanon, Syria, and Morocco, this collection offers another new perspective on the classic issues of the Nahda, such as literature, print culture, and nationalism, by exploring their significance to popular fiction, theater, cabarets, street culture, music, film, performance, and visual culture. More importantly, many of the book's contributions consider how these mediums and practices overlapped in the context of the public spheres of everyday life in cities, as well as rural contexts. With chapters on Baghdad, Damascus, and Morocco, the collection spotlights places that are often overlooked in the history of the late nineteenth to the mid-twentieth-century Arab region. By turning the focus to café goers, nightclub performers, filmmakers, and more, this collection expands the remit of who participated in the Nahda and in what ways they did. More importantly, this book's contributions endeavor to emphasize the central role that everyday audiences—from illiterate members and public spectators, to actors and dancers—played in engaging with, producing, and popularizing the Nahda as a movement, and the importance that entertainment events, activities, and spaces played in this process.

The Nahda and Everyday Entertainment

The Arab Nahda—it is often stated—arose from a regional engagement with practices of and views on modernization and social reform. Emerging from within elite and middle-class circles within Ottoman provincial cities like Beirut and Cairo, the Nahda was largely informed by wider political and sociocultural reforms, such as the Ottoman Tanzimat (reorderings) of 1839, 1856, and 1876, and influenced by the increasingly globalized phenomenon of capitalism and its concomitant industries: education reform, new communication technologies—like the telegram and printing presses, and transportation methods, like locomotives. The changing global political economy, its challenges and contentions, along with the increased British and European imperial interests in (and incursions into) the Ottoman world and the Arab region writ large, saw growing instances of fissures, factionalizations, and proto-nationalist sentiment among (largely non-Muslim) minority groups and residents in the empire's provinces.

As a result, new political and cultural ideas increasingly circulated and were debated among the Arab intelligentsia in the late nineteenth century, particularly in Cairo and Beirut but also in Damascus and elsewhere in the Ottoman dominions.[5] Concurrently, and largely as a consequence of these developments, a sense of Arabic national identity was formulated and experimented with, the key works of which would pave the way for later pan-Arabist movements of the mid-twentieth century. These debates, and others of the Nahda period, were negotiated within the context of classical Arabic literary revivals, poetry, translations, and language through print, theater, music, photography, and other mediums. The term *Nahda* is, therefore, often translated as "Renaissance" and this period is, sometimes crudely, seen as a pivotal moment when the Arab world entered the modern, global, capitalist system, incorporating its concomitant intellectual movements into their worldview.[6]

With the origins of its core projects emerging from among the Arabic-speaking intelligentsia of the Ottoman period, the Nahda has always had a difficult—some would even say hostile—relationship to entertainment. In so far as the Arab litterateurs of nineteenth and early twentieth century were interested in the "popular," it was in order to mold and educate the masses not to entertain them. Literary works and other scholarship produced by these elite thinkers were largely informed by the period's imperial reforms focused on questions of education, social relations, civic codes, jurisprudence, and moral behavior, among related concerns. For example, historians have explained how Nahdawi interests in the public were for purposes of social reform (*islah*) and benefit, as has been discussed in connection to public interest (*maslaha ʿamma*) and public benefit (*manfaʿa ʿamma*).[7] As Samah Selim argued in her work on Egyptian popular fiction, intellectuals saw themselves as thought leaders whose role was to reform the people. Selim explains, "[i]n turn-of-the-century Egypt, reformist intellectuals conceived of modern narrative in political and didactic terms. By educating and improving the collective character of the Egyptians, it would prepare them for citizenship in the modern nation-state."[8] The whole tradition, however, was founded on a worldview that "for the most part considered the cultures and life worlds of the masses with contempt and also with a certain fear."[9]

Popular entertainment, as a realm typically unconcerned with issues of morality and reform, has often been construed as antithetical to the aims of the Nahda. The former was too unruly to be useful to the burgeoning intellectual project. For instance, famed early Nahda historian Jurji Zaydan (1861–1914), who emigrated from Syria to Cairo in the 1880s, described contemporaneous Beirut society as being made up of three classes, the elites, the masses, and the upwardly mobile educated middle class. For Zaydan, the second class "*al-ʿamma*" were the commonplace "riff raff," craftsmen, merchants, and those with "menial occupations." This class, according to Zaydan, was made up of society's lost causes (the "immoral crooks," "idle vagrants," the drunkards, and the uneducated poor).[10]

For Nahdawi scholars, popular entertainment was a double-edged sword. Theater, in particular, presented a paradox. It had the potential to shape the morals of the general public in a positive way, but it frequently fell short of that potential.

In Muhammad al-Muwaylihi's *Hadith 'Isa ibn Hisham* [What Isa ibn Hisham Told Us], an Egyptian in the late nineteenth century guides a resurrected Pasha who had died earlier in the century—before the rapid spate of modernization in Egypt—through the new sights of Cairo. Among the many things the narrator shows the Pasha is a theater, which he extolls for its ability to shape the people. "This is a theater," he says, "something that Western peoples acknowledge as having educational and corrective qualities. It encourages virtues, exposes evil traits, and portrays the deeds of former generations so that people can be educated and learn lessons from them." The Pasha, though, is unimpressed. "How can you be making such claims when what I've been watching here doesn't resemble in any way what you've just been describing?" he asks, retorting,

> in fact, it's just the opposite. What I've seen here is just a repeat of what I've observed in the dance hall—drinking wine, flirting with women, portraying amorous situations in a highly suggestive manner, one that's designed solely to arouse people's passions, make such things more accessible and easy, and stir up lustful emotions.[11]

Despite its potentials, popular entertainment was failing to form a productive national subject and to promote a model for morally "good" behavior. Elite intellectuals often perceived theaters, alongside café culture, cabarets, nightclubs, and street performances as activities and spaces that were holding the people back and often actively promoting bad morals. In Egypt, Cairo's downtown district of Azbakiyya (or Ezbekieh) brought all these forms of popular entertainment together and quickly won a reputation as a place that corrupted the morals of all classes.[12] If we take the words of leading Nahdawi intellectuals at face value, popular entertainment in the Arab world was something that had to be reformed for the Nahda to succeed.

Yet, despite the loftier aims of Nahdawi intellectuals, intentions do not determine reality, and engaging mass audiences—many of whom were illiterate or uneducated—was not possible or effective through exclusively elite means and contexts. Publications switched hands and traveled into spaces that brought together the educated and illiterate, theatrical performances were rooted in and related to the literature, poetry, and plays being engaged with and translated by Nahdawi intellectuals, elite culture trickled down to street audiences and into the nightclubs and cabarets which, irrespective of their moral high ground, were regularly frequented and discussed by the literary elite. Despite the varied limitations on expressions within the public sphere in the late Ottoman context, streets and squares during the nineteenth century, the latter of which became popular additions to cities during the 1870s, as Till Grallert argues, were spaces in which different groups of city-dwellers—informed by their respective economic and sociopolitical concerns—negotiated the notion of "public" vis-à-vis regulation by Ottoman and associated authorities.[13] The importance of squares, as sites of political dissent, became particularly evident at the start of the First World War. Relatedly, Ilham Khuri-Makdisi has demonstrated how theaters long played an important role as places of public debate and opinion (which often resulted in state-mandated closures).[14]

Censorship and regulation, and the defiance of each, were always a part of the Nahda and its history. For instance, publishing in the Ottoman realms saw a variety of laws emerge during the mid to late nineteenth century that limited the nature of what could be published and complicated the publication and dissemination process for the region's privately owned presses. In 1857, Ottoman authorities instituted a law requiring printing establishments to acquire licenses and submit their works for pre-approval to the central press office. In 1865, another law was promulgated requiring all periodicals to obtain a license.[15] The danger of official sanction always loomed over publishers, but it is possible for present-day scholarship to overexaggerate censorship's effects. As Donald Cioeta has noted, in Beirut "there were only three suspensions before 1876 noted in literary sources, none involving disputes about censored material."[16] As Palmira Brummett has shown, despite various press laws during the Hamidian period (1876–1909), "the Ottoman press was not completely suppressed," while publishing continued to be perceived as a threat even after the end of Abdul Hamid II's rule in 1909 and with the purported "freedom" of the Second Constitutional period (1908–20).[17] People typically found ways around this censorship, such as moving their operations outside the Ottoman Empire or to Egypt, where, at the end of the nineteenth century, censorship of Arabic materials was more lenient.[18]

Public entertainment was also the subject of official scrutiny. Theater, in particular, caused authorities to worry, its reach as performance instead of literacy-focused was potentially wider than publications and more difficult to control. Scholars have noted how censorship laws during the Hamidian period were particularly strict about theatrical productions in Ottoman Istanbul, and other cities, whereby "any kind of moral indecency or political criticism was rigorously punished."[19] Of course, this did not mean that plays were not put on, but rather that they were often limited to specific translations and were heavily regulated by the Ottoman authorities. However, this regulation was not always consistent and was not necessarily the case for theaters in Khedival Egypt. As Adam Mestyan has explained, while theaters were perceived as dangerous places for rulers (for instance, as spaces where they might be assassinated), "khedivial theaters were mostly governed by unwritten rules."[20] Theater rules and regulations were not limited to Ottoman or Khedival authorities. In fin de siècle Egypt under British occupation, for instance, acting troupes were required to submit their scripts to British authorities before staging them. The most famous case of censorship was Hassan Marʿi's play *Dinshaway*, based on the controversial execution of four Egyptian villagers by the British in 1906. Even in the relatively laxer environment of Egypt, this was deemed too controversial a subject to address on stage and performances were banned.[21]

This volume acknowledges the importance of public entertainment in this period. Spectacle and performances were central aspects of life in the Ottoman Empire and the decades after its fall. Any study of the Nahda is incomplete if it does not consider popular culture. More importantly, overlooking popular culture or relegating it as peripheral and inconsequential to the sociopolitical significance or impact of the Nahda, problematically dismisses the collective agency of social classes beyond elite and middle-class groups. Additionally, while this volume turns to an analysis of the popular culture of entertainment in the wider Arab world, it does so with the understanding that this culture is far from stagnant. Nor is this collection about studying the popular culture of the Nahda as a self-contained end in itself. Rather, informed by recent studies that examine the "popular" in popular culture, this volume operates from the understanding that change, political or societal, "rarely happens without popular culture because culture is one of the modalities where the popular [. . .] is made material."[22] Thus, in focusing on the Arab Nahda as a movement related to the culture of popular entertainment, the contributions in this volume strive to reframe the Nahda as a phenomenon that belonged to, engaged, and was reconfigured by everyday mass audiences, rather than one restricted to the closed-off circles or venues of the middle class and elites.

Studies on Popular Culture and Entertainment

Despite (or perhaps because of) frequent condemnations of popular entertainment in Nahdawi texts, it has become an increasingly well-studied area in recent years. Egyptian popular culture, specifically, has become almost a subject area of its own. Since the pioneering work of Pierre Cachia, a significant amount of academic work has looked at the subject from the late nineteenth century until the present. Many of these studies have been focused on the contemporary era.[23] In his groundbreaking study on mass culture and Egyptian nationalism, Walter Armbrust explored the rise of mass media like radio, film, and television and the importance of public commentary and culture in relation to the ways in which modernist ideals were perceived by everyday audiences.[24]

More recently, scholarship has taken the late nineteenth and early twentieth century as their subject. Shifting away from a focus on the literary intelligentsia to consider the politicization of the public sphere via everyday media, Ziad Fahmy's *Ordinary Egyptians: Creating the Modern Nation through Popular Culture* used theater and music to document the birth of a popular nationalism in Egypt around the 1919 revolution.[25] While Samah Selim's *Popular Fiction, Translation, and the Nahda in Egypt* studies a rich archive of serialized popular novels at the turn of the twentieth century to sketch an alternative cultural history of the period—one that had often been ignored or marginalized.[26]

An increasing interest in the history of popular culture is also seen in scholarship dealing with other urban spaces in the context of the wider Arab world. Turning to a study of music through radio, recordings, and performances, Christopher Silver's *Recording History: Jews, Muslims and Music across Twentieth Century North Africa*, tells a history of nationalism and religious identity across Morocco, Tunisia, and Algeria through some of the region's biggest musical stars as well as the disparate voicees of musical composers, audiences, and nationalist figures.[27] Salim al-Tamari and others have used music and popular culture as a way to look at early twentieth-century Palestinian history.[28] Still, others have explored popular culture through the lens of folklore and traditional regional practices related to music and performance.[29] While Iran is beyond the scope of the present volume, one can note similar trends in the fields of Iranian studies with numerous recent studies turning to a close examination of music and popular culture pre and post the 1979 Islamic Revolution.[30]

Many recent studies have expanded their remits to include the Arab world (or Middle East) at large, with some even encompassing the advent of a modern global entertainment scene in which contemporary capitalist modes of production have generated a much more integrated culture across the world (though one that is also profoundly affected by postcolonial power dynamics). Andrew Hammond, for example, has published numerous works related to media, politics, and popular culture, including art, in the late twentieth-century Arab world, including North Africa.[31] Others have also focused on visual culture in the Middle East and the popular image's connection to everyday audiences in the public sphere.[32] Some have also addressed the topic from the context of the Arabian Gulf states, which have typically been overlooked in scholarship on the arts and popular culture.[33] With a few exceptions, the vast majority of these works focus on late twentieth century and early twenty-first-century popular culture.[34]

The present volume, while benefiting from earlier approaches both to the Nahda and to popular culture in the Arab world, endeavors to do something a little different. The book imagines the Nahda as a *popular* movement. It does not take the disparaging words of Nahdawi intellectuals about popular entertainment at face value. Instead, it proposes that the Nahda took on an alternative existence in the streets among everyday masses and was not limited to literary-scientific associations, publishing circles, and the realms of the educated elite. It asks what might happen if scholars turned their attention away from the classic foci of the Nahda to look at the broad sweep of "popular entertainment" including theater, nightclub singing, film, café culture, printed imagery, and more. Through this volume, we propose an alternative conception of what the Nahda was and what its key cultural contributions were.

Popular entertainment is frequently perceived as a form of "authentic" cultural expression, with historical connections to cultural traditions of the region. During the rise of anticolonial and anti-imperialist sentiment in Middle Eastern countries with the emergence of regional nationalist movements in the post-Second World War era in the 1950s and 1960s, and the growing significance of global solidarity movements, the view of popular culture as a repository of local (non-Western), folkloric expression and source material become increasingly prevalent among local agents of sociopolitical change. The cultural turn of the 1970s extended the importance of popular culture to the realm of academic pursuits as a way to write alternative, subaltern histories that challenge and problematize totalizing meta-narratives.[35] While these studies have been instrumental in shifting views on popular culture in academia, and in demonstrating its importance in the context of post-independence identity formation and revolutionary practice in the mid to late twentieth-century Arab world, the function of popular entertainment and culture from the mid-nineteenth to the early twentieth centuries was not the same as that of the later periods. The popular culture of the Nahda period was not just a repository of "folk tradition." Rather, it was a living, shifting entity—as much a product of modernity as the Nahda was. In fact, as Eman Elnemr has suggested in a talk on licentiousness in twentieth-century Egypt, there was something hypocritical about the Nahdawi condemnation of the purportedly loose morals of popular entertainment. Intellectuals of the period embraced the coming of capitalist modes of production when it suited them, but were scandalized by the bars, cabarets, and cafés that came as a result of the same forces.[36] The contributions in this volume strive to unpack, redress, and expand upon these views of popular entertainment, its audiences, perceptions, and manifestations in the context of the Arab Nahda.

Writing Popular Histories of the Nahda

Writing a history of popular culture and entertainment in the context of the Nahda in the Arab world is "a messy affair," as Till Grallert notes in one of this volume's chapters. The challenges are multifold, from the logistical question of locating sources and capturing ephemeral, transitory events or performances, to gauging audience reception when it comes to retellings and reports on occurrences or practices. Regarding troubles with primary sources, the majority of material from the period covered in this volume was created by a small class of people who, until now, have made up the primary focus of Nahda studies. These elite community members' attitude toward popular culture at the time was often antagonistic, condescending, or outright hostile.

To go even further, popular entertainment, in its fullest expression, is something that cannot survive in these written sources. These are largely studies of performances or other ephemeral moments of receptions, which occur in particular spaces, at particular times, among particular people. To work on popular culture means shifting the focus to audiences. Thus, one becomes concerned with the so-called masses, who are often excluded from historical sources or are cast as singular groups despite being made up of thousands upon thousands of multi-confessional, socio-economically diverse individuals living in the region's rapidly urbanizing centers, never mind the wider populations working the fields in rural settings.

The present collection's contributors, therefore, have had to be creative with their use of available, often unconventional, sources by reading them against the grain. From journal publications, posters, and advertisements to 78 rpm records and retellings of performances in publications (like the one that this introduction opened with), the source materials used in this volume's contributions also typically fall into the category of popular, even ephemeral, culture and demonstrate the importance of this material in the writing of alternative histories.

The chapters come together to present multifaceted, multivalent views that intersect in the public sphere and among mainstream audiences. In a Foucauldian sense, the history of popular culture is a discursive one that requires a consideration of transitory, ephemeral, affectual, and experiential practices and lived experiences, rather than the scholarly, established elite settings, disciplines, and meta-narratives. This means that this alternative history of the Nahda is unsettled and unresolved, unconstrained as it is by the idealized parameters of high-intellectual debate. But it is also revelatory. It shows what happens when the rarified debates of the Nahda—on language, knowledge production, feminism, nationalism, and morality—played out in the world in front of a variety of different audiences. Rather than being anathema to the Nahda, popular culture shows the Nahda in action and not simply as an intellectually constructed movement always-already set to guide us toward an imagined ideological endpoint.

The nine contributions in this volume show what this nontraditional approach to the Nahda and its sources can look like and what its benefits can be. In particular, these chapters expand the study of the Nahda period into places where it never usually goes both geographically and demographically. This volume does not merely look at the journals of the nineteenth century as historical sources, it asks how they were being read and who was reading them. This book also asks what was happening in cafés, nightclubs, and theaters. Given the diverse nature of the examples of popular entertainment being covered in this volume, including literature, visual culture, performance, and quotidian life, the book's approach is necessarily interdisciplinary, helping to open up the field of Nahda studies to underexplored connections with disciplines like visual studies, film, music, and theater. Contributors, experts from diverse fields, including art history, literary studies, Middle Eastern history, and media studies, each employ an interdisciplinary approach to their studies of specific facets of popular entertainment, while striving to read available source material in alternative ways.

The emphasis on this period's interconnectedness, specifically how a popular history of the Nahda challenges the often artificial disciplinary, cultural, and media boundaries placed by present-day approaches to the field, is made visible in this volume through the organization of contributions into three distinct, yet interrelated, parts. Contributions in the first part focus on the interrelated and popular issues of sexuality and morality as seen in the street culture and nightlife of various modernizing cities in the Arab world. Specifically, this part's essays underscore how these forms of entertainment did not conform with a prevailing bourgeois sense of morality or views of what was edifying or improving. One of the themes that runs through these essays is the role of women in these entertainment establishments, how they were both exploited but also given a space to voice their views of modernity and the changes that were happening in their contexts. In Chapter 1, Till Grallert explores many of these themes through a study of the challenges that faced popular entertainment in late Ottoman Damascus. Grallert's assessment focuses on sites of popular public entertainment like riverside cafés, marketplace taverns, theaters, casinos, and public gardens, as well as the streets, which saw the confluence of socially accepted and "illicit" activities among the city's diverse population. Capturing the continuous negotiations, and transgressions, of popular entertainment as it played out in these spaces, Grallert explains how normative views on issues of gender, class, and religion were constantly in flux and required renegotiations between the moralizing factions of Ottoman rule and members of the populace. In particular, he considers how illicit entertainment and other related activities—like the presence of women in public spaces during holidays—challenged state-mandated Islamic morality laws requiring their continued reiteration by the Ottoman state.

In Chapter 2, Walid El Khachab reflects on the nature of the Nahda as a vehicle, and what it might mean to view it from this media-centric perspective. Drawing on Marshall McLuhan's oft-cited quote "the medium is the message," El Khachab posits that the Nahda *is* the media. According to El Khachab, the Nahda as media—or vehicles of newness and modernity—disturbed the value systems that existed prior to the era of rapid modernization in the late nineteenth century. Hence, the moral anxiety experienced by elite members of Arab societies, as discussed in Grallert's chapter, emerged in response to the introduction of this new media. El Khachab analyzes the outcomes of changing views on morality within the Nahda, with special emphasis on the idea of *Khala'a* (libertinage or the French word *dévergondage*). He proposes that the proliferation of late nineteenth to early twentieth-century Nahda media, for example, vinyl discs, radio receivers, and films, transmitted *Khala'a* from the public venues of libertine entertainment, such as *café-chantants*, cabarets, and music halls, to the private spaces of largely bourgeois households. One of the far-reaching byproducts of the dissemination of *Khala'a* is the rise of Um Kulthum (1898–1975) compared to the downfall of Munira al-Mahdiya (1885–1965) as an outcome of the changes in the Nahda's entertainment market, which demanded manufacturing a "clean," "cultured," and "classy" singer.

Similarly dealing with issues of morality, illicit entertainment, and gender in Chapter 3, Pelle Valentin Olsen charts the development of Baghdad's modern nightlife during the early twentieth century. Olsen shows how these venues and the (mostly female) performers who appeared in them, although they were the subject of frequent moral condemnation and censure, acted as a lightning rod for some of the most important debates of the Nahda: nationalism, gender, women's roles in public space, religion, and the role of state in a modern society. Nighttime public leisure was not just about having fun. Or, to put it more accurately, having fun was not *just* about having fun.

Extending into a more focused assessment of entertainment activities in the context of theaters and related spaces, the book's second part underscores the interrelation between performance and a growing interest in popular public spectacle. Through examples of entertainment related to singing, acting, and music, essays in this part reframe and interrogate some of the classic narratives of the Nahda: from Eurocentric models of nationalism in the Arab world to debates about gender roles in the twentieth century. The contributors to this part use popular entertainment to consider these questions from alternative angles, taking, for instance, a more transnational approach to cultural production in the period by following the international tours of theater troupes in the first decades of the twentieth century.

Diana Abbani's contribution, Chapter 4, picks up from Olsen's study of Baghdad's nightlife and moves the reader's attention to similar contexts in Beirut. By studying a series of little-known interviews in the journal *al-'Asifa* with a wide cross section of Beirut's female entertainers (from the famous stars to the lesser-known dancers and singers), Abbani constructs a picture of Lebanon's early twentieth-century entertainment scene from an often-overlooked perspective. Although filtered through male voices in a magazine, Abbani comes as close as possible to showing what the Nahda looked like from the perspective of nightclub dancers—an extremely diverse group of people in terms of both class and ethnicity. Abbani shows that their experiences of the Nahda and their views on issues such as a woman's place in society and her role in the family were extremely complex.

Shifting the focus from individual performers to a consideration of groups and musical practices, in Chapter 5, Elizabeth Matsushita uses the revival of Andalusi music in the twentieth century to explore the complex position of North Africa and North African performance traditions in the Nahda. This chapter shows how North African cultural practitioners, who are often overlooked or relegated to the sidelines, negotiated the complex cultural dynamics of their own region and related to other areas in the Arabic-speaking world, all against a background of increasing French colonial domination. In demonstrating the connections practitioners established between Morocco, Algeria, and other North African regions, and related practices beyond these contexts, Matsushita's contribution also exemplifies the translocal nature of the Nahda's popular forms of entertainment and cultural production.

Similarly, Chapter 6 by Raphael Cormack casts the Nahda as a transnational movement by exploring the way that Nahdawi texts traveled through the peripatetic theatrical troupes at the turn of the twentieth century. In this chapter, Cormack, taking the travels of Sulayman al-Qardahi's troupe through the Egyptian countryside and North Africa, argues not only that drama is an unjustly overlooked arm of the wider Nahda project (one which brought in much broader audiences than printed texts) but that drama also allows us to think through how the Nahda moved widely across national borders and far outside the metropoles which are usually considered the centers of Nahdawi life.

Contributions in the book's third part pick up on the preceding essays' concerns, but extend them into the realm of media-specific productions through publications and film, and their relationship to the realms of the imaginary in connection to vision, spectacle, identity, and nationalism. Specifically, the essays in this part explore examples of works, from printed imagery and literature, to early Egyptian cinema, to consider these productions for their uses as popular forms of entertainment and their significance in promoting populist views among mass audiences. In Chapter 7, Hala Auji turns to a novel analysis of engravings in widely cited and studied Nahdawi journals like *al-Muqtataf* (Beirut; Cairo) and *al-Hilal* (Cairo). These late nineteenth-century journals have traditionally been considered for their literary and historical import and not their visual content despite the fact that these journals, and others, published a diverse array of imagery, from educational diagrams to illustrations of myriad people, creatures, places, and events. In assessing the diverse nature of these illustrations, which also included portraiture, and renditions of performers and mass entertainment spectacles, Auji argues that these images played important roles as forms of visual entertainment among literate and illiterate readers alike. Engravings were the tools through which ideas were being popularized as well as ends in of themselves. These images would have exposed readers (and onlookers) to new ways of seeing, imaging, and imagining notions about the fine arts, history, societies, technology, the world, and even space at this time.

Alaaeldin Mahmoud, in Chapter 8, considers works of modern Egyptian literature for their interest in and promotion of populist views on Egyptomania, which has traditionally been understood to be a fin de siècle European concept. Mahmoud argues that the earliest actualization of Egyptian Egyptomania (a response to an essentially Orientalist European preoccupation), can be traced to the prose and verse work by Egyptian scholar Rifaʿa al-Tahtawi (1801–73). Since the early twentieth century, ancient Egypt was cast in an anti-Orientalist/anticolonial fashion as evident in the early, yet not widely known, fictional works of the poet Ahmad Shawqi (1868–1932). Such a "nationalist" re-appropriation of (ancient) Egypt was further developed in Shawqi's later, and much better known, verse play *Masraʿ Kliyubatra* (*Death of Cleopatra*) (1927). Similarly, as Mahmoud shows, responses to particular aspects of Egyptomania like Tutmania and mummymania are to be found in poems by Shawqi, Bayram al-Tunisi, Yunus al-Qadi, Khalil Mutran, and others, and short stories, such as Mahmud Taymur's "Firʿaun al-Saghir" (1939) and Naguib Mahfouz's "Yaqazat al-mumya" (1939).

In Chapter 9, Thana al-Shakhs turns to film and its connection to the formation of a "national" Egyptian cinema in order to problematize what "national" even meant in Egypt during the early twentieth century. Thana argues that in early 1920s Egypt, then a nominally independent state under continued British occupation (as a "veiled protectorate"), Western films became increasingly popular. As a result, a local Egyptian film industry emerged within politico-economic conditions that propelled using such an industry as a springboard to propagate the popular ideas of "national identity," whereby filmmakers negotiated the populist expectations of mass spectators and their own, often elitist, views of Egyptian nationhood. Relatedly, she points to a popular controversy (popularized even more by the press of the time) that strove to classify Egyptian films from an Egyptian nationalist lens. According to this standpoint, films such as Aziza Amir's 1927 *Layla* and the 1930 film *Zaynab*, a cinematic adaptation of Muhammad Hussain Haykal's novel *Zaynab*, are accepted as "Egyptian" productions. Relatedly, the natural environment was key to the creation of a local film industry in Egypt. Specifically, the shift to the desert, in films like *Layla* and *Qubla fi al-Sahraʾ* (*Kiss in the Desert*), or from urban centers to the countryside, in *Zaynab*, was crucial to the cinematic representation of national identity.

Through these three sections, this book looks at the different ways that popular culture and entertainment can change how we think about the Nahda, and how popular culture from the Arab world can alter the way we look at popular culture more broadly. This volume also explores how the Nahda, which took place almost concurrently along with other "renaissances" around the globe since the last quarter of the nineteenth century and culminating in the first quarter of the twentieth century, was equally a transnational artistic movement, especially in its unique reception and re-creation of its own global/local popular and entertainment practices.

PART ONE

LEISURE & MORALITY

Chapter 1

PROPER FUN? STRUGGLES OVER POPULAR ENTERTAINMENT IN LATE OTTOMAN DAMASCUS (1875-1914)

Till Grallert

I went to the three theaters now existing in Damascus to see with my own eyes what is going on and observed unspeakable transgressions of humanity. Singers performed the most outrageous transgressions at all three places and some people assured me that after the audience (*al-qawm*) leaves the amusement venues of moral corruption, young men follow the girls to their places, where it happens, what happens until the morning (without prayer and without fasting).[1]

Throughout the ages, Damascenes of both genders walked the streets day and night for pleasure. During the hot seasons, they flocked to the cafés, orchards, and gardens along the rivers and in the green belt surrounding the city, where they engaged in all sorts of leisure and entertainment: eating, smoking, drinking, gambling, and dancing (Figure 1.1).[2] One could find numerous entertainment venues across the city, catering to the more illicit needs and pleasures of the townspeople. Such activities were for a large part checked only by the affluence of those willing to attend and the state of the roads and streetlights hampering nightly movement through the city.

The legitimacy of the Ottoman state, on the other hand, rested on the provision of safety and security, including the protection of public morality. Enforcement of these norms became an ever more important symbolic policy after the loss of large sections of the empire's non-Muslim populations to secessionist nationalist movements and competing empires in the course of the nineteenth century. As one consequence of the increasingly Muslim population, the Ottoman Empire sought legitimacy as a *Muslim* state—a quality that was formalized by the 1876 constitution.[3] Two of the most widely agreed upon Islamic norms are the ban of alcohol and extramarital sexuality. Particularly during the month of Ramadan and around Muslim places of worship, the state aimed at presenting itself (and its representatives) as pious Muslims and capable protectors of "public morality" (*adab 'umumiyya* or *akhlaq 'umumiyya*). To support this vision of a pious empire and a modern incorruptible state, officials and soldiers were repeatedly banned

Figure 1.1 Crowded riverbanks with the municipal garden to the right. *Damas - L'Entré Avec Le Barada*, Sulayman Hakim, Damascus, [1891?]. Getty Research Institute, 2008.R.3(A19), Box T56. http://hdl.handle.net/10020/2008r3a19.

from visiting cafés in uniform and while on duty. Reminders to the Muslim townspeople were posted in the streets, calling on them to keep the fast and behave properly during the holy month of Ramadan. Common targets for these policies were the purveyors of alcohol and gambling and, more generally, female presence in public places.

Trying to write histories of popular entertainment is a messy affair even for the medium-sized provincial city of Damascus and during the relatively short period of the last fifty years of Ottoman rule. It is an attempt to navigate multilayered quotidian practices of hundreds of thousands of townspeople during the age of reforms and rapid transformations on global, imperial, and local levels[4] through only one of the urban society's many constituent communities—and a tiny one for that matter: the newly emerging, literate, multilingual middle class of white-collar workers, officials, and entrepreneurs engaged in their time's new and developing media, the periodical press, as entrepreneurial publishers, editors, authors, and readers.[5] The surviving spoils from Beirut's and later Damascus' news press[6] nevertheless provide a vivid and unmatched insight into the daily affairs of urban populations at the end of empire and provide ample documentation for the middle class' vested interest in the state's modernizing ideology.[7]

This modernizing ideology and corresponding policies, inter alia, sought to establish control over social and urban places, negotiating the concrete meaning of the new and developing concepts of *a*, *the*, and *being public*. This is not the space to rehash the scholarly debates on Islamicate cities and the applicability of dichotomous concepts of public and private spaces rooted in Roman law to historical societies outside the Global North.[8] It must suffice to say the nineteenth-century eastern Mediterranean underwent profound social, economic, and political transformations, such as the advent of a new, bourgeois public sphere and modern governance, which resulted in the rapid development and evolution of the necessary vocabulary—an Ottoman-Arabic *Sattelzeit*.[9] Thus, the semantic layers of *a*, *the*, and *being public* were neither restricted to nor identical with ʿ*umumi* and *al-ʿumum*.¹⁰ While *al-adab al-ʿumumiyya* referred to universal moral values and general decency, *turuq ʿumumiyya* denoted streets of unrestricted access, while *al-manafiʿ al-ʿumumiyya* became the technical term for public works through alluding to the common good and public benefit.¹¹ Finally, *mahallat* and *buyut ʿumumiyya*¹² designated places of illicit entertainment and deviation from *al-adab al-ʿumumiyya*, which thus threatened the persistence of public order (*al-raha al-ʿumumiyya*) and, ultimately, the Ottoman claim to legitimate rule.¹³ Accordingly, the Penal Code of 1858 designated the violation of public order (*asayiş-i ʿumumi*) as one of three types of criminal felonies.¹⁴ Press codes prohibited anyone from inciting readers to violate public order and penalized contempt for moral values.¹⁵ Similar restrictions to one's liberty were upheld by the constitution of 1876 and 1908¹⁶ as well as legislation regulating public assemblies and freedom of speech.¹⁷

The concept of *the public*, being closely related to, if not outright dependent on, the notion of general equality of all, created a tension with the deeply stratified Ottoman society, an *ancien régime*, in which one's rights and social capital were based on multi-dimensional social relations of kinship, religion, profession, and so on, as well as property and payment of taxes.¹⁸ Within such a context, the state and the modernizers equated "public" interest more often than not with the elites and subscribed to a paternalistic stance toward "the (common) people"—be they framed as ʿ*amma*, *shaʿb*, or *khalq*—commensurate with established social hierarchies. A good example of this convergence between the new middle classes, old elites, and the state is the newspaper report cited at the beginning of this essay, which praised Sultan ʿAbdulhamid II (r. 1876–1909) for his piety and for enforcing a ban on everything contravening Islamic morals during Ramadan 1318 AH (December 1900/January 1901) before venturing into the previous description of popular entertainment.

Popular entertainment—the cheap, noisy, unregulated joys of the common townspeople—had the potential, if not tendency, of transgressing and, thus, constantly renegotiating normative boundaries of gender, class, and religion. It was, consequently, increasingly pushed to the margins, the side of the streets, the fringes of the city, and the nightly hours. For many of the educated elites the dangers were not limited to the morality of their fellow townspeople, but they framed their disdain at popular entertainment within the discourse on hygiene, contagious diseases, and public health.¹⁹ Yet, while the city saw repeated attempts to expel female dancers, criminalize the idle, ban the sale and consumption of alcohol, and prevent women from entering public places during holidays and at night, the constant reiteration of such policies, outlined on the following pages, attests to the resilience of social practices.

Sites of Popular Entertainment

Cafés and Taverns

Gathering outside, sitting down to chat, having a drink, playing a game of backgammon, listening to music or a story, or just idly watching neighbors and strangers passing by was certainly the most popular form of entertainment in Damascus. Hundreds of cafés lined the streets of the city.[20] They were often nothing more than small holes in the wall with wooden stools lining and encroaching upon the pavement, which severely impacted traffic across town and were a source of frequent complaints.[21] Officially prohibited by the empire's building and municipal codes[22] and shunned by the modernist discourse on streets as the clean and healthy arteries of the urban body, the municipality (*baladiyya*) repeatedly tried to enforce this vision.[23] By the 1910s, this was compounded by a distaste for and criminalization of idleness. But the practice was hard to control as it did not require fixed installations and patrons would return as soon as inspectors had left. Thus, cafés and the noisy crowds in front of them continued to be a major source of traffic jams for pedestrians, coaches, and beasts of burden alike.

The city also had a number of larger indoor venues, where people gathered well into the evening. The larger and, depending on whom one asked, more refined venues, sometimes called "casinos" (*kazinat*), were akin to clubhouses and located in the modern quarters of the city around Marja Square and Suq al-Khayl as well as along the banks of the Barada river to the west and northeast of the city—the Green Meadows and al-Sufaniyya outside Bab Tuma (Figure 1.2 and Figure 1.3).

Figure 1.2 Darwishiyya Street south of the future entrance to Suq al-Hamidiyya after remodeling according to the "new style" in the mid-1880s. Note the sign for "Cazino Munchie" on the left and the newly stratified traffic. Detail from *Street Leading to Straight Street*, Damascus, by American Colony, Jerusalem, [1886?]. Library of Congress, LC-M36-848[P&P], http://hdl.loc.gov/loc.pnp/matpc.07047.

1. Struggles over Popular Entertainment

Figure 1.3 View of Suq 'Ali Pasha with men sitting around a low table next to a water basin. Behind the basin, men sit in front of a café, Damascus, 1909. Ebay, 123069537097, http://www.ebay.com/itm/123069537097.

While a relatively recent development, they were hugely popular by the late 1870s and patrons flocked to them night and day save for the winter months.²⁴

Socially acceptable opening hours were a contentious issue. It seems that the threshold between virtuous and illicit entertainment was around two hours after sunset. Neighboring Beirut saw repeated attempts to enforce a curfew around this hour with commentators arguing that the current state of affairs with cafés across the city open until after midnight represented moral corruption (*fasad*) and disturbed public order.²⁵ On the other hand, an official claim that cafés offered "tavern girls" (*bint al-hana*, a clear reference to sex work) instead of coffee to justify a renewed curfew by imperial decree was rejected by the newspapers.²⁶ Crime statistics for the spring of 1909 included arrests of proprietors of cafés for violating the curfew and thus attest to similar regulations in Damascus.²⁷

Theaters and Cinemas

Theaters were a recent introduction to the city and of dual moral quality. On the one hand, the state and new elites deemed theater a respectable art form and of great educational value. Local literati authored original plays and wrote Arabic adaptations and translations of Western classics, journals published plays, and schools staged theatrical performances, sometimes in the presence of the highest-ranking officials in the province.[28] On the other hand, the new conservative journal *al-Haqa'iq* ran a long series of letters from 'ulama' in 1911–12 decrying the moral vices of acting (*tashkhis*, *tamthil*) in response to a performance of "Zuhayr al-Andalusi" by students of the Ottoman school in town.[29] Old and new elites certainly agreed that acting and performing on stage was a disreputable profession if conducted for popular entertainment and as a business.

The first theater in Damascus was established by Abu Khalil al-Qabbani (1833–1902)[30] with substantial political and financial backing from Midhat Pasha on rented premises inside the walled city in 1879[31] during the latter's tenure as vali of Syria. The venture, named *al-marsah al-'umumi*, was a financial disaster. Even though official support from valis continued after Midhat Pasha's ousting,[32] opposition from notables and 'ulama' allegedly grew to the extent that children sung taunts in the streets. By 1884, the theater had closed and al-Qabbani moved to Cairo, where he performed at the Opera House.[33]

A more successful venue with a dedicated auditorium for theatrical performances became the Ottoman industrial orphanage (*islahhâne* or *dar al-islah*). Also established during Midhat Pasha's tenure,[34] the *islahhâne* did not produce its own shows but was a venue for traveling troupes of performers.[35] It was joined in 1909 by the first purpose-built theater "Flower of Damascus" (*Zahra Dimashq*) on the Eastern side of Marja Square opposite the new town hall and operated by Habib Efendi al-Shammas.[36] Both venues hosted troupes from Egypt (including the famous Salama Hijazi)[37] and Anatolia[38] as well as local associations[39] and schools.[40] *Zahra Dimashq* also housed the first cinematograph in Damascus from November 1909 onwards. During the initial years, it mainly screened newsreels (albeit not necessarily of current events) introducing a potpourri of moving images from Istanbul, the Russo-Japanese war, or American weddings.[41] Within a year, they added film screenings during intermissions of theater performances.[42] Habib al-Shammas also leased the café in the municipal gardens outside Bab Tuma to the east of the city, where he introduced film screenings after sunset in summer 1910.[43]

Gardens

Popular as they were, cafés and taverns were spaces for exclusively male entertainment. But every spring, men and women, old and young, began to flock to the gardens and orchards around the city for leisure and respite from the heat and pollution of the streets. The most favored of these gardens were located in the Green Meadows to the west, along the banks of the Barada at al-Sufaniyya, on the slopes of Jabal Qasiyun to either side of Salihiyya Street, and along the Thawra River. Families, as well as single men and women, mingled rather freely at the ubiquitous evening picnics or went on an evening stroll. Nu'man Qassatli recounted in the late 1870s the customary schedule of the "seven Tuesdays, the seven Saturdays, and the five Thursdays" commencing with the Nayruz on

12 Adhar (March): on Tuesdays, the people would gather on the riverbanks at al-Sufaniyya. On Saturdays, thousands of men and women would visit the tomb of Shaykh Arslan and picnic in the Green Meadows to the west of the city. On Thursdays, they flocked to "al-Arbaʿin" on the slopes of Jabal Qasiyun.[44]

Little changed until the end of the Ottoman era, safe for the ever-increasing number of cafés, casinos, and theaters, most of which were concentrated along Darwishiyya Street, Marja Square, and Suq al-Khayl, as well as along the banks of the various rivers.[45] Most people fled the summer heat to the more pleasant climate of the gardens[46]—particularly when the month of Ramadan, with its general preference for nightly gatherings of families and friends for *iftar* and subsequent entertainment, coincided with the hottest summer months.[47]

Forms of Popular Entertainment

Available entertainments at the cafés and gardens included music, male and female dancers,[48] wrestling,[49] and *karagöz* (shadow play),[50] games such as the *jarid* on horseback[51] or backgammon, cards, and draughts,[52] as well as coffee, tea, *hashish*,[53] alcohol (see the longer section as follows),[54] and the water pipe.[55] An anonymous female traveler provided the following account in 1891:

> We had a pleasant drive, one afternoon during our stay, to one of the public gardens of the so-called Christians [. . .]. This was a beautiful little park, with the swift-rushing Abana running through it, and the air sweet with fragrance of roses [. . .]. [. . .] we saw many people (some men, but mostly women) sitting here quietly eating fruits and nuts, drinking lemonade, sherbet or arrack, and smoking the Turkish pipe [. . .]. These women were all dressed in white, but, unlike the Mohammedans, their faces were not covered [. . .].
>
> As twilight deepened, men came around with long iron poles and stuck them in the ground, and on the end hung a lighted lantern, so that before long the whole place was brilliantly illuminated and presented a very attractive appearance.[56]

Photographs show funfairs with wooden swings and (small) Ferris wheels with up to six pods carrying two people each surrounded by hundreds of men, women, and children. Some of these photographs were produced for the German troops in 1917 and, according to a note from a soldier, they depicted the celebrations at the end of Ramadan (*ʿid al-fitr*).[57]

It is important to note that neither gathering at night, nor smoking water pipes in public was restricted to men, nor was the consumption of intoxicating beverages restricted to non-Muslims. Unlike twentieth-century commenters want us to believe, this state of affairs was no novelty. Mid-eighteenth-century observers Ahmad al-Budayri al-Hallaq and Mikhaʾil al-Burayk already noted (and lamented) these popular forms of entertainment.[58]

Entertainment did not come for free. Idling at the small outdoor cafés might have required no more than buying a cup of coffee or a glass of tea at around Ps 0.25.[59] After sunset, prices doubled and at least some larger venues charged a mandatory cover.[60] Performers, such as storytellers, musicians, dancers, or puppeteers, charged additional payments to entertain the patrons. Gustav Bauernfeind, a painter of Oriental subjects from the Templar community in Haifa, who spent several months in Damascus and kept a diary of his expenses, provided a rare description of a *karagöz* performance in the mid-1890s. According to him, the show was attended by some 150 people with everyone paying Ps 0.50, which was split between the proprietor of the café and the performer. The latter allegedly played three venues every night.[61] This would mean that the performer made at least Ps 37.5 and up to three times this amount if the other venues were similarly spaced—a stately sum, when street vendors earned less than Ps 3 a day, unskilled workers made between Ps 6 and 8 per day[62] and low-ranking officials, such as policemen, clerks or corporals (*onbaşı*), nominally received monthly salaries of Ps 150–200.[63] Tickets for theater performances and film screenings were much more of a luxury, selling for at least Ps 2.5 to 6 for seats in the stands and Ps 19 and more in private boxes.[64]

The Fight over Popular Practices or How to Have Proper Fun?

Throughout his account, Nuʿman Qassatli eulogizes his fellow Damascenes as most virtuous and gracious people. Whereas for him the gardens and picnics resembled paradise on Earth, the authorities and many pious men (for women never surface but as subjects of restrictive policies) took the opposite stance and denounced them as the source of all vices. For them, gardens, cafés, and theaters outside the surveillance of the authorities and tight social control were the very locus of immoral transgression of propriety: sex, alcohol, and disregard for religion. Thus, in August 1878, a few months before Qassatli finished his book, the authorities issued calls to observe the rules of modesty and propriety in the gardens and to not engage in "acts violating human nature"[65]—a topos that would resurface again and again over the following decades.

Establishing Proper Public Gardens

Of course, soirees, and lavishly illuminated nightly receptions at the outlying gardens were considered perfectly proper as long as they were attended by members of the elites[66] or at least organized and supervised by the elites, such as charitable theater performances for the poor, organized by the wife of the Russian consul,[67] or the annual banquet for the soldiers to celebrate the arrival of spring, *ʿid al-khudar*.[68] Contempt was reserved for the unsurveilled gatherings of the populace at the margins of the city and the day, while modern cafés and public parks at prominent locations in the vicinity of the administrative centers, sponsored and operated by branches of the administration, became highly valued billboards of the city's enlightened elites.

Public parks were part of the modernizing project and the urban program of Ottoman modernity. They were frequently constructed adjacent to the new administrative buildings of municipal, district, and provincial authorities across *Bilad al-Sham* (the Levant) from urban centers such as Aleppo, Beirut, Hama, or Homs to smaller towns like Qatna or Bi'r al-Sab'.

In Damascus, three municipal gardens were built between 1879 and 1914. The first public garden (*al-junayna al-'umumiyya*) was initiated by Midhat Pasha and located on the southern bank of the Barada west of Marja Square. This garden with its large, two-storied municipal café opened to the public in June 1879. Two-hour performances of military music were staged three days a week at sunset. The garden and the surrounding area were illuminated during these evenings and large crowds of people promenaded in the park and on the banks of the river.[69] The venue became the site for many official rituals, including the annual celebration of Sultan 'Abdulhamid II's birthday and the anniversary of his accession to the throne or the reception of foreign dignitaries, such as the German Kaiser Wilhelm II in November 1898.[70]

The *baladiyya* completed the construction of a second municipal park on the banks of the Barada in al-Sufaniyya to the east of the city in 1887. It became a huge success with people flocking there in the summer evenings[71] and it remained a popular spot for gatherings for the next decades[72]:

> [T]he quarter of Sufaniyya had been full of dirt and waste and the location of the knackery and thus full of bad smells. But now at the beginning of the spring, one can see thousands of people (*al-khalq*) flocking to it and enjoying themselves at its beautiful spots and its gardens. The municipality built two stone bridges over the Sufaniyya rivers. The second was completed this year and is the site of a beautiful café. The rivers have been banked with stone walls and trees have been planted along the banks. Iron rails protect people from falling into the river [. . .] This [remodeling] has two advantages: improvement of public health and recreation for thousands of people (*bani al-insan*).[73]

The gardens in the west were extensively remodeled in conjunction with the construction of the first purpose-built town hall on the western side of Marja Square during the early 1890s. Many large trees were felled, and the second floor of the casino underwent major expansion works (Figure 1.4). Yet despite such works and their general popularity, the garden and the casino were demolished after only five years to make place for the New Serail in 1899.[74] In the absence of public gardens in the vicinity of the administrative center, the authorities made use of the "Gardens of the Provincial Treasurer" (*junaynat al-defterdar*) on the northern banks of the Barada further to the west. The site was one of the venues for the popular part of the official celebrations of the sultan's anniversary of his accession to the throne in 1902, when "some thousands" of people gathered after sunset to attend the performance of a troupe of singers.[75]

Figure 1.4 The new municipal café during remodeling, May 1894. Robert Edward Mather Bain, Government Cafe, Damascus. Library of Congress, LOT 3249-8, http://hdl.loc.gov/loc.pnp/cph.3c12360.

In 1907, new gardens were built next to *junaynat al-defterdar* with which they merged.[76] The joint venture became the site of major celebrations following the restoration of the constitution the next year[77] and the name gradually changed to the "National Gardens" (*hadiqat al-umma*)[78]—a name that had been used for the original municipal gardens in 1878.[79] During the height of the Young Turks' popularity, the gardens were called "Liberty Gardens" (*hadiqat al-hurriyya*) similar to the former Hamidian Gardens on Cannon Square in Beirut.[80] Originally private businesses, the gardens were generally considered municipal gardens and the municipal budget for the fiscal year 1326 (1910–11) earmarked a substantial sum for their upkeep.[81] The municipality did not operate the cafés itself but leased all three of them to contractors.[82]

Dissociating the Public from the Popular

Official contempt for cafés as places of immorality is illustrated by repeated attempts to limit the possibility for associations between them and the authorities in public opinion. Laws and policies prohibited various classes of officials—particularly those tasked with enforcing propriety as municipal bailiffs, policemen, gendarmes, and teachers—from patronizing entertainment venues while on duty or in uniform.[83] On occasion, such regulations were tightened and reissued in response to transgressions. As was the case in the aftermath of an alcohol-induced quarrel involving some gendarmes at a café close to the forces' headquarters in Damascus, only a week after the end of Ramadan 1308 AH (May 9, 1891).[84] In 1907, the Ministry of Public Education issued a blanket ban on teachers visiting places of entertainment even during their leisure time as their presence could be noted by parents.[85] This sentiment was shared by the towns literati as evident from the pages of the new dailies published after the Young Turk Revolution of 1908. *Al-Muqtabas*, for instance, complained in December 1909 that police took liberty literally and abandoned their posts while on duty instead of protecting the inhabitants. They allegedly gathered at theaters and all sorts of dodgy venues without even wearing their uniform.[86] One year later, the paper again complained that despite all laws prohibiting police, gendarmes, and municipal bailiffs from frequenting cafés in uniform and on duty, bailiffs were a common sight at these venues. *Al-Muqtabas* laments that thus the authority of the government was diminished in the eyes of the people (*'ayn al-nas*).[87]

The authorities' wariness of cafés as places of trouble and danger to public order was not entirely unfounded. Repeatedly, they were the sites of open rebellion of officers against the sultan and the state. The famous "1897 Coup d'État Attempt in Syria"[88] might not have indeed been an attempted coup d'état but this spark that did not ignite took place in an unnamed café. There, Lutfi Efendi, a lieutenant in the Ottoman army and stationed in Beirut, delivered a speech cursing a portrait of the sultan. Lutfi was confronted by other officers, quickly arrested, and sentenced to five months imprisonment.[89] One year earlier another lieutenant, this time from the 5th Army headquartered in the city, was initially supported by his comrades. Rising during an evening performance, he read a manifesto in Ottoman Turkish criticizing the person and rule of the sultan. The British consul reported "His Majesty was in fact most roundly abused by name and no opprobrious term which the Turkish language contains was omitted. His actions were adversely criticized, he was characterized as an oppressive and cruel tyrant and those who submitted tamely to such outrages were not spared."[90] When the police arrived, fellow officers insisted that the lieutenant continue his speech. Apparently to not further alienate the soldiers whose pay was in arrears for months, if not years, no immediate action was taken against the insubordinate officer. The authorities instead issued a statement that he had been drunk, deeming a violation of Islamic morals much less damaging than a direct challenge to public order.[91]

At the same time, the authorities acknowledged the need to accommodate the needs of army officers far away from otherwise restraining social networks for some entertainment (and a chance to spend their limited pay) by running its own cafés in the immediate vicinity of the barracks in Baramke.[92]

Regulating and Criminalizing Popular Behavior and Entertainment

Consuming alcohol and other intoxicating substances as well as the mingling of strangers of both sexes became the focal point of two concurrent developments in the elite discourse on popular entertainment. On the one hand, the empire increasingly sought political legitimacy as a Muslim state—a quality that was, inter alia, formalized in the 1876 constitution—after the loss of large parts of its non-Muslim populations. Thus, the enforcement of two of the most widely agreed upon Islamic norms, the ban of alcohol and extramarital sexuality, became an important imperial policy. These policies coincided with the month of Ramadan from the late 1880s onwards and aimed at presenting leading officials as pious Muslims and the state as capable protectors of "public morality." In 1887, the authorities posted large announcements in all major *suq*s of the city, calling upon every Muslim "to keep the fast of Ramadan [1304 AH] strictly and to behave themselves decently during the month."[93] In a show of propriety, cafés were not permitted to open during the day for the month of Ramadan, not even for non-Muslims or in predominantly non-Muslim areas.[94] The following Ramadan (May/June 1888), the authorities engaged in an empire-wide show of piety. As *Thamarat al-Funun* reported, Sultan ʿAbdulhamid II himself had:

> [H]eard that some women engage in fashion and behavior transgressing the religious norms. Thus, he issued orders to the religious authorities (*muhafazat al-din*) to ban such manners immediately. It is one of the duties of the believers of both sexes to ensure the implementation of religious rules during the holy month of Ramadan [. . .] and to enforce collective prayers in official offices and Islamic schools. This order, which puts things into the right places was communicated to the Ministry of the Interior and to the provinces to be implemented.[95]

The *vali* of Syria complied and issued orders to ban all behavior violating religious morals including all circumstances that could lead to the occurrence of transgressions. Policies specifically aimed at banning "some" women from the nightly gatherings of people on the banks of the River Barada and the adjacent gardens, where they did what the "old custom allowed them to do," as one author put it.[96]

On the other hand, a local modernist discourse in conjunction with numerous foreign proponents of a *mission civilisatrice*, be they French Catholic, Anglican or German Protestants, the Russian Imperial Palestine Society, or the Alliance Israélite Universelle, advertised very similar ideals of propriety in the name of human (and capitalist) development and progress. Its proponents increasingly perceived of idleness in terms of unproductive labor and a threat to future productivity through gambling away both health and money, which in turn would lead to destitute children roaming the streets and wives and daughters engaging in sex work.[97] The shared and common targets were cafés—broadly conceived as *the* locus of transgression—and the female presence and their appearance in public places. At times, one could readily observe a competition between all communities in the city as to who was the most pious in restricting women.

Banning the "Glass of Happiness"

The first reported ban of alcohol during the period under study dates to Ramadan 1292 AH (October 1875), when the Christian proprietor of a tavern in Suq al-Jimal and British subject complained that the police had attempted to subject his venues to the general inspection of cafés for a suspected breach of the prohibition of alcoholic beverages during the holy month.[98] Attempts to ban alcohol were repeated during the late 1870s and early 1880s. Yet the stance toward alcohol was far from unanimous among the townspeople. A petition called on the municipality to ban any alcohol from the *suqs* and quarters in the vicinity of mosques (which would have meant almost the entire city).[99] Others lamented that attempts to uproot the trade of alcohol and *hashish* in the gardens outside Bab Tuma failed due to the corruption of complicit officials.[100] Yet, a third author was outraged by police and gendarmerie ordering some literati—who habitually spent long nights in one of the pubs (*mahallat 'umumiyya*) drinking "a glass of happiness" (*ka's al-hana'*), as he put it, to cheer them up—to leave the place at once. Their congregation was prohibited, he went on, their community dispersed, and they themselves were thrown out of the place like criminals. He called on the authorities to henceforth publish a list of all places prohibited for literati in the official gazette.[101]

Six years later, in 1890, the State Council issued orders to close all shops and warehouses storing and selling intoxicating substances in the provinces of Beirut, Aleppo, and Syria.[102] Such a blanket ban was repeated immediately after the end of Ramadan 1320 AH (December 1902/January 1903), when the Ministry of Interior issued orders to all provinces banning the sale of alcoholic beverages and the operation of warehouses for storing spirits in places which would be "cursed by its fumes."[103]

Yet, drinking prevailed and prohibitions remained largely symbolic. Newspapers in Beirut continued to print advertisements for alcoholic beverages without any intervention from the authorities during the 1880s and 1890s.[104] The same letter that reported yet another pious ban of alcohol in May 1906, also related how three men had drowned over the course of the previous days. One had been trapped in the Sufaniyya River, where he had gone with a girl in the evening, while the two others had been drinking on the banks of the Barada and—drunk as they were—slipped and fell into the water.[105] In mid-December 1907, six weeks after the end of Ramadan, an apparently agitated "Rashid" reported on the outrageous transgressions of the laws established by the holy books, the messenger of God, and his prophets, which now proliferated throughout the city of Damascus and especially around Suq al-Khayl and Suq 'Ali Pasha northeast of Marja Square (Figure 1.5). There, he claimed, large crowds of drunkards gathered every day and, fearing neither God nor the commander of the faithful and his authorities, drank "the mother of all evils" (*umm al-khaba'ith*). Like many before him, "Rashid" called upon the vali to enforce divine laws (*hudud*), as well as Ottoman regulations, and to effectively end the sale of alcohol.[106] Four weeks later, the store of Dawud al-Maskubi in Suq al-Khayl, which specialized in foreign beverages and sweets, was burned down.[107]

The fight against alcohol did not come to an end with the Young Turk Revolution in July 1908 and the promulgation of general liberty. Immediately prior to Ramadan 1326 AH, which began in late September 1908, As'ad Bey (Darwish), newly appointed deputy commander of the gendarmerie and leading member of the local Committee of Union and Progress, endeavored to shut down some of the city's most (in)famous cafés and gambling venues: first among them the casino of

Figure 1.5 Suq al-Khayl, Damascus (Bain News Service). Library of Congress, LC-B2-4739-1, http://hdl.loc.gov/loc.pnp/ggbain.27716.

the gendarmerie itself, owned by ʿAbd al-Rahman Bey al-Yusuf, a leading local notable and the protector of the Hajj, the Café Dimitri on Marja Square, and the café of ʿAziz Efendi, superintendent of the police forces, in Suq al-Jimal. This blunt move and demonstration of power was the talk of the town,[108] but Asʿad Efendi fell from power within a month in the aftermath of the Rashid Rida affair.[109] None of the cafés was actually closed, and in January 1909, newspapers called on the police to shut down six of the most notorious cafés: Café al-Hammam in Suq al-Sinaniyya, Café al-Darwishiyya, the Café of ʿAmara, the Café of al-Kharrab in the vicinity of the ʿAziziyya Barracks at the intersection of Straight Street and Bab Tuma street, Café Bab Tuma, and Café Dimitri Faʿsi.[110] One week later, on the day of the arrival of the cover for the Kaʿba from Istanbul, the new governor Husayn Nazim Pasha—his predecessor Shukri Pasha had been recalled in the wake of the Rashid Rida affair—informed the owners of cafés pertinent for gambling that their venues will be shut down if they continued to harbor gambling.[111]

Despite all these attempts at enforcing moral rigor among the Damascenes, reports of drunken frolic and serious incidents resulting in the death of people through accident or outright murder continued unabated.[112] *Al-Muqtabas* reported in January 1909 that the number of misdemeanors and felonies under the influence of alcohol had increased to over sixty during the last month.[113]

Limiting Female Participation

Limiting female access to and regulating their behavior in public places and spaces outside domestic confines was the other side of the highly symbolic pious policies. In Ramadan 1309 AH (April 1892), the governor of Syria issued orders prohibiting women (ta'ifat al-nisa') from going out and strolling (tajawwul) through the alleyways and streets of Damascus during the nights of Ramadan.[114] In December 1900, the Ministry of Interior issued orders to all Muslims to observe the month of Ramadan 1318 AH. The orders were announced to the Damascene public by criers walking through every quarter of the city. Muslims were instructed to observe their duties, avoid amusement parks, and ban women from strolling the alleys in groups in contravention of the rites of the community. Every person was called upon to eschew anything that would transgress Islamic morals. The order also prohibited all games violating religion and morals.[115]

In the face of such policies, Christian authors began to call on their communities to regain the lead in moral affairs by likewise limiting their women's presence in public places. In March 1889, an anonymous Damascene called on the heads of the Christian communities to ban women from participating in the old custom of leaving the town in the evenings and to go to the gardens, where men, women, and children mingled freely without fear of association and without observing social hierarchies. Thereby the two patriarchates (Greek Orthodox and Greek Catholic) should follow the Muslim community, which some years ago prohibited their women from attending the picnics and excursions to the gardens as well as the Jews, who had adopted the Muslim model recently. This, he argued, would restore Christian honor in the town.[116] With reference to this letter, *al-Bashir* reported that the reason these transgressions occurred in gardens and orchards was the absence of guards supervising the entrances. According to the paper, Muslim men had originally banned their women from going to the gardens at night arguing that Muslim women, upon witnessing Christian and Jewish immorality, would themselves become morally corrupt.[117]

The Greek Catholic patriarch Butrus IV actually issued such a ban on women leaving the house on Sundays and during religious holidays twelve years later, in the runoff to Easter 1901. Framed as a measure to safeguard public morals, he adopted the argument that many vices originated from women going out and mingling with men during these holidays.[118] It is important to reiterate that such bans were largely symbolic. As we have seen, women of all religious communities flocked to the gardens outside the city and populated the cafés along the rivers' banks, during the evenings and nights. Often, but not exclusively, they did so in the company of their nuclear or extended families.

Naturally, the streets and public places inside the city were not restricted to male movement and particularly not in broad daylight. Many poor women had to work to earn a living, and many did so outside their own homes. Many were their household's only earners when husbands, sons, or brothers were absent with the Ottoman armies. Some were single widows; some were young girls. Both groups were financially vulnerable enough to work at proto-industrial manufacturers at lower wages than any men would.[119] Numerous girls attended the Christian and Jewish schools in the eastern parts of the city and the Midan (Figure 1.6),[120] as well as the increasing number of government schools for girls throughout the city.[121] Women regularly attended places of worship and *hammams*, some shopped for

Figure 1.6 Midan Road south of Suq al-Sinaniyya, Damascus. American Colony, *Street Scene in Old Damascus*, Jerusalem. Library of Congress, LC-M32- 413, http://hdl.loc.gov/loc.pnp/matpc.01145.

groceries, and all visited friends, neighbors, and relatives every now and then. Some women worked on the streets as peddlers, professional mourners, and compounders of plaster.[122] Finally, women participated as part of the audiences in the various spectacles staged in the city, as well as occasional outbreaks of violence (Figure 1.7 and Figure 1.8).[123] Altogether, the streets were certainly not an exclusively male space. So much so that the British consul deemed an order to ban women from the crowds watching the German emperor Wilhelm II visiting the city—in an attempt to prevent would-be assassins from hiding in female gowns—a laughable and absurd measure.[124]

The appearance of female bodies in public places was thoroughly regulated by customs and laws (as was men's attire, although much less restrictive).[125] Even though Nuʿman Qassatli lamented that Western fabrics and fashion encroached even upon women, he also noted that none of them left the house without wearing an *izar*, covering their bodies from head to toe, and a *mandil* (kerchief) that completely covered their faces (Figure 1.9).[126] Non-Muslim women equally adhered to this custom at least outside the majority Christian quarters of Bab Tuma.[127] Over the next forty years, female attire did not change significantly, except for an ever-growing variety of local- and foreign-made cloth.[128] Probably the only exception to the rule of covering one's face were Bedouin and generally peasant women temporarily staying in the city or living on the urban margins.[129]

Figure 1.7 Female spectators crowding the rooftops along Midan Road watching the Hajj caravan's departure, Damascus. Sulayman Hakim, *Depart à la Caravane par la Mecque*, [1890?]. Getty Research Institute, GRI, 2008.R.3(A19), Box T56, http://hdl.handle.net/10020/2008r3a19.

Being completely covered did not make women invisible or slip from male attention. On the contrary, since their attire was either colorful and vividly patterned (a fact often overlooked due to the hegemony of black-and-white photographs)[130] or plain white, women were easily spotted—and molested. Prevailing social norms as to the sanctity of female bodies and the prospect of immediate intervention from bystanders might have functioned as a disincentive to would-be assailants, but anecdotal evidence shows that sexual violence (*ghasabiyyat*) and "indecent acts" (*fi 'l shani'*, *fi 'l munkar*) were rather common.[131]

The Meaning and Extent of Liberty After 1908

After the restoration of the constitution in the Young Turk Revolution of July 1908, the meaning of "liberty" and "equality" and their respective implications for everyday life were far from clear and became hotly debated at homes, on the streets, at meetings of various associations, and in a rapidly expanding press. While "freedom" was generally welcomed, and some even called for the abolition of taxes, quite a few people feared this would mean the abolition of all norms and every order and, thus, ultimately the destruction of human society. At the core of these perceived dangers were transgressions of gender relations under the pretext of general equality of human beings: be it in densely packed crowds, evening

Figure 1.8 Detail from Figure 1.7.

meetings of associations that opened membership to women, or unveilings of women.

The question of female propriety under the liberties granted by the constitution became virulent within a few months, with the police in Istanbul having been ordered to arrest women in the markets for wearing make-up and for demonstrating in breach of Islamic customs (*'adat*). This matter gained prominence in the struggle between the reformers and conservatives in Damascus, when a group of leading *'ulama'*, newly organized as a "club" and forming a conservative opposition to the Committee of Union and Progress (CUP), petitioned the governor about one week before the beginning of Ramadan 1326 AH (September 29, 1908) to reform female attire and to prohibit women from wearing make-up. Their opponents from the CUP argued that the state had no right to interfere in matters of individual freedom and free choice and that neither the state nor the police should prevent women from walking in the streets. If at all, such matters fell to the authority of the religious communities. The CUP won, but only after threatening to use violence to quell opposition to the new regime.[132]

In early 1909, male members of the club of the medical college in Damascus followed precedent from Beirut[133] and went to a dance bar (*qahwat al-raqs*) in Bab Tuma where they verbally attacked two female dancers from Austria over their country's assault on the Ottoman Empire and called on all Ottomans to

Figure 1.9 Woman wearing a *mandil* on Darwishiyya Street, Damascus. Detail from *An Oriental Bazaar*, American Colony, Jerusalem, 1900. Library of Congress, LC-M32-411[P&P], http://hdl.loc.gov/loc.pnp/matpc.01143.

leave the place immediately. The affair was the talk of the town and rumors abounded.[134] The matter of female dancers gained further attention when the police became aware of them staying at the theaters (*al-tiyatirat*), taking money from the patrons for actions breaching common norms, and prohibited them from staying there. This step to criminalize the women was criticized by *al-Muqtabas* on the occasion of a dancer being arrested at the theater of the *islahhâne*, who claimed that her transgression of the new regulations was caused by direct instructions from the commander of the gendarmerie. Nevertheless, her protest was ignored, and she had to pay a fine. *Al-Muqtabas* called on the police to henceforth not engage in urban affairs, as the town was full of criminals who would never be prosecuted.[135]

In 1910, the *baladiyya* made another attempt to ban female singers and dancers from the theaters, at least during the month of Ramadan 1328 AH (September 1910).[136] To this end, the municipality and the director of police forwarded reports to the provincial administration council targeting singers, naked dancers, and prostitutes (*al-baghiyyat*) at Café al-Junayna[137] and other places for exhibiting immoral behavior, for causing dissonance (*tanafur*) among the male audience, and for a general corruption of morals (*ifsad al-akhlaq*). In consequence, the council banned female dancers and singers from exercising their trade at cafés not just during Ramadan, as the municipality had applied for, but permanently. *Al-Muqtabas* approved of this measure and wrote:

> We hope that the authorities will always persist in implementing this decision until Damascus will be different from the amusement park that is our neighbor Aleppo. Even though there are people who say that in these times amusements have become a necessity of life, those transgressing morals should be outlawed.[138]

An anonymous commenter praised the decision to fight the owners of cafés and theaters who had absolutely no morals and who aimed at destroying religion and the homeland. He argued that dancing and singing were particularly evil during the holy month of Ramadan and added that the provincial administration council and the *baladiyya* did well in banning such transgressions. The measure, he continued, was welcomed with approval by all communities and religions upon its announcement in the press. The people, however, wondered, why the owner of a single café was exempt from this prohibition:

> Allegedly, the female dancers at his place are no prostitutes (*liwati*) but we say that they are exactly of this profession and that their lewdness (*khala'a*) hurts us. Someone said that they are all the graduates of a single school and of the same teacher. Without doubt, they are all transgressors. It is not worthy of a director of the police that he should publicly defend such a transgression.[139]

However, as always, male demand and the female dancers' and sex workers' structural vulnerability prevailed.

Concluding Remarks

Ottoman Practicality and the Persistence of Quotidian Practices

In this chapter, I outlined some aspects of popular and public entertainment and how the question of *proper* fun touched interwoven layers of social, religious, and judicial norms. Popular entertainment, in all its vibrant diversity and with its potential for transgressing otherwise well-respected norms and boundaries, became the focal point of negotiations between and among established and emerging local elites, representatives of the state apparatus, and, ultimately, the common townspeople over the direction society should take in a period of rapid fundamental transformations. These negotiations took many forms—from quotidian practices to legislation and new institutions, newspaper editorials, and municipal policies. An expanding state apparatus increasingly aimed at governing the daily life of its subjects, who, in the process, became at least notionally framed as citizens and, occasionally, *a* or *the* public. Conceptual tensions between the deeply rooted social relations of the *ancien régime* based on kinship, religion, profession, and new ideas of political and social equality, paired with beliefs in individual improvement and societal progress through sobriety and honest labor, became pertinent to how people viewed leisurely activities. The state's legitimacy to rule and govern remained grounded in the established Ottoman circle of justice and the provision of public order (*al-raha al-'umumiyya*) grounded in moral values and general decency (*al-adab al-ʿumumiyya*). But competition with other imperial powers resulted in a shift toward a predominantly Muslim population through the loss of predominantly Christian regions in wars and to secessionist movements. The Ottoman state reacted by emphasizing its identity as an explicitly *Islamic* state. Regulating alcohol consumption and potential sexual encounters became the symbolically significant focal ground for claiming political legitimacy.

Faced with the social reality of blanked bans being impossible to impose, the Ottoman state chose two strategies: powerful symbolism and taxation. As we have seen, announcements of pious policies centered on the Islamic ritual calendar, particularly the month of Ramadan. But the state also tried to positively frame its constant defeat by designating special zones of propriety around places of Muslim worship. A zone of 200 yards around Muslim places of worship and Muslim quarters within which the sale of intoxicating drinks was prohibited had originally been introduced in regulations for the city of Istanbul in 1861.[140] In the early twentieth century, orders from the Ministry of Interior expanded this idea of "Islamic quarters and streets" or an explicitly "Islamic" space of propriety within cities to all provinces, while, in effect, backtracking on the universal applicability of their virtuous policies.[141] The measure was reiterated with a new police law, promulgated on August 17, 1907, and published in an Arabic translation six months later. This law repeated many of the earlier regulations prohibiting the transgression of public morals and it explicitly prohibited gambling and banned all "public venues" (*al-mahallat al-ʿumumiyya*) from the vicinity of places of worship, schools, and cemeteries.[142] The law, however, had mostly symbolic value and was not enforced in Damascus. In March 1912, a certain ʿAbduh Khayrallah complained that despite the prohibition of taverns in the vicinity of mosques and places of worship, a new bar had just opened in the Bab Misr neighborhood of the Midan quarter in close proximity to precisely such places.[143]

The second implicit admission of the immutable persistence of illicit pleasures and popular entertainment was that the sales tax on intoxicating substances accounted for a substantial part of the imperial budget.[144] Generating profits from the trade and consumption of alcohol and from suspected or actual sex workers made fiscal sense when the authorities proved unable and unwilling to effectively ban either practice.[145] The imperial model was also adopted on the local level. As we have seen earlier, ʿAbd al-Rahman Pasha al-Yusuf, the protector of the Hajj, was the owner of casinos and the British consul reported that "to his great discredit be it said, the Muhafiz el-Haj is one of the freest livers and hardest drinkers in this city."[146] In early May 1904, coinciding with the festive entry of the returning Hajj caravan into town, the vali was much praised for conceiving new measures to fight "the plague brought upon Damascus" in the form of female Jewish singers and the sale of alcoholic beverages. In addition to the symbolically significant appointment of special officials for enforcing public morality in the Jewish quarter (but not the prohibition of alcohol), the vali introduced a special tax on those profiting from the transgression of public morals. Henceforth, singers were supposed to pay the extraordinary amount of Ps 19 per night, or forty times the price of attending a *karagöz* performance, while sellers of alcoholic beverages were charged Ps

9.5.¹⁴⁷ The ban on the sale of alcoholic beverages at non-specialized stores in May 1906, published in close proximity to *al-mawlid al-nabawi* in 1324 AH, should, therefore, be read as an attempt to concentrate the alcohol trade at sites under the surveillance of municipal inspectors, while, at the same time, the authorities fostered their image of Islamic piety.

Chapter 2

IMMORAL ENLIGHTENMENT

MEDIA AND MORAL ANXIETY IN THE LATE NAHDA

Walid El Khachab

The Nahda movement could be characterized by its intense flux of translations and importation of modern technological and cultural products from Europe to the East Mediterranean Arab World as of the nineteenth century. Nahda studies usually focus on the content and ideas produced within these imported vehicles. This chapter attempts to address the materiality of the media themselves and assess the perceived moral impact of the value system inherent to these media, not just to the ideas carried by them.

Nahda studies acknowledge media inasmuch as it understands "serious" ideas akin to an indigenized version of European enlightenment to be disseminated in books or through print media, including books and newspapers. Al-Tahtawi's discussion of French constitutional monarchy in his book *Takhlis al-Ibriz* about his sojourn in nineteenth-century France is an early typical example of "serious" modern European ideas reproduced in Arabic in print media, which constitute the backbone of the Nahda's agency. The focus here is on the ideas produced within the print vehicle, and—sometimes on their materialization through institutions. The most recent example of English-language articulate scholarship in Nahda studies focused on ideas, major intellectual figures, and print media is Hussam Ahmed's *The Last Nahdawi: Taha Hussein and Institution Building in Egypt*, which is an intellectual biography of Taha Hussein and his role within modern Egyptian cultural institutions, rightfully emphasized in the book's subtitle: "Institution Building in Egypt."

The most recent example of Nahda scholarship in French is Randa Sabry's article "Passion des bibliothèques et quête du livre chez les voyageurs égyptiens partis en Europe au temps de la Nahda," ("Bibliophilia and the Quest for Books among Egyptian Travellers in Europe during Nahda"), which is yet to be published. In her survey of Egyptian travelers' accounts of their journeys to Europe at the turn of the nineteenth century, Sabry details the Nahda's men's views of libraries as being themselves a performance of modernity and points to the solace they found in these modern European institutions' acknowledgment of Arab cultural contribution to civilization, through their Arabic manuscripts and monographic collections.

In this chapter, I would like to shift the approach to the media themselves as well as to the ludic or entertainment-focused production within different media, which has also contributed to Nahda. I acknowledge the role of these media institutions rather than the ideas carried by them. I will focus on late Nahda, that is, at the turn of the twentieth century, and on entertainment, not on the cultural productions of "serious" intellectuals. This chapter is hence closer in its scope and its acknowledgment of pop culture's agency to Raphael Cormack's book *Midnight in Cairo*. Cormack details a fascinating account of nightlife in Egypt during the late Nahda era, with a cultural studies analysis of the agency of "The Divas of Egypt's Roaring 20s" as he puts it in the subtitle. The chapter, therefore, is part of the larger subfield of Nahda studies which addresses entertainment and pop culture and does not confine itself to the history of ideas advanced by "great intellectuals."

To quote McLuhan's proverbial formula, I would not argue that the medium is the message (of the Nahda).[1] Rather, I submit that the Nahda is the media, in the sense that the Nahda is not simply a set of ideas but an assemblage of ideas, practices, and values inherent to specifically modern media of the late nineteenth to early twentieth centuries. My thesis is that the media in themselves are a vehicle of newness that disturbed the value system established before the modernizing efforts of the Nahda. This explains the anxiety that Constantin Zureiq and Jacques Berque have noted in Arab societies' response to modernization. Both authors, one from the Arab cultural nationalism side, and the other from the side of Western postcolonial interest in emergent independent societies, have astutely identified this anxiety prevalent in Arab societies. Zureiq calls it *qalaq*,[2] while Berque calls it *angoisse* (anguish).[3] But both attribute it to an emotional reaction to colonialism and to the feeling of helplessness in the face of the overwhelming technological and material superiority of colonial powers, as well as of the realization of the wide gap between the colonizer and the colonized. I suggest that this angoisse—particularly on its moral level—is rooted in a broader sense of alienation in a world that was modernizing at a pace that disrupted traditional value systems and practices, thus generating anxiety, even before the advent of direct colonial rule.

The intermediality and multimediality of many late Nahda figures are in themselves a testament to the claim I make about the Nahda being closely associated with the practice of the time's new media. In this chapter, I will focus on figures of late Nahda at the turn of the twentieth century and its first decades, who are clearly part of popular culture but whose work and career intersect with the Nahda movement's "serious" highbrow culture.

Nahda was not simply about the manufacturing of a modern Arab identity, or the calls for establishing a modern democratic society, for secularism, and for modern citizenhood. It was also about the enthusiasm for books because they can carry novel ideas, or—for Conservatives—because they disseminate the cultural production of the venerable Elders (*Salaf*). But the liberal/conservative divide is also palpable in attitudes toward "new media" of the time. In late *Nahda*, that is, in the early decades of the twentieth century, modernists were often enthusiastic about the importation of any new technological/media innovation, on the grounds that if it is used in Europe, it will be useful in the Arab world and will be a further step on the way of emulating the "civilized" West. But for conservatives as well as the liberals preoccupied with the impact of modernization on morality, anxiety was expressed not only vis-à-vis the substance of the products and services carried by the new media but about the very media themselves. Similarly, major Nahda figures were not just reproducing the modernist propaganda of progress and civilization emulating the European historical path, they were also relishing in the reproduction of cultural products associated with new media for the sake of practicing them, even for non-serious purposes, such as popular entertainment. Hence, proponents of Nahda's modernizing work were enthusiastic about the introduction of telegraphs and trains because of their beneficial effects on trade, government efficiency, and social cohesion on the national level. But both Liberals and Conservatives experienced anxiety when the vinyl records, moving pictures, and the radio were introduced at the turn of, and in the early decades of the twentieth century. Records and radio were appreciated by the Conservatives because they allowed the mechanical reproduction and the wide dissemination of Quranic recitation, or because they made major statesmen's speeches widely available. But the possibility for records and private radio stations to disseminate songs promoting debauchery and discourses about love and romantic attraction was troublesome for many Nahda intellectuals and ordinary citizens. Movie theaters were notoriously the object of male anxiety about female virtue because they offered the possibility for both genders to meet in the dark, as per Sayed Darwish's song "Harrag 'Alaya Baba Maruhsh El-Sinima" (My Father Forbade Me to Go to the Cinema). Similarly, records allowed young men and women to access dubious and salacious songs otherwise available only in cabarets, such as the songs of the "X-rated" singer Sayed Shata from the 1920s famous for "Sa'it al-Haz Ma Tit'awwadshi" (A Happy Hour Cannot Be Missed), or Munira al-Mahdiya's Bacchic song "Irkhi El-Sitara illi fi rihna" (Drop Those Curtains), or even some of the Diva Um Kulthum's early salacious songs, for example, "El Khala'a wel-Dala'a mazhabi" (Libertinage and Coquetterie Are My Doctrine) (1926).

Changing Moralities of Media: The Rise of Khala'a

Modern media, or Nahda media, are addressed here as a complex conceptual assemblage, in the sense Gille Deleuze gives to the expression, that is, a set of interconnected figures both material and conceptual whose agency lies in their connectedness. Nahda media here refers to objects such as vinyl discs, radio receivers, and films; as well as to institutions and industries, such as cinema and broadcasting; and to consumption platforms associated with these, such as radio stations and movie theaters. Media are not just beheld to technology and to the market where they are turned into goods or vehicles for goods (e.g., for the entertainment industry or the information market). They are also a complex of producers and products at the same time, materialized in the physicality of their means of production and of their nature as commodities endowed with materiality. They are not just transparent vehicles of content; they are the vehicle, the material, and the content all at once.

The social and moral aspect of modernity is not easy to define. It is best approached as newness and importation of contemporary Western values and practices. Immorality, therefore, is not understood here as an absolute and universal set of practices and values, but merely as social practices and rituals that are perceived as generated by changes introduced by material modernization. An arch-example of moral effects of modernization is—as in Europe in the nineteenth century—the effects of social change due to the Industrial Revolution on personal and social investment in sex and alcohol, both being means for hundreds of thousands of individuals to cope with the anxiety resulting from massive industrialization and urbanization.

One concept best suited to introduce the discussion of social change in the sense of reshaping the value systems due to the material changes introduced by modernization is that of *Khala'a*. That concept can be approached as a conceptual assemblage of the Arabic equivalent of loose morals, libertinage, and the French idea of "dévergondage." It literally means "(moral) dislocation." *Khala'a* would be practiced in highly symbolic spaces such as taverns and brothels. In other words, *Khala'a* would be a practice reserved mainly for males as consumers, women involved being usually the producers of entertainment, song and dance workers, and sometimes, sex workers. It would be a practice reserved in these spaces where social conventions agree to the suspension of "good-mannered" social codes.

A literary example of *Khala'a* in Egypt in the mid-nineteenth century is detailed in Flaubert's writings and correspondence during his trip to Egypt, which were minutely commented on by Edward Said.[4] Flaubert's visit to the famed *'alme* or *ghazeya* Kuchuk Hanum is a pointed example of the practice of *Khala'a*. European writers and researchers have divergent opinions about Kuchuk's class, whether she was a street entertainer/prostitute (*ghazeya*) or a classy, indoor, learned dancer (*'alme*).[5] What is attested is that at his hostess' house, the young French traveler— who was not at the time the illustrious novelist—listened to a musical performance, watched belly dancing, drank wine, and had sex with his hostess. One should note that all this took place in the private space of Kuchuk's home in Upper Egypt and not in a public institution, such as a cabaret or a brothel. Said saw in that encounter between Flaubert and Kuchuk a metaphor of the Orientalist's voyeurism and debasing of the feminized Orient by a male-centered, self-indulgent colonial gaze. Beyond that analysis, I would suggest that the encounter informs the reader about the geography of libertinage in nineteenth century, early Nahda period in Egypt.

Contrary to some Orientalist assumptions, in tune with the far-right discourses in the Muslim sphere, those practices grouped here under the label of *Khala'a* have always existed in predominantly Muslim societies and were vibrant in nineteenth-century Egypt. They were just "policed" and "disciplined," usually through a specific tightly controlled urban distribution: need for brothels and taverns to have permits, pay taxes, and—in modern times—submit to food and public health inspections. Some streets were open for certain forms of libertine entertainment, such as public belly dancing. The confinement of "immoral practices" was socially and morally acceptable inasmuch as they were strictly confined in specific places: neighborhoods or streets or alleys in the city. It was actually with modernization which started aggressively under Napoleon, then under Mohammed Ali, that limitations were gradually put on public *Khalaʿa* in nineteenth-century Egypt.

The epitome of the importation of pre-Victorian and Victorian morality was under Mohamed Ali who banned public belly dancing, the public practice of prostitution, and exiled major Madames, forcing them to move to southern Egypt in 1834.[6] It is precisely as a direct result of this decree that Kuchuk Hanum was banished from Cairo to Esna in southern Egypt where Flaubert visited her. That decree was still enforced after Mohamed Ali's death by his successor Abbas Pasha, who was the ruler of Egypt when Flaubert met Kuchuk. The irony of Abbas Pasha being gay, famous for his orgies, and having been assassinated by some of his minions may have no place here. Suffice it to note that the ruler's logic seems to be based on an understanding of the tensions between private and public spaces. In line with centuries-old Arab cultural and social conventions, Abbas made sure that non-normative heterosexual practices—such as his gay sex—were not allowed in the public space, even though they were a poorly kept secret. In line with Victorian contemporary ideas, he was opposed to the presence of orgy-esque *Khalaʿa* in the public space but was the first to practice it in private. The libertine aspect here is of course not the gay sexual orientation, which together with bisexuality had its place within the distinction public-private space in traditional Arab cultures, but the practice of orgies.

In pre-Nahda times and around the time Nahda became a strong set of discourses, practices, and public policies in the second half of Mohammad Ali's reign, *Khalaʿa* was a transgressive practice, but a confined one both in time and space. It was tolerated because it was disciplined and controlled. The practice of *Khalaʿa* and the word itself made their way into the times of the late Nahda in the 1920s through to the 1940s. Nonetheless, I claim, it caused immense social and moral anxiety, not because of its mere existence—which was not new—but because of its association with modern spaces of libertine entertainment, and more pointedly, because of its production within modern media, which made *Khalaʿa* far-reaching and able to be consumed in private homes. Media, such as the vinyl disc, radio, and film were technological icons of modernity and were thus consumed as part of the performance of one's modernity. But they made libertine products such as *Khalaʿa* in music and belly dancing far-reaching, instead of being confined to an entertainment district such as Ezbekieh. With the rise of the modern media of the time, *Khalaʿa* could reach thousands in movie theaters and hundreds of thousands of good-mannered members of the bourgeoisie in the privacy of their homes, if they had a gramophone or a radio set.

In the following sections, I will briefly discuss a few examples which showcase the impact of shifting moral perceptions on the production and the consumption of certain cultural products, or on the evaluation of certain iconic artists' careers or works. These perceptions contributed to shaping the cultural products themselves, making them "cleaner" and as such, more suitable for the mass mediation of modern technologies of entertainment such as disc and film. The traditional comparison between the two major divas of late Nahda: Munira al-Mahdiya and Um Kulthum is a case in point. Another case is that of the tribulations of some early silent movies *fortunas*, involving two entertainment stars: Bamba Kashar and Fatima Rushdi.

The Morality of Aesthetics

At the meeting point of modernity-causing anxiety, morality and cultural production lies the issue of what one may call "the morality of aesthetics," or—even better—"the aesthetics of morality." Munira al-Mahdiya was the indisputable star of music and musicals at the turn of the twentieth century in Egypt. Her cabaret poetically named "Nuzhat al-Nufus" (roughly "The Pleasant Promenade of the Souls") was the Mecca of music lovers at the heart of the entertainment district of Ezbekieh. Her performances of musicals on stage were always major artistic and popular events. Munira al-Mahdiya's voice was characterized by a streak of hoarseness. This is not a casual detail, as it goes to the core of the aesthetics of morality. This claim of mine is confirmed by the significant number of historians and critics who underscored the fact that al-Mahdiya had a raspy voice, which one may call in today's terms, a smoky one. Critics often compared al-Mahdiya's raspy voice to Um Kulthum's clear, "pure" one. "Raspiness" is either explicitly or implicitly associated with both sexuality and social status in the discourses of Arab critics and cultural historians. It is assumed to be a sign of vulgarity and of unhinged "low-class" over-sexualization of the female subject. Therefore, it is safe to consider the raspy voice to be a feature of *Khalaʿa*.

Ratiba al-Hifni has written a major historical study of Munira al-Mahdiya's career, affectionately calling the diva "The Sultana" or "The Queen." Yet al-Hifni makes it a point to underscore the fact that: "Munira's voice characteristically enjoyed a natural hoarseness, which gave a special character to her performance [. . .] ranging from extraordinary force to affection and sweetness." She adds that Munira's voice had the cachet of ʿ*almes*.[7] The subtext here is that Munira's aesthetics were the expression of the lower classes' taste, where underscored explicit sexualization of the body, its movements, and its voice, is paramount, as in the singing-dancing performances of the public entertainers or ʿ*almes*. That cachet of her voice contributed to making her sexy, and—I argue—it is a major reason why that sexiness made her popular, attracted audiences to her theater and also made some of her records such as "Drop Those Curtains" major hits in terms of sales.[8]

But the end of the Second World War and the ensuing 1919 revolt demanding Egypt's independence from Great Britain led to the establishment of a new national bourgeoisie able to share power with the previous ruling class. From that newly formed bourgeoisie came the first government led by the nationalist leader Saad Zaghloul, who was of a relatively modest background compared to the aristocratic background of most previous prime ministers. The coincidence of the rise of a more morally conservative social stratum—often from a recent rural background, or an urban popular one—with the advent of modern Nahda media, such as the wax, then the vinyl disc, made it progressively harder for a "popular" (i.e., overly sexualized) voice to be morally acceptable for the disc industry, which relied considerably on the purchasing power of the new, rising middle class, headed by the newly formed national bourgeoisie. It was only a matter of two decades before tastes became less welcoming of *Khalaʿa* on disc, then even on stage. By the 1930s, it was the time of—not only a change in tastes and aesthetics—but of a shift in what was considered a morally and aesthetically good taste. That new, good taste was embodied by the new diva of the time: Um Kulthum.

In her book on al-Mahdiya, Ratiba al-Hifni quotes the prominent journalist Mostafa Amin, a close friend of Um Kulthum, who provides an account of one of the last theatrical performances of al-Mahdiya after her comeback in 1948. Amin claims he went upon Um Kulthum's insistence. The star wanted to encourage al-Mahdiya—her former rival—and paid for the baignoire seats herself. The journalist underscores that: "Her voice (al-Mahdiya's) was more akin to a broken record. Her voice has lost its sweetness, its smokiness, its alto melodiousness, and its attractiveness."[9] Once again, the charm of Munira's voice is partly associated with its smokiness, but here this smokiness is alleged to have disappeared. When one considers the unspoken of this testimony, that al-Mahdiya has grown older, one realizes that Amin is implying that what may have been taunting smokiness has become simply unpleasant hoarseness, one too obvious to hide the overtly vulgar sexual perception of the effect of al-Mahdiya's voice. And Amin's use of the metaphor of the broken record is aptly hinting to the "industrial" dimension of Munira's demise. She was finished as a stage performer, and even more so, as a recorded artist: her voice's very nature has become that of a broken medium.

Al-Hifni's account of the rivalry between al-Mahdiya and Um Kulthum may shed some light on the role played by *Khalaʿa* in the ascent of one and the downfall of the other. The author introduces several critical assessments of Munira's contemporaries, which often included comparisons between Munira and Um Kulthum. A critical account of the respective talents of Munira al-Mahdiya and Um Kulthum summarizes the reasons why the latter has dominated the collective Arab memory since the 1930s and 1940s. The anonymous critic from the *Al-Majalla al-Musiqiya* is adamant that Um Kulthum's style is aesthetically superior because of its respect of "good taste" and moral rectitude: "The Kulthoumian art is characterized by clean lyrics and amour courtois. It is far from—not only from permissiveness—but from all what contravenes to good taste."[10]

The medium of the human body (particularly the combination of voice and dramatic or stage performance) in its interaction with the medium of the vinyl disc and that of language creates a stressful assemblage from the point of view of the newly formed but steadily growing middle class in Egypt. Munira al-Mahdiya's art was not morally threatening, simply because of the vocabulary and the content of popular entertainment songs. It was more so because the female performer's body was "multiplied" by the vinyl disc. The vocabulary, however, became an issue of particular interest from the moral perspective. *Khalaʿa* songs included references to topics such as the consumption of drugs and alcohol, lying in bed, and having sex.[11]

Khalaʿa was produced on disc until the early decades of the twentieth century. Munira al-Mahdyia and other libertine performers were successful recorded artists. But the disc market expanded after the Great War and reached larger strata of the rising middle class of the time. After the First World War, migrations from rural centers to the cities and the establishment of major companies and factories as of the 1930s, which hired clerks and workers enlarged the ranks of the newly formed middle class. Furthermore, the government's expansion and its policies that led to the hiring of hundreds of civil servants enriched the numbers of this middle class. It is that market, more conservative than the smaller middle class before the First World War, that required less *Khalaʿa* on vinyl. By the time the national royal radio station was established in the 1930s, where music could reach thousands of households, music had to be further sanitized to suit the news mass audiences. Media moral aesthetics became a necessity driven by technological changes and the composition of the market's moral spectrum.

It is worth noting that the press was a seminal media in the production of Um Kulthum as the epitome of the anti-*Khalaʿa* artist. Her close friendship with influential journalists such as Mostafa Amin and Mohamad el-Tabei institutionalized her memory as a friend of learned, respected intellectuals, and earned her hundreds of pages written about her talent, her culture, and her good, morally impeccable, taste in the press, and later in books recapping the history or theory of modern Egyptian popular culture. While producing Um Kulthum as the respectable diva, the press moved gradually from producing al-Mahdiya either as the femme à scandale or as the established diva to producing her as a stage in the progress of the national art of singing, a predecessor to Um Kulthum.

The manufacturing of Um Kulthum as a "clean," cultured, and classy singer was in part a marketing strategy aiming, not only at making a diva but also at making her the marketable decent product that surely appeals to the ideals of the middle class shaped in the interwar period, particularly in terms of disc sales and radio presence. The press played a major role in this enterprise, through the writings of famed journalists among her friends and also through press photography, where Um Kulthum is portrayed next to writers and journalists. The carefully drafted discourse about Um Kulthum distancing her from *Khalaʿa* insisted on elements which appeal to a constituency moderately aspiring to modernity, with a strong attachment to conservative moral values. The poet Ahmad Rami wrote about Um Kulthum's language and elocution being far from colloquial and vulgar, and about her background in religious performance training, such as Quranic recitation, reminding the reader that she represents the ideal singer: "A Quran reciter, song/daughter of a Quran reciter."[12] Frédéric Lagrange's observation about Um Kulthum's background summarizes the combination she represented, appealing to audiences keen on modernization, but still with an attachment to high morality: "She is the first *mutriba* (singer) who is neither an *ʿalme*, not a *Sayka*, but a modern woman."[13] A woman who is modern, who frequents upper-middle-class salons, but who is also adamant about her culture and education, a tendency evidenced by the first salon she attends in the palace of ʿAli Abd al-Razek, the famed author of the controversial book *al-Islam wa Usul al-Hukm* (Islam and the Foundations of Government).[14]

Cabaret and Vinyl Nahda

I have written elsewhere about Um Kulthum being an icon of modernity (or the Nahda) in her early career in the 1920s and 1930s before she gradually became—and resolutely so, since the 1950s—an idol, and an incarnation of classical Arabic music. In her early career, Um Kulthum was an Egyptian incarnation of the Western New Woman of the roaring 1920s, often photographed in men's clothes, then in smoky pictures comparable to Marlene Dietrich's in the 1930s. This forgotten Um Kulthum has sung quite a few light, sometimes lascivious, songs in the 1920s.[15] In 1927, Um Kulthum recorded "Al Eih Helef Ma Yekalemnish" ("Really! He's Sworn not to Talk to Me") for the Odeon label. A famous case in point is the song titled "Libertinage (or Debauchery) and Coquetterie are my Doctrine." Interestingly, the concept of *Khalaʿa* is at the center of this song's title. The melody and the vocal performance themselves have nothing licentious about them and they sound like hundreds of light songs from the era. It is the lyrics—and particularly the refrain—that are audacious. The song is yet another nonchalant ode to the Beloved, describing his handsomeness and the magic effect his looks have on the locutor/singer. But the refrain—even though not performed in a morally outrageous manner in terms of excess of sexualization of the voice—is quite audacious as they elevate libertinage and debauchery to the highest standards of an individual's reclaiming of their moral freedom. They are proclaimed a doctrine.

Cultural critic and painter Bermalion El-Begmawy has published pointed research in a series of posts on his Facebook page about the year 1931 in Um Kulthum's career. His main argument is that 1931 was the most productive year of the diva: she recorded thirty-one songs in that year alone, and that she displayed her musical style at its best in these songs, demonstrating a shift from an older style to a newer one, less focused on vocal improvisation and ornamentation. Bermalion's subtle observation about the shift in Um Kulthum's style and the iconographic material he produces can be quoted here as further explanation of Um Kulthum's rebranding of her work away from *Khalaʿa* in order to make her song more sellable on record. "Libertinage and Coquetterie are my Doctrine" was produced a few years before 1931. But in that year, none of the thirty-one songs had similarly daring lyrics. The shift into the "new" Um Kulthum was achieved in 1931 both in terms of her more modern musical taste and her firm distancing of herself from *Khalaʿa*. This is translated into an impressive recording activity: thirty-one discs in one year, that is, so to speak, a record, for the time, which discs were recorded by at least four labels: Odeon, Pathé, Alamphone, and His Master's Voice.[16] A song more obviously debauched than Um Kulthum's "Libertinage and Coquetterie are my Doctrine" is performed about the same era, by Um Kulthum's predecessor, Munira al-Mahdiya "Drop Those Curtains." To measure how tame Um

Kulthum's song is, one needs only to compare it with the almost contemporaneous song performed by Munira al-Mahdiya, who, after being the incontestable diva of the Egyptian musical scene at the turn of the twentieth century, was already losing ground to her young competitor Um Kulthum. Al-Mahdiya, dubbed fondly "Queen of Tarab," as Cormack recalls, sings suggestively about the locutor's use of alcohol and cocaine and subsequent sex.[17] In my loose translation, the locutor says approximately: "Enough! You are turning my head / Remember the day we sniffed (cocaine)? / I drank and became so drunk I could not sit up straight / Then we closed the door and laid down."

The explicit nature of the lyrics is striking, with very few euphemisms and allusions depicting in four short lines sex and the use of cocaine and alcohol. The available recordings of the song performed by al-Mahdiya herself confirm indeed the *'alme* streak in her utterances, and her playfulness puts her closer to the cabaret style than to the variety show. The song was a major hit in cabarets and had a life on vinyl. However, by the 1940s, the song was remembered only by the title, because the bienséance would not appreciate it being played on vinyl or on the radio, which required "cleaner" family-friendly products.

The purpose of this discussion is not to comment on the morally liberated dimension of the liberal trends within late Nahda. Rather, its aim is to underscore the agency of the new media accompanying the dissemination of this type of music: the vinyl disc. Even with the process of institutionalizing Um Kulthum as the performer of clean music, or perhaps because of that process, the younger diva has reportedly purged herself of her own records legacy. Um Kulthum's awareness of the power of the disc and its perennity pushed her to allegedly attempt to collect and destroy the entire vinyl edition of her quite popular hit "Libertinage and Coquetterie are my Doctrine" at the time of the disc's release. It is indeed almost impossible to find an original vinyl disc carrying that song, which is available today thanks to the archival function played by YouTube. Very few original discs of that song have survived the deliberate destruction ordered and overseen by Um Kulthum, and one of them was fortunately used to upload the song to the YouTube platform.

Um Kulthum's efforts aiming at reshaping her image were not limited to preserving the aura of the moral performer, untainted by *Khala'a*. She also presided over the editing of some of her songs after the proclamation of the Republic in Egypt to remove couplets dedicated to the king. Here it was her political morality that was at stake. But in her defense, that was a common practice. Muhammad Abd al-Wahab, Um Kulthum's male rival, did little to preserve the memory of some of his *Khala'a* songs from the 1920s, such as "Fik 'Asharet Kutshina fi-l Balkuna" ("Come and Play a Game of Cards in the Balcony"). He too oversaw the purging of couplets addressed to the king from his songs. This purge was made to make the artists in tune with the new Republican political morality and also to make the songs eligible for broadcast on Egypt's national radio. This concern about broadcasting eligibility dictated the purging of salacious sexual language in the repertoire of Sayyid Darwish from the first quarter of the twentieth century, when it was appropriated by national orchestras and radio programs after the

1952 Republican coup. In all these cases, moral (social or political) considerations dictated by the nature of the media altered the production and distribution of songs.

Nahda on Stage and on Celluloid

Munira al-Mahdiya's short career in the movies provides another insight into the aesthetics of morality. She starred in only one silent long feature film *The Coquette* (al-Ghandura) in 1935, directed by Mario Volpi. Unfortunately, the film is lost and very few accounts of the picture reached us, just enough to know it bears some similarities with Alexandre Dumas the Son's *The Lady of the Camellias*. A notable account is published by an anonymous critic in *Al-Musiqa* Journal which focused solely on a critique of the lyrics and an analysis of the maqams (modes) of Daoud Hosni's music performed by al-Mahdiya in this musical dubbed on the film's poster: "Opera comique" because its production value as spectacular, and the dialogues overwhelmingly sung like an opera, yet the epithet "comique" suggests a happy ending (and not actual comedy). Another valuable testimony relates more specifically to the play also titled *The Coquette*. The film's screenplay is based on the play by the same title, which premiered ten years earlier, in 1925, starring the same Munira al-Mahdiya. This testimony is authored by the playwright Badiʿ Khayri himself. He insists that the play was famously associated with Munira al-Mahdiya's fame, has insured her considerable revenues, and he points to a salient piece of trivia regarding her wardrobe on stage. Munira, says Khayri, used to wear a *baladi* dance costume manufactured exclusively for her character, which was famously ornamented with actual gold sterling pounds, and which was deposited every night after the show in a bank's safe.[18]

In the absence of photos, let alone of footage from the film, it is hard to tell how visually shocking Munira al-Mahdiya was on screen. But the audiences of the time were either able to see al-Mahdiya's *baladi* gold sterling costume on stage, ten years before the film's release, or had access through gossip and word-to-mouth, or through press coverage to a description of the costume. That must have been a powerful example of the confluence of all the anxieties caused by modernization as focused on the female body: her sexuality displayed in a *baladi* attire, the literal commodification of that body manifested in the weaving of that attire in actual money, and the public display of all that in entertainment institutions created by modernity, such as the theater and the movie theater. Cinema here generated an additional source of anxiety, because of the medium's ability to trigger the multiplication of expositions of the female commodified body of the entertainer, thanks to the nature of the modern media and screen technology, which "atomizes" the body's image into twenty-four frames per second, then, through the power of the projector's shutter, projects and blows up that image on screen, in as many as theaters as there are copies of the positive.

Cinema was as terrifying for the newly formed middle class as were the wax then vinyl discs. Movies amplified the anxieties already triggered by theater, with the added concern about Egypt's image. Conservative and nationalist voices often viewed the figuration of a *baladi* dancer on screen to be detrimental to Egypt's international image. Once again, this concern was anchored in the female body, and—as with the performer's raspy voice—it was about sexual and class anxieties. The production of the *baladi* dancer's body on screen is a case in point in the expression of the anxiety vis-à-vis an uncontrolled production of desire and female sexuality made possible and wide-reaching by modern media, such as press photography and film. The matter was not simply a moral one where Conservatives seek to hide the female body. It was about the agency of modern media. Basically, bourgeois discourses implicitly distributed accepted spaces for female bodies: the *baladi* dancer's place is the cabaret; the décolleté of the new woman is however accepted on screen.

After being confined to a limited and specific time and space until the nineteenth century, such as taverns, *Khalaʿa* became more visible and socially acceptable or at least valued. It started to be associated not only with the "Red-light districts" of the cities but with the modern Western-fashioned institutions of entertainment such as theaters and cabarets. The Kit Kat cabaret, then Badia's casino became socially distinguished spaces in the early decades of the twentieth century, the former for the lower strata of the middle class, and the latter for the middle and upper middle classes. In both cases, it is the modernity of the institution, its copying of Western models, and being frequented by British Empire soldiers, officers, and bureaucrats who gave the space its social legitimacy.

One may argue that the *baladi* dance still known today as *raqs sharqi* (belly dancing) was invented by Badia Masabni. Wendy Buenaventura's ethnographies and histories of *baladi* suggest the movement from street to cabaret was more progressive and took more decades to be associated with one sole name.[19] One can at least argue that Badia is the one who accomplished the transition of that art from a street vulgar performance, or an *ʿalme* sophisticated house-confined entertainment into the cabaret dance that we know today, thanks to the institution of cabaret then that of cinema. The latter having polished the practice of *baladi* into an art somehow occupying the middle ground between the popular entertainment of belly dancing and ballet, with divas such as Taheya Carioca and Samia Gamal, both apprentices of Badia.

From its inception in Arabic, with the rise of the Egyptian film industry, cinema and *raqs sharqi* have faced a predicament understandable within the debates caused by the social and moral anxiety generated by modern media. The screening of the second Arab long feature *Leila* (1927), produced and directed by Aziza Amir, caused an uproar on many levels, one of which was triggered by the scene of a *baladi* dance performed by the diva Bamba Kashar (whose first name is probably an alteration of the French "Pimpant" for "vivid pink"). According to film historian Ahmad El-Hadari, some conservative voices at the time have expressed concerns in the newspapers that the *baladi* scene might damage Egypt's image on the global scene (already back then, that argument was made).[20]

One can understand the class dimension of that concern: a bourgeois expensive newly imported art, should exclude *baladi* local indigenous (read: low-class) practices, such as belly dance. But another dimension—I argue—was the horror triggered by the possibility for members of good, well-behaved, rising bourgeois classes, particularly good girls and good women, to watch belly dance. This practice—until then confined to streets, brothels, then cabarets—was about to gain a wide audience thanks to the new media of celluloid film. It is worth noting that Kashar was about sixty-six years old when she performed that dance on film and that she died in 1930, less than three years after the film was screened. The bourgeois anxiety vis-à-vis *baladi* dance was not triggered by the sexual nature of the actual performance of Kashar. This performance was undoubtedly a homage to her exceptional career as a dancer, highly praised by the Khedivial vice-royal House. Rather, the moral shock originated in the association of *baladi* dance with Orientalist clichés about the dancer being a metonymy of Egypt or at least of its women, and about her perceived loose morality.

One can understand within the same frame, the burning and destruction of the negative of Fatima Rushdi's first long feature *Under Egypt's Sky* (Taht Sama' Misr, 1928). Some sources state that it was the diva herself who burned it; other sources indicate it was the work of the diva's lover and producer, Elie Edrei. The film was completely erased from existence, and a few theories have circulated to explain the mystery. The most compelling and widely accepted ones are that the diva felt the film, directed by Wedad Urfi, was not made at artistic standards worthy of her talent and public persona. Another compelling—more convincing—theory purports that Edrei managed to convince Rushdi that her public image as a major theater, then movie star would suffer because of the lascivious seduction scenes in the film. A complementary theory argues that Rushdi's extremely wealthy businessman lover, Edrei, was so jealous that he did not mind burning the negatives himself and enduring the financial loss. The remaining stills from the film and its press dossier do not suggest that Fatima Rushdi's role required nudity. The available synopsis suggests, though, that the character of her rival in the film, that of a Russian debauched and seductress dancer who performs in cabarets in Paris and then in Alexandria is probably the culprit.

The identity of the body "immorally" on display on screen does not change the core argument, that is, that the medium is so powerful that the female body it reproduces can disrupt public moral order, to the point it warrants destruction. It is worth noting here that the high society of the late 1920s in Egypt did not find its morality threatened by the public affair of the pair Rushdi and Edrei, who were not married, nor by the fact that they came from different faith communities (she was Muslim, he was Jewish), but that the magnification of the star's body as a sexual object, thanks to the celluloid media and the institution of the movie theater, posed enough threat and anxiety that warranted the destruction of the film.

To Conclude

Based on the aforementioned, it is safe to claim that the moral-immoral agency of celluloid has a parallel to that of vinyl and the disc industry. Modern Nahda media have contributed to the dissemination of liberal Westernized practices establishing new forms of relationship between men and women: songs and films at the turn of the twentieth century actively promote romantic involvement between men and women outside the institution of family-supervised marriage. Nahda media have also contributed, to creating new attitudes vis-à-vis the relationship between public and private space when it comes to practices of pleasure, and the representation of these in cultural and entertainment productions: entertainment, music, particularly the morally loose, "libertine" trends became part of the private space thanks to discs and radio sets and could reach the "good bourgeois" class in its public spaces of entertainment, such as movie theaters, while libertine entertainment was only accessible if only deliberately were to travel to the confined space of specific "red" districts within the city. Nahda media did not just carry and represent these aspects of social and cultural change. They were themselves the social change, media were the Nahda. The media generated moral anxiety as a byproduct of their agency, hence the strong emergence of the concept of libertinage, *Khala'a*, present either explicitly or implicitly in some of the cultural products analyzed earlier, including Munira al-Mahdiya's song "Drop Those Curtains" and Um Kulthum's "Libertinage and Coquetterie are my Doctrine."

An eloquent coincidence, let alone a full-fledged irony, is that the poet who penned the latter two songs, Yunus al-Qadi, was also the one who wrote the famous patriotic poem *Biladi Biladi*, which has been the Egyptian national anthem for close to half a century. This coincidence of iconic productions of libertinage and nationalism confirms my argument that the Nahda was not just introduced through ideas expressed in various media. It was rather introduced through the very "practice" of the new media, even if the products were for entertainment ludic, and sometimes debauched, purposes and not for the purpose of serious enlightenment. Therefore, one may submit that major heralds of modern nationalism, such as the poets 'Abd Allah al-Nadim and later Badi' Khayri and Bayram al-Tunisi, as well as Yunus al-Qadi, were not just perceived as threats to the colonial established order, because of their patriotic poems, or—in the case of Nadim—because of the nationalist, anticolonial propaganda. They were also causing moral anxiety because of the playfulness and risqué nature of their non-political writings in the press and some of their lyrics available on records or even broadcast in the short-lived industry of the private radio stations in the 1930s.

Chapter 3

NOCTURNAL BAGHDAD

NIGHTCLUBS AND POPULAR ENTERTAINMENT

Pelle Valentin Olsen

In his 1935 book *Iraq from Mandate to Independence*, Ernest Main, a British official and correspondent for the pro-British English-language *The Iraq Times* newspaper, wrote extensively about Iraq's modernity and development. Main focused on the sights, scenes, and features that he considered to be important markers of Iraq's progress three years after nominal independence from Britain in 1932. In a section on entertainment and nightlife, Main complained that "the evening entertainments in Baghdad are not very varied." Without enthusiasm, Main described the dancing and singing of female performers in nightclubs as "exotic and strange to Western ears and eyes." Main was no more impressed with the "shrill and quavering" music than he was with the "monotonous singing and swaying of the women dancers."[1] Unlike Main, whose criteria for measuring modernity and progress meant that Baghdad did not live up to his expectations, this chapter approaches Baghdadi nightclubs, their audiences, and many performers, as a newly available, vibrant, and artistically sophisticated terrain of urban leisure and the production of popular culture and entertainment.

Following the British occupation of the three Ottoman provinces of Baghdad, Basra, and Mosul between 1914 and 1918, the Iraqi state came into being under a League of Nations mandate in 1920. The Hashemite monarchy of Iraq formally came into existence a year later in 1921 when the League of Nations mandate granted to Britain was replaced by a monarchy, headed by King Faisal I, but still administered and controlled by the British. British influence remained strong until the 1958 revolution which overthrew the monarchy. In the first half of the twentieth century, during the transition from Ottoman rule to British colonialism and eventually independence, Baghdad was an incipient space in the process of becoming a modern capital. As part of this process, a wide array of novel leisure venues and practices became available, first to Baghdadis, and later also to Iraqis living in other urban centers. *Malha*, the Arabic word used most frequently for nightclubs in Iraq, carries several meanings, including "amusement,"

I would like to thank Sara Farhan, Orit Bashkin, and the editors of this volume.

"entertainment," "diversion," and "distraction." This chapter focuses on the new forms of nocturnal amusement, entertainment, diversion, and distraction offered by nightclubs.

In the 1920s, during the mandate period, a growing number of nightclubs began to appear. As a result, certain forms of entertainment and leisure moved from Baghdad's cafés, the *maqahi*, to its nightclubs, the *malahi*. Simultaneously, male performers and dancers were gradually replaced by female performers, first from across the Ottoman Empire and eventually, beginning in the 1920s, from across Iraq, Egypt, and the Levant. Developing from performances on makeshift stages in cafés in the first decade of the twentieth century, some cafés gradually transformed into nightclubs while others continued to offer music, song, and dance until these activities permanently moved to the nightclubs that began to appear in the 1920s.[2] Several of the first nightclubs were open-air establishments with long rows of seats or benches rather than individual tables, which allowed for large audiences. In the 1930s, indoor nightclubs catering to a wealthier clientele began to appear.

Also in the 1930s, a small number of female performers, including Munira al-Huzuz (1893–1995), Sultana Yusuf (1910–95), Zakiyya George (1879–1966), Salima Murad (1900–74), and ʿAfifa Iskandar (1921–2012), became famous national divas. Raphael Cormack has pointed out that in Cairo's nightlife, "rigid identities and conventional barriers . . . were more fluid than anywhere else."[3] In Iraq as well, countless performers crossed boundaries relating to sect, class, and gender throughout their careers. However, nightlife relied on different forms of labor and exploitation, including sex work and this chapter also tells the story of Iraq's many less famous female performers who never became national divas. Although many female performers came from outside of Iraq, this chapter highlights the ways in which performers, Iraqi and foreign, participated in the creation of a specifically Iraqi version of global and modern entertainment practices. While many of these women, especially the first generation, except for the most famous ones mentioned earlier, have been forgotten or erased from national narratives,[4] they played a key role in the creation of Iraqi modernity and culture.

From the vantage point of the different classes and individuals who took part in it, the nightlife of nightclubs was a novel and exciting place, a place of labor and exploitation, as well as a place where popular culture and entertainment was produced, circulated, and consumed by many Iraqi men from different class and religious backgrounds. In addition, nightclubs were sites of social and political transformation and debates over the appropriate articulation of Iraqi culture and modernity as well as sites in which morality, sexuality, and gender were policed. While a growing body of scholarship has begun to excavate the overlooked and largely unrecorded history of nightlife, popular entertainment, and female performers in the Middle East,[5] barring one study, Iraqi nocturnal practices and institutions of leisure have been all but absent in the English-language scholarship on Iraq.[6] As pointed out in various ways by the chapters in this volume, writing the history of popular entertainment poses methodological challenges. Despite their enormous importance, scholarship on the lives of the many women who were integral to the creation of nightlife across the region, is still relatively sparse. With limited access to primary sources produced by the female protagonists of Iraqi nightlife, this chapter analyzes memoirs and historical accounts written by Iraqis involved in the county's nocturnal entertainment industry, police reports, poetry and fiction, and advertisements in the press.

In the 1930s and 1940s, at a time when Iraq was struggling against British colonialism and when the state, as well as those opposed to it, was working to consolidate what it meant, politically, historically, and culturally to be Iraqi, there was a synchronous attempt, from below and through popular entertainment and nightlife, to lay claims to Iraqi history and identity. This chapter shows that while nightclubs and many of the women who performed in them existed on the margins of society, female performers became complex representatives and embodiments of Iraqi modernity and culture, even as they were seen as deeply compromised and morally dangerous in the eyes of many. They were embraced, and in turn embraced and promoted popular and nocturnal expressions of national identity, culture, folklore, and history.

Throughout the first half of the twentieth century, the period covered in this chapter, Iraqi nightlife was fundamentally transnational and transregional with performers and musicians coming to Baghdad, first from across the Ottoman Empire, and later also from across Iraq. The transnationalism of female nightclub performers, the mobility and movement of precarious forms of labor, including sex work, offers an alternative perspective on elite and middle-class-focused understandings of movement, travel, and entertainment. At the same time, focusing on the history of nightclubs, their performers, and audiences expands scholarship on the process of literary and cultural revival referred to as the Arab Nahda (renaissance), which transformed cultural and intellectual production across the Middle East in the nineteenth and first half of the twentieth centuries.[7] By favoring elite and middle-class cultural production, such as print culture and literature, and its relationship to nationalism, secularism, and language, traditional accounts of the Nahda have paid only limited attention to popular culture and entertainment. In addition, geographically, the Nahda's center of gravity has often been associated with cities such as Cairo and Beirut. As we will see, Baghdad deserves to be included as a central location in the creation of a popular Nahda.

From Maqahi *to* Malahi *and from Boys to* Banat

During the late Ottoman period, before the emergence of nightclubs, Baghdad's limited nightlife was characterized by *maqam* performances, which in the Iraqi context, meant the singing of poetic verses structured by elaborate rules and conventions, and featuring male dancing and singing. *Maqam* performances like these generally took place in cafés and women did not start to perform on these public stages in Iraq until after 1908.[8] One of the first cafés to offer dancing was Sabi' in the Midan area of Baghdad; it was also the first establishment to be referred to as a nightclub (*malha*). It is not clear when exactly Sabi' became a venue for public musical leisure and entertainment.[9] However, it is certain that by

1907, Sabi' was putting on *maqam* performances and dancing boys, often dressed in women's clothing.

In an entertainment scene without female performers, these male dancers, often young boys, were popular. The word for this type of performer was a *sha'ar*. During his act, the *sha'ar* "puts makeup on his face, lets free his long hair" and is so "specialized in imitating female movements during his dance that one forgot that he was a man."[10] Some performed with fake breasts made out of different materials.[11] Most were accompanied by their own bands consisting of one or two members, most often a percussionist and a violinist.[12] Although these *sha'ar* performances were popular with audiences, the profession was socially frowned upon and *sha'ar* performers were associated with male sex work.[13] It is important to note that during this period in Iraq, same-sex and non-normative sexual practices had not yet been definitively linked to homosexuality.[14] It is difficult to ascertain whether and to what extent *sha'ar* performers were actually involved in sex work or if this was just an accusation made by those who frowned upon the profession. Spatially at the very least, they were close—both *sha'ar* performers and sex workers were associated with the Midan area, close to Baghdad's official and state-sanctioned and legal red-light district, *al-Kallachiyya*. While brothels and sex work were intensely debated topics, for most of the first half of the twentieth century, as described by Sara Farhan, Iraqi authorities favored regulation, reformation, and containment over criminalization and a complete ban, which did not materialize until after the 1958 revolution.[15]

While few details are known about the lives of Baghdad's *sha'ar* performers, some of them gained considerable fame. One male dancer, Na'im, is particularly well-known because of his tragically early death, which was memorialized by the Iraqi poet Ma'ruf al-Rusafi (1875–1945). Na'im, a Christian youth from Aleppo, was extremely popular and, according to Iraqi historian Sami Zubaida, seduced and charmed many of Sabi''s male patrons with his beauty and dance skills.[16] One patron in particular became so infatuated with the young Na'im that he offered him money and gifts to become his lover. When Na'im refused, the man showed up drunk at Sabi' one night during Na'im's performance and shot the performer dead.[17] The murder of Na'im was the talk of the town in Baghdad for several weeks. Shortly after the incident, which took place in 1907, al-Rusafi, who had been an admirer of Na'im's, composed two poems, "Wajhu Na'im" (Na'im's Face) and "al-Yatim al-Makhdu'" (The Defrauded Orphan), in which he lamented the performer's murder.[18] "Wajhu Na'im" begins with the following lines: "God abundantly blessed Na'im's face with beauty / a moon more powerful than the sunrise on a jet-black night (*bahim*) with his slender (*saqim*) figure he taught people true love."[19]

The violence faced by Na'im was likely a reality for many performers who existed on the margins of society. At the same time, however, the murder of Na'im symbolically ended male performances. While it was still possible in 1907 for al-Rusafi to cast Na'im unapologetically as the poem's male beloved and protagonist, his murder occurred at a time when, in Iraq and across the globe, as noted by several scholars, discourses and practices of sexuality and desire were changing and when sexuality, especially same-sex practices, was being regulated in new ways structured by European colonialism, regional empires, and discourses on progress and modernity. As noted by Afsaneh Najmabadi in the context of Iran, beginning in the nineteenth century, homoeroticism and same-sex practices became a sign of backwardness, requiring the heteronormalization of eros, sex, public space, and family life to achieve modernity.[20] Similarly, Joseph Massad points to the deep connection between Arab nationalist and modernist discourse and the regulation of sexuality, especially same-sex practices, in the nineteenth and twentieth centuries.[21]

As the *sha'ar*, both as performer and object of male desire, disappeared from public view, instead, for the first time, around 1908, Iraq witnessed the introduction of female singers and dancers and the concomitant rise of the nightclub, the *malha*, as a space separate from the café. *Sha'ar* performances did not disappear overnight, but the space of the nightclub quickly became associated with female performers and the articulation of heteronormative desire. Similarly, while the *sha'ar* and the sexual sociability associated with this figure disappeared from Iraqi nightlife and poetry, other same-sex practices and homoerotic desires did not. They were, however, displaced from public institutions of nocturnal leisure.[22]

Writing specifically about the *khawal*, the Egyptian variant of the *sha'ar*, Wilson Jacob notes that the figure of the *khawal* sheds light on a "terrain of gender, sexuality, and sociability that was in the process of rapidly receding" and that "the effect of colonial modernity in Egypt . . . was implicit in the vanishing of the cross-dressing sociality of the *khawal*."[23] In Iraq as well, elite and middle-class desire for progress and modernity took place at the expense of feminine, queer, and lower-class sexualized subjects, such as the *sha'ar*. As we will see in the following sections, female performers and the nightclubs in which they performed arrived both as celebrated representatives, fulfillments, *and*, in the eyes of many nationalist and cultural elites, corruptions of appropriate and virtuous Iraqi leisure and modernity.

Female Performers and Famous Divas

One of the first female performers to arrive in Baghdad was a woman from Aleppo, who performed under the stage name Rahlu. Sometime after her arrival in 1908, she was given the nickname *Jarada* (locust) because of her dancing style. The arrival of Rahlu caused a small scandal and fueled concerns about moral degeneration, which was reported in the Iraqi press.[24] Rahlu performed on a wooden stage, which had been set up for the purpose in the garden of the Sabi' café.[25] As demonstrated by historians of female labor migration, during the late Ottoman period and throughout the interwar years, women sex workers and performers migrated to cities across the Middle East.[26] A large number of female performers from cities such as Cairo, Damascus, and Aleppo, but also from further afield, came to Baghdad and other Iraqi cities.

Al-Shatt café, which was owned by a Jewish *maqam* singer, and which became a nightclub in 1916, had already set up a stage in 1913 and made the performer Tira al-Misriyya their main star. When al-Shatt became a nightclub, it was able to seat 700 people and was full almost every night. Some patrons even paid for entrance without being guaranteed a seat.[27] By the beginning of the 1920s, Iraqi women from all of Iraq's religious communities and provinces had replaced some of the foreign performers. During the mandate years, laws were enforced that made it difficult for foreign performers to obtain Iraqi visas and some foreign performers and sex workers were deported.[28] Iraqi police reports show that between 1929 and 1931, ninety-one foreign dancers (*raqisat*), a category different from that of sex workers (*mumisat*) entered Iraq. During the same time period, thirty foreign dancers left Iraq and forty-six were expelled for "inappropriate behavior" and "breaking the law."[29]

Sadly, very little is known about this first generation of foreign and Iraqi female performers. Since most, if not all, performed under stage names, it is only possible to conjecture about the geographical origins and life stories of most of these young women who labored in Iraq's newly established nightclubs and cafés. While it is not surprising that people, including women, traveled and moved for purposes of labor at a time when Iraq's Ottoman and early mandate borders were more porous than they are today, it is important to include the category of female performers in our understanding of movement and mobility during the period. In addition, it shows that Iraq was very much part of transnational entertainment labor networks. The arrival of these women fundamentally changed nocturnal leisure by localizing and, to some extent, normalizing a new form of public and heteronormative desire and female performance.

The outbreak of the First World War (1914–18) and the subsequent Iraqi revolt against the British in 1920, which was violently suppressed, temporarily put an end to the spread of nightclubs. However, after 1921, nightclubs began to appear all over Iraq. According to an Iraqi police report, in 1930, there were twenty-seven establishments in Baghdad offering singing and dancing.[30] The following year, similar establishments also existed in Mosul, Basra, Kirkuk, and Amara.[31] Until the early 1930s, almost all of Baghdad's nightclubs were located in the Midan area—an area associated with sex work and brothels. In the 1930s, however, many nightclubs moved to Bab al-Sharqi at the southern end of al-Rashid Street, which by then had become Baghdad's main thoroughfare and entertainment hub with many cinemas and cafés lining the street. From the outset, these new clubs were different from cafés. They were open from early evening and until midnight, many had indoor stages, and all charged an entrance fee.[32]

The emergence of these new nightclubs in the 1930s and 1940s happened at a time when nightclubs had to compete with a growing number of nocturnal or evening institutions of leisure, including cinemas and theaters. Targeting a different clientele, the second generation of nightclubs tried to distinguish themselves from the now large number of nightclubs by offering Western music and dance and by appealing to a growing taste and desire for exclusivity among Iraqi upper classes. Some of these new clubs were located inside hotels away from the crowded Midan and Bab al-Sharqi areas. For example, in 1947 an Iraqi Jew by the name of David Cohen established the Jawhara Café. Despite its name, the Jawhara Café was a nightclub, albeit a more luxurious one. Jawhara presented two programs every evening. The first consisted of several hours of traditional Iraqi music, singing, and dancing. The second part of the program, which is what distinguished Jawhara from Baghdad's more traditional nightclubs, consisted of "western" music and mixed-gender ballroom dancing.[33] The nightclub, which was situated inside al-Hilal Hotel, frequently invited orchestras from abroad and promised its clientele "the most splendid nights of sociability" and "enchanting tunes and beautiful female artists (*fannanat*)." Al-Hilal, an upscale hotel further distinguished itself by using the word *fannanat* (artists), rather than *raqisat* (dancers) or simply *banat* (girls), which was how female performers were referred to at most nightclubs.[34] The same period also saw the rise of casinos, which were essentially nightclubs. In an ad with the caption "Meeting Place of the Upper Classes" (*multaqa al-tabaqat al-raqiyya*), Saʿdun Park Casino invited "lovers of art (*fann*) and musical entertainment (*tarab*)" to nightly musical concerts and "eastern, western, and acrobatic dance."[35] Another establishment, Casino Baghdad, compared itself to the "nightclubs of Paris, Budapest, and Berlin."[36] Establishments such as Saʿdun Park Casino catered toward the growing middle and upper classes who perhaps did not want to be associated with the Midan area, its brothels, and working-class drinking establishments.

It was in these nightclubs that several Iraqi female performers rose to national and regional fame and became entertainers of a different kind. Partially due to their appearance on Iraqi radio, which began broadcasting in 1936, and in Iraqi and Egyptian films, these women managed to escape some of nightlife's connotations with moral ambiguity and sex work and enter the upper echelons of Iraqi society. Both radio and cinema provided Iraqis with access to the voices of performers and served as crucial vehicles for the dissemination and legitimization of popular culture. Those who rose to fame, the divas, became linked to cultural and political elites and the public sphere through their radio and nightclub performances. Most nightclubs employed at least one famous female performer and helped launch the careers of some of the biggest Iraqi stars, composers, and musicians in the 1930s and 1940s. The popularity and demand for nocturnal leisure in the form of nightclubs increased the demand for new songs and new styles of music. Many of the musicians and composers, whose careers and fame were a result of the increase in nightclubs and taste for modern music, were Iraqi Jews. The most famous among them were the brothers Salih (1908–86) and Dawud al-Kuwaiti (1910–76). From the 1930s onwards, the al-Kuwaiti brothers composed most of the music and wrote many of the songs that became the soundtrack to Iraqi nightlife. The most popular of these were performed by Salima Murad and ʿAfifa Iskandar. The al-Kuwaiti brothers came to Baghdad via Amara and started their career playing at the Jawahiri nightclub. They later opened their own club named Abu Nuwas and Salih al-Kuwaiti was put in charge of the Iraqi radio ensemble.[37]

Salima Murad and ʿAfifa Iskandar, arguably the two most famous Iraqi female singers, began performing at al-Hilal in the early 1930s. Murad grew up in a Jewish family in Baghdad and was given the nickname of Pasha by Nuri Saʿid (1888–1958), Iraq's prime minister. Salih al-Kuwaiti composed many of Murad's most popular songs. Salih al-Kuwaiti also composed songs for Murad's sister, Regina Murad.[38] Murad was one of the first female singers to appear on Iraqi radio and she organized a cultural salon in her home. During these private sessions, she entertained politicians and other important Iraqis from the upper social strata. She converted from Judaism to Islam and married the Iraqi singer Nazim al-Ghazali (1921–63) in 1953. When she retired from performing in the 1960s, she managed and directed a nightclub she had started with her husband. ʿAfifa Iskandar, the daughter of a female performer of Greek origin, went on to become one of the most famous singers in Iraq. Iskandar spent a brief part of her career in Egypt, where she appeared in movies alongside famed Egyptian performers Muhammad ʿAbd al-Wahhab (1902–91) and Fatin Hamama (1931–2015). Upon her return to Baghdad, Iskandar, like Murad, organized a cultural salon in her home which attracted prominent Iraqi cultural personalities.[39]

Murad and Iskandar, and others such as Zakiyya George, Sultana Yusuf, Zuhur Husain, and Munira al-Huzuz became the first divas of Iraqi music. The songs of many of these stars and the compositions of the al-Kuwaiti brothers are still popular today. When the most prominent Iraqi singers began having weekly performances on the radio,[40] it partially changed society's view of female performers. In their careers, these women crossed boundaries relating to sect, class, and gender. While most performers remained on the margins of Iraqi society, the ones mentioned earlier not only gained fame and personal wealth but also entered elite cultural and political circles. They hosted and were hosted by politicians, appeared on national radio and in films in Egypt and Iraq, and were embraced as important producers of Iraqi culture. In the process, as both Cormack and Hammad have shown in detail in the Egyptian context, the public as well as private lives of these female stars and the scandals imagined or real, in which they were involved, became intensely debated topics in the press.[41]

Although now largely forgotten, in addition to the divas mentioned earlier, many other female performers also became symbols and embodiments of Iraqi modernity and cultural innovation. One performer, who is now mostly forgotten, is Salima al-ʿIraqiyya. Beginning in 1945, al-ʿIraqiyya performed at the al-Farabi nightclub, named after the famous medieval Islamic philosopher and jurist who spent his life in Baghdad, and a number of other nightclubs in Baghdad until her retirement in 1954. According to an anecdote, al-ʿIraqiyya refused to reveal her real name and origins and would simply say, "*Ana ʾIraqiyya*" (I am Iraqi), whenever people asked her. Two performers who are also largely forgotten today are the two Jewish sisters, Salima and Sabiha Dijla (Tigris). The Dijla sisters migrated to Baghdad from northern Iraq with their family in 1940. Salima, the eldest of the two, first worked at the Dijla nightclub, which is how she got her stage name. Salima's younger sister Sabiha also took Dijla as a stage name although she never worked there. Salima Dijla began her career at the Opera nightclub and later joined her younger sister at al-Farabi. Despite her name's connection to another nightclub, however, it was at al-Farabi that Salima made a name for herself as a dancer.[42]

While many female performers never became famous outside of Iraq and while most never made it to Iraqi radio and cinema screens, they nonetheless took part in an important and performative celebration of Arab, Islamic, and Iraqi cultural pasts and localities. As shown by historians of Iraq such as Orit Bashkin, beginning in the interwar years, Iraqi officials, politicians, educators, and intellectuals from across the political spectrum, often in competing ways, attempted to determine and consolidate what it meant, politically, historically, and culturally to be Iraqi and Arab. According to Bashkin, during the years of the mandate and monarchy, the Nahda took on a more national rather than cultural meaning in Iraq. In the official Iraqi Nahda "narratives of revival," as Bashkin calls them, the Hashemite monarchy positioned itself as the pinnacle of Arab national awakening and guarantor of future self-determination.[43] However, Bashkin points out that competing Iraqi narratives pointed to the transregional origins of the Nahda, criticized the fact that the Hashemite monarchy had not managed to rid Iraq of British hegemony, or even suggested that an Iraqi Nahda had yet to occur due to the sheer amount of power concentrated in the hands of the monarchy and wealthy elites, the low level of education, and Iraq's modest publishing industry.[44] While pan-Arab and Iraqi nationalist visions existed in tandem, like elsewhere in the region, both visions often nationalized the past and projected it backward into an Arabized version of Islamic history, often downplaying Iraq's Ottoman past which was seen as a period of decline. The interest in the Arab and Islamic past and its famous figures found its ways into textbooks, literature, and new national histories and myths, and other cultural manifestations.[45] Most of these, however, targeted a middle-class audience.

Concurrently, this chapter argues, there was a synchronous, albeit less structured, attempt, from below and through popular culture and nocturnal institutions of leisure, to lay claims to Iraqi, history, identity, localities, and the national project more broadly.[46] More specifically, while most nightclubs, and the women and musicians who performed in them, were very much on the margins of society, they participated in a popular and nocturnal invocation of "Iraqi heritage," which encompassed an amalgam of Arab and Islamic, specifically Abbasid, literary and historical pasts. The nightclubs performers worked in carried names such as al-Farabi, Abu Nuwas (the famed Abbasid era poet), Dijla, Shahrazad and Alf Laila, both of which are references to *A Thousand and One Nights* and the heydays of Abbasid power in Baghdad under the rule of the Caliph Harun al-Rashid. All these names have connections to names of people from Islamic history and literary titles understood, partially due to the Nahda, to be Arabic classics. The performers used stage names that further connected them to Iraqi localities such as Salima al-'Iraqiyya, Salima Dijla, and countless others that tied these individuals to Iraqi history, geography, and culture past and present. In particular, the urban history of Baghdad has long been closely linked with the Tigris and the river has played a ubiquitous role in Iraqi poetry, autobiographical, and fictional writing from the medieval period, throughout the Nahda, and until the present day.

While official narratives, such as those found in Iraqi textbooks, literature, and official discourse produced during the mandate, undoubtedly had a great effect on the creation of an Iraqi version of the past and a new national identity and culture, it is important to note that people and institutions outside the state were also claiming this past and making it relevant through practices of leisure. In his revisionist account of modern Egyptian history, Ziad Fahmy has re-examined the creation of Egyptian national identity through a focus on popular culture. Using colloquial and non-elite oral, aural, and textual sources, Fahmy shows the extent to which popular culture shaped early Egyptian nationalism, culture, and identity.[47] Fahmy's emphasis on popular culture, often produced in colloquial Arabic and consumed by non-elite audiences in everyday settings, allows us to reconsider the actors, agents, and consumers of the Nahda from a more inclusive vantage point.

For the many men who visited Baghdad's nightclubs, the fact that they could sit in an establishment named after figures such as Abu Nuwas and listen to singers such as Salima al-'Iraqiyya, Salima Dijla, and Salima Furat, must have contributed to their sense of belonging, at least momentarily, to a city and a nation with a long history. Like the non-elite Egyptian female performers described by Cormack, who played a large role in the creation of modern Egyptian culture,[48] these Iraqi performers, both the national divas and those who are now forgotten, worked hard to create an Iraqi nightlife and, in the process, contributed to the creation of Iraqi modernity, culture, and identity, even as they remained complicated, compromised, and even dangerous symbols of modernity.

Dangerous Women: Dancing, Singing, and Sex Work

Beginning in the late 1920s, Iraqi cultural and political elites and educators wrote about, debated, and opposed nightclubs and the women who performed there as part of larger struggles over morality, productivity, and the future of the Iraqi nation. Some of the early opposition to nightlife combined moral and medical concerns. In 1934, Fa'iq Shakir, an Iraqi medical doctor, gave a speech to the Iraqi Children's Welfare Society about venereal diseases. In his speech, Shakir listed what he saw as the reasons why venereal diseases were widespread. In addition to the lack of medical facilities, Shakir blamed a number of social practices and institutions such as brothels and nightclubs. These, he argued, corrupted and led Iraqi male and female youth astray.[49] For others, the newly available distractions of leisure, including nightclubs, posed a threat to Iraqi society at large. One educator writing for *al-Mu'allim al-Jadid* (The New Teacher), the official journal of the Iraqi Ministry of Education, argued that "the abundance of bars, the many nightclubs in which dancers perform in revealing clothes, and the silly films shown in the cinemas are all clear evidence that we have not yet found a good way to spend our [leisure] time."[50] Press and literary campaigns also criticized leisure establishments, such as brothels, nightclubs, and casinos, where men and women mixed and engaged in what some saw as questionable behavior. These accounts negatively portrayed female performers, linked them to sex work, and warned against the alcoholism and moral corruption attached to nocturnal establishments of leisure.[51]

As described by Haytham Bahoora, the figure of the sex worker was a popular literary topic and trope in anticolonial Iraqi literature and poetry during the period, allowing Iraqi male authors to visualize the integration of women into "secular, urban, and middle-class notions of modern domesticity and respectability."[52] Since the figure of the female sex worker was a marginal character existing outside most forms of social and moral regulation, her use by male writers "reveals an unsettled economy of virtue whereby she could be at the same time instrumentalized for narrative purposes, pitied, and viewed as a threat to male dominance, suggesting a deeply embedded ambivalence toward women's equality and liberation in the cultural imagination."[53] As we will see, so-called progressive male writers deployed the figure of the nightclub performer in similar ways. The scarcity of Iraqi archival sources that deal with the lived and everyday experiences of female performers makes literature a supplementary site of information. However informative these sources may be, there are limits to what accounts produced by men can tell us about female performers. For example, the Iraqi poet Muhammad Mahdi al-Jawahiri (1899–1997), who frequented Baghdad's many cafés and nightclubs in the 1920s and 1930s, wrote several poems in which he praised the beauty of female dancers and singers. One of these poems is a tribute to the beauty of Badiʿa ʿAtish, a female dancer from Aleppo who performed at the ʿAzzawi café: "As you turn away / you show the eye the best / that it can see of a behind (*ahsan ma tara khalfan*)."[54] The poem captures the novelty and excitement caused by the presence of female bodies in public spaces. At the same time, the poem demonstrates well both the objectification of female performers and the exclusively male gaze through which we access the history of Iraqi nightlife. While the experience of female performers is absent from these texts or only available in a mediated form, they shed light on their representation as well as on the moral ambiguity and anxiety that existed around new spaces of public leisure in which women took part.

The short story "Talib Effendi" from 1923, written by the prominent Iraqi socialist intellectual, writer, and journalist Mahmud Ahmad al-Sayyid (1903–37), is a case in point. "Talib Effendi" describes the adventures of Talib, a tribal poet, who adopts the title of *effendi* (an Ottoman word used to describe members of the educated and professional class) after having discovered the sophisticated urban lifestyle of Baghdad. With his connections to both the British and Iraqi tribal sheikhs, Talib enters upper-middle-class life. In Baghdad, Talib encounters a Turkish Christian nightclub dancer, whom he believes to be the daughter of a general in the Ottoman army who has come to Iraq in search of her Arab roots. Talib spends a night with the dancer and gives her money, convinced that her wealthy family will pay him back. He soon discovers, however, that the dancer is really a sex worker awaiting deportation.[55] According to Bashkin's reading of "Talib Effendi," "the imagined biography of the dancer correlates with a Hashemite national narrative: she comes from Syria, homeland of Arab nationalism, and wishes to return to her Arab roots and forget her Ottoman past."[56] As previously discussed, the imagined journey of the dancer in al-Sayyid's short story was, in many cases, also a real journey taken by female performers and sex workers during the period. According to Bashkin, "Talib Effendi" is also indicative of narratives and plots used by some Iraqi national and urban elites to discuss and criticize Iraqi tribesmen and rural subjects.[57] At the same time, however, al-Sayyid's short story represents an example of how female performers were portrayed negatively and often depicted as sex workers. While Talib wishes to bring the performer, and the promise she represents to the Iraqi nation, into respectability through marriage, she deceives and takes advantage of him and is only interested in his money. As such, she poses a danger to the men, including al-Sayyid, working to create a strong Iraq state.

Another example of a literary depiction of nightlife can be found in novelist Dhu al-Nun Ayyub's (1908–96) short story from 1938, "Hinama Tathur al-'Asifa" (When the Storm Blows). Ayyub, an Iraqi communist, teacher, and prose writer, was born in Mosul and graduated from the Higher Teachers Training College in Baghdad. In the early 1930s, he wrote for *al-Ahali* (The People), the newspaper of the nonsectarian anticolonial group of the same name, and coedited the magazines *al-'Asr al-Hadith* (The New Era) and the communist *al-Majalla* (The Magazine).[58] In "Hinama Tathur al-'Asifa," two male Iraqi friends, low-ranking officials in one of Baghdad's ministries, visit a nightclub: "We entered one of the numerous large clubs that functions as a refuge for those seeking company and where people come to spend and lose money."[59] The two friends find an empty table and order two beers. The table next to theirs is occupied by a wealthy landowning sheikh "ruling over thousands of peasants."[60] The sheikh's wealth provides him with the constant attention of the club's owner and waiters. At his table, the sheikh is accompanied by several of "those dancers who are imported from Budapest and Prague [*waridat Budapest wa Prague*]" who look at him "with the eyes of a thief looking at an ownerless donkey loaded with jewels."[61] The derogatory comparison between the female performers and imported goods is not the only judgment that the text makes. One of the friends observes with disdain how the sheikh is unable to communicate with the dancers at his table due to his lack of foreign language skills. Mocking what he sees as the sheikh's lack of culture, education, and manners, the narrator tells his friend: "he [the sheikh] can't even write the language of his own country" and that someone like him "wouldn't burden himself with learning another language, not even for a dancer."[62]

The blurred boundary between performance and sex work was by no means a strictly fictional or Iraq phenomenon. In her study of mobile female performers in French Mandate Syria, Camilla Pastor de Maria Campos notes that foreign women were classified as *artistes* and regulated differently than local women, who were defined as prostitutes. While women belonging to both categories, according to Campos, were engaged in sex work, the former "escaped being prostitutionalized and thus retained control of material and moral resources denied to women defined as prostitutes."[63] Similarly, Campos shows that the demand created by new public entertainment spaces "presented women options to travel, work, and control their earnings and reputations, escaping regulated prostitution."[64] In her study of sex work and migration, Liat Kozma suggests that "women who migrated for prostitution often followed the migration of men—workers, soldiers, pilgrims, settlers, and sailors" and that we see these women as "actors in a global economy rather than objects of commerce."[65] In Iraq as well, nightclubs all over the country employed hundreds of mobile female singers and dancers. This began, as we saw, around 1908, but continued during subsequent decades.

Stories such as Ayyub's "Hinama Tathur al-'Asifa" and al-Sayyid's "Talib Effendi," voice important social critiques of wealth and the political influence of tribal sheikhs, some of whom were empowered by the British and the Hashemite state. It is interesting that they do so through descriptions of excessive and inappropriate behavior in or around Baghdadi institutions of nocturnal leisure. The fact that they do so provides us with an example of how, at least in the opinion of leftist Iraqi intellectuals, such institutions ought to be inhabited. In addition, fictional narratives such as the ones described earlier also offered a space where new practices of nocturnal leisure and novel urban identities and figures, including those of frequented and worked in nightclubs, could be described, debated, worked out, and sometimes excluded. While female performers arrived in Baghdad as representatives and a fulfillment of a heteronormative modernity in which men and women inhabited the same public spaces, they were also seen by some as corrupting and compromising that very same modernity. Although they contributed significantly to modern Iraqi culture, entertainment, and urban life, for many of the male figures celebrated as the producers and creators of Iraqi cultural and literary modernity, female performers represented a strange, complex, and dangerous form of modernity that could not quite be integrated into or made to fit their ideals.

Even for the Iraqi composer and poet 'Abd al-Karim al-'Allaf (1894–1969), whose historical works celebrate the skills of Iraqi female performers and the many innovations of Iraqi nightlife and music, the profession of female performers had to be sanitized. A poet and a composer, al-'Allaf began his poetic career reading fierce nationalist poems in the Haydarkhana mosque during the 1920 Iraqi revolution. Later in life, he wrote songs for some of the most famous singers in Iraq.[66] In his work, al-'Allaf was concerned with saving, even if only retrospectively, the reputation of many of these women and probably also his own profession by censoring out certain details or by only indirectly hinting at the links between nightclubs and sex work. While al-'Allaf must have been aware of the less glamorous and exploitative side of Iraqi nightlife, he is careful not to explicitly mention the gray zone that existed between nightclubs and sex work.[67] In addition, in many of his biographical descriptions, al-'Allaf mentions the beauty of specific performers, their ability to "drive men insane," their flirtation skills, and the many rivalries that erupted over who could attract the wealthiest clients.[68] While al-'Allaf does not seem to explicitly condemn women who were involved in sex work, he makes sure to mention that several female performers eventually got married and settled down into a life of domestic bliss.[69]

Even among the most famous and respected female performers, the association with sex work, moral corruption, and dangerous transgression was still present. According to Iraqi historian Sami Zubaida, there were rumors that Murad's sister Regina ran an upscale brothel in Baghdad.[70] There were also rumors that Murad too ran a brothel and a gambling den for Iraqi elites.[71] Unlike the short stories by al-Sayyid and Ayyub, which employ entirely fictional and non-Iraqi performers, in Eli Amir's (b. 1937) 1992 novel, *Mafriach Hayonim*, translated into

English as *The Dove Flyer* in 1998, descriptions of Salima Murad and other Iraqi performers appear throughout the narrative. Amir was born in Baghdad in 1937. Like most of Iraq's Jewish community, he left in the early 1950s and settled in Israel. Originally published in Hebrew, the novel narrates the hardships and joys of Iraqi Jewish life in the 1950s through a Baghdadi Jewish family. In the novel, the protagonist's father has an affair with Murad before he gets married. Murad is described as a "golden-throated enchantress," and a "sumptuous woman with dark hair, coal-black eyes, an enchanting smile, and a chiffony red silk dress worn with a charming nonchalance on her buxom body."[72] Baghdad is described as a place "where singers and dancers sell themselves to the highest bidder."[73] The Nakba and the creation of Israel in 1948 played a major role in the mass migration of Iraq's Jewish community in the early 1950s, including many of the Iraqi Jews who worked in nightclubs as performers, musicians, and owners. While some of the famous Jewish contributors to Iraqi nightlife are still remembered and celebrated, many of the less famous ones, like their non-Jewish peers, have been forgotten.

Conclusion

For most inhabitants of Baghdad and other Iraqi urban centers, nighttime remained designated for sleep and other forms of recreation and socialization within the private setting of the home. For some, night was a time of labor not associated with or reliant upon nightlife. Cafés had already expanded public leisure well into the evening and early night. Beginning in the first decade of the twentieth century, some cafés set up stages upon which musicians, male and eventually also female dancers performed. By the 1920s, Baghdad had a noticeable and growing infrastructure of nocturnal leisure. In other words, Baghdad had a nightlife. The women who traveled to Baghdad from abroad and from within the country were not without agency. While they inhabited a morally ambiguous position, they were agents and actors within larger patterns of migration and the global economy at large. While some had relatively short careers because they got married, left, or found employment elsewhere, most performers were active for a decade or more. Some worked only at one nightclub, but most circulated between several nightclubs in Baghdad and other urban centers, including Basra and Mosul.

Although the state and press were often critical of nocturnal practices of leisure associated with nightclubs and the women who worked there, politicians frequented the same institutions and appeared with the divas of Iraqi nightlife both in private and in public. At a time when their level of fame and respectability made it less problematic for political elites to do so, the most famous Iraqi singers respected, embraced, and used for national purposes. The stars of Iraqi nightlife were paid large sums to perform at private parties and celebrations such as weddings in the homes of wealthy Iraqis. While some female performers were able to amass considerable personal wealth, for the majority of Baghdad's many singers and dancers, life was a lot less glamorous. Although downplayed and forgotten, collectively, Iraqi female performers and the nightclubs in which they performed contributed to the creation of Iraqi popular entertainment and culture.

PART TWO

Performance & Spectacle

Chapter 4

FEMALE PERFORMERS IN BEIRUT (1900–1930s)

AGENTS AND METAPHORS OF SOCIAL CHANGE

Diana Abbani

Her club is odd in its name and girls. It is the first cabaret named after its owner in Beirut. The girls come from different nations and countries, among which the Turkish, the Greek, the Russian and the German. One can see various dances, hear different languages, distinct songs and melodies. Its audience wear different outfits: the *tarboush* (traditional cap), the *qubbaʻa* (hat), the *kaffieh* (Bedouin headdress for men), *ʻiqal* (headband) [. . .] the *ifranji* (foreign, European) pants, the *Shami qumbaz* (male robe), the Albanian trousers and the Arabic *ʻabaya* (long garment), all these outfits exhibited under its roof. The sound of *nargileh* (shisha), cigarettes being inhaled and coughs prevail [. . .] The Greek langue dominates among the garçons in East Arabic countries. Oud, qanun, daff, jazzband, taqatiq, foxtrot dance, rumba, tango and waltz, then turkish belly dancing and Albanian dabke. [. . .] Amidst all this noise [. . .], a client raises his voice calling: Quickly, *wahad ʻaraq* [one drink of Araq]![1]

In this rich testimony, the Beiruti newspaper *al-ʻAsifa* (The Storm) left a rare account of *salat Blanche* (performance hall), one of Beirut's few cabarets that was owned by a woman, Madame Blanche. Blanche was a Turkish dancer and singer who traveled through Syria, Paris, Latin America, North Africa, Baghdad, and Tehran and settled in Beirut during the 1920–1930s.[2] She was an entrepreneur with a strong personality, managing her cabaret and the career of various women singers in the city. Within a few years, she succeeded in rising to the top of Beirut's urban musical life, not only as a singer and dancer but also as the owner and manager of her *sala*, a domain previously reserved for men.

Her *sala* was a meeting point for many prominent politicians and journalists of the time. When interviewed by a journalist, the latter declared, "Who doesn't know Blanche? The name of Blanche has become international, with our respect to everything international . . . When you pronounce her name in any music club, people say: We know her . . . we really admire her . . . we have listened to her beautiful singing."[3]

This detailed description of her cabaret, captures the experience of a night out in Beirut in the first decades of the twentieth century, giving a sense of the general atmosphere in the city's entertainment venues, where many female dancers and singers found fame and success. In Blanche's cabaret, the nights were divided into two shifts (matinée and soirée) formed of several dances and singing acts. Although the program was varied, Sawsan was the star singer who attracted the most audiences with her "captivating voice."[4]

There were many other nightlife venues alongside Blanche's cabaret, raucous places where the noise of the crowds, the sound of glasses tinkling on the tables, and the laughing of women singers and the audience filled the space. Some venues, like *al-Parisiana* (owned by the Kraydiyya family) and *Kawkab al-Sharq* (owned by Ahmad al-Jak), were characterized by their combination of modern and traditional features, mixture of music genres, and audience from different social and religious backgrounds and origins, just as Blanche's *sala* was. These new spaces, with women artists on stage or walking between the tables amid the male audience, presented new forms of entertainment and socializing in the city. The reactions to these developments varied widely, and this chapter will look at discourse that arose around them in the press.

Since the end of the nineteenth century, Beirut had become a major Mediterranean port city. With its integration into the world economy and the proliferation of economic and political exchanges, it also witnessed the emergence of a new entertainment scene. An Ottoman capital since 1888, Beirut became the state capital of Greater Lebanon and, from the 1920s, the capital of the French mandate over Lebanon and Syria. Quickly, it positioned itself as a major city in the region competing directly with Cairo, Aleppo, and Damascus. It saw gradual improvements in street gas lighting and police supervision, as well as growing incomes and decreasing hours of labor, all of which encouraged more people to go out at night.[5]

Sahat al-Burj, the city's central square, baptized the *Martyrs Square* in honor of the Syrian and Lebanese nationalists executed by the Ottoman authorities during the Great War and witnessed the opening of new bars, restaurants, theaters, and cabarets. Marked by their cosmopolitanism and commercial character, these spaces were open to modernity and shaped the artistic and cultural scene. Dancing, music, comic songs, alcohol, and food were all consumed in Beirut's cabarets. They marked the city deeply, attracting different social classes from within Beirut as well as visitors from neighboring cities. Levantine, Egyptian, Armenian, and European singers and musicians all visited and animated the city's nightlife.

This chapter focuses on female performers working and performing in the city's cabarets, and traveling between other major Levantine cities. Based on research into recorded disks and the press in Beirut (articles, concerts, and phonograph ads published in Beirut's newspapers, *Lisan al-Hal*, *al-Ma'rad*, and *al-'Asifa*), it analyzes the rise of the female musical scene since the beginning of the twentieth century and its role in shaping the city, the society, and the musical traditions.

The chapter particularly looks closely at a series of articles in *al-'Asifa*, in which different female performers left short interviews about their lives. These are an important and rich source, as they show how these women, who worked in the public sphere performing in front of men in a traditional society that marginalized them, tried to shape their own images. The results were complex and the strategies were not always unified; these articles show the different ways that these women themselves constructed a narrative around careers and the broader musical scene.

Fin de Siècle Women Singers Circulating in the Region

For a long time in Beirut, female singers and dancers were considered to be working in a dishonorable profession. During the nineteenth century, women did not have access to the *café-chantants* in Beirut or the various Levantine cities. The only women who ventured into this world belonged to "lower social classes."[6] Very little information can be found on early twentieth-century female singers and dancers, their life stories, activities, or status within society. Before the First World War, almost the only reason to mention them was to criticize their decadent and corrupted world.

The European travelers visiting Beirut and the Levant region during the nineteenth century did leave brief descriptions of the female musical life in the area. They tended to use the term *'alma* to designate the dancers and singers who performed at cafés and private gatherings in the region. This term, probably designating, as it did in Egypt, a professional of dance and singing, had a largely pejorative connotation as suggested by its associated expressions such as *savante en l'art d'émouvoir* (expert in the arts of seduction) or *baladine* (street entertainer). These women were seen as people who sung lascivious songs and danced provocative dances.[7] According to these travelers, the *'alma* did not practice a profession respected by society.

In the local context, the term *'alma* was not used. In Beirut's press, the singers of the *café-chantants* were called *banat al-qahwa, banat al-alhan*, or *banat al-musiqa* (Women of the Café, Women of melodies, or Women of music).[8] These designations may have been different but they still reflected a close link between these women's professional activity and their social status—they were mostly considered indecent, immoral, and sometimes prostitutes.

Although this moral stigma affected many of fin de siècle women singers, a few managed to distinguish themselves as performers. These were mostly the women who sang for theatrical troupes and during the intervals of plays like the Jewish singer named Layla. Performing in Beirut's *café-chantants* and wedding ceremonies for wealthy families, Layla enjoyed great success in Beirut and Cairo at the end of the nineteenth century.[9] But it was for her theatrical appearances that she won praise from the press. They especially liked her interludes at the plays of the Damascene playwright and composer Abu Khalil al-Qabbani (1835–1902) and the Egyptian singer Salama Hijazi (1852–1917), both pioneers of Arabic musical theater in Egypt.[10]

Another Levantine singer, originally from Beirut, was also a star of Abu Khalil al-Qabbani's troupe in Egypt, *al-mutriba al-shahira* (the famous singer) Malaka

Surur.[11] Malaka was the head of a Syrian women's ensemble, *Jawqat al-Hisan* (The Beautiful Women's ensemble) that came from Syria with al-Qabbani to sing at the end of his plays in Cairo.[12] She joined his troupe, along with Tira Hakim, another Levantine singer, and accompanied him to the 1893 Chicago World's Fair in the United States as part of the Ottoman mission.[13]

Like Layla, Malaka reflects the change in the status of women singers whose success was regional, and they became more appreciated by the intellectual elites and the *udaba'* (men of letters) who acclaimed their talent in the press. The Egyptian press praised Malaka for her dazzling and impressive singing, as well as her presence on stage, especially that she was one of the first unveiled women on stage.[14] She was multitalented and was also particularly admired for playing the *qanun* (a stringed instrument). The *al-Bashir* newspaper even attributed the success of al-Qabbani's troupe in Egypt more to her presence than to his acting.[15]

By the end of the nineteenth century, several Levantine women became famous singers circulating through the emergent nightlife in Beirut, Damascus, Aleppo, Baghdad, or Cairo. Many women played instruments, including the *oud* (a fretless lute), the *qanun,* and a number of different percussion instruments, forming musical ensembles that accompanied the female singers in front of an exclusively female audience at weddings and later on in front of a male audience in the *cafés-chantants*.

In this early period, most of the female singers were Jewish or Christian, like Jamila, Rahlu, and Rujina, who were from Wadi Abu Jamil, Beirut's Jewish neighborhood. An Egyptian actor, Omar Wasfi (1874–1945), recalled the absence of Muslim women singers in Beirut when he visited the city in 1897.[16] With al-Qabbani, he was on a trip looking for Malaka Surur, singing at the time in Aleppo. While passing by Beirut, he wanted to visit its famous *cafés-chantants*. But he was informed that they were all closed because it was a Saturday and all the singers were Jewish.[17]

The Rise of the Female Scene

In the early twentieth century, the record industry began to take off. A few of the most famous singers of the time released records during the first recording campaigns with Gramophone, Odeon, and Baidaphon, like *al-sitt* (the lady) Hasiba Moshe, Badriyya Sa'ada, or Tira Hakim.[18] They recorded mainly wedding and cabaret songs called *ṭaqatiq* and *qudud* (popular light women songs), in which they talked about the bride, her wedding preparation and wedding night, about love, separation, marriage life, and also about more obscene subjects. Some women singers also recorded what we could call "art music" including *qasa'id* and *adwar* (complex musical settings in which improvisation and a degree of virtuosity were given a prominent role).[19]

Through these records, as well as the movement of female singers between the Levant and Egypt (sometimes even as far as Iraq and North Africa), a new popular music-consuming public was created. 78-rpm records circulated through the region, crossing boundaries of geography, class, and gender. The phonograph and the recordings could travel to the private homes of people of all social classes, to places where professional musicians would never venture. Because of their portability and their availability, phonographs also provided women with access to different kinds of music, especially the songs that were sung in the cabarets and entertainment venues, from which they were often excluded—implicitly or explicitly.

Moreover, the transformation of music from a medium of artistic creation and celebration into a more public commodity marketed at a wider spectrum of society enabled the emergence of new social spaces, experiences, classes, and modern tastes.[20] These changes offered new opportunities in commercial entertainment to women of different classes who ventured into the music scene and marketed their artistic talents. More women participated in plays, animated the nights in Beirut's leisure venues, and recorded with multinational and local record companies. Entertainment in Beirut flourished after the First World War, responding to the tastes of a society in search of new modernity. With the time and means for leisure, middle-class men and women spent their nights socializing and entertaining, creating a new audience and a new way of life to experience the city.[21]

Along with these changes, a new musical genre appeared in Beirut under the French mandate, the socio-satirical monologue. Inspired by the French commercial and popular music of the Parisian music halls, it presented a new kind of music to the city, one that corresponded to its modern rhythms and way of life. The monologue was characterized by its light musical composition and varied colloquial texts dedicated to the entertainment. Its success and popularity make it a highly profitable commodity that was in vogue until the end of the Second World War. The key figure behind the rise of this kind of songs was the famous Beiruti poet and *chansonnier* Omar el-Z'enni (1895–1961), followed by many others. He criticized the changes in the city's customs and habits, particularly the westernization (*tafarnuj*) of the society and its decadence (in his monologues "Shubban Chic" [Young Chic Men] and "al-Dunya Crisa" [The World's in Crisis]), class inequalities (in "Law Kunt Hsan" [If I Were a Horse]), or the political corruption and the French domination (in "Shuf Tfarraj" [Look Around You] and "Hasib Ya Frank" [Watch out, Franc]).

In this popular entertainment boom, female celebrities, especially Egyptian ones, became big business, taking Beirut's musical venues by storm. The concerts and performances of Badi'a Masabni, Munira al-Mahdiyya, Sarina, Na'ima al-Masriyya, Fathiyya and Ratiba Ahmad, Nadira Amin, Fatima Sirri, and Fatima Rushdi among others would be regularly announced in Beirut's newspapers.[22] Female singers with a male musical ensemble performed in front of men, women, or mixed audiences in Beirut's cabarets. In private, women from elite circles also began organizing private parties where they socialized and played music themselves (mainly on the piano).

All of this blurred the boundaries between male and female repertoires, between the private and public worlds as well as between art and popular music. The influence of Western music hall traditions during the 1920s and 1930s also began to find its way into the Beiruti nightlife. The early twentieth-century tavern singers or dancers, *banat al-musiqa* or *al-qahwa* became *artistat* (*artistes*), an expression that still contained certain pejorative connotations, but emphasized the artistic aspects of their profession and reflected the impact of growing westernization on popular culture.[23] The most renowned singers, who, at the turn of the century, would have been called *al-sitt,* gradually became known as *mughanniyyat* or *mutribat* (professional singers), expressions that reflect the increasing professionalism and growing respect for their professions. Sometimes some expressions such as "Madame" and "Demoiselle" (lady and young lady) were also used as a mark of respect, particularly for European artists and educated, bourgeois women who played and sung during literary evenings, without necessarily being professional singers or musicians.

During this period, a new generation of singers such as Laure Daccache [Lur Dakkash], Marie Jubran, Fayruz al-Halabiyya, and later on Nur al-Hoda strived to escape the negative image attached to *banat al-musiqa*, associated with vice and prostitution in the popular imaginary. They tried to present themselves as "modern" singers worthy of respect. They challenged the negative image of female artists working in the entertainment world in front of a male audience. Most of them sang the traditional repertoire but they also recorded social, political, and nationalist songs. Somewhat counter-intuitively, they released several songs that criticized society's modernization, attacked the local authorities and the French mandate, and reclaimed independence. These sociopolitical songs echoed intellectuals' debates about society's decadence, women's role in modernity, and the dangers of women's autonomy.[24]

Laure Daccache (1917–2005) greatly represented this new generation of singers who tried to sell themselves as the modern face of the new Beirut. Accompanied by her father, she marked the local scene differently. She symbolized the new Beiruti woman, free and modern, and above all "respectful." She was, therefore, more appreciated by the society. She was a pioneer in promoting herself in the press, probably due to her father's initiative.[25] She participated in concerts organized by the intellectual elite and collaborated with many musicians qualified as *udaba'*. She was part of Beirut's intellectual and middle-class circles and distinguished herself from cabaret artists, especially that she composed her own songs. She did not record the type of obscene Egyptian *taqatiq* that were popular at the time, but mostly art music like *adwar* and *muwashshahat*,[26] as well as satirical songs.

But this reputability had limits. Although Laure was among the first women, if not the only one, to be considered in the 1930s as a composer [*musiqiyya*], she never became a widely known composer. Like many Levantine singers, she moved to Cairo and adopted Egyptian singing, but there, she did not succeed to compete with the rising stars of Cairo's musical scene.

The Depiction of Female Artists in the Press

With the increase of women in the entertainment scene, female artists became a huge talking point in the press. Often, they were the target of moralists, who criticized the rapidly expanding entertainment scene and its prominent stars.

In the early twentieth century, dancers and singers had often been accused of using their bodies as instruments to earn money. Since they exposed themselves publicly and used their bodies and voices, which were often considered as a source of shame, these women were accused of immorality and even compared to prostitutes. In an article entitled "al-Maraqis fil qahawi al-'umumiyya" (Dancehalls in Public Cafés), the editor of the daily Beiruti newspaper *Lisan al-Hal* attacked immoral entertainment venues which were harming and destabilizing society.[27] Unaccompanied by men, female artists were considered to be prostitutes, while cabaret owners were accused of "immodesty and greed." The editor called upon the authorities to levy taxes on nightclubs and to bring them under control. He addressed young men, instructing them to stay away from three main vices: women, alcohol, and entertainment venues. This kind of criticism was typical of Beirut's press of the time. It was a standard part of classic Nahda discourse, concerned with the city's modernity and progress amid the various political and social changes. It is also related to the Orientalist discourse, which linked the lack of progress of the region and the nation to medical, hygienic, and sanitary backwardness.[28]

For many writers and journalists, the cabarets and music halls, with their female stars, represented a perverse kind of modernity, set against the desirable aspects of modernity—publishing houses, universities, and intellectual gatherings. The stigmatization of social vices was thus brought at the heart of the moralists' modernity project in Beirut.

Women Tell Their Own Stories in the Press

The growing presence of female audiences in certain entertainment places, considered as male spaces, also formed a subject of controversy, particularly during the mandate period. Some theaters presented sessions only for women or for families. More women entered the public sphere, transgressing the traditional boundaries that had been set for them. For a woman, attending places of entertainment was often considered as a scandalous act in conservative circles, another reason for the growing criticism of these places.

With the rise of the female musical scene during the 1920s and 1930s, the press could no longer neglect or simply criticize these performers. New sections covering their life and stories emerged in many journals and magazines. *Lisan al-Hal*, the newspaper which had warned men to stay away from music halls, now had weekly adverts for concerts. In a dedicated section, *al-Ma'rad* newspaper published photos of dancers and singers, mostly European, who were performing in the city.

In this period, women were gaining some control over depictions of their own images too. For the first time, the faces of women artists were published in the press. This gave performers a chance to present themselves. The pose, the staging, the look, and the costumes, all these elements contributed to the construction of their modern representation. These unveiled women were often dressed in "decent" and modern outfits, few of them in *décolleté*. Standing, sitting on the floor or on armchairs, sometimes with accessories representative of their modernity several looked straight at the camera with a gesture marking their determination and their freedom; their photos were confrontational.

But despite the various changes in the city and despite the new opportunities that female singers had, public opinion about women's performance was still ambivalent. Some singers, for instance, were respected and appreciated for their education and talent (like Fayruz al-Halabiyya or Laure Daccache), but many others were still despised or considered immoral. Female performers had to walk an almost impossible tightrope. They were caught between the public desire for modern, alluring female artists and pushback from people with conservative opinions about women exposing their bodies and their voices to men in public spaces.

In 1932, *al-'Asifa* newspaper dedicated a weekly page, *Min Layali Bayrut* (Of Beirut's Nightlife) interviewing different dancers and singers performing in Beirut's nightclubs such as *Kawkab al-Sharq* and *Parisiana*. *Al-'Asifa* was a weekly political and literary newspaper founded in 1932 by the journalist and short story writer Karam Melhem Karam (1903–59). His journal was quite avant-gardist in its subjects, critique, and caricatures. He was also very critical toward the local authorities and the French mandate; therefore, the journal was often banned for its political standpoints, and Karam was imprisoned many times. He commented extensively on the social changes the city knew since the arrival of the French mandate, among them its nightlife and singers. In one-page interviews, accompanied by a photo, women were given in *al-'Asifa* the space to construct their own images, in their own words. This chapter will close by looking at the various strategies that they used.

We should still be careful not to overinterpret these stories. Despite the fact that *al-'Asifa* was giving these women a voice in the public sphere, this space was still, in many ways, subordinated. These women's testimony appeared in a newspaper run by men, edited by men and addressing a male-dominated audience. Through these interviews, *al-'Asifa* was trying to satisfy its readers' curiosity about the fascinating but forbidden world of *artistat*. Even if the interviewed artists had control over their words as they appeared on stage, the context dictated much of how they were received. Theirs was the voice of a stage performer—it was not considered authoritative or rational; on the contrary, it was seen as emotional and personal.

The context also bound them in other ways. One of *al-'Asifa's* main goals was to raise awareness against the difficulties and problems of this world, which provoked society's fascination and curiosity. The purpose of these interviews was, in part, educational and the female performers were often seen as examples for the young to avoid. They had left their domestic sphere to venture out alone in search of work, money, or pleasure. This was not always presented as a wise idea. Still, these articles remain a unique resource for the study of the lives of female performers in the 1930s. In different accounts, we can see the different approaches that they took.

Proud to be Singers

Several of the performers who were interviewed for these sections, such as Marie Jubran, Fayruz al-Halabiyya, or Badi'a Masabni, highlighted their personal strength and said that they were satisfied with their profession (or at least had no regrets about it). These confident women were mainly singers. They were the most famous and respected ones, probably from higher social backgrounds, or knew a social rise due to their talent and success. These were the kinds of women who gain public acclaims; few had been able to influence public opinion, even becoming advertising spokeswomen and role models of a kind. These were also the women who knew fame in Cairo and other Levantine cities, and who recorded with major record companies, which could explain their confidence and lack of regret. Apart from the famous dancer Badi'a Masabni, they were mostly singers and not dancers.

Marie Jubran (1907–56), also known as Marie *al-Jamila* (The Beautiful), was a Levantine singer of great talent. Born in Beirut, she began her early career in Palestine. She performed in the most famous venues of the region like *Kawkab al-Sharq* in Beirut during the Syrian Revolt, *Bismar* in Damascus, *al-Shahbandar* in Aleppo, and *Salat Badi'a* in Cairo. She was best known for her improvisation and interpretation of classical forms of Egyptian musical genres. She came into her interview with *al-'Asifa* confidently. She did not seem to be concerned by those who looked down on singers, declaring frankly, "If I wasn't a singer (*mutriba*), I would have wanted to be one."[29] *Al-'Asifa*'s journalist introduced her with respect, praising her policy of only buying national fabrics and presenting her as a patriotic model to follow. So, she could even say some risqué things about her personal life—that she did not want to marry anyone, for instance, and preferred to stay single so that she could keep working freely.

Nina Khayyat, known as both *Kawthar al-Arab* (The Nectar of the Arabs) and *Kawkab al-Parisiana* (The Star of the Parisiana), was also proud of her career.[30] She played an important role in Beirut's musical scene in the late 1930s to early 1940s. A pupil of Wadia Sabra (1876–1952), the famous Lebanese composer and founder of Beirut's Conservatory, she was first trained on the piano. She then continued her studies at the Oriental Music Club of Beirut.

In *al-'Asifa*'s interview, her image seems far from the stereotypical illiterate and uneducated woman artist-victim of her past. On the contrary, she claimed to be a singer who received a good musical education at one of the best musical schools, the Institute of Oriental Music in Egypt under its best teacher, Daud Husni (1870–1937). She emphasized her freedom and professionalism by evoking her great success in Egypt, whether at the radio or in concerts.[31]

Nina Khayyat's career seems indeed established and recognized, and not limited to the cabaret world, which explains her confident voice. She participated in the first Lebanese talkie *'Ala Hayakil Baalbek* (The Ruins of Baalbek) in 1936. She sang at the radio and in various venues in Egypt and Palestine, before becoming the first woman singer whose voice reached Beirut and Levantine listeners via radio al-Sharq (Radio-Orient) in 1938. *Al-Idha'a*, the Radio-Orient magazine attested to her talent while presenting her as a singer who impressed the famous Syrian musicians Sami al-Shawwa (1889–1965) and Camille Shambir (1892–1934), who advised her to go to Egypt, where she met Egypt's most notable musicians.[32] Yet, and despite these praises, Nina Khayyat's name disappeared from the press during the 1940s, and she was slowly forgotten.

The Sad Life Story of an Artist

Although some of the biggest stars of the cabarets spoke with triumph and pride, most did not. For the most part, their stories were filled with emotion of sadness, desolation, and regret. Bahiyya Amir, an Egyptian actress, dancer, and monologist who was performing in Beirut in 1933, confessed: "the actress is the unhappiest woman in the world. I worked so hard to get into this profession, but now I curse the day I followed my heart and not my reason. Every woman working in this field feels the same."[33]

Strangely, the cabaret—the place where women performers spent most of their time and where all their stories were shaped—is seldom mentioned in any of *al-'Asifa*'s interviews. On the contrary, most of the artists worked hard to depict themselves as "ordinary" women far from the cabaret. The stories they narrated talked about their personal feelings and inner lives, not their place of work.

Many artists portrayed themselves as victims of social and economic conditions that forced them to work in these places. They criticized their profession, directly, echoing the general pejorative image of female performers in the most conservative sections of the press. An Armenian dancer from Aintab (present-day Gaziantep, Turkey), Jamila Yaldız harshly attacked the dancers of her time accusing them of obscenity.[34] She lamented that many were obliged to practice this type of profession just to survive. Jamila deplored her "sad" life and her work as a dancer and singer. When asked about her early life, she smiled a melancholic smile; a tear fell on her cheek and said:

> I will not say what the other girls said about their love and passion for this art. As my work is not out of love, but out of need, poverty and misery. I think most of my colleagues took to the stage like me, out of need, poverty and misery, and not out of love for this art.[35]

Her hope was to escape her misery, even if that meant death, as it seemed more merciful to her eyes than the public exposure and social stigma that she constantly faced: "I wish to escape in any way that can save my dignity and my mother's life. I am sick of being looked at all the time. To inhabit a grave is better for me than this miserable and tough life,"[36] she admitted.

Other singers tried to emphasize the fact that they were forced to dance and sing to earn a living. Stella al-Istambuliyya, a Jewish dancer and singer from Turkey, declared:

> Although I live from my dancing, I despise it and hate it. I dance to earn my living; otherwise I would have chosen a different profession. It is a profession of fatigue, misery, despair and humiliation [. . .] because everything we earn doesn't bear comparison to what we risk in our dignity. This smile you see on my face is not a smile from the heart, how would it be? When I dance on the stage, I feel as if I am a dying bird who dances out of pain.[37]

Like Stella, many artists depicted their performing life as a façade that covered their internal suffering, and as means of living or a way to overcome the misery of poverty and stigmatization.

These interviews revealed another common aspect of their hopes and dreams. Most of them claimed that they wished to settle down, put an end to their career, get married, and someday, have their own family just like other women. For example, Malaka Jamal, a Beiruti dancer asserted that her "life is a series of sorrow, whenever it passes through my mind, it breaks my heart."[38] When asked about the dancer's wish, she replied: "A dancer only wishes to love and be loved, just like any other woman, because she is even more sensitive and delicate [. . .] My work is my 'master' (sayyid) and I hope that, after being completely fulfilled by my art, to become the wife of a beautiful young man, respectful and open-minded."[39]

Like Malaka, Sawsan, the famous singer in Blanche's cabaret did not only wish to escape the cruel musical scene, but she also longed to become part of the most respected "class," the intellectual elite. Sawsan refused to give any detail about her "miserable" childhood and early life: "The story of my life is so painful; it makes me sad to talk about it, I prefer not to disclose it please, as I wish to bury the past forever."[40] She also felt uncomfortable revealing what she wished to be if she wasn't a singer because it was far from her reality:

> This question embarrasses me a lot. If I need to give you an answer, I would say I prefer to be in my home, away from all the noise and the people. I was very close to achieving this wish in the past, this past that I refused to reveal to you. I would also have wished to be a writer and a journalist.[41]

The majority of these stories reveal the everyday struggles many women performers were living through, fighting to gain a certain social recognition and to prove their respectability. By putting their suffering on display, they broke the silence that had been forced upon them.

For all these women, singing and dancing was their world. For some, it was a source of pride, and for others, it was a source of suffering. Paradoxically, for a few, it was both a burden and liberator at the same time. It was the place that limited their everyday life yet released their soul for a few moments. Just like the Egyptian singer Buthayna affirmed:

> I don't regret being fond of singing, as when I sing, my soul flies high like the soul of a poet. I forget all what happened to me and see myself above the people wandering in a never-ending space. I adore this art, and the one who adores their art needs to sacrifice what they cherish the most.[42]

Conclusion: A Press that Stigmatized Female Performers

Al-'Asifa's interviews reveal the ambivalent relationships between women artists, their profession, and their body and voice. On the one hand, their femininity and sexuality allowed them to live; on the other, it was a source of disrespect. These artists tried to neutralize and sometimes even deny the femininity of their body and voice in order to counterbalance the image of immorality. While describing the vocal capacities of Fayruz in one of the ads, her voice was compared to men's voice, hence reducing the sexual dimension by getting closer to the image of male singers and appropriating male traits.[43] Others exposed themselves as women workers who make a living through their performance. Like men, they work in the public sphere; their bodies and voices are their productive force. They thus insinuated that their work is neither sexual nor shameful, but simply their tool for living, hence their appropriation of a masculine identity. Hence, the importance of *al-'Asifa*'s testimonies which give a fascinating—if sometimes conflicted, complicated, and compromised—window into the lives of female performers from their points of view. Sometimes, this view is surprising—they did not necessarily have happy or fulfilled lives.

In the various testimonies they left, these women performers used different strategies to try to counter the negative image and the existing constructions of gender and body on female artists. As Karin van Nieuwkerk argues in her work on female performers in Egypt, by going out into the public world, women were accused of leaving their families, sullying their virtue and the honor of the family.[44] To defend themselves, they often tried to construct a self-image of a working woman who was obliged to work in the public field to overcome the social and economic difficulties. They hoped for an image framed by a family or a man. By reconstructing their image within the family, they thought of regaining a more respectful image.

Some women artists revealed aspects of their private life to prove they were just like any other women who respected social values. Others wanted to prove that by going on stage, they didn't necessarily transgress the moral codes or commit sexual sins. Most of them wanted to become mothers and housewives, they said, in an attempt to gain respect by using the image of the respectful wife and the mother to define their identity. The Egyptian dancer Hikmat Fahmi wished to become an "honorable housewife and the mother of honest sons."[45] Bahiyya Amir also confessed that she wished to become a "housewife and a mother who would nurture her kids with her kindness and affection, and they would fulfill her with their loyalty and gratitude."[46] But because of their economic situation, these performers were forced to work in such places to make money and survive. They tried to construct a self-representation of the mother or the wife in the private sphere, in contrast to their image of working women in the public space. They thus tried to protect their reputation as respectable women, asserting that their singing and dancing were only a means of subsistence.

By talking to the press, especially within a respected newspaper like *al-'Asifa*, these women performers transcended their social confinement: they began to acquire a public "presence." They claimed their names and their voices. They assumed their presence in the public sphere while accepting their own responsibility over their acts and choices. By simply speaking to the press, these women, whose voices were not respected and often silenced, and whose singing was related to their level of dignity, were then speaking in public and indirectly challenging the silence forced upon them.

The drive behind publishing these interviews was probably a combination of a desire to stimulate male readership and at the same time indirectly suggesting the illicit behavior that *other* respectable women need to avoid. This goal seems to point out the risk that women would encounter if they ventured out of their private sphere and especially into the obscene world of artists and cabarets.

Therefore, they are seen and portrayed as having voluntarily challenged and transgressed social norms to find themselves on the margins of society. By acting in the public sphere, they already lost their femininity and humanity. Following their lead will incline the same destiny marked by regret and obscenity. Such a discourse was certainly the result of the entry of women into the public sphere. But it was also related to the rapid urban changes and especially the massive westernization of the city following the French domination and the rise of these entertainment venues where these women danced, sung, and shaped the musical scene.

Nevertheless, this abundant flow of adverts, interviews, and coverage shows that the relationship between women artists, the press, and society was beginning to change. It was now possible for female singers to be either admired and appreciated by society, or, at least, to attract their interest and curiosity. This will greatly impact the status and life of women singers for the next generations.

Chapter 5

ANDALUSI MUSIC AS CULTURAL RENAISSANCE IN TWENTIETH-CENTURY NORTH AFRICA

Liz Matsushita

In early twentieth-century North Africa, Arab-Andalusi music was experiencing a revival, first in the form of popular urban musical associations, then by the 1920s via national radio broadcasts and phonograph recordings. This musical renaissance took on a special significance in the context of the spread of European colonialism in the Maghreb, namely the establishment of the French and Spanish Protectorates in Morocco in 1912, and the Arab "classical" musical genres became points of civilizational pride in the face of foreign domination and cultural encroachment. This chapter will examine the spread of Andalusi music in Morocco, Algeria, and Tunisia as a Maghrebi manifestation of the Arabic Nahda: the notion that Arab culture contained profound resources that actively pushed back on notions of Western modernity and Arab-Islamic decadence. In the process Andalusi music became an avenue through which to express notions of national and civilizational revival, modernity, and pan-Arab identity. Practitioners and theorists of these musics often intentionally forged connections with their counterparts in the Middle East, dialoging with musicians and writers in Cairo and Beirut and in the process creating a transnational imaginary of Arabic musical renaissance. At the same time, it is worth asking: What alternative or counternarratives to a purely "Arab" Nahda were at work in North African musical spaces, and what other sources of musical renaissance were popularized in this same moment? Through an examination of musical programming, revivalist associations, radio, and musicology in the early to mid-twentieth century, a period spanning the colonial to the early national eras, this chapter will trace a multifaceted Nahda in North Africa rooted in the region's profound cultural memory, one forged at the interplay of local and transnational Arab identities and yet often defined against the non-Arab identities of the Maghreb.

The Nahda

The Arabic Nahda, or renaissance, has been the subject of copious writings over the last century. Traditionally, this cultural and intellectual movement has been squarely situated (1) in the Arabic-speaking East (namely Egypt and Syria/Lebanon), and (2) in literary genres. Yet North Africa has been left out of many of these historical conversations, a trend that is admittedly not isolated to the Nahda. Historically at the margins of the Arabic-speaking world, the countries of the Maghreb—Morocco, Algeria, Tunisia—typically remain afterthoughts in surveys of Middle Eastern (or even "Middle Eastern and North African") history. In M. M. Badawi's influential writings on modern Arabic literature, he notes that this literature developed first in the centers of Cairo and Beirut, then gradually spread to "other" parts of the Arab world. Interestingly, he claims North Africa and the Arabian Peninsula did not make "their distinct literary contributions" until sometime after the Second World War.[1]

In the introduction to her book on the "transcolonial Maghreb," Olivia Harrison points to the ways in which the Maghreb has often been marginalized in the literature of the Arabic-speaking world or analyzed solely in relationship to France. As such, scholarship has reproduced the notion of an isolated and even undifferentiated Maghreb, while flattening the varied histories of the countries that comprise it or overlooking the dense networks of exchange between the Maghreb and the rest of the Arabic-speaking world.[2] These types of narratives eschew a more capacious understanding of literary and artistic contributions and the often-flourishing intellectual life of Maghrebi cities throughout the nineteenth and earlier twentieth centuries. These contributions and their local and transnational manifestations should also be considered in the histories of the making and unmaking of pan-Arab and transnational imaginaries, especially those that potentially decenter the *Mashriq* (or east) as the locus of all Arab nationalism.

Music and musical performance have also tended to be overlooked as major sites of nationalist and pan-Arabist aspirations. The revivalist period of Andalusi music stretched from the late nineteenth century, a period of expanding European colonialism in the Maghreb (Algeria was first occupied by the French in 1830, and Tunisia was acquired as a French Protectorate in 1881), through the high colonial period of the interwar era, and into the early national period, when Arab-Muslim identity and Andalusi musical heritage became centerpieces of state-building projects. In the space that follows I aim to give a brief overview of this sweep while focusing on a few prominent examples of Andalusi music as renaissance. My hope is that this discussion will contribute to conversations in this collection that reframe and expand the Nahda to include musical performance, preservation, and scholarship, while also more broadly interlinking Maghrebi and North African histories with those of Egypt and the Levant.

Specifically, I will ask how we can take the phenomenon of Andalusi musical revival—musical associations, public performance, radio programs, phonographs, and scholarship—as part of the broader Nahda, while also being attentive to the particular dynamics that were at play in the North African situation which mark it as distinct from the *Mashriq* (the eastern Arabic-speaking world). This includes the ways in which Arab identity took on particular valences in colonial and postcolonial North Africa, due in part to a stifling French racial model and a subsequent nationalist backlash, that resulted in state-building projects around music and culture elevating Andalusi music to the exclusion of musics associated with ethnic and racial minorities. I argue that despite or even because of these contingencies, Andalusi musical revival can be considered alongside and with the Nahda as a stakeholder in the broader transnational project of Arab(ic) cultural efflorescence as a political argument, rooted in claims to both tradition and modernity, and set against a backdrop of colonial encroachment and nationalist state-building. At the same time, such a privileged focus on Andalusi music and heritage tended to obscure the multiethnic and diverse musical landscape as it existed in these countries in favor of strategically elevating a particular identity and history; in this way, like other Nahda forms, Andalusi performance and knowledge production made intentional moves toward a postcolonial narrative that was selective and, consciously or not, often in dialogue with European discourses on what constituted classical music, high culture, and modernity.

Andalusi Music in the Colonial Era

During the period of French colonialism in North Africa, musical life underwent many dramatic transformations. Part of this was attributable to the intense interest that the French took in "native" music genres, which accelerated after the establishment of the Moroccan French Protectorate (1912–56).[3] The French authorities in Morocco, in accordance with the unofficial colonial policy of associationism, viewed traditional Moroccan culture in its many facets (arts and crafts, Islamic practice, urban architecture, music) as something to be preserved and maintained, protected from the corrupting influences of modernization and assimilation.[4] This translated into a proliferation of colonial scholarship on these very topics, as defining and delineating these cultural objects was crucial to serving as caretakers to their "authenticity." Much has been written on these colonial efforts, although somewhat less so on musical preservation and scholarship.[5] Yet as I argue elsewhere, music constituted part of this same colonial edifice, predicated on establishing expertise on Moroccan and Maghrebi culture as an avenue to greater colonial control.[6]

One of the ways this was achieved was through an almost exclusive focus on two primary musical genres, in Morocco, Algeria, and Tunisia: Andalusi music and Amazigh (Berber) music. "Andalusi music" referred to the musical traditions believed to have been directly inherited from al-Andalus, the Islamic kingdoms of Iberia dating from the eighth to the fifteenth centuries. The enduring power of this cultural and spiritual heritage in the Maghreb can be attributed primarily to two things: first, al-Andalus retained a profound significance in Arab and Muslim memory across the Mediterranean, as the locus of an Islamic Golden Age that saw Islamic civilization at its peak, politically, militarily, culturally, artistically, scientifically, and intellectually. Second, many North Africans traced their family lineages to al-Andalus, and to the mass migrations that occurred from the Andalusi cities of Seville, Córdoba, Granada, and Valencia to the North African urban centers of Fez, Tétouan, Tlemcen, Algiers, and Tunis from the fourteenth to sixteenth centuries. Many of these cities claimed to retain pure vestiges of this "lost" Andalusi culture in their art, architecture, cuisine, and music. This cultural memory was heavily concentrated in the Arabic-speaking populations of urban centers.

The musical mapping of the Maghreb into Andalusi music and Amazigh music, then, was intentionally reflective of the French comprehension of the region's racial landscape as being comprised of "Arabs" and "Berbers," which, in turn, informed French colonial policy in myriad ways. In Algeria, where the French presence in North Africa began with the occupation of Algiers in 1830, the colonial racial model was part and parcel to the "Kabyle myth," which postulated that Berber-speaking peoples of the Kabyle mountain region were more assimilable to French culture than the urban Arabic-speaking peoples of Algiers, who were deemed to be more "fanatically" Muslim, and variously ascribed other negative traits such as decadence, intolerance, moral weakness, and effeminacy.[7] This translated to the cultural and political elevation of Kabyle Berbers, including a whole cadre of men who were educated in French schools and sought roles in French administration. By the time Morocco was colonized in the early twentieth century, many French officials believed that the assimilationist model in Algeria had been a failure, as colonial control there remained tenuous and embattled, and much of the "native" culture and landscape had been erased. These included men like Hubert Lyautey, who had been stationed in Algeria and Madagascar before being named the first resident-general in the Moroccan Protectorate, and thus he pursued so-called "associationist" political and social policies in Morocco that sought to maintain an administrative and cultural separation between Europeans and Moroccans.

Meanwhile, the Arab-Berber racial myth was by this point firmly established in the colonial mind and indeed was seen as even more necessary to policy considerations due to Morocco's larger proportion of Berber-speaking areas vis-à-vis Algeria. In Morocco the prevalence of the Arab-Berber paradigm led to distinct and separate policies applied to Berber-speaking peoples, culminating in the infamous "Berber *dahir*" or decree of 1930 that implemented separate law codes in Berber regions. As Jonathan Wyrtzen has described, this *dahir* was a major spark for the Moroccan nationalist movement, which formally began in the 1930s and led to the official establishment of the Istiqlal Party in 1944, as a mostly Arab political leadership that protested French ethnic policies and rallied around the idea of a united Moroccan-ness, shared by Arabs and Berbers alike.[8] However, by the early post-independence years of the 1950s and 1960s, this same Arab political leadership set out to systematically suppress the Amazigh language and culture, viewing these as reminders of colonial intervention and threats to Moroccan unity under the banner of Arab-Islamic identity.

Colonial-era musical manifestations followed this ethno-racial dichotomy almost to the letter. French-sponsored musical events, such as the "Three days of Moroccan music" concert series in Rabat in 1928 and the Fez Congress of Moroccan Music in 1939, were programmed to showcase Arab-Andalusi and Amazigh musical performances as the primary, and wholly distinct, components of the Moroccan musical landscape. Often programs would be explicitly labeled as such: an "Arab" portion of the program and a "Berber" one.⁹ French scholarship on Maghrebi music repeated the same pattern. Prolific musicologist Alexis Chottin's comprehensive works on Moroccan music, the *Corpus of Moroccan Music* (1931–3) and the *Tableau of Moroccan Music* (1939), were both expressly divided into Arab and Berber volumes.¹⁰ While more "popular" musical genres, such as the *aïta* category of urban sung poetry or the chants of Sufi brotherhoods, also made appearances in such manifestations, the overwhelming majority of colonial representations of Moroccan and Maghrebi music was predicated on this dichotomy, with Andalusi music serving as a stand-in for Arab Morocco.

What is worth noting here is the extent to which Andalusi music became the primary representative of Arab music and behind that an "Arab" identity, in the colonial mind but also in North African and nationalist circles, despite the diversity of musical practice among Arabic-speaking populations. As a musical tradition that could be understood as "classical," Andalusi music served as a particularly potent avenue toward advocating for Arab North African heritage, a heritage that was deeply rooted in North Africa's Andalusi history but also one that stretched across the Mediterranean and instantiated links with the rest of the Arabic-speaking world. Thus, in the twentieth century, this art form that had traditionally been practiced by limited circles in closed events began to reach the masses, extending beyond an urban elite or small cadre of learned *shaykhs*, via public performances, concerts, recordings, and radio programs. This was accompanied by an increase in scholarly writings on Andalusi music by Maghrebi writers from the 1920s onward that circulated among an Arab elite, within North Africa but also abroad. This kind of broad-based investment in Andalusi music formulated a musical Nahda in the colonial and postcolonial Maghreb.

Al-Andalus, the imagined origin of this set of musical traditions, was the name given to the Islamic kingdoms of the Iberian Peninsula (modern-day Spain and Portugal) as they existed from 711 to 1492, including the legendary Caliphate of Córdoba (929–1031) which witnessed an efflorescence of scientific, artistic, architectural, and scholarly achievement. Often heralded as an Arab-Islamic "golden age," the loss of al-Andalus to the Christian Reconquista of the fourteenth to sixteenth centuries became a major subject of Arabic poetry and literature, particularly the "city elegy" genre, in ensuing centuries. The Reconquista also resulted in successive waves of migration from the major Andalusi centers of Córdoba, Seville, Valencia, and Granada to North African cities, where, it is popularly held, these migrants retained the traditions of their former home and passed them down over the generations. Several scholars have written about imaginaries of al-Andalus in the musical and literary realms. Jonathan Glasser's *The Lost Paradise* explores the rich and complex history of Andalusi revival in North Africa, particularly the myriad musical associations that were founded from the early twentieth century onward. Significantly, despite new forms and audiences that were made available under colonialism, this musical revival was not simply a colonial project or a knee-jerk response to colonial domination. The "associative movement," or the granting of a formal administrative structure to support local associations as social and recreational formations, began in France in 1901, and immediately afterward was taken up in Algeria, spawning countless amateur musical associations comprising both *pied-noir* and indigenous Algerian groups. However, as Glasser notes, the association form was likely simply a more formalized, state-backed framework for a phenomenon that had already been occurring, namely the formation of indigenous musical ensembles and recreational clubs dating to the nineteenth century.[11] Specifically, the associative movement furthered opportunities for those dedicated to the project of *reviving* Andalusi music. Yet Glasser gestures to an interesting interplay here: while the project of revival was rooted in notions of a timeless and unchanging tradition, it was simultaneously a move toward modernity via the musical association form. As a modern construct, the amateur musical association entailed new forms of interaction, participation, and the physical movement of Andalusi music into new performance spaces.

The imaginative geography of al-Andalus must also be considered here, especially as we seek to place regional geographies in conversation with each other. Many scholars have investigated the deep and multifaceted histories of Andalusi memory and nostalgia throughout the region, concentrated in but not limited to the Maghreb. Jonathan Holt Shannon has traced the legend of Ziryab as progenitor of the Andalusi *nuba*, or suite form, and the circulation of Andalusi nostalgia discourses across the Mediterranean, from Morocco in the Maghreb, to Syria in the Levant, to Spain in Europe.[12] Eric Calderwood's book on "colonial al-Andalus" specifically examines the case of the Spanish Protectorate in Morocco, and how successive Spanish colonial governments drew on an imagined, shared Andalusi heritage to facilitate Spain's occupation of Morocco. Interestingly, this investment in Andalusi identity was not solely Spanish and colonial but also inveighed the participation of Moroccan nationalists who worked with Spanish authorities on projects of Andalusi cultural revival, including music.[13]

Hence the revival of Andalusi musical heritage in the Maghreb was linked up to the larger imaginary of Arab and Muslim space across the Mediterranean. The discourse of al-Andalus as a lost paradise, an imagined Arab golden age that represented the pinnacle of Islamic civilization, had a broad appeal as a kind of decline narrative, which allowed those speaking from various locations to articulate their visions for contemporary Arab-Islamic society.

While in the Moroccan Protectorate there was a shared investment in Andalusi musical revival between indigenous elites and European officialdom, in the settler colony of Algeria musical life tended to follow the highly segregationist model of wider Algerian society. Despite its assimilationist tendencies, the vast influx of European settlers to Algeria over the course of the latter nineteenth century led to the entrenchment of a *pied-noir* society that was segregated from indigenous Algerians, often racist in its orientation, and frequently at odds with both Muslim society and the French metropolitan government. As colonial society invested in Algeria as a European space, socially and sonically, the musical landscape came to mirror the sociopolitical one. French musical periodicals and societies focused almost exclusively on European classical music and scarcely acknowledged native Algerians, let alone Algerian musics. These included the *Revue musicale de l'Afrique du Nord*, inaugurated in 1910 as the official publication of the Conservatory of Algiers, and included round-ups of concerts and performances in all major North African cities, including Tangier, Oran, Algiers, Constantine, and Tunis. As such it claimed a pan-North African focus, and underscored the existence of a "musical public" among the European settler community throughout North Africa, one that was in dialogue across both urban and colonial boundaries.

This kind of exclusionary and bifurcated cultural landscape could only contribute to a strengthening investment in Andalusi music as the "classical" music of indigenous Algerian society, the mirror-image classical genre to that vaunted in European circles, an investment that grew as the country approached independence. Indeed, the Andalusi revival movement was particularly pronounced in urban Algeria, with amateur musical associations founded by Algerian Muslims and Jews spreading throughout the first few decades of the twentieth century and musical transcription and scholarship efforts being spearheaded by enterprising Algerian musicians and musicologists from Edmond Yafil to El Boudali Safir, making their way into the new technological forms of the radio and the phonograph recording by the 1920s.

Despite the conflicting colonial attitudes toward Arab music and culture across the North African colonial states, a common and intensifying investment in Andalusi musical revival and preservation stretched from Morocco to Tunisia throughout the early decades of the twentieth century. The participants in this revivalist movement were often in dialogue with each other and with musicologists and musicians from the *Mashriq*, which exercised its own gravitational pull despite the vibrancy of Maghrebi cultural and intellectual life. The strengthening of public investment in Andalusi music as an important manifestation of Arab achievement and sophistication led, in the immediate post-independence years, to a kind of re-entrenchment of the Andalusi movement that took on new dimensions as it became linked to state-building projects. In the next section, I will discuss some of the primary venues through which Andalusi musical revival arose in the early to middle decades of the twentieth century, considering this alongside the framing question of how musical performance and knowledge in North Africa were discursively linked to the Arabic Nahda.

Andalusi Musical Performance

Andalusi musical performance in a variety of venues became a means of disseminating the art form to a wider public, while also investing that public in attendant ideologies of Arab civilizational decadence and revival. This broader dissemination was part and parcel to what Jonathan Glasser has defined as Andalusi revival dating to the turn of the century, in which Andalusi music became "the object of a revivalist project in a newly emerging colonial public sphere" that "sat at the nexus of scientific, aesthetic, and colonial discourses that went well beyond specifically musical matters."[14] Glasser points out also that it is necessary to interrogate the very notion of a "revival," as it invokes the possibility of a pristine past that is being recovered, whereas in reality revival was just as much about creating something new; this was especially the case with the "revived" Andalusi musical repertoire and the new technological mediums that disseminated it. It suffices to say here, however, that whether or not a pure Andalusi tradition was being recovered, Andalusi music as a practice and discourse became a central preoccupation of elite circles even as it also reached a wider popular audience who consumed its sounds and ideas through the radio, the phonograph, and the public concert space in the early decades of the twentieth century.

Scholars like Ziad Fahmy and Chris Silver have demonstrated how music and popular culture are potent sites at which to explore processes of nationalism and identity formation. Fahmy introduced this argument in his work *Ordinary Egyptians*, which demonstrated how forms of mass culture including music contributed to the making of a national community that transcended ethnic and religious divides in early twentieth-century Egypt.[15] Silver more specifically investigates popular music, musicians, and recordings in the Maghreb, including renowned Jewish Moroccan musician Samy Elmaghribi, as catalysts to a broader and more inclusive form of Moroccan nationalism in the years leading up to independence.[16]

With Andalusi performance, there was simultaneously a capacious appeal to a broadly defined North African heritage and a somewhat exclusive musical space that privileged certain class and ethnic backgrounds over others. I will explore this in more detail in the following sections; however, here, I want to carry Fahmy's arguments into the sphere of Andalusi music in the Maghreb and situate that within the framework of Andalusi revival as Nahda. Central to this position is the ubiquity with which Andalusi music began to appear in North African cities by the middle decades of the twentieth century, a crucial political moment of embattled colonial rule and strengthening nationalist movements.

Musical Associations

As noted earlier, musical associations became a major vehicle for the preservation, practice, and promotion of Andalusi music in early to mid-twentieth-century North Africa. However, the performance groups varied widely from the more "modern" (in terms of size, instruments, and performance practice) to the more traditional. One of the earliest of these that gained recognition and renown was El Moutribia in Algiers, founded by Algerian Jewish musician Edmond Yafil and French musicologist Jules Rouanet.[17] Yafil, who was a prolific musicologist in his own right and produced a sheet music series entitled "Repertoire of Arab and Moorish Music" that included many selections from the *nuba*, led this ensemble until 1923 when he was appointed the chair of Arab Music at the Algiers Municipal Conservatory; at this point the singer Mahieddine Bachetarzi took over. French colonial surveillance often made mention of happenings in the Algerian theater, monitoring for any potentially anticolonial activity or ideology, and especially for any indications of pan-Arab unity developing between Algerian groups and those in Morocco, Tunisia, Egypt, Syria, and Palestine. Bachetarzi, who in addition to heading El Moutribia was also active in staging theatrical productions and tours, was monitored along with Algerian public reaction to his plays; according to Arabic newspaper *Er Rihala* his stage works "should be able to play a large role in the education of the native masses," indicating at least the perception of a broad and inclusive reach for his works.[18]

By the 1920s, several other amateur Andalusi associations were cropping up in Algeria. Together, these associations represented a shift not only in performance practice but also performance space: increasingly, Andalusi music was now being played not in cafés and private homes but in concert halls.[19] Similarly there were many active Andalusi ensembles in the Moroccan Protectorate, led by a *ma'alem* or master musician and an often-shifting lineup of musicians. Hadj Othman El Tazi, Faqih M'tiri, and Mohamed Brihi each led ensembles in Fez, some of which continued after their leader's deaths. Many also engaged periodically with French colonial events: all three of the earlier performed at the Fez Congress, and M'tiri was selected along with several other musicians to represent Morocco at the 1932 Cairo Congress of Arab Music, a selection overseen by the Service of Native Arts head Prosper Ricard. The French concern with curating the most "authentic" assemblage of Moroccan Andalusi musicians for this event led Ricard and his colleagues to convene multiple meetings in Fez and Marrakech, even as that authenticity was likely called into question by the inorganic and interventionist nature of their formation.[20] Similarly, for the Fez Congress, "representative" Andalusi orchestras of various North African cities were called to play, though it is not as clear who comprised each one of these; ensembles from Algiers, Tunis, Tlemcen, and Marrakech performed (though due to "political reasons" no such orchestra was invited from Tétouan, the Spanish Protectorate capital), as well as the performing ensembles of the Protectorate's conservatory system.[21] This conservatory system, which specialized in traditional Andalusi music and had schools in Rabat, Fez, and Marrakech, yielded another avenue through which a greater swathe of young Moroccans could be initiated into the art form, expanding the field from the more traditional methods of *shaykhs* and apprentices.

Radio

The radio in colonial North Africa began largely as a tool for colonial states to spread ideology; early radio broadcasts in the Maghreb were French-run, and the TSF (*télégraphie sans fil*, or wireless) was also heavily promoted as a pedagogical tool in colonial schools, through which it disseminated lessons on history, geography, and music that were largely in accordance with colonial narratives.[22] Yet at the same time the radio became one of the more accessible mediums through which "ordinary Maghrebis" could listen to Andalusi music, as well as other indigenous musical genres. In Morocco, the colonial office the Service of Native Arts set up a broadcasting station, Radio-Rabat, in the French Protectorate's capital in Rabat. The station included a large concert hall set up to accommodate musical ensembles, adjacent to a glass-windowed cubicle from which the operators gave signals to the musicians.[23] A British BBC announcer with an interest in Arab music, Philip

Thornton, described receiving a tour of the facilities in the mid-1930s and being immediately impressed both by the sophistication of the proceedings and the "atmosphere of charming informality" that still distinguished it from his London offices. Performances of Arab and Andalusi music were regularly broadcast via Radio-Rabat, executed by local musicians of some renown, in some instances members of the sultan's private orchestra. One such performer was Idris ben Abdelali El Idrissi, a voice professor at Rabat's Conservatory of Moroccan Music, who himself contributed to Arabic musical knowledge, as will be discussed later.

Of course, the overall programming of these colonial stations remained Western music—throughout the 1930s, the vast majority of the broadcasting day consisted of European classical compositions, contemporary pieces, "dancing jazz," and popular songs from Europe and the United States. There was, however, a daily two-hour "Arab music concert" in the afternoons on Radio-Rabat, likely what Thornton witnessed on his visit, as well as an additional hour in the evening.[24] The evening concert would sometimes be specially broadcast from Fez instead of Rabat, at the auditorium of the Batha Palace, which would also serve as the main venue for the Fez Congress of Moroccan Music in 1939. But despite the imbalance, these regular opportunities to hear musicians of traditional Arab and Andalusi music on the radio expanded the reach and accessibility of this once-exclusive art form and moved the music into new spaces both literally and figuratively.

Reflecting the differing political situations, the main Algiers radio station in the 1930s dedicated little to no time to Arab music in its broadcasts, only holding a semi-regular "varied Oriental music" hour. However, beginning in the 1940s, the scholar and musicologist El Boudali Safir began producing radio programs for Radio-Alger in Algiers, including inaugurating the Arabic language radio channel as its literary and artistic director, which broadcast talks on literature, theater performances, and music.[25] In this way the radio could serve not only to play Andalusi music for a wider audience but also to educate the public on the history and theory of Andalusi music and its local and national variations. Safir also created three musical ensembles for the radio channel: one devoted to Andalusi music, one to popular music, and one to modern music. This was part of a lifelong project of Andalusi revival: like contemporaries in Morocco, he undertook a project of transcribing the *nuba* of the Algerian Andalusi genre and recording them in studios across Algeria, including Tlemcen, Oran, Bougie, and Constantine. Safir's dedication to promoting Andalusi music to the Algerian public continued into the postcolonial era, when he served as the director of the National Institute of Music, and organized the first three festivals of Andalusi music in Algiers.

Safir's radio programming was accompanied in written form by his articles on Algeria's "classical music," some of which were published in the colonial periodical *Documents algériens*. The use of the French word for "classical" and its Arabic translation is noteworthy and was quite frequently used to describe Andalusi music in the context of North Africa; in its way, this attribution fitted Andalusi music into preexisting understandings of an elite and traditional canon, parallel to and reminiscent of European classical music, and further underscored the

Andalusi movement as a revivalist project rooted in a vaunted cultural past. In a 1949 article entitled "Arab music in Algeria," Safir wrote, "Bedouin or Berber are distinguished from properly Arab music, called classical or Andalusi, dear to the refined city-dwellers of the great cities, and which marks a relatively recent stage in the evolution of Oriental music."[26] He went on to say, "Under its current form, it is in Muslim Andalusia that Arab music perfected its contours. It is on the edges of Guadalquivir, it is in Córdoba, it is in Granada, that it succeeded in achieving its evolution." Safir's article makes the familiar claims of many scholarly writings on Andalusi music in the era, such as that Andalusi music, whose distant roots are in Arabia, with influences from ancient Greece, was shaped, developed, and transformed in medieval al-Andalus and then brought to the major urban centers of the Maghreb through the migration of Andalusi refugees during and after the Reconquista.

Another point of interest in this standard depiction was that Andalusi music was something especially valued by "refined urban-dwellers," to be heavily differentiated from folk, popular, Bedouin, and Amazigh genres. Manoubi Snoussi, the Tunisian musicologist, drew a similar distinction to much more dramatic effect in his 1961 article "Tunisian Folklore," which sought to edify a French audience in an amusing way on the folk music of the Tunisian countryside, which with the phenomena of urbanization and modernization was in danger of dying out. Snoussi's fictionalized account imagined a *tabbal* (player of the *tabl*, a large percussion instrument) and a *zakkar* (player of the *zukrah*, a reed instrument) who had recently moved into the big city in search of work, and found that their rustic rural music had no audience among city-dwellers. Instead, the Tunisian urban populace were only interested in Andalusi music. "The city-dwellers, however impassioned for music, showed themselves to be inaccessible to the charm of the nostalgic tunes of the mountain," Snoussi narrated, from the perspective of the two rural musicians.[27] As such, the musicians seek to reproduce Andalusi *nuba* fragments on their instruments, but find it prohibitively difficult to do so: "the elegant line and the cleverly mannered forms of the music of the city-dwellers ... a veritable ordeal to try to reproduce, with my rustic instrument, the melodic nuances so ingeniously gradated that these people of such complicated tastes are looking for."[28] While purporting to inform the readership of the characteristics and challenges of folk and Bedouin music, and even lamenting its disappearance, the article also subtly served as a mouthpiece for the superiority of Andalusi music and its strong associations with sophistication and culture in the Arab city. Andalusi music, specifically the Tunisian variant of *ma'luf*, was the popular and preferred genre for the urban middle and upper classes. By Snoussi's fabular account, we can also surmise that urbanization led to greater segments of the city, including working classes and rural migrants who increasingly came into contact with urban populations, being exposed to and influenced by Andalusi music, recognizing its value even if it remained an exclusive art in practice.

Snoussi himself made notable use of the radio in promoting Tunisian music and educating the public on Tunisian genres in the postcolonial era. Having gotten his start as the young secretary to the French musicologist Baron Rodolphe d'Erlanger, who settled in Tunis in the 1910s and became a prolific writer on Arab music, Snoussi went on to oversee the editing and publication of the latter volumes of d'Erlanger's massive *La Musique Arabe* series after the scholar's death in 1932. The last d'Erlanger volume was released in 1959. In this way, Snoussi was heavily involved in the French-influenced musicological world of colonial Tunisia through independence, despite the fact that his work for d'Erlanger is often not properly credited. In the 1960s, Snoussi produced a series of radio programs for Radio Tunis entitled "Initiation to Tunisian Music," with 188 episodes total over the course of a few years.[29] The episodes were divided into five principal themes, of which the lengthiest were "classical music" (forty-seven episodes) and "Islamic liturgy" (ninety-five episodes). Snoussi's classical music broadcasts, which began in 1963, were devoted to *ma'luf*, the Tunisian version of Andalusi music. This included discussing and demonstrating, via the radio broadcast, the principal modes (*maqamat*) of *ma'luf*; the primary instruments (oud, rebab, qanun, nay, tar, darbuka, and naghgharat); and the *nuba* composition. In this way Andalusi music was both literally sounded on the radio airwaves and also defined, described, and dictated to a broad listening audience.

Indeed, *ma'luf* was a major subject of learned inquiry and public promotion in twentieth-century Tunis (and, as musicologist Mourad Sakli notes, was primarily referred to as such until the early decades of the twentieth century; the term *Arab-Andalusi* then became more common as a generalized term). The idea behind initiatives like Snoussi's radio programs, as well as Rashidiyya Institute concerts and Salah El Mahdi's national musical patrimony collections (discussed more later), was that Tunisia's musical heritage was simultaneously unique and linked to a wider transnational Arab culture.

Andalusi Musical Knowledge

In the early to mid-twentieth century, scholars from the Arab world engaged in the study of Arab and North African music, in diverse ways, and their work resided in uneasy tension with European musicology on Arab music. Yet it was not—and cannot be read merely as—a response to European musicology, but was actually crucial to the production of musical knowledge and the making of modern musicology as a whole. In this sense, my reading of musicology in North Africa follows Omnia El Shakry's work on the social sciences in Egypt: much of what might on the surface be considered merely a response or a co-optation of European scholarly practice by North African practitioners was in fact a discrete field rooted in a precolonial canon, that also in many ways contributed to the development of European knowledge.[30]

Like French musicology, Arab and North African musicology was heavily invested in the definition of distinct ethnic genres predicated on racial and ethnic categories, and as such their work similarly served to reinforce and perpetuate these categories. Yet while the French promoted racial distinctions in North Africa as a means of dividing and controlling potentially unruly colonial populations, North

African writers had a different set of premises. Their work was both a continuation of a centuries-old Arabic musicological tradition, and a future-oriented knowledge production that participated in a nationalist political project. The ethno-racial hierarchy they established thus served as a vision for the postcolonial landscape: a triumphalist Arab hegemonic project that marginalized minority ethnic identities in North Africa, most notably the Amazigh.

Thus within this body of scholarship is visible the articulation and production of racial, ethnic, gender, and class categories, in ways both similar to and different from the production of such categories in French musicology. Arabic treatises on music were in dialogue with European scholarship, yet to an extent were also independent developments, part of a continuous scholarly tradition dating back to the Arab and Muslim theoreticians of the medieval era. The work on Andalusi musical repertoire, in particular, frequently and self-consciously attached itself to this centuries-old scholarly canon, while also actively engaging with colonial scholarship.

The Nuba

Besides performance, one of the most meaningful ways that Andalusi revival took on dimensions of political claim was in knowledge production. One of the central tenets of Andalusi revival was the collection and transcription of the *nuba*, the classical song suites that comprised the core repertoire of Andalusi music, believed to trace directly back to al-Andalus but scattered and lost over centuries of principally oral transmission. There were several figures throughout the colonial and early national periods who attempted to collect the *nuba*, both North African and European. The French spearheaded a transcription project through musicologist Alexis Chottin, who presented the *nuba oshshak*, one of the eleven surviving *nuba* suites, in his 1931 volume of the *Corpus of Moroccan Music*. Meanwhile, the Spanish toiled away at their own *nuba* collection project from their capital in Tétouan, in collaboration with Moroccan informants, a fact that Spanish musicologist Patrocinio García Barriuso boasted of while attending a French-sponsored musical conference in 1939. The inter-colonial rivalry over musical preservation and promotion in North Africa had, of course, quite a different aim than that of those North Africans who also studied the *nuba*.

In fact, Mostefa Aboura, an Algerian schoolteacher residing in the border town of Tlemcen, began his *nuba* collection project as early as 1900, an ambitious endeavor that was as Jonathan Glasser termed it "an ingathering of scattered, unruly, endangered musical knowledge."[31] Aboura's project went through many iterations over the ensuing decades, and much of what he recorded shifted out of sight after his death in 1935; a planned presentation of his transcriptions, to be introduced by his longtime collaborator Mohamed Ben Smaïl at the 1939 Fez Congress of Moroccan Music, never took place. However, as Glasser outlines, Aboura's project—as well as L'Andaloussia, the musical association that he and Ben Smaïl founded in 1925—played an important role in the broader Andalusi revival movement of urban Algeria and Morocco in the early to mid-twentieth century. L'Andaloussia became one of the most active amateur musical associations in Protectorate Morocco, frequently invited to perform at French musical manifestations as one of the principal representatives of Andalusi music for a broader audience: they performed at the "Three days of Moroccan music" series in 1928, at the Morocco Pavilion at the 1931 Paris Colonial Exposition, and made multiple performances at the five-day Fez Congress of Moroccan Music. At this latter event, the Spanish musicologist Patrocinio García Barriuso, in attendance as the sole delegate from the rival Spanish Protectorate, gave a generally favorable review of their sound but criticized elements of their authenticity, including the orchestra size and the use of European instruments. García Barriuso complained that they thus had the "veneer of an Arab orchestra while its ensemble and repertoire is not very different from a Jazz-band," and the enthusiasm with which the crowd received their performance was evidence that Moroccans were losing their taste for traditional music.[32]

As noted, El Boudali Safir also made strides toward *nuba* transcription in his own city of Algiers. The act of collecting and transcribing the "lost" and "scattered" song forms was a claiming of sorts for various actors working from various positions. While the scholarly pursuit of knowledge about North African society and culture fulfilled colonial aims toward achieving discursive mastery over their holdings, for savants like Safir and Aboura the *nuba* project contained seeds of revival, heritage, and a learned avenue through which to seek Maghrebi society's path forward by tracing the civilizational path it had left behind.

The collection of the *nuba*, as well as the broader Arabic musicological project it intersected with, was certainly in dialogue with colonial efforts and influenced by the practice of European musicology and its essentializing categorizations of non-Western music. However, Arabic musicology was also profoundly and self-consciously engaged with a longer trajectory of Arabic scholarship on music that dated to the precolonial era, in fact even to centuries earlier. Frequently North African scholars invoked this intellectual genealogy and made calls for a revival from the decadence which musical culture had been allowed to fall into.

Arabic Musicology

Throughout North Africa in the early to mid-twentieth century, an academic subfield on "Arabic musicology" blossomed, one that drew on the canonical texts of much earlier Arabic scholarship but that was also consciously attached to modern intellectual idioms. These musicologists, whose primary focus tended to be Arab and Andalusi music, were often in dialogue with European musicology and particularly those colonial musicologists who took Maghrebi music as their field of study, yet their work was by no means a simple response or co-optation of European science. Rooted in the work of medieval scholars and in dialogue with scholars from Egypt and the Levant, Arabic musicology can instead be understood as an intellectual instrument of modernity that implicitly or overtly advocated for the strength and renovation of Arab society and civilization. This strength was manifest in the sophistication and prestige of its music, as well as in the advanced scholarship that analyzed and historicized it.

Idris ben Abdelali El Idrissi, mentioned earlier as one of the regular performers on Radio-Rabat, was also a musicologist and scholar. He gave a presentation at the Fez Congress of Moroccan Music in 1939 on *aïta*, and authored two texts on musical life in contemporary Morocco that focused mainly on traditional Andalusi music. In the introduction to his book *Uncovering the Secrets of Music* (1939), El Idrissi invoked the names of the great Muslim scholars of the past who had written about music, including Al-Kindi, Al-Farabi, and Ibn Sina, and wrote: "I aspire to inscribe my name following those whom History has recorded, and of which she has retained the memory of their great qualities of heart and mind."[33] He went on to say that progress in the realm of knowledge, both scientific and artistic, was key to the advancement of a nation and to the unity of that nation—essentially, that it was a patriotic act. Without it, he said, a nation cannot aspire to "civilization" and risks being erased from history.

El Idrissi refrained from any specific statements about Morocco as a "nation," likely due to his close relationship with colonial authorities, and instead referenced a broad pan-Arab, pan-Islamic geography. He invoked the names of great Arab and Muslim scholars from across the globe, those who already formed a canon of Arabic intellectual genealogy, including Al-Farabi and Al-Kindi, both ninth-century scholars based in Baghdad. He continued this pan-Arab narrative when he recalled the birth of Arab song, "hidâ," in the pre-Islamic Arabian desert. This was a form of sung poetry that was said to have developed on the arduous journeys of trade caravans, intended to align with the rhythmic walk of the camel. In this he traced a direct line from this earliest known form of Arab music to the Arab music of Morocco in the present, a common trope in Arabic musicology.

Those writing in the immediate postcolonial period also sought to establish a transnational genealogy for local classical music. In Tunisia, the national government commissioned an ambitious recording project of Tunisian musics under the direction of the head of the Service of Fine Arts, musicologist Salah El Mahdi. In his preface to the second volume of *Al-turath al-musiqi al-tunisi* (*Tunisian Musical Heritage*), El Mahdi discussed the *nuba*, *muwashshah*, and *zajal* musical forms, all of Andalusi origin, and wrote:

> Nearly all the pieces published are known throughout North Africa, with slight modifications in interpretation according to the region. This is why we think that by publishing them we are doing a service to our Tunisian compatriots as well as to the other inhabitants of the Maghreb, who will thus be able to come to know an important part of a common musical heritage. We think we shall also be useful to our other Arab brothers by showing them an aspect of the Arabic artistic heritage, and to all those who are interested in art as the manifestation of the soul of peoples and civilizations.[34]

By orienting his project toward multiple audiences, moving outwards in concentric circles—Tunisians, Maghrebis, Arabs, and the world—El Mahdi articulated the ties of affinity that existed between the local and transnational. Tunisian Andalusi music, or *ma'luf*, was understood to be primarily the heritage of Tunisians themselves, and as such comprised a part of a national cultural project to recover and record its melodies for posterity. Yet a "common musical heritage" also existed with the other nations of the Maghreb, under the wider umbrella of Andalusi music. And beyond that, Arabs throughout the Middle East and North Africa region would appreciate this branch of the wider tree of "Arabic artistic heritage." The project of Andalusi documentation and revival was thus a simultaneously local and transnational affair, one that had the capacity to articulate multiple political projects at once, and the instantiation of these projects perhaps reached its height in these early years of independence.

Conferences

Musical conferences were one of the primary modalities through which modern Arabic musicology was given shape, particularly as these tended to bring together scholars and musicians from a wide pan-Arab geography. The Cairo Congress of Arab Music in 1932, discussed in detail by A. J. Racy and Mahmoud Guettat, was the most famous such event: a massive undertaking sponsored by the Egyptian government and largely organized by Egyptian musicologist and minister of education Mahmoud Ahmed El-Hefny, the Congress elicited the participation of delegations from multiple European and Arab countries, as well as representative Arab music ensembles from Egypt, Syria, Iraq, Lebanon, Morocco, Algeria, and Tunisia.[35] Most of the delegates who sat on important committees were European; however, several Algerian and Tunisian delegates were in attendance, and the Lebanese musicologist Wadia Sabra played a significant role in debates over the standardization of scales and the use of Western musical instruments in Arab music.

The Cairo Congress's object was "Arab music" writ large and, despite the acknowledgment of distinct regional differences, there were efforts to approach something like a standardized category that encompassed the entire Arab world. Within this, the inclusion and spotlighting of multiple Maghrebi musical ensembles, who represented regional variations of Andalusi music, is noteworthy. From Tunisia, the ensemble was led by the *rebab* player Mohamed Ghanem and Khemais Tarnan, a renowned oudist who would go on to perform with the ensemble of the Rashidiyya Institute in Tunis. The Rashidiyya was founded just two years later, in 1934, with the objective of reviving and promoting *ma'luf*, the Tunisian variant of Andalusi music.[36] From Morocco, the ensemble was largely comprised of noted musicians from Fez, including Faqih M'tiri, who fronted an ensemble popular in Fassi circles. However, as noted the Moroccan ensemble itself was cherrypicked by French Protectorate authorities as the best "representative" of authentic Moroccan Arab-Andalusi music, belying colonial intervention.[37]

As Mahmoud Guettat has argued, the Congress betrayed a general lack of attention to Maghrebi music as distinct from the more spotlighted *al-musiqa al-sharqiyya* (*Mashriqi* music), despite the attendance of North African ensembles and delegates (the latter of whom, as he also points out, were present under the banner of the French delegation). Conversations at the Congress largely omitted the specificity of Maghrebi melodic and rhythmic modes.[38] Further, as Guettat rightly indicates, the intellectual work often solely attributed to scholars was often actually a joint effort with Arab musicologists and musicians. This includes Congress co-organizer Rodolphe d'Erlanger's interlocutors Iskandar Shalfun of Egypt and Ahmad al-Wafi of Tunisia, and the aforementioned Manoubi Snoussi, d'Erlanger's assistant and the inheritor of his musicological project.

Less well-known but significant in its own right, the Fez Congress of Moroccan Music was held in the historic Moroccan city just seven years later and included several of the same actors. The Fez Congress was co-sponsored by the French Protectorate government and the Moroccan sultan, yet was largely planned by unofficial colonial state musicologist Alexis Chottin. The programming of the event was reflective of French scholarly and official attitudes toward Moroccan culture and music which followed the ethno-racial divide presupposed by French observers since the nineteenth century: music was almost wholly classified as either Arab-Andalusi, Amazigh (Berber), or "popular." Like several other French-sponsored musical events during the colonial era, the Fez Congress's programming followed and thus reinforced this musical model. However, the conscious and intentional contributions of numerous Moroccan and Algerian scholars and musicians cannot be overlooked, nor the ways that they pursued their own ends through shared participation in a colonial event. Multiple North African scholars and officials gave presentations on Andalusi music, in both French and Arabic (the second day featured an Arabic-language panel), and a special sub-commission on Andalusi music comprised of both French and North African delegates was assembled and presented its report. Other more popular and folk Moroccan genres were highlighted as well, but Andalusi music was central; Patrocinio García Barriuso, who left one of the few extant accounts of the Congress in detail, perceived it to be the conference's main focus. Hence, via the participation of a cadre of learned and elite Moroccan and Algerian participants, as well as several orchestras from different Maghrebi cities, Andalusi music took preeminence in the proceedings largely through the designs of the Moroccan and Algerian participants, thus allowing it to prefigure a postcolonial nationalism predicated on Andalusi revival and classical Arab-Islamic heritage as state identity.

Conclusion

While North African writers and musicians did not often explicitly ascribe the label of Nahda to Andalusi musical revival, the notion of Arabic cultural and intellectual renaissance broadly construed was at the very core of the movement. Throughout the early decades of the twentieth century, musicians in the urban centers of Algeria, Tunisia, and Morocco formed ensembles that, while based on earlier forms of musical practice, fit themselves into the modern social and cultural landscape in transformative ways. This included adopting the association form introduced by the French government in Algeria, moving into new, more public performance spaces, undertaking theatrical tours, and participating in colonial-sponsored musical events and conferences. This also included appearing on radio airwaves on Arabic music hours. Alongside the advent of new technological and social forms of musical practice, there came an increase in scholarly production on Andalusi and traditional musics in North Africa that simultaneously dialogued with the modern European field of musicology and attached itself to a centuries-old genealogy of Arabic writings on music, stretching from the Maghreb to the *Mashriq*.

Where in the colonial period the sustained practice of Andalusi musical preservation and dissemination could be seen as a form of heritage protection in the face of European encroachment, this practice took on new dimensions and aims with the establishment of independent postcolonial states in the 1950s and 1960s. The promotion of Andalusi music, including the formation of state orchestral ensembles, conservatories, didactic radio programs, and transcription and collection projects like that of Salah El Mahdi, served the needs of fledgling governments seeking to re-inscribe notions of North African autonomy, Arab identity, and Islamic modernity that could be decoupled from European configurations and colonial impositions. As noted, Andalusi music was a particularly potent genre with which to achieve these goals, as it broadly invested in the pan-Arab ideology of the postcolonial moment while also staking claims in a more locally cultivated, authentically Maghrebi heritage. At the same time, this exclusive investment in Arab and Andalusi heritage was accompanied by the tacit or active suppression of minority identities, and the visibility and audibility of Amazigh, Sufi, Bedouin, and Black African musics decreased following the end of colonialism and its ethnographic interest in non-Arab genres.

In more recent decades, Andalusi music, while still regularly practiced and publicly performed, has taken on a more antiquated quality, while national identities have expanded to become more multicultural. In Morocco, the official recognition of Tamazight as a national language in 2011 after decades of Amazigh activism, the rejoining of the African Union in 2017 and a subsequent, if superficial, turn toward pan-African identity, and a general disillusionment with pan-Arabism has manifested musically in a vibrant and diverse festival culture that often spotlights and celebrates these once-maligned "minority" musics, most notably Amazigh and Gnawa. Yet renewed investments in, and reinterpretations of, Andalusi music and heritage have also cropped up in the twenty-first century as avenues to cross-cultural dialogue, including musical projects that attempt to reach across the Islam/Western divide and recover shared histories in North Africa and southern Spain, particularly in the wake of 9/11 and the sharp increase in Islamophobia in the West.[39] In this sense the lifespan of Andalusi revival tends to ebb and flow with historical timelines, mapping onto salient political projects at strategic moments. In the period under discussion, the revitalization of Andalusi music in Morocco, Algeria, and Tunisia was a branch of the broader promotion of Arab civilizational inheritance that took on a new urgency with the spread of European colonialism.

Chapter 6

ON THE ROAD

SULAYMAN AL-QARDAHI AND THE TRAVELING
THEATRICAL TROUPES OF THE NAHDA

Raphael Cormack

In 1964, the Egyptian playwright, journalist, and writer Tawfiq al-Hakim (1898–1987) published his memoirs, *The Prison of Life* [*Sijn al-'Umr*]. In this book, he looked back at a long and extremely successful career. His novels, *Return of the Spirit* [*'Awdat al-Ruh*] (1933) and *A Bird from the East* [*'Usfur min al-Sharq*] (1938), had been some of the most prominent and influential works of the interwar period. After the Free Officers Revolution of 1952, he became a leading cultural figure in postcolonial Egypt. By the time these memoirs were published, his position as a grand old man of Egyptian culture was secure; his contribution to the country's artistic life could hardly be disputed.

In *The Prison of Life*, he recalled the momentous occasion when he encountered "art" (*al-fann*) in person for the first time. It happened, he said, in the Nile Delta town of Disuq, where his family was living in the early twentieth century. At this time, the small town was graced by a visit from "the theatrical troupe of Shaykh Salama Hijazi or—more likely—one of the troupes which imitated him, put on his plays, and took his name as they traveled through the countryside."[1] Al-Hakim does not give a precise date for this event but he does say that he was just a young child—therefore it probably occurred in the second half of the first decade of the twentieth century.

Salama Hijazi (1852–1917) was one of the biggest stars of the Arab stage at the time, particularly renowned for his beautiful singing voice. Hijazi's visit to Disuq would have been a significant event. In al-Hakim's vivid, stylized description of the events, the itinerant troupe's entire stay became a theatrical event. They set up a temporary wooden stage in town, decorated it with fabrics and gas lanterns, and prepared to put on a musical version of *Romeo and Juliet*, called, in Arabic, "Martyrs of Passion" [*Shuhada' al-Gharam*].[2] Everyone was excited at the company's arrival and, as they walked through the streets before the show, "crowds of people stood in rows to watch them, as veiled women looked out from behind their windows."[3]

The young Tawfiq al-Hakim was lucky enough to secure an invite to the performance itself and, although he could not follow the plot in detail, he remembered being amazed by the spectacle—the singing, the costumes, and the sword-fighting displays in particular. When he came to write the story of his life, he identified this dramatic moment in a small town in Egypt as the beginning of a lifelong obsession with the theater and the arts.

Traveling theater performances like this one al-Hakim witnessed as a child played an extremely important part in the development of Arabic drama from the late nineteenth century onwards. They brought plays into areas far beyond the centers of the Nahda's print culture—Cairo, Alexandria, and Beirut—going into the countryside to perform in front of rural audiences and crossing national borders with their work. They were pivotal in spreading some of the most important texts and ideas of the Nahda into places they had not been before. In the process they influenced people like Tawfiq al-Hakim, introducing them to a new form of entertainment that they had not seen before. Yet, in scholarship on the Arab Nahda, there have been few detailed studies of the role and wider impact of theater troupes like these.

This is a subject which merits a large, in-depth study, to examine the activities of individual theater companies closely and trace their influence and reception in cities and the countryside across the Arab world. This would allow us to plot the different nexuses with more clarity—how they worked, who was involved, and who saw the performances. In this chapter, I will examine some of the sources that can be used to build a picture of the traveling theater scene and outline the potential of a larger work on the subject.

Theater and the Nahda

Theater is, in many ways, the Nahdawi genre par excellence. In drama, the complexities of the Nahda's educational project and its intersection with the goals of popular entertainment are clearest. Theater is increasingly becoming a focus of scholarly work on the Nahda. Since Muhammad Yusuf Najm's 1956 work *al-Masrahiyya fi-l-Adab al-ʿArabi al-Hadith*[4]—the first book to give a comprehensive picture of the rise of theater in the nineteenth-century Arab world and still a canonical text—several others have appeared. In English, there are in-depth studies such as Philip Sadgrove's *The Egyptian Theatre in the Nineteenth Century, 1799–1882*,[5] Carmen Gitre's *Acting Egyptian: Theater, Identity, and Political Culture in Cairo 1869–1930*,[6] and Adam Mestyan's *Arab Patriotism: The Ideology and Culture of Power in Late Ottoman Egypt*[7] (which dedicates several chapters to theater and will be discussed later). In Arabic, Sayyid ʿAli Ismaʿil has written numerous books about the development of theater in the nineteenth and twentieth century, including *Tarikh al-Masrah fi Misr fi-l-Qarn al-Tasiʿ ʿAshar*[8] [The History of Theater in Egypt in the 19th Century] and *Masirat al-Masrah fi Misr: 1900–1930*[9] [The March of Theater in Egypt: 1900–1930] (the latter is one of the few books to talk about traveling troupes).

The majority of work on the history of theater has dealt with Egypt but it has not been the only focus of study. North African theater history is also a growing field, after landmark texts on Tunisian theater by Moncef Charfeddine and M.

M. Driss, Khalid Amine and Marvin Carlson released *The Theaters of Morocco, Algeria and Tunisia: Performance Traditions of the Maghreb*[10] in 2011. Ali al-Raʿi's *Al-Masrah fi-l-Watan al-ʿArabi*[11] [*Theater in the Arab World*] also outlines the theatrical history of all the countries of the Arab world.

Increasingly, theater is being seen as an integral part of the broader Nahda project. I would go even further than that and say that it is *the* quintessential genre of the Nahda. Drama encapsulates the missions, the tensions, and the problems of the Nahda more than anything else. Simply materially speaking, theater was a pivotal part of the Nahda; plays and theatrical scripts made up some of the key texts of the period. Play scripts were produced at a staggering rate—many published on small private presses, some not even published at all (merely acted on stage). Many were written by some of the most significant Nahdawi figures of the time—Najib al-Haddad and Farah Antun, among other things, were both prolific writers and translators for the stage.

In fact, plays were so widespread that some of the most prominent literary texts of the Nahda may have actually been better known in their theatrical versions than in their originals. Rifaʿa Rafiʿ al-Tahtawi's influential translation of Fenelon's epic *Telemaque*, for instance, was published as a book in 1867. Just two years later, a dramatic version was published by Saadallah Bustani which immediately became extremely popular. As Peter Hill has observed, "The play would later go on to great success on the Egyptian stage from the 1880s to the 1900s, entering the repertoire of famous Syrian troupes like those of Sulaymān al-Qardāḥī and Salāmah Ḥijāzī."[12] This theatrical version of *Telemaque* proved to be enduringly popular with Egyptian audiences. As late as 1918, it was still being performed on theatrical tours by one of the country's most important troupes.[13]

But the importance of theater goes much further than that. It is a microcosm of the Nahda itself. Drama was seen as a perfect vehicle to promote the moral and ethical development of the masses. Late nineteenth-century theorizing is clear that the role of theater was "refining" [*tahdhib*] the morals of the general public— the playhouse was like a school for the general populace. Al-Tahtawi's travelogue of his time in Paris, *Takhlis al-Ibriz fi Talkhis Bariz* [*Extracting Pure Gold in the Overview of Paris*], is one of the earliest Arabic works to discuss proscenium arch theater and the first to talk about it at significant length. In it, he extolls the benefits of theater and, in particular, he claims that it had the ability to promote the Muslim ideal of "praising the good and censuring the bad" by putting examples of each on stage before an audience.[14] In the decades after this work was published, the idea that theater was primarily designed to improve the moral condition of the people. Books like Ali Mubarak's *ʿAlam al-Din* [*The Sign of Religion*] and al-Muwalyihi's *Hadith ʿIsa Ibn Hisham*, written in the late nineteenth century, both repeat the ubiquitous claim that theater's primary benefit was in its ability to improve the masses. The narrator in Muwaylihi's work tells the resurrected Pasha that theater "encourages virtues, exposes evil traits, and portrays the deeds of former generations so that people can be educated and learn lessons from them."[15]

Well into the twentieth century, the view that theater's function was primarily moral and social function still dominated the thinking of Egyptian nationalist writers and thinkers.¹⁶ Theater offered a potential place to shape and educate the general population. Like the journals discussed in Chapter 7, it could be an important public benefit (*maslaha ʿamma*). As such, it was a vehicle for a larger project that was central to the Nahda that can be (somewhat crudely) summarized under the flag of bringing "modernity" to the Arab world.

Lofty as the idealized model of theater might be, entertainment is always impossible to control. The desires of an audience are unpredictable and seldom conform to the desires of the theorists. We all fall short of the glory of God and theater was often found to be wanting. In al-Muwaylihi's *Hadith ʿIsa Ibn Hisham*, the Pasha who witnesses the theatrical performance sees no possible benefit in the theatrical performance he witnesses. He tells the narrator: "In fact, it's just the opposite. What I've seen here is just a repeat of what I've observed in the dance hall—drinking wine, flirting with women, portraying amorous situations in a highly suggestive manner, one that's designed solely to arouse people's passions, make such things more accessible and easy, and stir up lustful emotions."¹⁷

Proponents of the theater were adamant that the problem was not with the theater itself, merely with the way that people in the Arab world had adopted theater. The narrator in al-Muwaylihi's text assures his interlocutor that in Egypt drama is "in its initial stages, the beginning of its emergence. For that reason, we need to excuse the shortcomings that we can see here. People are unaware of its true essence and effects."¹⁸ Others complained that people in Egypt did not understand how useful theater could be. Many were annoyed that audiences only came to see the musical sections and were not interested in the true theater itself (whatever that was). Farah Antun said that Salama Hijazi had "killed the art of theater in Egypt. They say this because the audience do not go to the theater to hear the plays but to hear his songs."¹⁹

These writers were committed to the idea that theater could be a great moral benefit if only it was done right. But they were fighting a losing battle. Performance, as a medium, cannot be controlled. It shows things as they are, not as they are meant to be. Audiences of performances are never a blank slate to be educated, they have some control over what is shown to them—the financial concerns of the troupes alone are enough to make them think twice about what to put on.

Of course, the relationship between theater practitioner and audience is a complicated one. It would be simplistic (and fundamentally illogical) to say that dramaturges are simply giving audiences what they want. It is a matter of give and take, in which audiences, actors, writers, critics, and others all brought something to the table. There was a constant tension throughout the Nahda between what audiences *should* want (moral improvement) and what they actually *did* want (simply put, entertainment). The public's seeming unwillingness to be "improved" annoyed many intellectuals.

Theatrical performances show a different kind of movement to the Nahda of printed texts. The purity of the Nahda's cultural-moral theories is compromised by the act of staging a text. This chapter turns its attention to the traveling theater troupes like the one that al-Hakim witnessed as a child to open up new ways of looking at the Nahda as a whole. Theatrical audiences that were not simply the educated and literate populations in large urban centers like Cairo, Alexandria, and Beirut; they were rural and transnational. The nexuses of influence were new and different. These troupes and texts traveled through the turn-of-the-century Arab world in surprising ways. This chapter is an attempt to tell this story and give Nahda scholarship a new focus.

Sulayman al-Qardahi—A Pan-Arab Dramaturge

Our guide through the peripatetic world of Arabic drama is Sulayman al-Qardahi (d. 1909), one of its most successful proponents in the late nineteenth century. Arabic theater has been transnational from its inception. Since 1847, the generally accepted date of the performance of the first Arabic play—Marun al-Naqqash's *al-Bakhil* [*The Miser*]—troupes have moved frequently from country to country.[20] Al-Qardahi was no different. His professional life was typical of the constant wanderings that characterized the theater of this time. He was born in Mount Lebanon in the 1850s. In the mid-nineteenth century, this area (particularly Beirut and Damascus) was cradle of Arabic drama, producing the most important early proponents of the form—Marun and Salim al-Naqqash, Abu Khalil al-Qabbani, Iskandar Farah, and others. Al-Qardahi, though, had an atypical early life; as a child he was orphaned and sent to France for his education. In the late 1870s, he moved to Egypt and began to take part in a variety of theatrical activities, both amateur and professional. In 1882, he set up his own dramatic troupe in Alexandria.

By the 1880s, Egypt was beginning to supplant the Levant as the center of Arabic drama. Levantine troupes were moving their activities to Cairo and Alexandria for a variety of reasons both political and economic; Egypt was going through something of an economic boom in the late nineteenth century and its laws on censorship were more liberal than then the rest of the Ottoman Empire. For much of the 1880s and 1890s, al-Qardahi dominated the Egyptian theater scene, putting on a string of extremely successful productions and helping to launch the career of the singer Salama Hijazi in plays like *Telemaque* and an Arabic version of Verdi's opera *Aida*.[21]

Al-Qardahi was just one person in the transnational theater network of the late nineteenth century. In her book, *The Eastern Mediterranean and the making of global radicalism*, Ilham Khuri-Makdisi noted the potential political power that these constantly mobile could wield. As well as noting the birth of a transnational dramatic corpus in the late nineteenth century, Khuri-Makdisi argues that it developed into a specifically radical movement. In the early twentieth century, she says, "the making of a transnational network of actors who were constantly on the move and were often in close contact with radical leftist circles in Beirut, Cairo, and Alexandria must have privileged the incorporation and integration of radical global and internationalist elements into the theater's repertoire."[22]

Al-Qardahi's career in the late nineteenth century is a central focus in Adam Mestyan's 2017 book *Arab Patriotism*. Mestyan argues that al-Qardahi contributed to the creation of a burgeoning Arabic-language patriotism in Egypt, through his plays about the Arab hero Antar ibn Shadad and the Caliph Harun al-Rashid.[23] By the early 1900s, al-Qardahi was one of the Arab world's most famous actors and producers.

Al-Qardahi had a long and successful career. Two specific performances toward the end of al-Qardahi's long and successful career in the theater demonstrate the unexpected ways that the Nahda traveled at the beginning of the twentieth century. The first instance, a performance of *Othello* in the early twentieth century, illustrates the rural movement of theater in the Arab world. The second, a performance of Najib al-Haddad's *Salah al-din al-Ayyubi*, shows how the theater traveled across borders in the early twentieth century.

Othello in Sohag

It has long proved difficult to show how people in rural areas experienced the Nahda. Broadly speaking, aside from a small section of the local elite, the majority of people living in the countryside—often illiterate or largely uneducated—have been left out of the histories. As Ussama Makdisi recently observed, "classes of people were generally excluded from having their voices heard in the Nahda's secular and communal public spheres [...] the poor and indigent [...] marginalized rural communities or tribes [...] peasants."[24] Of course, the intellectuals of the nineteenth and early twentieth century did not entirely ignore the countryside. In fact, the *figure* of the "peasant" increasingly came to embody the rising of new nations and a new consciousness across the region. As Samah Selim showed in *The Novel and the Rural Imaginary in Egypt, 1880-1985*, in the late nineteenth century, "reformist and nationalist intellectuals became increasingly preoccupied with the peasantry's role in the project of national renaissance." One does not have to go far to see this in action. Selim, for instance, discusses the portrayal of peasants in the work of Yaʿqub Sanuʿa and ʿAbdallah al-Nadim in the nineteenth century, but it continued well into the twentieth century in works like Muhammad Husayn Haykal's *Zaynab* and its subsequent film adaptation. Arguably, it continues to this day.[25]

But, in places like Egypt, people who lived in rural areas were largely made into metaphors. As elite writers in the urban centers were using the countryside largely as a foil for their own ideas about issues like modernity and nationalism, the active participation of actual "peasants" in the intellectual currents of the time was notably absent.[26]

Despite the apparent silences, it is clear that people in the countryside engaged with the intellectual world of the Nahda in some of its own ways. The book trade, for instance, has been used to look at the Nahda's impact on rural areas. Ami Ayalon has used memoirs by Taha Husayn and Sayyid Qutb to show that itinerant booksellers spent time in rural communities; they would stay for a few days, selling books or lending them out for a small fee. The journals that were being produced in increasing numbers at the turn of the century largely had a readership in the urban centers where literacy was higher. But there is evidence, from readers' letters and elsewhere, that they did circulate in the countryside.[27] Still, while there was clearly some access to printed material in rural areas, it was limited in size and, in some cases, subject matter. When Taha Husayn lists the kinds of books available from these itinerant peddlers, he mentions folk tales, tales of historical wars, Sufi poetry, works of magic, and more.[28] But, as Pierre Cachia notes, there was "not a single translation among them."[29] Taha Husayn's list is not one that conjures up images of the Nahda, as it is traditionally painted. Ayalon concludes that in a number of ways, "the countryside would remain for a long time . . . at the margins of the developments which the introduction of printing spawned."[30]

Performances, however, like the one that Tawfiq al-Hakim saw were relatively common. From the late nineteenth century onwards, there were a number of theatrical companies that specialized in these kinds of countryside tours. Muhammad Yusuf Najm's *al-Masrahiyya fi-l-Adab al-'Arabi al-Hadith* mentions five such troupes—Jawq al-Surur al-Watani led by Mikha'il Jirjis, Jawq al-Kamal al-Watani led by 'Ali Hamdi, Jawq Shubban Misr al-Watani led by Ibrahim Hijazi, Jawq al-Ittihad al-Watani led by Dawud Sulayman, and al-Jawq al-Misri al-'Arabi led by the singer and actor al-Shaykh Ahmad al-Shami.[31] The troupe of Ahmad al-Shami became particularly famous in the early twentieth century. It is here that the nightclub owner, Badi'a Masabni, got her first full-time job.

It would not be far-fetched to speculate that these theatrical tours had precedent in the tours of shadow plays (Khayyal al-Zill) or farce players (Mahabbazin or Awlad al-Rabiya) through the Egyptian countryside. Although little evidence of pre-modern itinerant performances survives, the legacy of these performances may have endured into the twentieth century even as the genre of entertainment changed.

Fortunately, though, a number of accounts of the performances given by theatrical troupes do survive. The unpublished memoirs of C. R. Ashbee, held at Cambridge University, for instance, gives a detailed description of a show by Munira al-Mahdiyya's troupe that took place about an hour from Cairo on April 18, 1917. He left a detailed description of both the setting and the audience. The stage was erected outside the village school, he said, and "the hangings were of gorgeous colors, in bright Arabic patterns; they were fastened to great masts and hung on 4 huge palms trees, through the open tops of which you saw the stars." The show lasted for around five hours and the audience "were mostly farmers, students and shopkeepers, there were some 600 altogether, all men. I and a Frenchman were the only westerners present."[32]

Yusuf Wahbi (1898–1982), another pioneering Egyptian theater practitioner, encountered Sulayman al-Qardahi's troupe as a child and told a story in his memoirs, just as Tawfiq al-Hakim had. Wahbi was one of Egypt's most important actors, directors, and producers from the early 1920s through into the 1950s and 1960s. When he was a child, he had an experience very similar to Tawfiq al-Hakim's when he witnessed a traveling troupe as it came through town. Wahbi, like al-Hakim, gave no precise date for the performances but, also like al-Hakim, it must have occurred at some point in the first decade of the twentieth century.

In Sohag, a city in Upper Egypt, the young Yusuf Wahbi saw al-Qardahi's troupe put on a performance of *Othello* in Arabic. The company made a splash as they came into town, walking up and down the corniche, announcing in loud voices the plot of the play that they were about to put on. In the evening, they set up a makeshift stage and performed their play in front of a large, enthusiastic crowd. The young Wahbi was, like al-Hakim, extremely impressed with the show and it proved to be a pivotal moment in his life. "On that night," he said, "my love of acting was born."[33]

Wahbi's account of al-Qardahi's performance of *Othello* in Sohag reveals a lot about this crucial but often overlooked site of reception for some of the period's most important texts. It is through them that people in the countryside who do not often get written into the intellectual history of the period—the farmers and shopkeepers of Ashbee's narrative—encountered the Nahda. Performance, by its nature, always transforms a text and here it was no different. This was not a passive site of reception; both audiences and performers were involved in the creation of the performance.

Audience interaction, for instance, was a common part of Arabic theater at this time. Youssef Wahbi's memoirs recall one particularly striking example of what must have been a very common practice. During the performance of *Othello* by al-Qardahi's troupe, the actor playing Othello speaks the lines "if you ever see something that makes the heart fall apart/ look in to it and you will find that a woman is the cause." After he pronounced these lines, Othello turned to the women's box and said, "apologies ladies, these are the playwright's words, not mine."[34] (Evidence that despite what C. R. Ashbee said about the audience in the play he saw, women were at least sometimes present in the audiences.)

What happened around the play—before, after, and between scenes—was just as important as what went on during it. As Ashbee noted, performances could go on for as long as five hours, and they often included much more than just a play itself. The academic Sayyid ʿAli Ismaʿil, in his study of Ahmed al-Shami's troupe, quoted at length from a newspaper report in 1912 describing a performance in Beni Suef. The main event was an Arabic version of Victor Hugo's play *Mary Tudor*, but alongside it there was a whole evening of entertainment, including "monologues filled with advice for the youth" and "a short comic farce" (*fasl hazli*) at the end of the play.[35] Likewise, after Munira al-Mahdiyya's play that C.R. Ashbee witnessed in the 1910s, there was a singing encore at the request of the audience.

There was one particularly important genre of performance that seems to have been unique to these traveling countryside troupes: the promotional pre-show parade. Both Yusuf Wahbi and Tawfiq al-Hakim were particularly struck by the sight of the troupe entering town, dressed in their costumes, and announcing that they would be putting on a play. This was clearly a crucial way for these traveling troupes to drum up support and these living adverts had to be both striking and memorable. Yusuf Wahbi left behind a particularly vivid description of al-Qardahi's troupe and their advert for *Othello*:

> The image of this amazing, unusual scene is still etched in my memory. There was a parade, surrounded by a crowd of tens of the young men of Sohag,

traveling up the Nile corniche. At the head was a giant man with a black face, bushy beard and hair . . . He had a long sword around his waist . . . behind him was a woman with her hair blowing in the wind, her chest and neck radiant with diamond necklaces. Following her were men wearing embroidered clothes that I had never seen the likes of before and women whose dresses threw up dust as they trailed along the ground.

Once the troupe had made this impression, they proceeded to explain the plot of the play in a way calculated to appeal to the residents of Sohag. Othello, the play's complex protagonist, was painted as a powerful Arab hero who stood up to the Europeans. Yusuf Wahbi quotes their words from (distant) memory:

Good people of Sohag, this is the hero Othello; behind him is his wife Desdemona and his entourage . . . He is the mighty Moroccan [al-maghribi al-jabbar], who has crossed the seas, destroyed walls, set fire to the cities of the Franks, and plunged their castles into destruction.[36]

This Othello was an Arab hero. This is a common theme in al-Qardahi's work. In the 1880s, Adam Mestyan argued, al-Qardahi was using the character of ʿAntar as an onstage representative of Ahmed ʿUrabi and the rising national consciousness of Egypt. The Arab warrior of legend was a cipher for the revolutionary Egyptian army officer ʿUrabi, fighting (in one version of his story) against a Turco-Circassian elite. "In my interpretation, both ʿAntar and ʿUrābī represented fighters who resisted oppression and injustice," Mestyan argues, pointing out al-Qardahi pointedly thanked ʿUrabi for his support for the theatrical venture after a performance of the play at the Opera House.[37]

Al-Qardahi, then, has a history of using his plays for political ends. In the early 1900s, his Othello (judging by Wahbi's description of his pre-show advertisement) was being used to represent a rising Arab nation standing against the forces of European colonialism. By doing this, al-Qardahi was presaging Khalil Mutran' landmark 1912 translation of the play, ʿUtayl. In this later work, Othello's character was used as a way to "write back" to Britain's national playwright. Mutran foregrounded Othello's Arab identity, going as far as to say that Shakespeare's writing had a particularly Arab sensibility and even speculating that he may have taken the story of Othello from an Arabic work. Both Mutran and al-Qardahi were laying claim to this great figure in European literature and putting him into the service of a new rising nation.[38]

In 1912, Mutran's version of Othello, like al-Qardahi's portrayals of ʿAntar ibn Shaddad, was performed at the Cairo Opera House in front of a crowd of dignitaries and notables. But before this, al-Qardahi had brought Shakespeare's famous "moor" through the small towns and villages of rural Egypt. The Nahda was not confined to large metropoles like Cairo nor to elite venues like the Opera House. The intellectual and cultural trends that started in the nineteenth century reached far into rural areas, reforming themselves as they went.

These traveling troupes have the potential to tell a very different history of Egypt's late nineteenth and early twentieth-century culture. It is one in which the rural population is not entirely cut off from the developments of the Nahda, rather it participates in them. Othello, in his political guise as an Arab hero, was popular in rural areas, just as he was in the cities—assuming, as aforementioned, that the choice of plays was in some ways dictated by their popularity among audiences. The rural inhabitants of Egypt, thought by many at the time to be apolitical and apathetic, rushed to see this play, whose geopolitical overtones were clear as day.

Saladin in Tunis

Sulayman al-Qardahi traveled far and wide, not only through Egypt's countryside but further across the Arab world. In the late nineteenth and early twentieth century, he made his way abroad too, visiting the Levant, France, and North Africa. In the first decades of the 1900s, territorial nationalism was becoming increasingly important, but theater companies like al-Qardahi's were building a pan-Arabic popular culture that moved beyond borders and nations.

At the end of 1908—not too long after performing his version of *Othello* in Sohag—Sulayman al-Qardahi arrived in Tunisia with his theatrical troupe. In December of that year, he gave a set of performances in Sousse before moving on to Tunis at the beginning of 1909. Arabic-language theater was almost unheard of in Tunisia at the time. Al-Qardahi and a few other troupes who came from Egypt are credited with creating Tunisian theater, with some justification—there had been very little that could be classified as Arabic proscenium arch theater in Tunisia before his arrival.[39]

Al-Qardahi performed the tried and tested repertoire that had made his troupe popular in Egypt. He put on a production of his version of *Othello*, which had impressed the people of Sohag as well as an Arabic translation of the opera *Aida*. He also put on a version of one of the early twentieth century's most popular Arabic plays—Najib al-Haddad's *Salah al-Din al-Ayyubi*, a dramatization of an episode in the history of the Crusades based on Walter Scott's *Talisman*.[40]

This was one of the most popular plays of the late nineteenth century in Egypt. It had been one of Salama Hijazi's most well-known roles and Odeon Records had released his versions of songs from the play in the early twentieth century.[41] Unlike the jealous lover Othello, whose heroism is at best complex, Saladin was an unambiguously noble and virtuous Arab hero. Written for performance in Egypt in 1893, at a time when a British army of occupation was present in the country, it dramatized the story of an Arab leader who bested an English king, both morally and militarily.

The action begins with Saladin recalling his victories over the Franks in verse—describing how he went from Alexandria, through Gaza into Syria and conquered the city of Jerusalem. He soon discovers that his great rival, Richard the Lionheart, has been taken ill with a terrible fever. The honorable Saladin disguises himself as a doctor and cures the English king, saving his enemy's life.

At a time when European powers were beginning to make more imperial incursions into the Arab world, a noble, successful, powerful Arab leader proved popular with Arab audiences. From the late nineteenth century into the 1930s, novels and plays about Saladin proved consistently popular. Samuel England has examined the journey of Walter Scott's novel about Saladin into Arabic, first through a translation by Yaʿqub Sarruf, serialized in the Egyptian press from 1886 to 1887, then in Najib al-Haddad's stage version. In the early twentieth century, subsequent versions of Saladin's story were published in Arabic, most prominent among them were Jurji Zaydan's 1913 novel *Salah al-Din al-Ayyubi* and Farah Antun's 1914 play, *Salah al-Din and the Kingdom of Jerusalem*.

Saladin, the Arab hero standing up to European Crusaders, became an important figure in the cultural imagination of Nahdawi writers and intellectuals. As England recently argued, the popularity and importance of plays about Saladin can help pave a way toward a new understanding of the Nahda's formal priorities—the novel no longer needs to be taken as the ultimate Nahdawi literary form. The public nature of drama made it central to the wider project of the Nahda and its relationship to the ordinary population of the Arab world.

Plays like the one that al-Qardahi's troupe performed in Tunisia are part of a "more fluid processes of adapting texts, for the express purpose of engaging audiences in organized gatherings of performers and citizens." The "printed, bound text" need not be the only focus of our critical work on the Nahda. England suggests that the setting of a theater, in which "the playhouse becomes a large, capacious court," implies a contemporary political reading more than the novel does.[42]

Looking at the travels of al-Qardahi's troupe—from Syria to rural Egypt and then to Tunisia—it also becomes clear that this theatrical movement traveled extremely widely, from the urban to the rural and across several national borders. If Saladin started to become a pan-Arab political figure at the turn of the nineteenth century, he has drama to thank for it. For it was drama that carried his story widely throughout the Arab world, as it also carried the story of others like Othello.[43]

Al-Qardahi's tour in Tunisia was successful. Things went so well for them that the Bey of Tunis gave him a medal, endowed him the noble title of Bey, and granted him an unspecified sum of money "for his efforts in establishing Arabic theater in Tunisia." But the success was short-lived. On May 5, 1909, al-Qardahi unexpectedly died and was buried in Tunis. Within weeks, the sad news had reached Cairo.[44]

But al-Qardahi's influence did not end with his death. The troupe that he had brought with him to North Africa remained. Taking the name *al-Najma* (The Star),[45] its members continued putting on plays and even incorporated Tunisian actors into their ranks. Fittingly, the first play that this new troupe put on was *Othello* (under its alternative title *al-Qaʾid al-Maghribi*—the Maghrebi leader).[46]

For decades after al-Qardahi's death, Saladin remained an important figure on the Arabic stage. In 1918, the singer and actress Munira al-Mahdiyya toured in the Egyptian countryside. She played three nights in Assiut in May of that year and one of the plays that she performed was the ever-popular *Salah al-Din al-Ayyubi* by Najib al-Haddad. In the mid-1920s when George Abyad's Egyptian theatrical troupe toured Iraq they put on (among other plays) their version of Farah Antun's

Salah al-Din al-Ayyubi and the Kingdom of Jerusalem.[47] *Othello* too maintained some level of popularity through the early twentieth century, though not on the level of Saladin.

It was through the al-Qardahi's tours, and others like them, that these two figures spread through the Arab world into sometimes unexpected places. It was also through these theatrical performances that people who are not usually given a place in the story of the Nahda—including the illiterate, rural populations, and women—engaged with some of the period's most important texts.

This chapter has scratched the surface of a much larger story, one that is full of complexity and historiographical challenges. As Tawfiq al-Hakim's memoirs which were quoted at the beginning show, the world of traveling troupes was sustained by rumor, bombast, and exaggeration. He could not even remember, many years later, whether the performance that he had seen was by Salama Hijazi's famous company or just one of the many companies that imitated it. After all, this was a business that relied on getting a good audience, so publicity (whether entirely honest or not) was a crucial part of their activities.

Nonetheless, this overlooked world of traveling popular theater at the beginning of the twentieth century reveals a crucial aspect of the Nahda. This is the story of the Nahda as it was experienced by audiences in rural communities and as it moved across national boundaries. This theater both reflected and shaped the cultural developments of the period.

Epilogue: The 1920s and 1930s

The period after the First World War was a golden age for Arabic drama. It was also a time of unprecedented mobility for Arabic troupes. Before, many had gone on tours; by the 1920s, it was expected that Egypt's large theatrical troupes would spend part of the year—often in the summer—on the road in the Arab world. All of the biggest stars of the early twentieth century did it—Munira al-Mahdiyya, Najib al-Rihani, Yusuf Wahbi, Fatima Rushdi, George Abyad, and more. Building on the steps made by troupes like al-Qardahi's, a huge number of professional companies were formed and dramatically expanded the geographical reach of Arabic theater, spreading a nascent pan-Arabic culture as they went.

Although Egypt and Greater Syria saw the largest part of this theatrical activity, many companies began to branch out too. Touring troupes, in the 1920s, started to make the long trip to Baghdad, where they were welcomed enthusiastically by the Iraqi public. In the middle of this decade, Yusuf Wahbi's company traveled as far away as South America, putting on his plays for diaspora Arab audiences there. The tour proved so successful that Najib al-Rihani embarked on his own South American tour soon afterward.

Tunisia too, where al-Qardahi had given his final performances, saw more traveling actors and theater practitioners arrive. In 1921, the legendary actor and troupe leader George Abyad came to the country to become "the head of the first state-supported theater in the country."[48] He also opened an institute to train Tunisian actors, producing some of the biggest names in Tunisian theater, including Sheikh Ibrahim al-Akoudi and Mohammed Bourguiba (brother of the president-to-be Habib Bourguiba). His stay in Tunisia lasted a year and a half and a 1970 biography claims that he "accomplished [his task of] building Tunisian theater on the same basis as Egyptian theater." (Though others are more cautious about making such grand claims.) [49]

The theatrical tours of the 1920s spread Arabic drama further across the Arab-speaking world than it had ever been before. They also managed to create something resembling a unified Arabic theatrical culture. The most striking example of this appears in the memoirs of Najib al-Rihani, the biggest comic theater star of the early twentieth century. Al-Rihani was known for his onstage creation, Kish Kish Bey, the wealthy 'umda ["mayor"] from the Egyptian countryside who came to Cairo and fell into the clutches of its big-city pleasures. Created in the 1910s, this character became the star of innumerable farces, revue shows, and, in later years, films. His antics were already a much-loved feature of the Cairo stage by the early 1920s.

When Najib al-Rihani took his troupe to Palestine in this decade, he encountered something strange—someone else had already been touring the area as Kish Kish Bey before he even got there. He soon discovered that an actor called Amin 'Atallah had taken his famous character and was marketing himself in the region as "the real Kish Kish bey." The Palestinian playwright Nusri al-Jawzi recalled that "Najib al-Rihani's character, Kish Kish Bey, had a huge impact on Palestinian actors." Later, when al-Rihani traveled to South America he found that even across the Atlantic Ocean, other Kish Kishes had appeared. Amin 'Atallah's nephew George had taken up the family business of impersonating Kish Kish Bey and was making a good career for himself. Kish Kish, a character who had started life as quintessentially Egyptian, was now a global phenomenon, influencing a whole generation of theater makers.

These traveling troupes left their mark on the places they traveled through in a variety of other ways too. Nusri al-Jawzi recalled that theater practitioners in Palestine began to mimic the styles of acting that they saw these troupes perform. He also added that these traveling companies often gave Palestinian actors the chance to get on stage themselves: "A lot of the time," he recalled, "these troupes lacked one actor or more and they borrowed local Palestinians to fill the gaps."[50]

But sometimes things did not go so smoothly. Plays that were big hits in Egypt turned out to be controversial as they traveled abroad. In her memoirs, the theater troupe leader Fatima Rushdi recalled one incident during the 1920s in Beirut at the performance of a play about the First World War Ottoman governor of Syria, Jamal Pasha. In the 1910s, he had earned the title Jamal the Bloody, for the ruthlessness with which he put down Arab nationalist revolts. During a performance of the play in Beirut, a commotion started:

> One of the audience members went as far as to pull out a gun and shoot at Aziz ['Id, the actor playing Jamal Pasha]. He was so affected by the amazing acting that he imagined that he really was gazing upon "Jamal the Bloody," not upon an actor. After he fired the bullets, he kept ranting and raving, throwing terrible

insults and abuse at Jamal Pasha, until some people around him calmed the man down.[51]

This was not the only time that these traveling troupes touched some political nerves. When they traveled in Palestine, the issues were particularly prominent. Fatima Rushdi, whose troupe had been shot in Beirut, was attacked in the press in Palestine for putting on two Arabic plays in a Jewish venue. "Where is Fatima Rushdi's patriotism," one newspaper asked. "Is there an Arab anywhere, with Arab blood in their veins, who would put on two shows like this?"[52]

Before the age of the film, and apparently independently of printed texts, there was a vibrant transnational Arabic culture, based in the world of theater. By looking at drama, new nexuses emerge, new sites of exchange and influence appear, which make us look at the Nahda from a very different geographical perspective.

PART THREE

MEDIA & THE IMAGINARY

Chapter 7

INCREDIBLE PRINTS

THE INTERSECTION OF KNOWLEDGE AND ENTERTAINMENT IN JOURNAL ILLUSTRATIONS

Hala Auji

A June 1894 article from the Arabic illustrated journal *al-Mathaf*, published in Alexandria, describes the experience of walking through the various displays and pavilions at the world fair Exposition International d'Anvers held in Antwerp that year. The most noteworthy of these installations, according to the article, is a floating castle hanging from a hot air balloon that fair visitors can ascend to:

> And the best of what can be seen there, which amazes the mind and catches the eye, is the castle hanging in the sky; rises only with air via a single *muntad* [airship] wrapped three times in Chinese silk; it is tethered to the ground with twenty cables connected to four ropes and nets divided across [the sphere] [...] as you can see in the picture [*sura*] that is published in this issue [...].[1]

The engraving featuring this site appears on the issue's next page with the caption "this is the picture of the lofty castle" (Figure 7.1). Taking up a quarter of the page's layout, the printed image illustrates the text's description. The image shows the castle—held aloft by a single balloon and lines of rope—hovering over the fairgrounds that appear minuscule in comparison. While it lacks the details and refinement one would see in a drawing, painting, or photograph, the engraved illustration captures the "spirit" of the experience through a distorted perspective that lends a sense of the great distance between the airship and ground. Through this image, the journal's editors seem to ask readers—regardless of their literacy—to visualize or imagine the excitement of the fair, and the experience of floating in a castle. Thus, while depicting a distant event in Belgium, the engraving brings readers closer to experiencing a spectacle that they would not have otherwise seen (whether visually or in person).

This chapter explores similar engravings across a variety of illustrated Arabic periodicals in the later decades of the 1800s, which engaged middle-class and everyday audiences in visual and conceptual experiences pertaining to knowledge, spectacle, and art. At this time, engravings became important fixtures in myriad

Figure 7.1 Engraving of "the Lofty Tower" picturing the world fair at Antwerp in 1894. *Al-Mathaf* 1, no. 16 (1894): 122. Bayerischen Staatsbibliothek München, 4 A.or. 3805 w, 122.

Arabic journals published since the 1870s in eastern Mediterranean cities like Beirut, Cairo, and Alexandria. Journal images, like their accompanying articles, were not limited to any specific genre. Many were portraits—of historical and contemporary figures—as well as renderings of monuments, cities, flora, fauna, scientific diagrams, and any conceivable topic of interest from this time. These images also made an amalgam of imagery accessible to popular audiences, which they would not have been able to see otherwise. Although photography, art galleries, museums, panoramas, and world expositions were certainly available to many of Europe's urban (even rural) publics, this was not necessarily the case for all people living in Khedival Egypt and Ottoman Syria at this time. For many of these regions' non-elite publics, reproductions of photographs, paintings, and other published imagery were the closest they would get to the original objects or contexts.

While seemingly disparate, these engravings all relate to interests among Arabic publishers to engage a wide readership, from erudite middle-class generalists to everyday, often illiterate, audiences. The popularization of science, language, technology, and other fields determined by late nineteenth-century publishers, editors, and scholars as ones necessary for social reform and civilizational progress (key tenets in Nahdawi thinking) was central to the publishers' goals of public benefit (*maslaha 'amma*). Indeed, Arabic periodicals from the late nineteenth century have served as important markers of Nahdawi perspectives on modernity, cultural progress, and social reform.[2] Yet, the wider significance of engravings printed in these publications is only recently gaining serious consideration in studies on the Middle East and Ottoman contexts.[3] Journal editors foregrounded printed images—alongside textual descriptions—as important new modes of entertainment, visualization, and teaching. Images included an array of scientific diagrams, many of which depicted microscopic particles and processes invisible to the naked eye, like figures showing the way light passes through a microscope or an image of the different stages in a plant cell's division. Engravings also illustrated "exotic" flora and fauna, many of them foreign to the Levantine landscape, like American condors and whales. Concurrently, many engravings captured subject matter that was popular among audiences in Europe, North America, and the Ottoman metropoles at the time, such as Orientalist imagery of global ethnic groups or renditions of the latest technologies like the telegraph. Some of these illustrations—such as early diagrams showing the first use of the telephone in 1876—also included textual descriptions explaining how the image can be used to help "the pen describes the telephone's make-up and bring the mind closer to an understanding of its meaning/workings."[4]

As this chapter will show, through the use of engraved illustrations, publishers were also interested in less lofty ambitions like popular entertainment, and not just social reform or education, perhaps in the hopes of ensuring commercial success. Specifically, engraved images comprised views, subjects, and renderings that were popular with mainstream audiences in metropoles at the time. These included images like the "Lofty Tower" (seen in Figure 7.1) showing spectacles at world fairs, as well as engravings of stages and performers, costumes, Orientalist landscapes and cityscapes, and even satirical cartoons/caricatures,[5] to name a few. In fact, one can say that the prevalence of imagery and subject matter related to optics—from illusions to new imaging technologies—demonstrated a preoccupation with issues of vision and visuality that were popular with everyday global audiences at the time, from fairgrounds to the streets. Concurrently, engravings intended for didactic purposes, like diagrams, may have also been perceived as forms of visual entertainment at a time when technology, science, and the arts of illusion were popular among everyday viewers, many of whom were illiterate.

In this chapter, I approach this line of inquiry through a varied selection of engravings from some key illustrated Arabic periodicals printed during the late nineteenth century—c. 1871-96—in Beirut, Cairo, and Alexandria. The selection of images that I study here, which is by no means a comprehensive overview of such examples, comes from a few of many illustrated journals in circulation at the time, which, in turn, belonged to a small subset among a larger group of non-illustrated periodicals from this period. Specifically, I focus on journals that not only utilized engravings as a part of their content but rather went the extra steps to engage with these images in accompanying texts. These journals include *al-Jinan* ("The Gardens," 1870–86, Beirut[6]), *al-Tabib* ("The Physician," 1878–95, Beirut[7]), *al-Muqtataf* ("The Selections," 1876–83, Beirut; 1884–1952, Cairo[8]), *al-Hilal* ("The Crescent," 1892–present, Cairo[9]), *al-Mathaf* ("The Museum," 1894, Alexandria[10]), and *al-Bayan* ("The Bulletin," 1897–8, Cairo[11]). I examine the visual conventions of illustrations and what the journal editors/publishers might have intended with the inclusion of such engravings, and how these images were used to negotiate various views on science, art, and spectacle as part of the journals' broader aims of not only popularizing knowledge, taste, and civilizational discourses but also serving mass entertainment purposes.

Periodicals and Everyday Audiences

Printed images in Arabic publications produced at eastern Mediterranean presses became prominent in Arabic books and periodicals toward the late 1800s. At this time, the Arabic publishing industry, which emerged in the Ottoman context in the early to mid-1800s, grew exponentially with the rise of an urban middle class of merchants, scholars, and industrialists, who established private Arabic presses in Beirut, Cairo, Alexandria, Istanbul, and other key urban centers throughout the Ottoman Empire. Periodicals, which were cheaper and easier to produce than book volumes, were central publications for many of the private presses burgeoning in the region at this time. These periodicals were largely funded by annual subscriptions (although some periodicals in circulation were state funded) and were published serially. For many of these weekly, monthly, and bimonthly journals, magazines, and newspapers, circulation and subscription numbers were not limited to a particular geography. Rather, presses often solicited the assistance of news/sales agents (*wukala'*) living across and beyond the Ottoman region, in centers in Europe, South America, North America, and even parts of South Asia.[12]

Periodicals, particularly those covering literary-scientific content, many of which included illustrations, served as an important new genre through which ideas of the Nahda were negotiated, debated, and spread. With essays covering a wide span of issues—from medicine to literature—these journals demonstrated a view of the sciences and the arts as interconnected and universal fields of inquiry. Although some publications took on more political stances by the early twentieth century, the majority of the periodicals produced in the Ottoman realms were careful to avoid testing subject matter and were prevented from publishing political material due to censorship laws. While these laws varied across the course of the nineteenth century, for presses in Ottoman territories, these restrictions became more explicit and stringent during the reign of Sultan ʿAbdulhamid II (r. 1876–1909).[13] After the British occupied Egypt in 1882, as a "veiled protectorate" under Khedival rule, many publishers, particularly those from Christian communities (such as those in Syria), immigrated to Egypt and established their presses in Cairo and Alexandria, purportedly to avoid Hamidian restrictions and religious persecution.[14]

Despite varied regional challenges to press freedom, production, and profit, a few of which I touch upon in this chapter, periodical presses, in theory, were interested in speaking to a mass audience, and not a coterie of elite readers. Periodical publishers and editors saw themselves, and their publications, as mouthpieces for modernization through the circulation of ideas on social and cultural progress, reform, and change. Given these individuals' social and class status, education, and, to a large extent, wealth, they typically believed that they were duty-bound to serve the public interest. The first press editors/publishers, who typically included venture capitalists, came from middle-class professions as doctors, teachers, engineers, and lawyers, and considered themselves "men of letters" (*udabaʾ*).[15] By the 1880s, these editors, as scholars, took on the role of the "journalist (*sihafi*) and/or the public writer (*katib ʿamm*)."[16] In their self-proclaimed "new public role," these *public* scholars fashioned a "self-image"[17] as purveyors of social reform, progress, and civilizational discourse in the interest of "public benefit (*maslaha ʿamma*)."[18] For those working in Syria and Egypt before the 1900s, the figure of the public scholar was being conceived of in a transitional moment of overlaps between imperialism and colonialism, printing practices and scribal traditions, and guilds and professionalized labor.[19]

The public—for these editors—was largely made up of fellow middle-class readers, men and women, not just in Khedival Egypt and Ottoman Syria, but also in the international locales where journals had agents. Yet, despite the claims to public duty and while publications were geared toward nonspecialist readers, they were not targeting the indiscriminate masses: publishers expected readers to pay for issues via subscriptions. Scholars of Arabic publishing history, like Ami Ayalon, explain that only a small subset of Egyptians and Syrians purchased periodicals during the late 1800s.[20] Indeed, looking through any issue of the journals in circulation during the late 1800s, a reader would come across a letter from the editor(s) asking subscribers to pay their dues.[21] Literacy rates were also very low throughout the 1800s until at least the mid-twentieth century.[22] Nonetheless, from what we know of reading practices at this time, journals—and their content—may have had a wider—specifically more generalist—readership than their circulation numbers suggest. Public spaces, within which periodicals circulated by the late 1800s, were sites of sociability and intellectual exchange. As Shirine Hamadeh explains for the eighteenth-century Ottoman world, public "spaces of sociability," like coffeehouses, baths, and theaters, brought together different classes of society, yielded various forms of social encounters, and facilitated public debate, and the "expression of political opinions" long before the emergence of modern developments.[23] These remained important spaces for public discourse in the nineteenth century and were meant to be accessed by generalist audiences.[24]

Although periodicals were not affordable for the masses—as they remained financially accessible to elite and middle-class readers—they did not circulate in a vacuum nor were they limited to exclusive spaces. While it is not always clear how publications circulated among individuals (beyond the listed subscribers), scholars have evidenced that publications were shared and discussed in varied settings, like reading rooms, private salons, and bookstores.[25] Some scholars also suggest that periodicals were read out loud and shared in street cafés and town squares.[26] Periodicals were also likely shared within the privacy, and gendered spaces, of the home where they were read with or by family members, specifically women, of various ages and levels of education. Thus, despite restrictive Hamidian publishing laws in the late 1800s, privately operated journals and presses managed to circulate their publications within these diverse public and private contexts, with these printed pages serving as important spaces for critical engagement as well as entertainment.[27] As Stephen Sheehi argues, the new print media allowed for a "textual space" that yielded a "new form of public space and civil society," which let regional (and international) groups of readers—of various levels of literacy—engage with a wide range of material in "dialogue [via correspondence, questions, and commentaries] with the editors, authors, and experts."[28] I would add that journal engravings also played an important role in this "textual space" as an integral component of reading that extended to orality and visuality, for which traditional, logocentric, literacy was not required to enjoy the novelty, contemporaneity, and entertainment value of periodical illustrations.

Illustrating Arabic Journals

Of the various kinds of periodicals circulating at this time, from pamphlets and broadsides to newspapers and journals, the journal format was the one that included imagery and was often interchangeably referred to in historical sources and on publication mastheads or title pages at this time as *jarida*, *majalla*, *sahifa*, or *jurnal*.[29] Although, in the early decades of the Arabic periodical press (until the early 1900s) few illustrations made their way into journals, due to the serial nature of periodicals subscribers could eventually have issues bound into larger volumes, creating books that could serve as visual and textual compendia. The paucity of engravings, the difficulty in obtaining them, and, relatedly, their possible excessive cost, rather than a lack of interest in them, seem to have been the contributing factors to the low image-per-issue rate in the late 1800s when illustrated journals were first gaining popularity.[30]

The number and nature of engravings that appeared in journals not only varied from one publication to the other but also remained largely inconsistent within the production life span of individual productions. Journals with larger subscription numbers and, thus, more funding, tended to showcase more images—largely encompassing a variety of subject matter and engraving methods—than smaller, shorter-run (and likely underfunded) publications. For example, *al-Muqtataf*, with approximately 1,600 regional subscribers by 1892,[31] typically published around five or six images per issue by the time its editors relocated production to Cairo in 1884. While this might not seem like an exceptional number, it does give a sense of the typical frequency of illustrations in periodicals when compared to other periodicals at the time that claimed to be "illustrated journals."[32] The Alexandria-produced bimonthly journal *al-Mathaf* usually only included one engraving per issue during its short-lived history (lasting only a year), despite referring to itself as an illustrated periodical in its masthead (*jarida musawwara*). Interestingly, the images that were most frequently published in the periodical press were actually advertisements found in newspapers. Similarly, many journals also included illustrated advertisements. Yet when the various journal issues were bound, the end pages with advertisements were typically removed. Thus, the bound volumes available to researchers today are not very accurate indicators of all the imagery that individual issues may have included in the form of ads.[33] Granted, imagery used for advertisements at this time was often repetitive across issues, and editors did not employ this imagery with the same intentions as other engravings used for didactic or entertainment purposes. While not all journals explicitly dealt with, or engaged, printed imagery, many periodicals, even if they were largely unillustrated, did include printed portraits at a time (examples of which are discussed later on in this chapter).

Journal editors understood that images had a certain draw with their audiences. The importance of illustrations for regional publishers, for example, is evident in a message to readers that appeared in an issue of *al-Muqtataf* from 1882:

> [there has been logistical and financial] difficulty in procuring illustrations and diagrams that are needed to help describe [visualize] the journal's content [. . .] by God's grace we have contracted one of Europe's most prominent publishing societies, which will furnish us with all our [visual] needs.[34]

Speaking to readers about illustrations almost two decades after *al-Muqtataf* was first published (as an illustrated journal from the start) the journal's editors seem to be responding to possible criticisms about the quality (or dearth) of illustrations. The more likely scenario is that the publishers wanted to encourage subscribers to keep paying their dues, and thus spoke of improvements and enhancements to justify the cost. Whatever the impetus was for this announcement, it makes clear that illustrations played an important role in the nature of the journal and audience expectations. Thus, despite their limited or inconsistent appearance in Arabic publications before the 1920s, engravings were often sought when it was fiscally and technically possible. For press editors/publishers, journal illustrations played a central role in popularizing content, from the scientific and industrial to the literary and historical, which would have otherwise been esoteric or inaccessible to the average generalist reader (and any illiterate sub-audience). The printed images helped to turn Arabic periodicals into both visual compendiums of popularized encyclopedic knowledge and sites of imaginative pictorial entertainment for a general readership. While it is challenging to pinpoint the reception of images, and how popular they may have been to contemporaneous readers, the nature of the imagery used and the subject matter it covered certainly speaks to both the publishers' interests in popularizing knowledge as well as popular interests via mass entertainment, of which vision and visuality played a central role.

Although the desire to include images in journals is evident, the previously mentioned announcement in the issue of *al-Muqtataf* from 1882 makes clear that early journals seem to have faced various challenges when it came to procuring illustrations. Publishers of the early Arabic press faced many technical and logistical challenges.[35] These hurdles were not just about the problem with acquiring engravings. Obstacles included all facets of letterpress printing, from deficiencies in metal typefaces to a shortage in skilled labor, including typefounders, composers, and printers.[36] These struggles, until the late 1890s, included problems acquiring and producing engravings. While records on this aspect of Arabic publishing are limited to a few announcements in journals, it seems that presses struggled with locating adequate engravings that could capture or keep up with the wide array of modern inventions, discoveries, and interests related in their journals' articles and reports. As was the case for *al-Muqtataf* by the early 1880s, European or other Western printing or scientific societies were the ways in which presses could acquire up-to-date illustrations for their publications.[37] While it is difficult to ascertain which European presses, or related societies, Egyptian and Syrian publishers turned to at this time, it is clear that there was a translocal network within which publishers (and engravers) engaged in the circulation of engraved blocks and lithograph plates. In some cases, it seems that publishers also commissioned artists from, or based in, places like Italy.[38]

Despite these challenges, presses often found creative workarounds and appear to have relied quite frequently on the exchange of engraving blocks. Images were often reproduced across different issues of the same journal (to illustrate different articles) or shared by different presses. For instance, an illustration showing the different sizes of the sun as seen from the planets in the solar system is repeatedly used in at least three different articles: in an *al-Muqtataf* article about the sun and surrounding planets from 1876, and in two essays from *al-Tabib*'s serial discussion of extraterrestrial life (in the December 1884 and January 1885 issues).[39] Engraved blocks were also borrowed from local providers, often by different presses. For instance, an engraved portrait of Egyptian education minister Ali Pasha Mubarak (d. 1893), reproduced alongside his obituary in an 1893 issue of *al-Muqtataf*, includes the credit line "the image is borrowed from" one Dr. Muhammad Duri Beyk indicating that by the 1890s, at least in Egypt under British occupation, printed imagery became important enough to be (informally) considered intellectual property (Figure 7.2).[40] These are just a few examples of this practice, which would have been common at these presses where publishers were trying to keep up with print schedules and could not afford to frequently commission new imagery for each article. The emergence of new printing technologies, such as photo engraving and lithography, allowed for the cost-efficient production and use of photographic reproductions, which were not only used to print photographs

Figure 7.2 Portrait of Ali Pasha Mubarak. *Al-Muqtataf* 8, no. 3 (1893): 289. American University of Beirut/Library Archives.

but also extended to creating photo-engraved plates of paintings and drawings in print.

It is also clear that many engraved plates were produced by engravers in Egypt or Syria who had likely been educated in art/painting schools or workshops.[41] Although these engravers frequently copied illustrations found in European or North American publications (only occasionally mentioning their sources),[42] these artisans, by the later decades of the century when informal views on intellectual property were gaining traction, frequently inscribed their names on their productions.[43] This, too, indicates the increasing importance of engravers (often interchangeably referred to, at this time, as a *naqqash*, *haffar*, or *musawwir*[44]) and their engravings, thus showing the growing market for local illustrations in publications. While absent in the current historiography of modern art from the region, engravers were likely working within similar contexts and networks as their more well-known contemporaries, like the famed Syro-Lebanese artist Daoud Corm (1852–1930). In many ways, engravers became the popular artists whose names and works were seen by everyday audiences and who may have been better known to larger swathes of readers than the names or works of artists who did not produce material for the print industry at this time.[45]

Engravings as Popular Entertainment

Engravings were diverse in content and illustration method—an amalgam reflective of the divergent themes in the journals' articles and reports. As previously mentioned, while many were geared toward knowledge dissemination, such as technical diagrams of inventions—like the telegraph, camera, and telephone—or scientific explanations, like planetary orbits, not all of these images focused exclusively on utilitarianism or even public benefit. Engravings included portraits, of historical and contemporary figures like Catharine the Great or Rifaʿa al-Tahtawi, ethnographic imagery of Amazonian tribes, and a wide array of subject matter, many of which would have been found in spaces of popular public entertainment, from theaters to expositions. For a present-day reader flipping through issues of the different journals from the late 1800s, the diverse nature of the imagery in these publications might at first seem haphazard or unthematic, paralleling the typical understanding of these periodicals as being digests that covered sundry topics from the literary to the scientific, and everything in between.

However, a closer look at specific journals and the images featured in their issues demonstrates that images followed certain themes from one publication to the next, although such themes were sometimes inconsistent and frequently overlapped across each of these periodicals. Earlier publications like *al-Jinan* (Beirut), most well-known for publishing Salim al-Bustani's serial novel *Asma*,[46] included a medley of "beneficial" and entertaining content. *Al-Tabib* and *al-Muqtataf* typified the publications emphasizing science, exploration, and industry, with the former also including reports on literature and home-making/child-rearing (geared toward female readers), thus imagery tended to focus on technology/machinery, inventions, astronomy, discoveries, and medical practices, alongside the occasional illustrations of flora, fauna, and portraits of intellectuals/political figures. In fact, of all the illustrated journals published at this time, *al-Tabib* and *al-Muqtataf* featured the most diverse set of engravings. *Al-Hilal* focused on matters of civilization, archaeology, and history, with engravings being largely limited to portraits, besides the occasional illustration accompanying an article. Contrarily, *al-Bayan* highlighted issues of currency and contemporaneity. While its publishers sometimes included the occasional portrait, engravings were of novel, such as a man using a stereoscope, and unconventional, typically unseen, content like lightning. *Al-Mathaf*, while not often dealing with objects or museums, did encapsulate the era's attitude toward collecting—ethnography, novelty, and curiosities—alongside a focus on art and cultural institutions, including illustrations of buildings, such as the School of Fine Arts in Vienna and artifacts, like an Alhambresque ceramic vase. Thus, for the large part, images that appeared in each journal often related to each publication's dominant themes.

What the engravings had in common was that they belonged to a group of imagery that was circulating in publications produced at various sites in Europe, North America, and the broader Ottoman region. While illustrated journals were examples of nineteenth-century popular publications across the world, the Arabic journals examined in this chapter all relied on images/articles that came almost exclusively from Western contexts, if they were not original, local productions. Given the political and social connections that presses and/or their owners had on markets/publishing industries in France, Britain, and North America, it is not surprising that the majority of translated articles, stories, engravings, and even the concept of literary-scientific journals themselves were informed by sources from these locales.[47] Yet this was not simply about Egyptian or Syrian publishers wanting to copy or mimic Western sources, rather the publishers viewed themselves as participants in contemporaneous global capitalist interests in issues of social reform, technological change, urbanization, and industrialization. Ultimately, when it came to engravings, editors of the Arabic periodicals took as much care and deliberation to their inclusion as they did with writing, translating, and editing articles, stories, and reports.

Seeing and Imagining the Unseen

Editors deployed images in journals for multiple purposes. Most were geared toward "public benefit" as previously discussed, as was the case for the use of diagrams and other descriptive illustrations, which served pedagogical and didactic roles. Diagrams were a central pictorial mode across the varied illustrated journals, including subjects like microbiology, industrial history, anatomy, and technology, and featured most prevalently in journals, such as *al-Jinan*, *al-Tabib*, and *al-Muqtataf*, concerned with discoveries, medicine, science, and industry.[48] Printed diagrams played a central role in the experimentation process by showing readers how images could be used to teach themselves about the workings of the world around them. In an 1876 issue of *al-Jinan*, a diagram of Earth's orbit around the sun features prominently and is used in the accompanying text to describe this year-long journey in detail, along with an explanatory caption (Figure 7.3). While diagrams related to astronomy were particularly popular, technical diagrams became the norm in journals like *al-Muqtataf*, like an image featuring the various components of telegraphic communication (Figure 7.4). Focused on issues of biochemistry and other fields deemed pertinent to medicine at the time, *al-Tabib* features various diagrams of microbiology, such as an engraving showing what types of bacteria would look like when seen via a microscope (Figure 7.5). By the 1890s, as printing

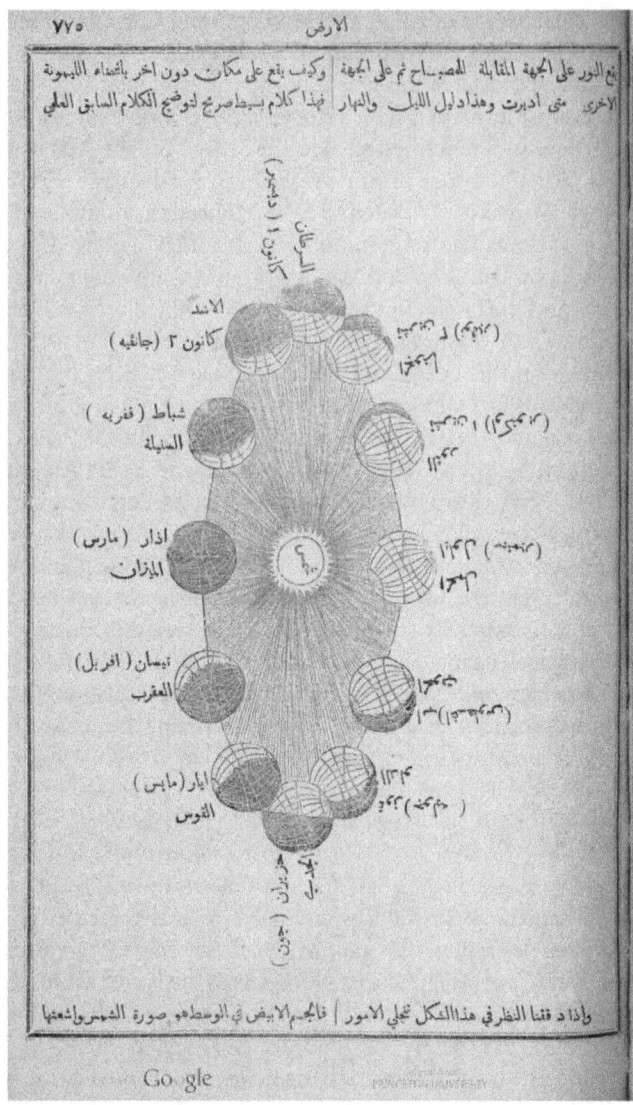

Figure 7.3 Celestial diagram of Earth's orbit around the sun. *Al-Jinan* 8, no. 22 (1876): 775. Public Domain, Google-digitized. The digital image of this work was produced by Google, Inc.

technology developed, so too did the nature of diagrams and what they depicted. For example, an article on lighting in *al-Bayan*, from 1897, includes a reproduction of one of the first bolts of lightning caught on camera (in Paris) and images of static electricity (produced by exposing photosensitive plates to electric sparks) as a way to explain how lighting works (Figure 7.6).[49] Diagrams like these, some of which emulated examples found in more specialized publications at this time, were

Figure 7.4 Diagram of telegraphic equipment. *Al-Muqtataf* 1, no. 8 (1876): 182. American University of Beirut/Library Archives.

meant for a generalist reader who was probably learning about this process for the first time. These images exemplify nineteenth-century constructivist approaches to scientific inquiry that no longer limited knowledge production and dissemination to the level of discourse but emphasized the use of measuring tools through which investigations of phenomena could take place even beyond the confines of the laboratory.[50] Diagrammatic engravings revealed the mechanics of how things, that many readers had likely not seen nor heard of, work.

Figure 7.5 Page from an article featuring a diagram of different bacteria as seen via a microscope. *Al-Tabib* 11, no. 10 (1884): 182. Tübingen, Universitätsbibliothek, ZE 42.

It is clear that the editors viewed diagrammatic knowledge, and engravings in general, as important disciplinary tools that can be used to direct and control a viewer's gaze and understanding. Diagrams were sometimes accompanied by descriptions of how "reading" such imagery in a scripted fashion would facilitate an understanding of the content being discussed.[51] Several diagrams published in journals also described the very modes of capturing such imagery through newly developed tools, like telescopes, photographs, and microscopes. Engravings depicting the mechanics of invisible processes (like electromagnetism) or microscopic particles invisible to the naked eye, provided a way of "seeing" that was previously unimaginable and unfamiliar to the general reader. In their

Figure 7.6 Photoengraving of electric sparks. *Al-Bayan* 1, no. 10 (October 1897): 407. Digitized by Universitäts- und Landesbibliothek Bonn (urn:nbn:de:hbz:5:1-251075). Image in the Public Domain.

descriptions and imagery, it is clear that journal editors were committed to separating what they saw as fact from fiction, and, more specifically, avoiding and refuting any views of the world that did not conform with their modern, Western, understanding of knowledge.

Yet, despite their purported transparency or "scientific" objectivity, journal diagrams, and other images, were likely viewed and misunderstood, in many ways, and belonged to broader experiences in an era of subjective perception. Scholarship on visuality and perception during the nineteenth century has demonstrated how modernity's excessive visual stimuli expose viewers to "reception in distraction."[52] Speaking of North American contexts in the mid-1800s, Shelly Jarenski explains how mass-media visuality brought with it "new cognitive and emotional reactions [that] many felt in the face of mass-media visuality [which] resulted in certain aesthetic environments marked by convergence, illusion, and virtuality."[53] Relatedly, Jonathan Crary has explained how the "rise of attentive norms and practices" in the early 1800s brought about the notion of subjective vision—in psychology, philosophy, neurology, early cinema, and photography—as modernity's tools of vision through which it seeks to control and experiment with the viewers' attention and perception.[54] Both Crary and Jarenski speak to the mobility of "the visual experience" whereby mass-made images are "abstracted from any founding site or referent."[55] Through everyday experiences of mass media, spectators (like Arabic illustrated journal readers and audiences) experienced an overlap of multiple visual forms from uncertain and unstable perspectives. Despite the disciplinary, or didactic, nature of purportedly transparent, objective, and utilitarian mechanically produced images, from photographs to diagrams, these visual examples of mass culture had the potential to continuously ruin "certainties and stabilities."[56]

Thus, while Arabic journal editors frequently couched their illustrations and descriptions of discoveries, technologies, and phenomena in "objective" scientific language, it is not guaranteed that readers, particularly those less familiar with the content in publications, were completely grasping the complex visuals, descriptions, and arguments being made.[57] What can be ascertained is that images were seen, even if not fully understood, and these engravings would certainly have raised questions for readers, or at least served as fleeting amusements. Even if readers could not read, or understand, the complexity of the accompanying texts, the engravings lent viewers the ability to at least envision or imagine a new "reality" from previously unimaginable and unfamiliar perspectives. One can say that this way of seeing, which was not possible in everyday life, disoriented readers by upending the very notion of what vision meant—almost magically—rendering the invisible, visible.

This is particularly true of visual renditions of celestial bodies in a variety of "views." Imaging, or imagining, the universe certainly parallels the scientific and literary interest in outer space at the time, both real and imagined. In an 1877 report in *al-Muqtataf* on American astronomer Asaph Hall's detection that year of one of Mars's two moons an illustration of Earth at different distances was published with a caption reading "Mars at its furthest, intermediary, and closest distance" (Figure 7.7). Another example (from *al-Bayan*) compellingly depicts the view of Earth from the moon (Figure 7.8). The eeriness of the moon's topography captured in this image is compounded by the insurmountable impossibility of experiencing this view. These engravings enhance the distance between subject and observer while simultaneously making it present in materiality of the engraving. One can imagine how viewing these images—with their unstable perspectives—ruins the observers' sense of certainty about their experience of the world, even while the articles themselves attempt to ground their analysis in empiricism.

Figure 7.7 Diagram of "Mars" from three distances. *Al-Muqtataf* 2, no. 5 (1877): 113. American University of Beirut/Library Archives.

Novelty, Spectacle, and Exoticism

In addition to commonly recurring engravings related to industry, technology, and all sorts of "modern" scientific inquiry, as previously noted, journals included images of myriad subject matter. Looking through journal issues, one can find illustrations of obelisks, Roman sculptures, and various "unusual" flora and fauna (like the zebra), alongside historical and contemporary events, reproductions of photographs taken

Figure 7.8 Image of "Earth from the moon." *Al-Bayan* 1, no. 1 (March 1897): 31. Digitized by Universitäts- und Landesbibliothek Bonn (urn:nbn:de:hbz:5:1-251075). Image in the Public Domain.

during inaugurations of sites or canals, sailboat races, and depictions of pavilions at world fairs, to name only a few. What many of these engravings had in common, if one were to separate them from the category of diagrams, is that they dealt with issues of novelty and spectacle, as well as exoticism. Although they served a general pedagogical purpose, these images were not typically meant to be read in conjunction with the text or used to understand complex descriptions. Rather, these kinds of engravings made otherwise distant or inaccessible forms of spectacle and popular entertainment accessible to journal audiences.

Many of these illustrations included Orientalist and colonialist understandings of cultures and society. Images of "curiosities" or the "exotic," often depicting ethnic or racial "others," served as extensions of spectacle and entertainment. For instance, an early issue of *al-Jinan* (1871) included two engravings of the Black performers Millie and Christine McKoy (1851–1912), who were born conjoined at the pelvis, sold into slavery at birth in North Carolina, and lived their lives performing on various stages.[58] The two engravings in *al-Jinan* are stylized renderings (likely copied from printed drawings circulating in British journals, and not actual photographs) depicting the sisters performing on stage. One engraving depicts them from the front wearing a double-bodice dress and two sets of boots (Figure 7.9). While the second image shows them with their backs to the viewer, but this time they are barefoot wearing only a short undergarment, insinuating that they were topless (Figure 7.10). These engravings simultaneously render them as "detached" objects of study and sexual fantasy.[59] Adding to the sexualization, fetishization, and "enfreakment"[60] of the McKoys is the fact that they are referred to in the singular, as "Millie Christine," and not as two individuals. The sexualization and racialization of female performers was not uncommon in mass media at the time, and these images should be seen alongside parallel practices in photography in which bodies of non-White women were fetishized through the use of costumes and other related tropes found in Orientalist photographs as well as images produced in Ottoman and Egyptian photography studios.[61]

Racialized imagery, then understood as ethnographic inquiry into different human and civilizational "characters,"[62] extended to other kinds of engravings. For instance, an 1885 article from *al-Tabib* includes a series of faces meant to distinguish between external differences in skin color and facial features as clues into the "order" of "human species" supported by a system of visible and invisible patterns. These views mirror contemporaneous Western ideas of "racial sciences" at the time that were reported on in journals like *al-Muqtataf*.[63] These characterizations also reflected opinions of some Arabic journal authors and editors, particularly in Egypt, who saw themselves as being different from other "primitive nations."[64] In 1896, *al-Hilal* published a series of articles focused on Sudan with images depicting women and children from different cultural groups in Africa, particularly Nubia, which, some argue, Egyptians believed to be the rightful colonizers of at the time (and not the British).[65] Relatedly, *al-Bayan*, in 1897, published a series on "The Egyptians" that mapped out different religious groups, "tribes," and rural communities as a form of ethnographic census including population numbers, education levels, and cultural practices. The engravings accompanying the text only depicted images of non-urban groups, specifically members of nomadic communities (*badu* also referred to as *'arab* in the articles) (Figure 7.11), *fallahin* (Egyptian peasantry) (Figure 7.12), and the Amazigh (as *barbar*) (Figure 7.13). These images should not be viewed in isolation. Rather, they are best understood alongside the copious number of similar photographs and drawings that were being produced and circulated (as *cartes de visites*, or through print like postcards and journal illustrations) by photography studios in Europe, Egypt, and key cities in the Ottoman world at the time.[66]

Engravings of racialized "Others" seem to parallel those of the colonial apparatus that Timothy Mitchell describes as producing "mirrors of truth" (like exhibitions

Figure 7.9 "Image of Millie Christine while she dances." *Al-Jinan* 2, no. 18 (September 15, 1871): 620. Public domain, Google-digitized. The digital image of this work was produced by Google, Inc.

and photographs) where "detached" scientific inquiry reproduces Orientalist images of the other as pedagogy.[67] These engravings were also about popular entertainment paralleling similar content exhibited and experienced at world fairs. In fact, the illustrations in Arabic journals belonged to a growing visual corpus of Ottoman and Egyptian photographs, paintings, and prints of rural groups, farmers, peasants, and members of purportedly "primitive" societies, in which these communities

Figure 7.10 "Image of Millie Christine from her back." *Al-Jinan* 2, no. 18 (September 15, 1871): 621. Public domain, Google-digitized. The digital image of this work was produced by Google, Inc.

were categorized, depicted, and differentiated according to then-recent methods in taxonomy, ethnography, and history steeped in Western ("universalist") civilizational discourses, which were popularized in the press and through expositions. While paintings, photographs, and photographic albums, such as artist Osman Hamdi Bey's (1842–1910) production for the 1873 Vienna Exposition of popular "costumes" of social groups within the Ottoman Empire,[68] circulated among largely elite or middle-

Figure 7.11 Engraving of a group of people accompanying an article on Egyptians. *Al-Bayan* 1, no. 11 (November 1897): 427. Digitized by Universitäts- und Landesbibliothek Bonn (urn:nbn:de:hbz:5:1-251075). Image in the Public Domain.

class Ottoman, European, and North American audiences (in print and exhibitions), similar renditions—of Egyptian and Syrian subjects—in Arabic journals were made accessible to non-Western, everyday audiences.

Taswir (Picture-Making) for the Masses?

Art for the masses may not have been the journal editors' exact understanding of the role of visual content that they included in their publications. However,

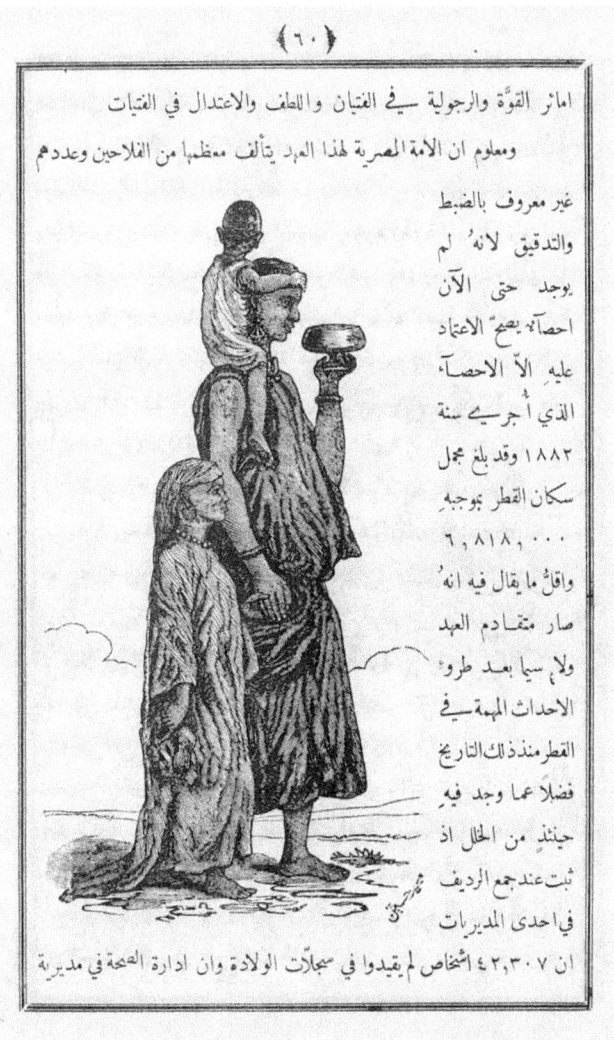

Figure 7.12 Engraving of three figures accompanying an article on Egyptians. *Al-Bayan* 1, no. 2 (April 1897): 60. Universitäts- und Landesbibliothek Bonn (urn:nbn:de:hbz:5:1-251075). Image in the Public Domain.

through their journal content, editors were interested in engaging with, and even popularizing, contemporaneous views on visual/artistic practices as important markers of taste and, by extension, civilization and progress. *Al-Muqtataf*, for instance, published an essay "The Fine Arts" (al-Funun al-Jamila)—in two parts— by Egyptian engineer and student at the School of Fine Arts (Paris) Ahmad Fahmi in February 1887.[69] Illustrated with two engravings, one a photographic reproduction of the Apollo del Belvedere sculpture in the Vatican and an engraving of the "Death

Figure 7.13 Engraving of a North African figure accompanying an article on Egyptians. *Al-Bayan* 1, no. 3 (May 1897): 114. Digitized by Universitäts- und Landesbibliothek Bonn (urn:nbn:de:hbz:5:1-251075). Image in the Public Domain.

of Socrates" based on a 1787 oil painting by French artist Jacques Louis David (1748–1825), the article locates a Western civilizational understanding of "fine art" as part of the liberal arts purportedly originating in Greek culture. Fahmi's ultimate aims in approaching *al-Muqtataf*'s editors was to expand on the fine art's intellectual and civilizational value to the public, "that its [fine art's] benefits might reach all children of the Arab nation and become as widely known as the other fields of knowledge."[70] *Al-Muqtataf*'s editors, in the footnotes, also point readers in the direction of other articles on philosophy and aesthetics, and "people's tastes in beauty."[71] Another, though little-known, article evidencing interests in popularizing art was published a few years later in *al-Mathaf* in 1894. Entitled "Fann al-Taswir" (Art of Image-making), the article (whose author is not listed) describes *taswir* as: "an art of *tamthil* (mimesis) *al-ashbah* (spirits) [semblances] through light and shadow and color."[72] Although this text also underscores the

Figure 7.14 Engraving of Madame De Staël. *Al-Muqtataf* 7, no. 11 (1884): 347. American University of Beirut/Library Archives.

importance of Greek painting, "Fann al-Taswir" does not necessarily extoll the fine art's philosophical connections like Fahmi does. In fact, it traces a history of *rusum* (drawings) across various media in time, grounding the practice in the traditions of ancient Egyptians, Persians, and Akkadians, in addition to those of the Greeks and Romans.[73] What both of these articles indicate is how academic and philosophical discussions of *taswir*, and the fine arts more broadly, were explicated and demystified within the context of illustrated periodicals.

This interest in popularizing the value of the fine arts can also be connected to the use of portraiture in journals. Mass-produced portraits—of local and foreign authors, intellectuals, and political dignitaries across time—made using various modes of printing, particularly engravings produced for and used in periodicals, became increasingly popular by the late 1800s (Figure 7.14; see also Figure 7.2). Although printed portraits—of non-imperial individuals—were initially introduced in book publications at local and regional presses, oftentimes in the form of author portraits, this particular genre became rather widespread in the publishing industry, intersecting with and informed by a similar popularity in studio photography. The popularity of printed portraiture was also informed by the sociopolitical importance of this genre within (and beyond) imperial Ottoman circles at this time, whereby, printed, photographic, and painted—as watercolor on paper and oil on canvas— portraits of rulers and other important courtly figures served increasingly central roles as diplomatic gifts.[74] However, while imperial and elite paintings, and photographs, were not typically circulated among the everyday populace, it was through journal portraits—as printed galleries—that mass audiences were able to appreciate and engage with this artistic genre that was gaining regional recognition at this time. In the absence of public painting and portrait galleries at this time in Egypt and the Ottoman realms, printed portraits (and other images) in journals were the way in which public audiences had access to the "fine arts" that were being discussed and popularized in the periodical press. Some engraved portraits were even detached from their pages and found their way onto everyday locations like storefront window shutters.

Further connecting portraiture and *taswir* to everyday (commercial) life in Egypt (and the region), the editors of *al-Mathaf*, in a note to readers from August 1894, attempted to convince subscribers to pay their dues by announcing a prize of a painted portrait for each individual whose account is fully paid. Editors claim to have come to an agreement with various artists/painters (*musawwirun*) in Europe to gift each subscriber—who paid all their dues to date—with a photo-sized oil painting (based on a personal photo portrait).[75] These are but a few known early examples of journal publishers drawing on the social (and commercial) value of the visual arts as a way to engage a broader audience, whose members may not have previously had access to these ideas or images.

Conclusion

Engravings in illustrated Arabic periodicals sought to engage the vision—and attention—of contemporary observers in often divergent ways that were typically not possible in everyday life. While journal editors often shared their views on the images, and accompanying articles, in their periodicals, it was not always clear how readers perceived journal content. Although some readers (deemed qualified enough by the editors) had opportunities to publish their views in the journals, editors rarely published letters from readers nor did they seem to really care how the material in their publications was received. As a result, we can only conjecture how the regional public viewed, engaged with, appreciated, or even understood, these images. However, the simultaneous presence of varied modes of representation, printing techniques, and ways of seeing/reading—across key journals in the region that were circulating around the same time—might have made for a disjointed (though amusing) visual experience. Engraved images rendered visible, conceivable, and even accessible, an array of otherwise unimaginable, unknown, and unseen objects, people, places, topics, and phenomena, from observing a distant Earth on the surface of the moon to examining an instrument able to zoom in on objects invisible to the naked eye, and everything in between.

These images as part of publications that circulated from reading rooms, salons, cafés, and squares, to private spaces of the home, should be read as part of a wider, growing interest in mass culture and entertainment at this time. Engravings, and their accompanying articles, reflected and engaged ideas, events, inventions, performances, fashion, and technologies that readers and everyday audiences were also coming across while living and working, or simply passing through, urban centers. They also emulated, reproduced, and expanded upon images that were circulating by other means, through photographs, postcards, oral descriptions, and live performances. When studied as part of a growing network of mass-produced culture and entertainment, that entailed textual, visual, performative, and oral engagements, illustrated journals can be better understood for their visuality at the time; despite their role in Nahdawi intellectual history, and the persistent logocentric views in which these histories are told, illustrated periodicals did not always require literacy to be enjoyed by readers.

Chapter 8

EGYPTOMANIAC EGYPTIANS? ANCIENT EGYPT IN THE POPULAR LITERARY IMAGINARY IN TWENTIETH-CENTURY EGYPT

Alaaeldin Mahmoud

Introduction, or Is Egyptomania an Orientalist Construct?

From antiquity to the modern times, historians, geographers, philosophers, theologians, travelers, musicians, artists, and littérateurs have been fascinated with the idea of ancient Egypt. Greco-Roman and Judeo-Christian traditions were specifically the primary sources that have fueled the imagination of the Old World's populations concerning the idea of Egypt. Ancient Egypt's popularity in Greek/Hellenistic historical writings by Herodotus, Diodorus Siculus, Strabo, and Manetho, and more illustrates the turned-into-Western Greek/Hellenistic worldview of Egypt inasmuch as the ethnic worldview of the ancient Greeks themselves.[1] Hellenizing Egypt meant "westernizing" not only ancient Egypt but also an age-old appropriation of it. Peculiarly, a westernized Egypt influenced rather than being influenced by its westernizing force. It is with such westernization of (ancient) Egypt that Egyptomania was catapulted into existence.

Although it is broadly claimed that Egyptomania as a term was born recently—in 1925 (which is a significant date in its own right), interest, fascination, and obsession with Egypt was restored in the wake of the European Renaissance. In this ambience, there was a revitalized interest in Egypt as an atavistic civilization viewed as one principal source of ancient Greece/Rome civilizational advancements. During the European Renaissance, growing popular interest in occultism in early modern Europe unearthed a corresponding interest in ancient "esoteric" Egypt or "Egyptosophy." Associating ancient Egypt with the occult and the esoteric in the European Renaissance imaginary gave rise to the construction of an imagined Egypt, an Egypt which has, in turn, continued to bring about a form of Western Orientalism.[2]

Orientalizing (ancient) Egypt blossomed as subsequent "waves" of modern European Egyptomania. Another milestone wave of Egyptomania is consorted with the publication of the *Description de l'Égypte* (1809–28), concurrently with the discovery of the Rosetta Stone and the translation of the Egyptian hieroglyphics by the French scholar/Orientalist Champollion.[3] Like that of the Renaissance, the French Orientalist version of Egyptomania was not exclusively scholarly. Through the increasing numbers of travel accounts made accessible to the French (and European) readerships, French diplomats and adventurers wrote about their encounters with the Orient. The publication of Vivant Denon's "imperial romance" *Voyage dans la Basse et la Haute Égypte pendant les campagnes de générale Bonaparte* in 1802 was a smashing success—commercially speaking. The French and European reading masses who read *Description* and Denon's *Voyage* were fascinated with "[t]heir spectacularly illustrated folios [which] captivated an entire continent with detailed color images of pyramids, crocodiles, mummies, and harems."[4] The scholarly *Description* and the popular *Voyage* as well as the many other travelogues and narratives would set forth and illustrate what Said described as a "textual attitude to the Orient."[5]

"Egypt Craze" in the Western/Globalized Popular Entertainment Industries

Egyptomania was closely associated with modern entertainment since the development of the latter as a global industry. One giant step toward modern European Egyptomania is concomitant with the life and work of the Italian explorer and archaeologist Giovanni Belzoni (1779–1823). Once a circus strongman who toured Europe for his performances, Belzoni decided to visit Egypt to propose setting up a hydraulic machine to Egypt's viceroy. In a turn of fate, Belzoni became involved in the Egyptian antiquities "business" (and archaeology later on), as he got contracted by the British consul Mr. Henry Salt to make "researches for antiquities, which were to be placed in the British Museum."[6] Although some are ambivalent about evaluating Belzoni's career, it is important to note that it is he who opened new horizons for the display of ancient Egypt throughout Europe (and later around the globe).[7] To put "displaying ancient Egypt" into effect, Belzoni managed to exhibit his collection of Egyptian art and artifacts in William Bullock's "Egyptian Hall," located in Piccadilly Street, London in 1821.[8] The smashing success of these "Egyptian" exhibitions, especially in Britain and later in America, not only heralded the emergence of a new version of Orientalism—an "Orientalism-for-profit,"[9] but also dramatically introduced ancient Egypt into the world's emergent global popular culture.

Imagining Ancient Egypt in a Nahda-imbued, Modern Egypt

Worldwide fascination with Egypt materialized itself both in the more scholarly Egyptology and in the lighter Egyptomania; that was by the rise of global cultural capitalism. Modern Western obsession with Egypt became part of a burgeoning global popular culture. However, the global-ness of this popular culture often seemed to mean nothing more than Western-ness. Western Egyptomania was, in many ways, a parallel phenomenon to Western Orientalism. In the many forms of Western, modern entertainment—such as exhibitions, dance, theater, revue, popular fiction, film, and more—ancient Egypt was instrumentalized in such ways that further nurtured an already Western, Orientalist image of Egypt. Images and representations that invoked mystery, unruliness, irrationality, lust, and more of the Oriental "other" were well invested in the Western, modern entertainment scene.

As Egyptomania traveled the world, largely carried by Western capitalist imperialism, new forms of non-Western, non-Orientalist interest in ancient Egypt grew. However, even as Egyptomania spread through geographical spaces like Russia and Eastern Europe, whose designation as "Western" is debatable, or in the nations of the Global South such as India and South Africa, it was largely present due to Western cultural and/or colonial influence.

While Egyptology and Egyptomania could be used interchangeably; it is worthwhile to emphasize their interconnectedness in the context of global popular entertainments. When it comes to the escalating interest in ancient Egypt—that mounted to be an "Egypt craze"—that swept over the globe's four corners, especially in the early 1920s onwards, there has been a consistent pattern in how non-Western nations approached ancient Egypt: it usually began with Egyptological interest triggered by the touring Egyptian artifacts collections since mid-nineteenth century, and then it was followed by an Egyptomaniac fever among either secret or underground movements/groups or in the various forms of (global) popular entertainment, as in the cases of Brazil and Japan.[10]

With the advent of the nineteenth century, ancient Egypt grew to be displayed worldwide. The rise and the swelling trend of world exhibitions, museums, and galleries, in addition to global tourism, all contributed to globalizing a once-Western Egyptomania. Thanks to this global popularity acquired by all things Egyptian within the world's popular culture, many non-Western nations started to take note of ancient Egypt. In Russia, for instance, Egyptomania was taken note of via Italian and French influences following Napoleon's Campaign. Similarly, the Campaign intrigued Brazil's King Dom Pedro I to purchase the first Egyptian collection in 1824; housed now in Brazil's National Museum.[11] Another roaring wave of global Egyptomania followed when Howard Carter discovered King Tutankhamun's tomb in 1922. It was such a global event that it drew the attention of the entire world to ancient Egypt and its civilization. In response to this, Chinese scholars began to note the European fascination with ancient Egypt. In the first three decades of the twentieth century, and for China to appear connected to global civilization, many Chinese subscribed to a popular pseudoscientific theory that civilization had spread to China from Mesopotamia.[12]

However, Egyptomania in both Ottoman and post-Ottoman eras, especially from the second half of the nineteenth century until the early decades of the twentieth century, offers an intriguingly special case. Throughout the Ottoman history of Egyptomania, European influences were present and cannot easily be downplayed. Since the sixteenth century when the black market in Egyptian mummies was endemic in Europe, ostensibly for medical and entertainment purposes, the Ottomans, who were Egypt's rulers then, passed laws to control the illicit trade in mummies.[13]

Given that the Ottomans did neglect the heritage of ancient Egypt, the collective belief (in Europe) that Egyptian antiquities were abandoned property fueled European obsession with ancient artifacts, including mummies (leading to the growth of a lucrative market of all things Egyptian in Europe). There are several possible reasons for the Ottoman negligence of Egyptian antiquities (and of the ancient Egyptian civilization altogether). It could be attributed to some medieval Islamic worldview that viewed ancient Egypt as the land of tyrant pharaohs, idolatrous slaves, and unscrupulous polytheistic clergy. Equally, the Ottomans' disinterest in ancient Egypt could duly be comparable to other Eastern nations such as India, China, or Japan, whose image of ancient Egypt was not central in their popular imaginary as it has always been in Western Europe, where ancient Egypt was envisioned as an "intimate stranger" or Europe's "own cultural *shadow*."[14] More interestingly, the Ottoman colonial encounter with Egypt may have brought about "othering" of Egypt, both ancient and modern, in the establishment of their colonizing "self." To illustrate, in *Hac Yolunda* (On the Way to the Pilgrimage), published later in 1922, which describes his travel to Jeddah via Egypt, the Ottoman Turkish military doctor Cenap Şehabettin depicts the "locals" in Egypt as backward, idle, and self-indulgent.[15] This, in turn, could have led to a disinterest in the country's ancient civilization.

In the nineteenth century, a nascent "Egyptian" Egyptomania would soon rise out of this atmosphere of neglect. It is true that the discovery of Tutankhamen's tomb in the early 1920s was a paradigmatic turning point in the way modern Egyptian elite and public alike perceived their ancient Egyptian past. However, the history of this phenomenon goes back further than the 1920s, to the long-term, deep ruptures inflicted upon the modern Egyptians' perceptions of their homeland in the wake of the French Expedition of 1798.

Whether the birth date of the Arab awakening/enlightenment era, best known as *al-yaqaza* or *al-nahda*, was specifically in 1798 or most probably later than this date, it is established that some sort of an Arab "renaissance" was around and about since the second half of the nineteenth century in the Ottoman *velayat* (provinces) of Egypt, the Levant, and Iraq. Under the Ottoman rule, up-and-coming feelings of nationalism were experienced by the Arab intellectuals and men of letters in Egypt, the Arab *mashriq* and North Africa. Interestingly, *adab* (which could only conveniently be translated as "literature") writers sought to rediscover and get inspired by select works of Arab *turath* (heritage). With the invention of presses and the availability of patronage, especially in Khedivial Egypt, Egyptian writers of *adab* passionately began their journey to re-visit the masterpieces of classical Arabic literature, whether in verse or prose.

Amid this aforementioned age of new cultural production, interest in ancient Egypt grew, particularly among the late Ottoman Egyptian elites of the nineteenth century. One man who steered the way was the young Egyptian Azhari Shaykh Rifaʿa al-Tahtawi (1801–73), whose somehow ubiquitous remarks on ancient Egypt could have been one small step for him, but certainly a giant step for modern Egyptian Egyptomania. Privileged to be mentored by the enlightened Shaykh Hasan al-ʿAttar (1766–1835) besides a cohort of leading French Orientalists such as Silvestre de

Sacy (1755–1838), Joseph Reinaud (1795–1867), and Edmond-François Jomard (1777–1862), al-Tahtawi put his best foot forward to introduce formative changes in historiography and spawn "an interest in ancient Egypt in the Islamic scholarly community."[16] With an eye-witness to the demise of a dying age and the birth of a new one, al-Tahtawi introduced to his readers an ancient Egypt that was typically commensurate with a burgeoning Nahda ideology. The earliest mark of al-Tahtawi's Egypt-themed interest could be traced back to 1827, when he published his Arabic translation of Joseph Agoub's (1795–1832) poem "Dithyrambe sur l'Égypte," in which Egypt was depicted in a romanticized fashion as "the mother of gods, heroes, and sages."[17] The Egypt that would appear afterward in al-Tahtawi's non-translated poems was not, by all means, dissimilar to the Egypt of the nostalgic Agoub.

Rifaʿa al-Tahtawi was the herald who presaged the rise of Egyptian nationalism in modern Arabic literature.[18] Through him, it is possible to trace the history of nineteenth-century Egyptomania, literary imaginary, and, even, the Nahda. For al-Tahtawi, ancient Egypt—or rather his own image of it—was an intrinsic part of his literary and reformist Nahdawi enterprise. Similar to Agoub's Egypt, al-Tahtawi's ancient Egypt, as envisioned in his verses and so-called anthems, evoked feelings of national pride and euphoria, awe, or sometimes nostalgia.[19] In his non-poetic work, al-Tahtawi's instrumentalization of ancient Egypt in his Nahdawi venture is even more usable. In his *al-murshid al-amin lil-banat wa-al-banin* (The Reliable Guide for Girls and Boys) (1872), he dedicated a brief chapter to define and explain *tamaddun al-watan* (civilizing the nation) to his targeted young readers. For him, for *al-watan* [ostensibly modern Egypt] to be civilized, "the manners and the customs" [of modern Egyptians] needed to be "improved;" in addition to acquiring "perfection in education," they need to be encouraged to "gain virtue, secure urban scruples, and promote their prosperity."[20]

In *Manahij al-albab al-Misriya fi mabahij al-adab al-ʿasriya* (The Paths of Egyptian Minds in the Joys of Modern Arts) (first published in 1869), al-Tahrawi thoroughly developed his view of ancient Egypt's primordial *tamaddun* (civilization). He illustrated the causal relationship between the ancient Egyptians' *tamaddun* and their diligence by highlighting their accomplishment of extraordinary works such as the pyramids, the great obelisks, paintings, and magnificent statues, besides the representation of sloth and indolence as statues of dull-looking persons, with their head down, assuming a dog's lazy seated position.[21] Obviously, his ancient Egypt/Egyptomania (and that of his contemporaries) was largely, if not exclusively, aspirational and teleological: what the Nahda enterprise needed was (an image of) a civilized, progressive, and industrious ancient Egypt; one that could stand defiantly against the current Orientalist image of ancient/modern Egypt and serve as a model for the modern nation.

Al-Tahtawi also had a number of newly Egyptomaniac contemporaries and disciples, notably Muhammad Shihab al-Din (1795–1857), Salih Majdi (1826–81), ʿAbd Allah al-Nadim (1843–96), and ʿAli Fahmi Rifaʿa (1848–1903). These writers chronicled the history of Egypt in poetry, contextualizing the historic accomplishments of ancient Egypt within Egypt's long history. In the poetic oeuvre of those Egyptian authors who were productive in the last quarter of the nineteenth century, ancient Egypt was never the sole subject or theme, in contrast to literary works that would appear later by early twentieth-century Egyptians, but it did begin to feature in different ways. Cast in a late Ottoman fashion, Shihab al-Din's Egypt, for instance, a land of ancient wonders which are only comparable to other great relics of the past like Yemen's Ghamdan Fortress, Mesopotamia's Taq Kasra (i.e., Arch of Ctesiphon), as well as the Quranic *Iram Dhat al-'Imad* (Iram of the Pillars) and the Throne of Balqis (Queen of Sheba).[22] In comparison, 'Ali Fahmi Rifa'a's ancient Egypt, although personified in his 204-line poem "'Arus al-afrah" (Bride of the Jubilees) (published in 1874), represents only one era in Egypt's long three-era history: Pharaonic, medieval, and modern times. In pursuit of an *a la mode* verse chronicling of Egypt's history, a less-known poet like 'Ali al-Khashshab was keen to cite in his nationalistic *ruba'iya* (1879) some details related to ancient Egypt like the Pyramids Builders and Sesostris I, along with the Ptolemies and the Romans, the Arabs like 'Amr ibn al-'As, the Umayyads, the Abbasids, Ibn Tulun, the Ikhshidids, the Ayyubids, the Turks, and the Circassians, as well as the French Campaign, to conclude with the Muhammad 'Ali dynasty.[23]

The Egyptomaniac Shawqi

It was with the young yet more renowned court poet Ahmad Shawqi (1868–1932) that Egyptian Egyptomania would undergo a paradigm shift. Contrary to his predecessors whose Egypt-related verse celebrates ancient Egypt only as one "stage" of the country's long history or a brief episode in a longer chronicle, and unlike the globally rampant international Egyptomania, Shawqi started to create a specifically Egyptian Egyptomania, stimulated by "a search for a long-lost identity" rather than a pursuit of the exoticism, mystery, or esotericism of ancient Egyptian civilization.[24] As a literary forefather, Shawqi's Egyptomania positions him neither with the late Ottoman Egyptian poets who feature Egypt in their literary work nor with the (Orientalist) Europeans whose image of ancient Egypt certainly differs than, if not perceivably contradicts with, how the Egyptians of his time began to perceive their country and its (ancient) history.

In his first lyric epic poem with the title "Kibar al-Hawadith fi Wadi al-Nil"[25] (Major Events in the Nile Valley), Shawqi began to shape this new form of Egyptomania. Recited at the International Congress of Orientalists in Geneva in 1894, Shawqi's poem was not simply another poetic chronicle of Egypt's glorious history, but rather an anticolonial aesthetic-intellectual manifesto that could be cast as one of the Nahda's earliest manifestations of Pharaonism. This manifesto was not only a counternarrative to the Western perception of ancient Egyptian history as disinterested taxonomy and mythological fantasy but also a political and legal Egyptian decolonization strategy.[26] Putting this strategy into aesthetic practice, Shawqi sang the Pharaonic, Ptolemaic, and Islamic heroisms of Egypt while accentuating that Egypt's invaders: the Hyksos, Achaemenid Persians, Romans, the Crusaders, the Circassian Turks, and Napoleon's French army—were all oppressors who were endured and eventually overthrown.[27]

The very recital of "Kibar al-Hawadith fi Wadi al-Nil" by Shawqi in an "international" scholarly Congress/exhibition in Continental Europe is significant. Shawqi was writing back directly to the European Orientalist/colonial narrative (bearing in mind that Egypt was a British colony, or more accurately, a "Veiled Protectorate" at that time) that objectified ancient Egypt's antiquities and history as profitable material for colonial gaze. Shawqi and other Egyptian intellectuals of the Nahda would embark on an anticolonial Nahdawi version of Western/globalized Egyptomania.

This, however, was only half of the story. Evidently, turn-of-the-century Egyptian writers and intellectuals came to be more induced that the classical Arabic verse of the time was no longer the best or the only literary medium to popularize ancient Egypt for their targeted new mass local readerships, and it seems that Ahmad Shawqi was no exception. In response to this conviction which might have been dictated by the world literature vogues of the day, the emergence and exponential growth of popular Arabic fiction in fin de siècle Egypt signaled taxonomic transformation in the way the Nahda writers re-appropriated their history of ideas, aesthetics, and position-in-the-world.

In contrast to his 1894 epic "Kibar al-Hawadith fi Wadi al-Nil" that targeted a Congress of Orientalist intellectuals, Shawqi's early attempts in popular Arabic fiction, first launched by his publication of his Egypt-themed fictional works (or so-called "Pharaonic quartet"), obviously targeted mass readership. This is materialized by publishing his first novelette 'Adhra' al-Hind aw Tamaddun al-Fara'ina (The Maid of India, or the Civilization of the Pharaohs) in late 1897. Before its publication, Shawqi published it as serialized in Al-Ahram newspaper. His second and third novelettes, Ladiyas aw Akhir al-Fara'ina (Ladiyas or the Last of the Pharaohs) and Dal wa Tayman aw Akhir al-Fara'ina (Dal and Tayman or the Last Pharaohs) (1899) were serialized too as they appeared first in Al-Mawsu'at journal since late 1898 until early 1900.

As Egyptomania and Egyptology went in tandem worldwide, it is worthwhile to note that Shawqi's Egypt-themed popular fiction attempts were similarly responses to Orientalist or "foreign" Egyptological work. In the significant disclaimer in his own preface to 'Adhra' al-Hind, Shawqi suggests that the novelette could, in part, be written in response to Ferdinand de Lanoye's book Ramses le Grand, ou l'Egypte il y a trois mille trois cents ans (1866), translated as Ramses the Great, or, the Egypt of 3300 Years Ago in 1869.[28] With his assertion in the novelette's preface that 'Adhra' al-Hind was an endeavor to explore ancient Egyptian historiography that was still in its infancy,[29] Shawqi created his special formula for an emerging Arabic popular fiction: the combination of fact with fiction, or Egyptology with Egyptomania, in a way that should appeal to both elitist and populist audiences. He chose to set the story in a variety of exoticized settings such as India's Eight Jungles and the ancient Egyptian metropoles of Memphis and Thebes, to the dismay of the literary critics of the day.

Rather expectedly, the publication of Shawqi's 'Adhra' al-Hind was fuel for one of the Nahda's literary feuds between Ibrahim al-Yaziji (1847–1906) and Shakib Arslan (1869–1946), when the former dismissed the novel for wishing to represent the "myths and falsehoods" of Ramses II's (known as King Sesostris) time by depicting "jinn, goblins, magicians, astrologers and talismans, as well as descriptions of fantastical creatures' marvels."[30] He added that one cannot find anything in it that the current fiction writers are eager to incorporate in their work such as "insightful morals, literary themes, or historical facts"[31] In response to this vilifying critique, Arslan argued that in order for writers to meet the requirements of the time, they cannot avoid using "neologisms" that their Arab ancestors were ignorant of such as "al-ra'i al-'am" (public opinion).[32] This critical feud relating to Shawqi's Egyptomaniac popular fiction reveals how the early endeavors in writing popular fiction were received by the Arab critics of the day, one consequence of which was the insistent exclusion of it in the Nahda's canonized literary repertoire.

Shawqi was not writing in a vacuum. Across the world, rapid dissemination of knowledge of Egypt produced by the Egyptological breakthroughs of the French Campaign savants and later writers, also coincided with "the rise of a mass market for popular fiction," brought about a surge in new literary genres such as "short stories, mysteries, historical novels, occult fiction, and science fiction."[33] Egyptian-themed popular fiction was a thriving, lucrative business for European writers, especially in the last two decades of the nineteenth century; whose Egyptomaniac novels were bestsellers globally such as H. Rider Haggard's *She* (1886) and *Cleopatra* (1889), and Anatole France's *Taïs* (1890). Another significant author in world popular fiction is the German Egyptologist and novelist Gerge Ebers (1837–98). Ebers was of particular interest to the Nahda writers such as Jurji Zaydan (1861–1914), whose historical novels show "striking similarities" with Ebers' historical romances, and Ahmad Shawqi,[34] whose early novelette *Dal wa Tayman aw Akhir al-Fara'ina* (1899) was a free adaptation of Ebers' Egyptomaniac romance *Eine Ägyptische Königstochter* (1864), which he had read in Arabic translation.[35]

A closer examination of Shawqi's early attempts in Egyptian fin de siècle popular fiction reveals much about how the Nahda littérateurs approximated popular entertainment in regard to Egyptian Egyptomania. Shawqi's choice to serialize his novelettes in well-circulated journals served to meet the needs of the new mass readerships, largely housewives.[36] Conscious of the dissimilarity between his elitist audience in the 1894 Congress of Orientalists in Geneva and the new populist women and juvenile readerships, Shawqi played up his literary Pharaonism in a "lighter" tone, in contrast to the solemner tone of his "Kibar al-Hawadith fi Wadi al-Nil."

Eager to contribute to *al-adab al-asri* (contemporaneous literature), Shawqi served his readers with stories set in Orientalized-like, exotic settings, cast in a hybrid form that combined the old form of the [Arabic] *maqama* and the new form of the [European] novel,[37] and written in a style more accessible to the mass readerships of the time. In chapter I titled "Jazirat al-'Adhara" (The Virgins' Island) in *'Adhra' al-Hind*, Shawqi described the young virgin girls as "moons, rising day and night, impregnating space and time with light; they were all harbored in an erected-on-water palace, accommodated therein as the Gemini would accommodate its stars, that palace was built with crystal and alabaster, furnished with all sorts of jewels, worn with non-Arab fragrance and amber."[38] In such prose which may appear extravagantly pretentious in the eyes of the contemporary reader, Shawqi, with an observant eye on the taste and expectations of his readers, treated them with fiction written in a style that invokes the famed Arabic *maqamat* and the mysterious (Orientalist at times) ambience of *Alf Layla wa Layla* (the Arabian Nights) stories.

Still, how Shawqi imagined and represented ancient Egypt history and historical figures, especially in his early literary works, was evidently and largely subject to the influence of (French) Orientalism.[39] Shawqi's alleged disinterested Orientalist Egyptomania was, in fact, a kind of de-Orientalized Egyptomania, where political undertones underlay all his Egyptian-themed literary works.[40] In *'Adhra' al-Hind*, for example, he alluded to ancient Egypt's glory under Ramses whose military campaigns reached as far as to Sino-India, while in *Ladiyas, Dal wa Tayman*, and even in *Shaytan Binta'ur* (The Satan/Demon of Pentawer) (1901–2), there are noticeable political allusions to the 'Urabi revolt and the [British] occupation (1881–2), together with his critique of life in Egypt politically, socially, and economically.[41] Shawqi's anticolonial, de-Orientalizing attitude and re-appropriation of ancient Egypt were dictated by his dual role as a Nahdawi intellectual/writer and a poet in the Khedivial court of 'Abbas Hilmi II.[42] In his dedication published in *'Adhra' al-Hind*, Shawqi panegyrized the Khedive as one of Egypt's greatest "Pharaohs" in way that could not be fully comprehended by the novelette's defenders and detractors alike.

Born and raised in the Khedivial court, Ahmad Shawqi appears incapable of relinquishing so-called "courtly" themes and settings easily in his early fictional attempts. Like Ramses II, the "royal" protagonist in his first novelette *'Adhra' al-Hind*, whose unsurmountable military achievements are recounted in a pride-invoking air, the Pharoah Hamas (Ahmose), the protagonist in the second novelette *Ladiyas*, is portrayed in similarly pompous, heroic terms. The heroic Pharaoh rescues Ladiyas (perhaps Lydia), the princess of Samos, from the Persian Prince Bahram who she thought to be her rescuer from her cousin Poris, who kidnapped her. Princess Ladiyas marries the Pharaoh after killing Bahram in a duel.[43] In what looks like bringing Egyptology and Egyptomania together, apparently in appeasement of both his *waly al-ni'am* (Chief Patron or Benefactor, i.e., Khedive 'Abbas Hilmi II) and his "new" readership, Shawqi combined his interest in the splendor of ancient Egypt (the royal/courtly in particular) with the supernatural, that is, "the popular taste for magicians' tales in *'Adhra' al-Hind* and *Lādiyās*."[44] In *Ladiyas*, for instance, the events were narrated preposterously—Hamas (Ahmose) got involved in a fight with a lion, "where he vanquishes the beast, mounts it, and then flies it to his destination amid the people's shouts of praise and joy."[45]

Shawqi and Cleopatra

No ancient Egyptian historical figure could reflect the demands of fin de siècle mass readerships, spectators, and audiences converging with Orientalist/colonial Egyptomania more than Queen Cleopatra VII (r. 51–30 BCE), the last queen of the Ptolemaic dynasty of Egypt. Her historically famed beauty, shrewdness, and feminine power, her legendary love story with Mark Antony, along with her tragic suicide all provided an incomparably rich material through time for European/world artists and littérateurs to depict the story of her romantic love and unfortunate death. Evidently, the first Arabic writer to represent Cleopatra in modern Arabic literature is Ahmad Shawqi in his 1894 epic "Kibar al-Hawadith fi Wadi al-Nil."[46] At that early stage of his literary career, Shawqi's literary depiction of Cleopatra as a wanton, shrewd temptress whose playful ways contributed to the fall of the Ptolemaic dynasty in Egypt was a predominant, unchecked Orientalist influence. Conversely, after thirty-three years, the more mature and de-Orientalized Shawqi would write an Arabic verse drama masterpiece under the title *Masra' Kliyubatra* (*Death of Cleopatra*) in 1927. In contrast to his 1894 Cleopatra where he seemed to adopt the standpoint Italian writers such as Dante, Petrarch, and Boccaccio had of her as "a corrupted enemy of Rome,"[47] the Cleopatra of Shawqi's *Masra' Kliyubatra*, rewritten of Shakespeare's *Antony and Cleopatra* (first published in 1623), was recast as a woman torn between love for her own country and love for Antony in an allegory of the Egyptian struggle for independence from the British.[48]

With the publication of Shawqi's *Masra' Kliyubatra*, he has evidently opened a new chapter in his relationship with his audience. The very choice of the artistic medium was significant: in the late 1920s when Shawqi's verse play was published, Arabic-language theater has already become, by far, one of the most liked and sought-after forms of popular and mass entertainment. Translated or freely adapted plays, largely European classics, were already been served to an avid and loving Arab audience on almost a daily basis in the theaters of Cairo, Alexandria, and other urban centers in Egypt. In such a thriving ambience of mass entertainment, Shawqi saw it necessary to establish the connection between his presumably elitist literary text and theatrical performance when he decided to give permission to Fatima Rushdi's theatrical troupe to set *Masra' Kliyubatra* for stage in the forthcoming season.[49] To Shawqi's satisfaction, when Fatima Rushdi's troupe performed the play on January 19, 1930, the advertisement described the play in terms most appealing to the entertainment-enamored theatergoers of the time: "In *Masra' Kliyubatra*, there exist comedic scraps, melodious tunes, spiritual dances, Pharaonic landscape, singing treasures, bulbul-like rhymes, historical exhortations, musical cadences, and hellish snakes."[50]

Tutankhamun and the Modern Egyptomaniac Egyptians

The discovery of Tutankhamun's tomb in November 1922 by the British archaeologists Howard Carter and Lord Carnarvon was immeasurably a global event that took the entire world by storm. This outstanding discovery caused a qualitative shift in worldwide Egyptomania, and the Egyptian version of it was no exception. The list of the Egyptian and even Egypt-based poets, novelists, dramatists, writers, and translators who responded to the momentous event with Egypt-themed literature is long. Leading literary journals such as *al-Hilal, al-Muqtataf, al-Risala*, and *Abullu* (Apollo) hastened to publish poems, short fiction, excerpts from verse plays, and literary translations that either commemorated

King Tutankhamun himself as in Shawqi's poems "Mafakhir al-faraʿina" (Feats of the Pharaohs) (*al-Muqtataf*, 1923), "Tut ʿAnkh Amun wa-hadarat ʿasrih" (Tutankhamun and the Civilization of His Time) (*al-Muqtataf*, 1926), or Khalil Mutran's "Nashid Tut ʿAnkh Amun" (Tutankhamun's Anthem) (*al- Hilal*, 1924), or holistically celebrate ancient Egypt's landmark accomplishments such as the pyramids, the sphinx, Egypt's colossal temples and magnificent statues. That was in effect through the publication of Egypt-themed poems by prominent poets as Hafiz Ibrahim, Wali al-Din Yakan, Ibrahim Naji, and Ahmad Zaki Abu Shadi.

In more popular or rather a low-brow-ish vain, renowned colloquial Egyptian poets such as Bayram al-Tunisi (1893–1961) and Mohammad Yunus al-Qadi (1888–1969) also wrote poems on the occasion to commemorate the ancient Egyptian king and promote Egyptian nationalistic ideas. These poems were particularly appealing to the Egyptian public in the early years of the twentieth century. Like that of his fellow classical Arabic Egyptian poets, al-Tunisi's poetic envisioning of the young ancient Egyptian king was instrumental in voicing the current, largely political state of affairs. Lambasting modern Egyptians for turning their glorious king who used to have an "army" and "garrisoned troops" into a "mummy," al-Tunisi bitterly concludes his poem "Tut ʿAnkh Amun" (Tutankhamun) by describing the Egyptian king as "sightedly asleep yet in a blind land."[51] Al-Qadi's Tutankhamen, in contrast, gained unprecedented mass popularity to the extent that Munira al-Mahdiya and Naʿima al-Misriya, two Egyptian divas of the day, competed in singing two *taqtuqas* (light popular songs) commemorating the ancient Egyptian king.[52] Apparently in pursuit of the vogue of the time, al-Qadi's Tutankhamen *zajal*, sung by Munira al-Mahdiya, has clear political implications that were in tune with an emergent neo-Pharaonism that as Frédéric Lagrange puts it, "infiltrated the hearts of people who considered the pharaohs as their ancestors."[53]

Global factors that include the rise of progressive ideas such as national freedom and self-determination, the end of an annihilating world war that coincided with an upsurge in cultural capitalism's highly lucrative popular entertainment industries, combined with local factors such as a looming revolution against British colonialism coupled with intense nationalistic sentiments all informed how ancient or Pharaonic Egypt should be envisioned in the cultural production of modern Egyptians, both high- and low-brow, particularly in the 1920s and 1930s. One of the best literary works that represents the era's Egyptian Egyptomania (materialized as Pharaonism) is Tawfiq al-Hakim's chef-d'oeuvre novel *ʿAwdat al-Ruh* (*Return of the Spirit*), written in 1927, and published in 1933. Al-Hakim's Egyptomania is not illustrated only in his allusions to the myth of Isis and Osiris, and the recurrent use of the *Book of the Dead*, but also in the way ancient Egyptian mythology is re-envisioned to propagate a parallel "rebirth" of the modern Egyptian nation "after millennia of national eclipse,"[54] which would only be realized by the modern Egyptians' 1919 revolution.

Along with al-Hakim, there are other writers who invested in Pharaonism aesthetically, whether in their dramas as in the works of ʿAli Ahmad Bakathir and Ahmad Zaki Abu Shadi or their fiction as in the work of ʿAdil Kamil and Naguib

Mahfouz. Although such aesthetic investment was predominantly engulfed in political overtones, there existed a few instances of exaltation of Pharaonism for ostensibly apolitical, aesthetic reasons. Together with the politically charged Pharaonic poems of Shawqi, Hafiz Ibrahim, al-Tunisi, and al-Qadi, there were likewise poems (and other literary works) which celebrated ancient Egyptian art (mainly sculpture) from a particularly aesthetic perspective. Khalil Mutran's "Waqfa fi Zil Timthal li-Ra'msis al-Kabir" (Standing in the Shadow of the Statue of Great Ramses) (al-Muqtataf, 1924), "Isis aw al-Husn al-Khalid" (Isis, Or Immortal Beauty) (al- Hilal, 1928), along with Abu Shadi's Egypt-themed pictorial poems published in al-Muqtataf and Abullu in the years 1929–34 were written in commemoration of immortal (majestic) beauty embodied in ancient Egyptian sculpture and architecture. Such exaltation of, or obsession with, the legendary beauty of ancient Egyptian art has been common in the work of authors, say, from Belzoni to Hafiz Ibrahim, yet the difference made by the work of Mutran and Abu Shadi and their likes lies in the emphasis laid on the extraordinariness, miraculousness, and immortality of the ancient Egyptian art in general.

An omnipresent and eternal ancient Egypt was not limited to ancient Egyptian art; it also embraced the ubiquity of ancient Egypt (civilization) itself. What is common in Egypt-themed fictional works published in the mid and late 1930s such as Mohammad 'Awad Mohammad's "al-Maqama al-Haramiya" (The Pyramidic Maqama) (al-Risala, 1934), Naguib Mahfouz's "Yaqazat al-Mumya'" (The Awakening of the Mummy) (al-Riwaya, 1939), Aziz Ahmad Fahmi's "Wahi Nefertiti" (Nefertiti's Revelation) (al-Risala, 1939), and Mahmud Taymur's "Fir'awn al-Saghir" (The Young Pharaoh) (1939) is not only that the Pharaonic spirit is still alive or the enduring presence of ancient Egypt in today's Egypt[55] but also the idea that ancient Egypt is universal and global, with charms and wonders that appeal to everyone. The author of "al-Maqama al-Haramiya" uses the Arabic maqama form and even the celebrated narrator Isa ibn Hisham to present a debate between the Great Pyramid and one of contemporary America's skyscrapers. Irrespective of the immediate message that portrays the ancient Egyptian civilization as superior to the modern "American" civilization, a subtler message implies that ancient Egypt is not appreciated per se, but also, more importantly, if compared with another civilization, especially the Western civilization. A similar juxtaposition is illustrated in Taymur's "Fir'awn al-Saghir." America is present here again, but this time as "a beautiful, mature and overpowering American divorcée, who combines a mystical enthusiasm for things Egyptian with high-class seduction."[56] Although Taymur chooses to cast the story into a soap-opera-like form that could even be labeled as a "romantic kitsch," most probably to appeal to the avid readers of the popular fiction of the day, he appeared to emphasize a more serious message: an eternal Egypt is present, with its "unique and uniquely abiding civilization."[57]

On a similar vein, global appeal to ancient Egypt as represented in modern (short) fiction is likewise exhibited in one of Mahfouz's early short stories titled "Yaqazat al-Mumya'." Obsession with Egyptian antiquities shows in the characterization of the Francophone Turco-Egyptian protagonist. The recurrent theme of eternal Egypt is emphasized by highlighting some striking resemblance between a wretched Upper Egyptian peasant and Hur's newly discovered mummy. To label Mahfouz's story as a work representing Egyptian mummymania is a statement to ponder upon. It could be argued that "Yaqazat al-Mumya'" is the earliest Arabic literary work to feature ancient Egyptian mummies. In this piece of work, Mahfouz managed to mingle features of global Egyptomania/mummymania with those of an idiosyncratic, nascent Egyptian mummymania. While he did not miss to accentuate the enigmatic and mysterious ambience that shrouded the discovery of the ancient Egyptian tomb/mummy, Mahfouz was likewise keen to give voice to his neo-Pharaonism through his Egyptian mummy mouthpiece. The very resurrection of the mummy echoes al-Hakim's return of the Pharaonic spirit in his debut.

Chapter 9

THE EARLY EGYPTIAN FILM INDUSTRY AND THE FORMATION OF NATIONALITY

STUDYING MUHAMMAD KARIM'S *ZAYNAB* AS A VISION OF MODERN STANDARDS

Thana al-Shakhs

Egypt is known for being one of the most important gateways to the film industry in the Arab world. Despite its centrality to the history of Arabic cinema, determining the starting point of Egyptian cinema is often viewed as problematic because the formats and technologies of filmmaking, as a new form of art, were introduced to Egyptian audiences by British and French investors during the British occupation. Early films produced in Egypt by British and French companies presented the local culture and characters through colonial vision. Even when local companies were established, a British influence over film content remained hard-wearing. Therefore, determining the starting point of Egyptian cinema became an attempt to identify the cultural shift from following colonial examples to inventing a local vision. Critics interested in the history of Egyptian cinema such as Ahmad El-Hadari and Mahmoud Qasim suggest that local Arab cinema in Egypt started in the 1920s, thus sidelining earlier iterations as ones produced by "foreign" filmmakers. The origin of filmmakers became a major concern, especially that early practices in filmmaking were produced by conceivably Egyptians of foreign origin. This issue of origin occurred later when the notion of national identity and authenticity developed and resulted in a revision of the history of local cinema and re-classification of films.

To understand the historical context of the birth of Egyptian cinema, the main historical events ought to be listed. Egypt, while remaining an autonomous province in the Ottoman Empire with Khedival rulers, came under the British "Veiled Protectorate" in 1882. After the First World War and the first Egyptian Revolution of 1919 against the British occupation, Egypt's independence was declared in 1922 while several regional Arab countries, some of which were former Ottoman territories, including Syria, Lebanon, Algeria, and Tunisia, were still under colonial rule.[1] Thus, Egyptian cinema was born during a period of ardent resistance against the colonial, political, and intellectual dominance of Britain and France on one hand, and the long influence of the Ottoman Empire on the other hand.[2]

British and French companies produced films in Egypt with a colonial perspective such as *Fi Bilad Tut Ankh Amon* (*In Tutankhamen's Country*) by a British company and the French unpublished film on Prophet Muhammad's story. Other foreign companies such as Condor Film run by the Palestinian-Chilean brothers Ibrahim and Badr Lama were also criticized for offering a colonial perspective by adapting European, especially British, materials and misrepresenting local characters. On their part, Egyptian filmmakers of the early twentieth century such as Youssef Wahbi and Aziza Amir sought to offer what was a perceivably original reflection of local identity to reject the image presented by French and British film companies. Egyptian cinema's early efforts were celebrated by other Arab countries under colonial rules as a step toward self-representation that objected to colonial representation. Ella Schochat illustrates the wide-reaching impact of Egyptian cinema in the region; she writes, "The French in the Maghreb, for example, formed a 'special department' on African problems that was 'responsible for setting up a production center in Morocco whose official mission was to oppose the influence of Egyptian cinema.'"[3]

This chapter focuses on the early filmmaking practices and films produced after the British recognition of Egypt's independence in 1922 and before the 1952 revolution when the process of Egypt's transition from a constitutional monarchy to a republic started and was officially declared on June 18, 1953.[4] By investigating the role of the early Egyptian film industry in forming a public perception of local identity, this chapter considers the interaction that occurred between film production companies and the public, from members of the general audience to middle class and elite intellectuals. Although we can claim that all types of art involve a level of interaction with the public and cultural taste,[5] the film industry, as a popular entertaining platform, relies more on attracting crowds and creating positive reactions that increase ticket sales and profits. Additionally, cinema has an intellectual impact on a wide-scale audience, including the uneducated population, because it deals with local concerns, struggles, and dreams. This focus on national representation and concerns leads the study to avoid discussing films shot in urban settings where the influence of the Western lifestyle appears. During the early independence era in the twenties and thirties, intellectuals tended to show a modified and developed version of their nation to counter the colonial representation. Thus, rural settings that exemplified local concerns and lifestyles became more problematic. This chapter attempts to answer questions such as how the rural setting presented in early independence Egyptian cinema served in creating an imaginary image of national identity. The study does not attempt to reveal a concrete definition of nationalism during that early era after independence but to shed light on the public conception of national identity.

This chapter will discuss the intellectual environment that informed the formation of early Egyptian cinema and the varied local concerns that were negotiated through, and in response to, film productions. I will focus on films that were shot in the Egyptian desert and the Nile Valley for two main reasons. First, the environment that was chosen by filmmakers was meant to create an illusion of "originality" or "authenticity" given the mostly imported nature of film and cinema as imported mediums and forms of entertainment. In deserts and Nile villages, native Egyptians lived with no access to modern standards available in Egypt's urban centers in which local Egyptians were introduced to foreign practices. Accordingly, filmmakers presented this environment as a valid context of authenticity. Second, films that were shot in Egypt's local landscape are the ones that most scholars of Egyptian cinema recognize as the first authentically Egyptian films. Thus, the chosen environment, I mean desert and Nile villages, played an essential role in the classification of films, as Egyptian or otherwise, which is a controversial practice because it does not follow a fixed set of standards. Changes to these standards often occur as a result of developing the conception of national identity, which is a political process. However, important works such as Mahmoud Qasim's *Mawsu'at al-sinima al-'Arabiyya* (*Encyclopedia of the Arab Cinema*) classified films into two main categories: Egyptian films and European films that involved colonial perspectives.[6] The process of classification went through a long-term dialogue between films and local reception, including critical and popular reactions. Even though film classifications appeared later after the time of film production, they are still valid to examine the reception process.

The following sections will include brief discussions of Aziza Amir's *Layla* (1927), Ibrahim Lama's *Qubla Fi al-Sahra'* (*Kiss in the Desert*) (1927), and his *Ghadat al-Sahara* (*Belle of the Desert*) (1929). This chapter also takes up a detailed discussion of the 1930 film *Zaynab*, because it shows an important transition of film location from the desert to the Nile Valley. The film, which was directed by Muhammad Karim and produced by Youssef Wahbi's Ramses Company for Cinema Production, was adapted from a local novel written by Muhammad Hussein Haykal.[7] The novel's first edition was published in 1914 under Haykal's pen name "Masri Fallah" (Peasant Egyptian).[8] While the 1929 edition was published under his name, one year before the release of the film,[9] the second edition of the novel was widely celebrated by local media, especially since Haykal was a co-founder and the editor-in-chief of *al-Siyasa al-Usbu'iyya* newspaper which represented the Liberal Constitutionalist party. Under the impact of his political and intellectual position, the novel was received as a sincere conception of national identity.

Early Film Practices and the Intellectual Reality in Egypt

During the late nineteenth century and the beginning of the twentieth century, Egypt's intellectual reality was influenced by two major factors: Ottoman traditions and the British colonial system; the local experience of modernism was born out of this combination. Additionally, Western-style education became more popular among elites due to the mounting number of European schools in Egypt, leading, in turn, to a growing tendency among Egyptians of the time to pursue their education in Europe. Although most Egyptian intellectuals received local education in their youth, they were introduced to Western higher education later. Leading intellectuals such as Taha Hussein, Ahmad Hasan al-Zayyat, and Ibrahim Naji have a level of appreciation for Western modernism along with their local tradition. The role of capitalism must not be underestimated in this process because intellectual institutions are most often private organizations that seek benefits to ensure their survival and future development. Higher education institutions, press houses, theaters, and cinema perform as a means of both enlightenment and economic development. This starting point justifies the imitation of Western intellectual trends and artistic production by the film industry during this historical era.

Under these intellectual and social conditions, the moving picture first arrived in Egypt in the late nineteenth century when the French brothers Auguste and Louise Lumière brought their motion picture camera, the Cinématograph, to Alexandria.[10] During this time, silent films were primitive in their technique with no subtitles, while occasionally a recorded music was played to accompany the show. Such films were screened for free in cafés. It was a way to attract customers, encourage them to linger, and increase the owner's revenue. Foreign films, especially French and British films, became increasingly popular. However, there was sometimes a cultural gap to bridge between Egyptian viewers and the aesthetic and context of these foreign films, which required that café owners occasionally hire commentators to explain the films.[11]

As cinema became more popular, through the emergence of cinema houses, owned by French, British, or other foreign companies, competition for local audiences increased. As a means of entertainment, cinema houses sought profits and expansion, and advertisements became necessary. Under such circumstances, local Egyptian cinema emerged. In an article published in 1932 in *al-Sabah* magazine, cinemagoer Hassan Eid writes about his experience when he first visited Ramses Cinema in Cairo, which was founded by the local actor, director, and writer Youssef Wahbi in 1931. Eid confirms that this cinema's seat capacity and the number of films it displayed were comparable to those of foreign cinema houses in Egypt. He interviewed the manager, who explained that the house was less popular than those of foreign companies because the latter are stronger in the market. The manager also claimed that other companies intentionally created obstacles to obstruct Ramses Cinema's expansion into the local market, such as covering over this local cinema's printed film advertisements or increasing the costs of the foreign films that were available for local cinemas to purchase rights to project on their screens.[12] The domination of foreign companies on the local market led local intellectuals to view supporting Egyptian filmmakers and cinemas as a form of nationalism. This included the publication of articles in support of local filmmaking as integral to national identity, as seen in Salah Abu Sayf's article "Al-sinima fi Misr sina'a qawmiya yajib himayatuha,"[13] (cinema in Egypt is a national industry that must be protected), which was published in *al-Sabah* magazine in 1932.[14]

The competition between local and foreign companies led to concerns with the classification of films. However, it was difficult for critics to classify Egyptian films and foreign films produced in Egypt. To illustrate, in his *Mawsu'at al-sinima al-'Arabiyya*, 1994 edition, and *Dalil al-aflam fi al-qarn al-'ishrin fi Misr wa al-'alam al-'Arabi* (*Twentieth Century Films' Guide of Egypt and the Arab World*), 2002, Mahmoud Qasim considered the documentary film that reports the discovery of Tutankhamun's tomb, *Fi Bilad Tut Ankh Amon* (In Tutankhamen's Country), shot in 1923, to be the first Egyptian film. Assigning the film status as the first Egyptian film was a decision influenced by Ahmad El-Hadari's *Tarikh al-sinima fi Misr* (*The History of Cinema in Egypt*) (1989). However, Qasim determined later that the film's perspective on Egypt was distinctly foreign. He believes that true Egyptian cinema was launched with the 1927 films: *Layla* and *Qubla Fi al-Sahra'* or *Kiss in the Desert*.[15] He updated his *Mawsu'at al-sinima* in 2004 with a new classification. Qasim's works, especially *Tarikh al-sinima al-Misriya* (*The History of Egyptian Cinema*), are critical references in this study as the author was exposed to a rich archive of materials related to cinema and literature. He offers an extended list of early Egyptian films considering the chronological order and gives details about the casts, production companies, and examples of intellectual reactions as published in the local press. Focusing on the local film industry, Qasim disconnected between Egyptian films and foreign films produced in Egypt, revealing the standards of the local intellectual stream as seen in local magazines.

This disconnect between foreign and local industries was determined by two factors: the origin of the producer and the contents of the film. The documentary film, *In Tutankhamen's Country*, was directed by Victor Rosito, an Italian expatriate living in Egypt who had no experience in filmmaking. Additionally, the film was funded by British investors. Thus, Qasim classifies it as a colonial film but says it was the first film *about* Egypt. Qasim confirms that such colonial work misrepresented Egyptians, however, he did not offer further details on this comment.[16] On the other hand, *Layla*, filmed by the local producer Aziza Amir, shows an appropriate representation of Egyptian national identity. However, Qasim does not offer further details on how *Layla* represents the national identity.[17]

Layla succeeded, in the eyes of local media, in representing the national identity because it proves the local capacity to establish a local film industry. The film was directed by the Turkish-Egyptian director Wedad Urfi, who was later replaced by Estafan Rosti, and the last part of the film was directed by Aziza Amir.[18] The film was produced by the Isis Film Corporation established by Aziza Amir with the contribution of Wedad Urfi, who had experience in production and direction in a French company. Urfi came to Egypt as a representative of the French film production company to produce films about Egypt's Pharaonic and Arab history. Ironically, in his interview with *al-Masrah* magazine in 1926, he showed no interest in joining local actors in the project. He justified that the company had first-class professional actors and no need for new participants.[19] He later collaborated with Amir in their production of *Layla* and participated as a director and lead actor alongside her. In 1927, another interview with Urfi showed a completely different point of view about Egyptian actors. He expressed his great admiration for *Layla*'s cast and crew, especially Amir. He confirmed that based on his long experience in the industry, he could tell that Amir was an exceptionally smart actress.[20] Urfi's opinion as an experienced director was influential, considering the competition between foreign and local filmmakers. Local efforts got to their way to create wide-scale recognition.

However, Amir's ambition was concerning for some of the film critics; *Ruz al-Yusuf* published an article in which an unidentified author questioned the goal of the film. The author quoted Amir's perceptions of the film as a national project and argued that Amir was not up to this serious venture. Fame and money, the author went on to state, were very likely Amir's goals in this adventure and that involving the nation's reputation in the project would be a huge risk. For this particular critic, foreign spectators were also cited as a major concern for they may use the film to critique Egyptian culture and identity. The author continues by referring to the manager of the Cinema and Acting Company, Tal'at Harb,[21] who says that Egypt does not have the professional capacity yet to start film production. The author was aware of the national responsibility held by filmmakers. Therefore, he was against the risk.[22] Three months after the publication of this article, another article was published to describe the first show with the title, "'Aziza Amir ba'd kasb al-ma'raka" ("Aziza Amir after Winning the Battle"). Put in the words of this unidentified author, "the walls of Metropole Cinema were shaken by the audience's applause."[23] He, or she, continues to claim that the film was a foundation of a local film industry, produced and directed by Egyptians. He describes Amir's reaction, smile, and tears when she was asking congratulators for feedback to consider in future projects.[24] This success occurred by the public support and verification of the quality of the film. Thus, the film was described as a successful representation of national identity.

While *Layla* was received by audiences and critics as a national project, *Qubla Fi al-Sahra'* or *Kiss in the Desert* was more controversial in terms of its national identification. Qasim explains that the film is directed by Ibrahim Lama, who is originally Palestinian and produced by Condor Film, established by the Lama brothers, the main characters were Badr Lama and the foreign actress Yvonne Goeine. He adds that the film is directly adopted from *The Son of the Sheik*, a novel written by Edith Maude Hull and an American film directed by George Fitzmaurice.[25] In an article published in *Ruz al-Yusuf* magazine without an identified author, the film was described as a dangerous representation of Egypt. The author approved that the film was not Egyptian as claimed in the film advertisement. He, or she, confirms the foreign origin of the film company, director, and cast and notes that the producer created a false impression regarding the origin of the film when he changed the director's name from Abraham to Ibrahim, to match local names. Additionally, he used the photo of Ibrahim Zulfikar, the only Egyptian actor in the film who performs a secondary role before the photo of the main character in the advertisement sequence. This false advertisement proves that the local origin of a film was a key factor to attract spectators. The author continues that the content of the film proves European ideation about Oriental cultures as it represents locals as gangs who risk their lives to steal unworthy belongings from tourists. He highlights the colonial vision in discussing the costumes used in the film that represent Moroccan soldiers in the French army more than Egyptians. The observations shown in the article confirm the strong presence of European filmmakers and spectators that contributes to misrepresenting the local culture.[26]

The debate over what determined Egyptian filmmaking practices reveals the significance of intellectual independence in assigning a film as Egyptian, which was no less important than political independence at that time. Thus, establishing a local film industry was a dream of the young generation who admired this new entertainment means brought by foreign filmmakers to Egypt.[27] According to Mahmoud Qasim, in the early thirties, filmmakers were keen to inspire public support of local cinema as a nationalist mission. He explains that this nationalist mission was the responsibility of both local filmmaking companies and the viewing public. While the role of filmmakers was to use available techniques to produce films of the best possible quality, the audience's task was to contribute to publicizing local production.[28] The audience's corroboration ought to promote the local film industry, not simply a few individual films. Thus, the artistic value of a film was less important than its expression of national identity. The Egyptian film industry was characterized in some press coverage, quoted by Qasim, as representative of Egypt to the world.[29] The author offers an example of a film advertisement that confirms the Egyptian origin of the filmmakers, cast, dramatist, story, language, locations, and budget. This confirmation is followed by a call for the national support needed to promote the local industry.[30] Even when Egyptian films were released that did not meet the audience's expectations, as in the case of *Su'ad al-Ghajariya* (*Su'ad The Gypsy*), released in 1928, newspapers encouraged the audience to watch it for a week to support local production.[31] Notably, the nationality of the film was determined by the origin of the company, cast, and budget. This classification is justified by the need for a starting point from which the local cinema will start, even though the influence of Western intellect on Egyptian filmmakers was acknowledged by the press.

Early Critical Practices

Colonial history and the fresh sense of independence influences early critical practices. Critics objected to the impact of Western culture on films classified as Egyptian, especially since cinema was introduced to the local market by British and French companies and local filmmakers were still charmed by Western education and lifestyles. Additionally, cinema was originally a field dominated by almost the exclusive purview of Western filmmakers. Egyptian filmmakers learned the principles of cinema from the Western experience. Critics noted this powerful influence. For example, in his comments on *Ghadat al-Sahara* (*Belle of the Desert*), released in 1929, Qasim remarked that the desert costume worn by the Bedouin was accompanied by Western-branded accessories such as jewelry and shoes. He added that Arabic coffee was served in German cups and consumed in one gulp after raising the cups in a toast-like attitude, which is not an Arabic custom. Furthermore, the few tents on the film's set, allegedly there to house the whole tribe, as well as the lack of water, trees, or desert animals, show an unrealistic image of desert life.[32] Despite such a cultural disconnect between the filmmakers and the content, Qasim still considers the film to be Egyptian. He believes that showing a favorable and generous view of the local characters stands in opposition to colonial presentations of Egyptian character, which were negative and belittling.

However, he mentions that a betrayal that is part of the film's plot supports a bigoted colonial image, as it attributes immoral qualities to Egyptians.

This glimpse at an early example of critical practice establishes some standards of evaluation to which the local film industry would respond. Critical discussions published in local magazines show that critics believed that successful presentations of Egyptian identity ought to involve anticolonial images. The mission of establishing anticolonialism in Egyptian films was highly valued and placed creativity and other factors commonly considered part of good filmmaking in a secondary position. The national image as portrayed on film was meant to reach beyond the borders of Egypt and inspire worldwide consideration of the country and its people. Therefore, critics were concerned with modifying reality to match an idealized portrayal but still somewhat authentic representation of local values, culture, and lifestyle. The critical voices influenced the public's reaction to films. Some articles in the newspapers were published without the authors' names making these individual observations seem like sincere defenses of national character.[33] Thus, the intellectual support of cinema involved the mission of resistance against colonial representation of Egyptians. Such a concept played an important role in forming the public reaction to films and offered national standards to which film producers ought to aspire.

Accordingly, two opposing but interrelated factors influenced cinematic practices: seeking an ideal representation of characters to fulfill the resistance mission and the powerful impact of Western culture on local filmmakers. Considering that literary authors, critics, and filmmakers had received their education abroad or in foreign schools in urban settings following Western principles, the ideal representation of characters, though idealized, could not be free from Western standards, or more precisely "modern" standards. The conflict between local tradition and modern principles appeared in Egyptian films, especially that filmmakers tended to produce their works in locations such as deserts and farms focusing on a simple and an uneducated population and their lifestyle. This environment allows filmmakers to criticize the native reality and its tradition. However, tradition has the quality of maintaining local morals which filmmakers highlight in their idealized representation of national identity. In other words, the goal of delivering a virtual image of local identity affected the fictional characterization. To illustrate, an identified critic criticized *Qubla Fi al-Sahra'* because it presented Arabs as bandits; local police lacked work ethics, and some actresses dressed in indecent costumes.[34] For this point of view, the focus on the characters' morality is more important than the offered story. When immoral attitudes became controversial, and characters were idealized, conflicts between characters lost their interesting complexity. Involving immoral actions, such as banditry, within dramatic conflicts is unavoidable. Thus, flat characters and simple plots were popular. Filmmakers focused on presenting beautiful natural scenery as a part of producing an ideal image of Egypt, and the visual aspect of some films became more creative than dramatic events, as seen in *Zaynab*.

Early Egyptian cinema adapted Western literary and film sources and shifted the stories, culture, names, locations, traditions, and other geographically and culturally specific details to align with Egyptian social norms. *Qubla Fi al-Sahra'* is a good example of this adaptation since it was adapted from Edith Maud Hull's novel *The Son of the Sheik* (1925), which was produced as an American silent film in 1926. Thus, the visual aspect played a considerable role in this cultural translation from Western to Egyptian. However, the introduction of new cultural values accompanied the process. Modern values were presented as a necessary adaptation to the coming historical and intellectual era and gained legitimacy by depicting carefully crafted conversations about local tradition and religion.[35] To illustrate, the popularity of romantic films titled after the names of female protagonists, as seen in *Zaynab*, reveals a new tendency, at the time, to prioritize individualism and personal dreams over the more traditional valuing of community well-being over individual happiness.

Zaynab

The film *Zaynab*, the first film adapted from an Egyptian novel, was produced in 1930. People were inclined to respect the film adaptation because it was written by Muhammad Hussein Haykal, a nationalist figure and an important politician. The book was not considered a remarkable work in Egyptian literature until the publication of the second edition in 1929 and the film production in 1930. Both the novel and the film were followed by intellectual celebration by Haykal's weekly political journal *al-Siyasa al-Usbu'iyya*. Additionally, in 1930, Hamilton Gibb, an English Orientalist and a colleague of Haykal, published an argument that claims that *Zaynab* is the first authentic Egyptian novel.[36] Elliott Colla justifies this political intellectual celebration; he writes,

> The 1929 reproduction of *Zaynab* in print and in cinema needs to be understood in light of the 1919 Revolution and the subsequent shift from popular, direct politics to the representational, party politics of the Egyptian Parliament. This was a shift in which the struggles between the British, the King, the dominant Wafd party and the smaller opposition parties necessitated rapid shifts in representational strategies. It partly explains why, after letting his novel lie dormant for so long, Haykal would resurrect it so quickly to remake the Pharaonic face of his Liberal Constitutionalist party into that of a Muslim peasant.[37]

However, this celebration did not reveal the fact that the plot lacks twisted turns of events. In an article published in *Ruz al-Yusuf* a few weeks after the first show under the title "*Zaynab* 'la al-shasha al-bayda," the writer, unidentified, confirms that the film was boring in a way that the audience might take a nap, according to his or her expression, while Zaynab walks to the local market because it shows too many photos of the landscape before she arrives. Despite the writer's awareness that the film was meant to advertise the Egyptian landscape, he still complained about the lack of interesting events.[38] Thus, the film failed to entertain the audience. However, the media successfully managed to introduce

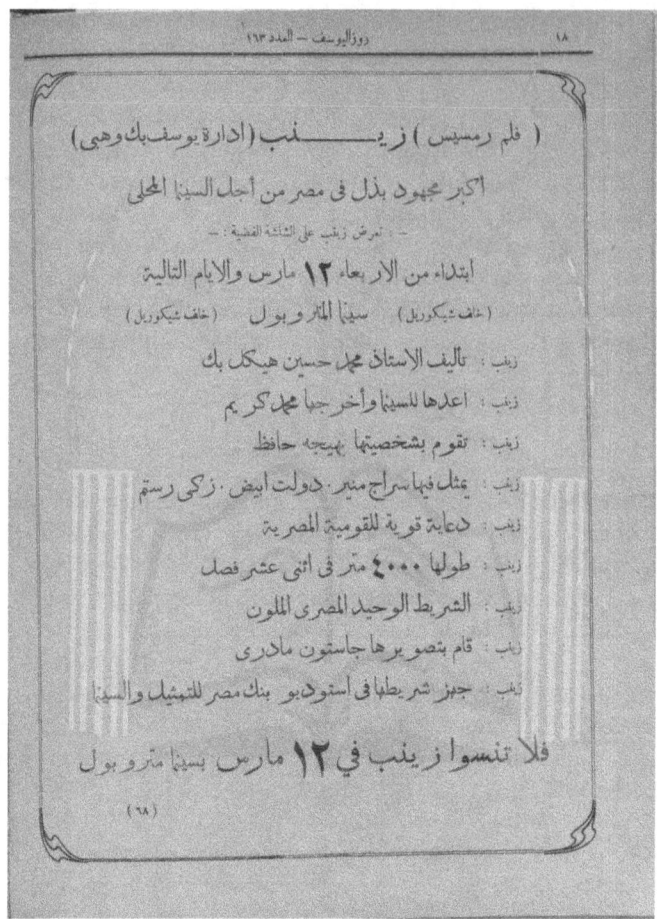

Figure 9.1 *Zaynab*'s film advertisement, *Ruz al-Yusuf*, March 11, 1930. Al-Babtain Library for Arabic Poetry, Kuwait.

it as a crucial moment in the local cinema history, as seen in the advertisement (Figure 9.1).

In addition to the political aspect, the fact that the film was adapted from a local novel, *Zaynab*, created a positive impression among intellectuals. Salma Mubarak and Walid El Khachab demonstrate that in the early twentieth century, there was a common assumption that literature is superior to cinema. Accordingly, cinema relied heavily on novels to invest them with intellectual validity.[39] Additionally, novels were considered a legitimate source of realistic visions that function as an important reference for the local filmmakers.[40] The authors insist that successful films in this era needed to portray realism as well as deal with social concerns, just as novels did. Thus, the early Egyptian film industry used literature, including Western works, to justify the validity of the content presented and to inspire an intellectual consideration of a literary cinematic narrative. However, film producers were very selective in choosing their literary sources, and here the filmmaker's voice appears.[41] One may argue that by adapting literature and relying on the public's tendency to respect it without question, filmmakers were easing their sense of responsibility for their films' portrayal of conflict, characters, and events.

While announcing Haykal's name in the second edition increased the popularity of the novel, one must not disregard the pen name effect. The author identified himself as a "Peasant Egyptian" creating an impression that it represents the thoughts and ideas of the average Egyptian citizen even though he wrote it while he was in Europe. This pen name functioned to hide the actual gap between his lived experience and the story he tells. This gap existed between most intellectuals, including authors, critics, journalists, and filmmakers, and the average public, or, in this case, peasants. Although Haykal's pen name does not involve a sincere realistic representation from the artistic perspective, it serves a radical political goal and attempts to redefine Egyptian identity. Haykal writes that he has intentionally used the word *Egyptian* prior to *Peasant* to avoid using the former as an adjective. In Arabic, adjectives follow nouns, and having the word *Egyptian* first means that the novel is not about an Egyptian who is described as a peasant. Accordingly, the pen name is translated into "Peasant Egyptian" where the adjective is peasant, and the character is Egyptian.

Haykal intends to distinguish between two types of local identity: peasants and landowners versus upper-class nobles who often have foreign roots and claim eligibility to rule.[42] According to this, Haykal argues that Egyptians are the natives who are rooted in the Nile Valley landscape, while the upper-class nobles are excluded. Thus, the author's conception of nationality stands on a political shift, not a simple representation of lower-class individuals. Before discussing the film in greater detail, it is important to look at the significance of the rural setting.

Rural Narrative in the Novel and Film[43]

In the nineteenth century, agriculture, always paramount in the Egyptian economy, developed significantly and became the choice sector for investment. The Egyptian countryside, stitched with farms, was the iconic image of Egyptian life and culture and also an ever more dominant theme in the social discourse and political ideology throughout the twentieth century. Since peasants were marginalized for centuries, this shift in focus had substantial repercussions and brought about a new conception of local identity.[44]

Local literature also turned its focus to peasants and rural settings. In Haykal's introduction to *Zaynab*, the author explains that he wanted to produce a rural narrative to educate people in cities about their country.[45] The rural narrative does not speak to peasants but about them. Presenting rural life as an essential part of the local heritage leads to romanticizing its images, values, and conflicts to create a respected vision of the national identity that can be world-widely accepted and embraced and stand against Egypt's colonial image. Hence, the word *peasant* became a national watchword. However, the intellectual mission of rural narratives—educating urban society about rural life—requires a focus on stable elements such as cultural tradition and landscape but cannot involve the complexity of conflicts. This idea will be further discussed in the section about how the novel presented national identity.

This intellectual vision influenced the local film industry, at the time still dominated by foreign investors and expected to reflect the national resistance against colonialism. The countryside appeared as an appropriate setting for creating a national vision and describing the conflict between past and present. Mubarak confirms that the words "peasant" and "countryside" were used frequently in films produced in the 1930s and 1940s even though their content was often primarily about urban life.[46] Capitalism and the influence of the Western civilization explains the popularity of urban content in the local film industry. Even in such contexts, filmmakers showed the needed recognition of the role of peasants and the countryside to support the nationalist mission.

In *Zaynab*, both the novel and the film, landscape was prioritized over story and character. The full title of the novel is *Zaynab manazir wa akhlaq rifiyya*, or *Zaynab Rural Landscapes and Manners*, while the film was introduced as an advertisement for rural landscape in Egypt. The story is flat and lacks plot development or conflict. The description in the novel highlights the beauty of the pastoral scenery since Haykal belongs to a landowner family in the Delta and spent a considerable period of his life in the countryside. In his introduction to the novel, Haykal confirms that he wrote it while he was in Europe yearning to be home. He adds that whenever he saw the beautiful natural landscapes of Switzerland, he went to his notebook and wrote passages of the novel.[47] Haykal's sense of belonging and yearning motivated him to compete with the European landscape with an imaginary version of his native landscape, a fact that will be demonstrated later. Such a context justifies the romantic filter through which Haykal viewed the Egyptian countryside and how that vision influenced his writing.

The 1930 version of the film was also produced with a similar motivation. Muhammad Karim was abroad when he decided to adapt the novel. In his memoir, the director writes about a sense of belonging and yearning like that of Haykal, feelings that motivated him to adapt the novel.[48] Unlike Haykal, however, Karim had never been in the countryside before making the film. When he traveled to Haykal's town, he was surprised by a reality that did not match the novel's description. He found that the peasants lived in a dirty environment that was hard to romanticize. He saw the squalor as an obstacle to overcome. He paid to have the streets washed and the animals cleaned.[49] He also filmed some scenes on the well-fostered private property of Muhammad Haqqi in the village of Inshas.[50] Karim exerted considerable efforts in choosing the film locations to depict agrarian beauty. He succeeded because most critics agreed that the visual images of the film were its best element, though the story was weak.[51]

This focus on visual imagery over plot is true of the novel as well, in which extended passages of well-crafted prose describe the landscape, while the development of character and the plot was weak, a minor concern to the author. Thus, both the author and the director followed the same aesthetics. While, in his introduction, Haykal confirms that he wanted to educate Egyptians about their land, the fact that the description is less than truthful suggests that he was more interested in encouraging them to take pride in their origins than in educating them about the realities of rural life. Karim responded to Haykal's call and followed in his footsteps. Although Karim realizes that the novel does not show the reality of peasant life, he understands that such a modified image is important to amplify the idea of the countryside as the nation's iconic representation. The purpose of both works was to create an inspiring idea, not an actual vision of the real Egyptian rural landscape. The "invented" landscape helped the novel and the film gain the attention of others; developing honest national self-awareness was still not a major concern. The priority of spreading an idea of an idealized Egypt beyond its borders was created by a sense of belonging and the importance of resisting the image of Egypt as a colonial entity. Additionally, romanticizing the land fits well with the yearning that modern Egyptians, including the author and the director, experienced when they were in Europe and urban centers, and motivates them to return to their origins. This sense of belonging explains what Mubarak noticed about the contents of the films produced before 1952 in which characters leave the countryside only to return and help create positive change.[52]

Critiques

As the visual aspect of this film improved the image of Egypt successfully, critics focused on the story, which presents hopeless love when the peasant young woman Zaynab falls in love with Ibrahim, another peasant young man, but marries Hasan in an arranged marriage. She does not resist the marriage, though her yearning for Ibrahim disrupts her married life devoted to her duties as a wife. She cannot overcome her misery, gets sick, and eventually dies. Qasim confirms that the story was a real story that happened in the village of Kafr Al Ghunamiyya in 1896.[53] This confirmation shows, at least, that the story is plausible within the cultural context.

Raja' al-Naqqash offers an interesting insight into the topic of hopeless love shown in *Zaynab*. He confirms that the film represents the beginning of a dominant stream in early Egyptian cinema. After the success of *Zaynab*, Karim directed *Dumu' al-Hubb* or *Love Tears* in 1936, adapted from the French novel *Sous les Tilleuls* (1832) by Jean-Baptiste Alphonse Karr, translated to Arab readers by the Egyptian writer, poet, and translator Mustafa Lutfi al-Manfaluti under the title *Magdoline* or *Under the Shadows of the Linden Tree*. Al-Naqqash explains that during this era, the Egyptian society rebelled against the traditional conservative rules, and the topic of emotional suppression was increasingly popular among local writers, especially authors who are influenced by the Western romantic stream. Thus, such popularity influenced Egyptian cinema production.[54]

Qasim informs that some critics, such as Habib Jamati, supported the story of the film while others believed that the story misrepresented the local culture.

Qasim discusses an article written by an anonymous writer using the pen name, *Misri* "Egyptian," who insists that the film must not be screened outside Egypt because it offers an inappropriate image of Egyptians. He argues that local traditions, religion, and morals were misrepresented, which would adversely affect Egypt's reputation, especially since Egypt was in a crucial moment creating her space among civilized nations. The author insists that the traditional mores presented in the film do not exist in real society. The writer does not justify this point but moves to the negative influence of this traditional image on outsiders who may see the film. In terms of religion, the author points out a woman's right to choose her husband in Islam. In discussing the moral tone of the film, he criticizes the scenes where the married woman, Zaynab, meets with her beloved, asserting that such actions are not appropriate and should not be attributed to an Egyptian woman.[55]

This reading of the character's conflict as an immoral attitude clarifies the lack of development in Zaynab's story. Plots progress through decisions that are made in reaction to events. Such decisions are controlled by motivations, and characters are very likely to make mistakes, resisting obstacles to fulfill their needs or desires. However, this national mission that expects the cinema to offer an ideal image of society and individuals rejects the use of mistakes and even obstacles in plots as they reveal weaknesses. Haykal was very careful in writing his novel. Zaynab does not make any strong protest against her marriage. She tries to accept her reality, but her emotions remain bound to her beloved. Haykal offers a simple conflict between tradition versus modernity represented by arranged marriage versus individual choice. For some critics, such as the one who writes as Egyptian, even this simple conflict was inappropriate for the era. The critic denies the continued existence of arranged marriages and says that shedding light on this issue does not help the nation in finding its space among modern urban societies. He writes his article with the Western readers in mind who would evaluate the local culture as uncivilized with outdated attitudes. He writes:

> Islam gives a girl the ultimate freedom in choosing her husband, and she can refuse marriage proposals [. . .] does Haykal deny that he writes about the mores of Islamic society where women do not have the freedom to choose a paramour and approach him? . . . Here, the Ministry of Interior which has the agency of monitoring morals must not allow exporting the film beyond Egypt's borders because the presented mores, attributed to Egyptians, will be ridiculed. We must understand the local culture as part of modern principles offering an honorable image to foreigners.[56]

Although the rural narrative is very important in raising others' considerations of Egypt's land and heritage, this heritage along with its traditions, contains, and practices might be used against Egypt. Thus, the critic *Misri* wanted Egypt to be presented as ideal, moral, religious, civilized, and modern, even if the story was about a simple peasant in the countryside.

This cultural complication that emerged after independence in 1922 suggests the reason for the shift from story to landscape, especially in the rural narrative where the modern standards are broken. The stability of the story and lack of developing events represent the silence that hides traditional complexity, which might be seen as weaknesses. Intellectuals, authors, filmmakers, and critics were still concerned about the unmodern version of Egypt. They understand its significance in building the national identity, but they use it as an abstract idea that avoids real representation and honest details. They want this heritage to appear as a beautiful background for modern reality. As the previous discussion showed, peasants in the film represent the subject for the expected viewers who were modern Egyptians and Westerners.

Haykal's Nationalism

Benjamin Geer offers a detailed study of Haykal's essay collection *Fi Awqat al-Faragh* or *During Free Times* where the latter discussed Qasim Amin as a model of local reformists and offered his notion of national literature that explains his conception of nationalism. I will highlight two important points that not only framed his notion of nationalism but also clarified the significance of the rural narrative in Haykal's literature. First, nature influences residents, more specifically natives. Second, national literature requires localism. While the first theme appeared clearly in his article about Qasim Amin,[57] the second dominated his discussion of the other article, "National Literature." In terms of the former, Haykal explains that the natural environment shapes the native character. Egypt has sunny, clear, and warm weather throughout the year. Native Egyptians have the same qualities. They are calm and submissive which allowed them to be led by foreigners throughout history. They have no ambition to change their reality. Haykal explains that Egyptian reformers such as Qasim Amin were introduced to different civilizations and environments, specifically French. Thus, Egyptian intellectuals educated abroad brought home new values such as being energetic, bold, ambitious, and imaginative.[58]

When discussing the values of localism, Haykal states that the problem of Egyptian literature, and Arabic literature in general, is that writers ignore the specificity of the local characteristics and assume that Arabic or Islamic civilizations represent one nation. Accordingly, Arabic literature, exactly like history, was written to please the ruling civilization. Haykal does not ignore the common characteristics among Arabic and Islamic nations, but he insists on the missing aspect of literature: locality. Accordingly, in *Zaynab*, he shed light on the local geography and setting, using localism as a means of nationalism.[59]

This national character is attributed to the environment of the Nile Valley where the population density is high. Notably, the author does not consider the desert a social environment that represents Egypt, but as a space that isolates the Nile Valley's social environment from its neighbors.[60] For him, the desert contributes to reducing the possibility of larger social interactions that allow change and development. Thus, the national image of Egypt appears in the agrarian environment and peasant character.

Although the novel was meant to represent the national identity in Egypt in the Nile Valley, the influence of French literature appeared clearly in the main character's monologue.[61] Haykal does not see any issue with such a foreign influence since he believes that European, specifically French, culture and literature helped create a bold, ambitious, and imaginative national character, and such characteristics play an important role in honing the skills of Egyptian national writers.[62] That is to say that during Haykal's time, Egyptian literature was still heavily influenced by European cultures, and the national character was less of a consideration among educated Egyptians who drew on European qualities, such as being bold and ambitious as seen in Haykal's article, to benefit their nation.

Zaynab *and National Identity in the Film Industry*

The most important influence Haykal had on the film industry in Egypt was moving the settings from the deserts to the Nile Valley since the image of the desert was a very important component in Western films and literature about Middle Eastern societies. Egyptian filmmakers followed models produced by Western producers until they were introduced to the rural narrative by Karim who adapted *Zaynab*. Qasim mentions that Egyptian cinema started with *Layla* in 1927.[63] *Kiss in the Desert* was also produced in the same year as *Layla*.[64] Both films were shot in the desert, according to the Western concept of a "typical" Middle Eastern environment, a notion popularized with the 1923 film *In Tutankhamen's Country*, in which the discovery of Tutankhamun's tomb took place in the Egyptian desert. Additionally, the desert romance genre appeared in Western literature and films such as in Edith Maud Hull's novels *The Sheik* (1919), and *The Son of the Sheik* (1925), which were produced as American silent adventure/drama films, in 1921 and 1926. *Kiss in the Desert* contained comparable content as a romance action film. Such influence was unavoidable during the establishment of the local film industry, and the emphasis on the desert landscape in Western films about the Middle East does not deny its significance for the national identity. The discovery of the tomb had a direct impact on the concept of Egyptian nationalism as it celebrates Pharaonic heritage and civilization. Thus, the move from the desert to the Nile Valley was a very important step in the development of nationalist film as it replaced the colonial imagination with local reality and helped Egyptians re-identify their national character.

In *Zaynab*, Haykal offers two types of Egyptian characters: the narrator Hamid, the rich educated landowner, who is introduced to urban life and French intellectuality, and the subject Zaynab, the simple young peasant who is tied to tradition and longs for modernism. Although Hamid represents the main character in the novel, he was excluded from the film, since he only observes and has no influence on the story. Hamid likes Zaynab, and they have a short romantic interlude; however, the fact that they belong to different social classes keeps them separated. They have no intention to develop their feelings. Zaynab chooses Ibrahim, a simple peasant, who experiences difficulties similar to those of Zaynab's family. Furthermore, Zaynab's husband Hasan was wealthy, and the class difference might explain the distance between the couple. She was chosen by Hasan's mother to be an obedient wife, and Zaynab maintains that role without further development. Zaynab herself was not open to either Hamid, the narrator, or Hasan, her husband. Haykal writes that we yearn to find our beloved among those who belong to our class because they are our people whom we love and trust in the first place.[65] Thus, there are two types of identity: the first represents the average population and the second embodies elites, and the possibility of interaction and exchange does not exist.

Class differences determine social and political roles. The lower-class national character is not ready to be active or influential. Meanwhile, the average Egyptian is miserable and pathetic whereas elites or modern intellectuals can offer support and sympathy as leaders. The film attempts to clarify the need for change in local society, and this change could benefit from the conception of modernity, as seen in Western cultures.

In the novel, readers get a clear idea about the role of class hierarchy that complicates the conception of national identity in Egypt during the early twentieth century. Hamid, the narrator, represents the higher class with his wealth and education. Accordingly, the film has adapted Hamid's vision to represent the lower class. The absence of the narrating character only eliminates the direct style of subjectivity; while Zaynab is presented to readers through Hamid's view in the novel, Zaynab as a character appears as seen from a distance or a class gap in the film.

ʿAli al-Raʿi discusses Hamid's vision in the novel. Although he spends time with peasant girls as a means of entertainment, he appreciates their innocence and spontaneity which the higher class lack.[66] The fact that he sees positive qualities reveals a unique consideration that has not existed among high-class individuals at that time. The tendency to reconsider the peasant character was the promising intellectual shift in the novel. However, Hamid's standards of judgment were influenced by his favor of Western values over local tradition. Peasant girls gain his consideration because they are less conservative and more open to physical communication with him unlike the higher class, veiled ladies. Thus, peasants' qualities result only from their exclusion from the conception of the ideal Egyptian who guards social and religious values which are the subject of a critique in the novel. Otherwise, Hamid still believes that shortening the distance between him and such lower-class servants negatively affects his pride and reputation as a landowner. Despite peasants' exclusion from noble standards, they are still under the influence of the local culture and passively play their roles, as seen in Zaynab's character who performs her role as an obedient daughter and wife until she dies out of her hopeless love. While they do not obtain the honor of the higher class, they still experience the consequences of traditional values.

Hamid's conception of Egyptian identity is influenced by European colonialism. Readers can recognize the Western logic in presenting positive and negative qualities in both the higher and the lower classes. On one hand, the average higher-class character is backward whereas the lower-class community is passive. On the other hand, wealth exposes individuals to intellectuality and civilization as appeared in Hamid's character who was introduced to Western thinking, while poverty excludes peasants from the prestigious and conservative society. This colonial vision underestimates the local tradition and involves a conception of modernism following Western standards. Although Hamid had been excluded from the film, his vision as a narrator appeared as a guideline for the director. According to Karim's memoir, one of the obstacles he needed to overcome was the congregation of peasants at the film locations.[67] Excluding real peasants from the screen was important to create a new version of them. Similarly, Zaynab's character was understood only through Hamid's vision.

Despite the colonial perspective in the novel, Haykal took a step toward a new perspective when Hamid shows sympathy toward poor peasants. In this stage of using the Western logic to develop self-awareness, sympathy serves to create a romantic vision but does not seek a radical change of social classes. Al-Ra'i demonstrates the contradiction in Hamid's character as he is emotionally involved with peasants' struggle but keeps his role as a landowner who maximizes the profits and accordingly the workers' efforts. The author adds that Hamid does not show any interest in improving the life status of his peasants. He is content with his generous sympathy, and for him, no further action ought to be expected.[68] Maintaining class differences is important for the higher class who seeks wealth development. Additionally, linking poverty to a passive character justifies the class hierarchy. Al-Ra'i believes that Hamid's sympathy plays an important role in romanticizing the rural reality and presenting its beautiful simplicity. The peasants' miserable reality has not been taken seriously. For al-Ra'i, Haykal offers unconditional celebration of the current reality without intention of change.[69] The alleged sympathy is not more than a necessary romantic trace. Thus, the long description of natural views in the novel serves in promoting such an honorable aspect of the gloomy scenes. The intense focus on the beautiful surroundings makes the tragic story become less miserable. Characters' tears become a part of the intended romantic image.

The average population's identity was an interesting subject in the film industry, but filmmakers were interested in elite spectators, such as influential critics. Consequently, elites participated through their comments and critiques in creating a cinematic vision about the identity of the average Egyptians who, so far, are voiceless. The elite's vision was meant to counter colonial representation and became a starting point to future development. But how is this different from colonial representation? Although creating the national identity seems very similar to the colonial representation of an uncivilized population, Egyptian elites have different goals and styles. The main objective of these films was to create an idealized image out of local social values to gain worldwide consideration. Here, the demand for a "modern" representation increased because film producers depend on the consideration of viewers and critics who follow Western standards. In terms of the style of presentation, authors and filmmakers promoted the sense of belonging and sympathy for the struggle of the average individual. Their intention to create works of positive vision and their emotional involvement in the lives of everyday Egyptians explains the presented image, even if it lacks truthfulness. The representation of the national identity in early local cinema attempted to offer awareness of the lower-class population and claimed that their issues became one of the main topics in critical discussions. Did it succeed?

Conclusion

The conception of national identity out of the political complications was not possible in the early post-independence era. One of the major political concerns was to distinguish Egyptians from outsiders or those who must not be considered Egyptians. Excluding communities that had lived in Egypt long enough to be merged with natives, such as high-class nobles of foreign origin, was a crucial step to justify the eligibility of a new version of political power. The conception of national identity cannot be separated from the notion of foreignness. Additionally, the colonial experience raised a local sensitivity to foreigners' presence, especially Europeans. The awareness of national complexity led to identifying subcategories: foreigners, Egyptians of foreign origins, and native Egyptians, who are classified into elite and average.

The idea that the nation must be controlled by authentic Egyptians created a political eagerness for dominating all institutions in the nation. Thus, early Egyptian cinema was restricted by political visions. Creativity and entertainment became less important than opposing colonial representation. Media, which was also influenced by political visions, played a significant role in setting standards for cinema production. Accordingly, the concept of nationalism in early film production was much affected by the notion of authenticity. The desire to present a superior version of authentic Egyptians was the main objective. The strong presence of European companies in several fields including cinema placed the authentic notion within a constant dialogue with Western spectators. An insistent question is repeated by critics, what would Westerners say or think when they watch this version of "us"? Which put more obstacles limiting the needed freedom for creativity. The constant dialogue between media and produced films modified the notion of nationalism. That is to say that an ideal representation of national identity is beyond reach.

CONTRIBUTORS

Diana Abbani is a social historian of the Modern Middle East. She is currently working as the science communication coordinator for the project Merian Centre for Advanced Studies in the Maghreb (MECAM) at the Forum Transregionale Studien. She holds a Ph.D. in Arabic studies from Sorbonne University, and previously received postdoctoral fellowships from the Forum Transregionale Studien and the Fritz Thyssen Foundation as a EUME fellow. She has published on Beirut's popular and material culture, the implications of social, political, and technological changes, as well as the emergence of music industries and entertainment in Beirut. She is preparing a book, which focuses on alternative narratives in Beirut's musical scene, uncovering the forgotten stories of people who were affected by sound transitions and revisiting the experiences of those marginalized by official narratives.

Hala Auji is an Associate Professor of Art History and the Hamad bin Khalifa Endowed Chair for Islamic Art in the Department of Art History at the School of the Arts, Virginia Commonwealth University in Richmond, Virginia. Informed by her interdisciplinary background in graphic design, criticism and theory, and art history, Auji's research explores the history of the book, print culture, cultural modernity, museum practices, and portraiture in the Islamic world, with a focus on Arabic-speaking communities of the eastern Mediterranean. Her work evidences intersections between book history, manuscript studies, art history, design history, comparative literature, and Islamic and Middle East studies. She is the author of *Printing Arab Modernity: Book Culture and the American Press in Nineteenth-Century Beirut* (2016). She received her Ph.D. in Art History from Binghamton University, State University of New York.

Raphael Cormack is an Assistant Professor of Arabic at the University of Durham. He was previously a visiting researcher at Columbia University in the City of New York and holds a Ph.D. from the University of Edinburgh. His work focuses on performance and popular culture in the Arab world. His most recent publication was *Midnight in Cairo: The Divas of Egypt's Roaring 20s* (2021). He has also edited two collections of Arabic short stories translated into English, *The Book of Khartoum* and *The Book of Cairo*.

Till Grallert is a social and media historian of the Arabic-speaking eastern Mediterranean from the nineteenth century to the present. He is currently a Marie Skłodowska-Curie postdoctoral fellow at the University of Hamburg and computationally investigates the ideoscape of early Arabic periodicals at scale.

He previously worked at the Orient-Institut Beirut and Humboldt-Universität zu Berlin, where he established a prototypical scholarly maker space for fostering computational tool literacy in the humanities. He holds a Ph.D. in History with a thesis on the streets of late Ottoman Damascus from Freie Universität Berlin (2014) and an MA from the School of Oriental and African Studies (2008), University of London. Till is interested in global digital humanities and the epistemic violence of the post-digital moment.

Walid El Khachab is an Associate Professor in the Department of Languages, Literatures, and Linguistics and coordinator of Arabic Studies at York University, Canada, and director of the Arab Canadian Studies Research Group (ACANS). In the sixty book chapters and academic articles he has published thus far, he explores film, media in general, literature and their interface with history, Sufi culture, and the sacred at large, particularly in Arabic-speaking contexts. His work appeared in journals like *Comparative Studies of South Asia, Africa and the Middle East*, *Sociétés & Représentations*, *CinéMas*, and *CinémAction*, among others. In December 2022, he published his latest book titled *Muhandis al-Bahja* [The Engineer of Joy] by Dar Elmaraya in Cairo on the Egyptian prominent comedian Fu'ad al-Muhandis (1924–2006).

Alaaeldin Mahmoud is an Assistant Professor of English in the Liberal Arts Department at the American University of the Middle East in Kuwait. He is a former Fulbright visiting scholar at the Ohio State University. He is an established translator who translated books on travel writing, fiction, and literary studies, notably his translation of *Other Renaissances: A New Approach to World Literature* (Kuwait, 2014). His scholarly interests include the literary and cultural history of the Nahda and literary translingualisms. His work appeared in edited volumes such as in *The Routledge Handbook of Literary Translingualism* (2021) as well as in journals such as *Middle Eastern Literatures*, *Comparative Literature Studies*, *Hungarian Cultural Studies*, and *ALIF: Journal of Comparative Poetics*. His latest published books are *Nusus ʿAbd Allah al-Nadim* (The Texts of ʿAbd Allah al-Nadim) in two volumes: *al-Diwan al-Shiʿri* (The Complete Collected Poems) and *al-Athar al-Nathriya al-Kamila* (Complete Works in Prose) (Cairo, 2020). He is also a member in international organizations like International Comparative Literature Association (ICLA) and Middle East Studies Association (MESA)

Liz Matsushita is a historian of the Modern Middle East and North Africa. She has been a Fulbright scholar in Morocco, has taught at Claremont McKenna College, and is currently a visiting Assistant Professor of History and Humanities at Reed College in Portland, Oregon. She received her Ph.D. from the University of Illinois at Urbana-Champaign in 2021. Her research focuses on the politics of music in colonial and postcolonial North Africa, particularly how musical performance, practice, and scholarship served crucial roles in both imperial systems and state-building projects in Morocco and Tunisia.

Pelle Valentin Olsen is a cultural and social historian of the Modern Middle East. He received his Ph.D. from the University of Chicago (2020). He is at work on a book manuscript entitled *Idle Days and Nights: Leisure, Time, and Modernity in Iraq*. Currently, he is a Marie Curie postdoctoral fellow at the University of Oslo. His work has appeared in edited volumes as well as in the *Journal of Middle East Women's Studies, Arab Studies Journal, Journal of Palestine Studies, Middle East Critique, Regards, Journal of Arabic Literature, Journal of Social History,* and elsewhere. *Palestine in the World: International Solidarity with the Palestinian Liberation Movement*, coedited with Sorcha Thompson, was published in 2023 by Bloomsbury/SOAS Palestine Book Series.

Thana Al-Shakhs is an Assistant Professor in the Liberal Arts Department at the American University in the Middle East (AUM) in Kuwait. She previously worked at Louisiana State University (LSU) during her Ph.D. preparation and at Princess Nourah Bint Abdul Rahman University (PNU) in Riyadh. She earned fellowships to participate at Digital Humanities Summer Institute, University of Victoria, BC held in the summer of 2017 and the Institute for World Literature held in the summer of 2015. Thana is interested in performance studies including cinema studies, transcultural poetics, and digital humanities. She published an article titled "How Can Digital Tools Develop Poetic Analysis? Vocal Analysis of a Sample of Suheir Hammad's Performance Poetry" at *Interdisciplinary Digital Engagement in Arts & Humanities* (IDEAH • Vol. 1, Iss. 1) May 2020. She holds a Ph.D. in Comparative Literature, a minor in English, with a dissertation on transcultural poetics and the role of performance comparing *muwaššah* poetry with examples of contemporary ex-phonic poetry from Louisiana State University, Baton Rouge, USA (2019), and an MA from the Department of Arabic Language and Literature at King Saud University, Riyadh, KSA.

NOTES

Introduction

1 'Abd Allah al-Nadim, *al-a'dad al-kamila li-majallat al-Ustaz*, vol. II (Cairo: al-Hay'a al-Misriya al- 'Amma lil-Kitab, 1994), 986.
2 Keith Watenpaugh, *Being Modern in the Middle East: Revolution, Nationalism, Colonialism, and the Arab Middle Class* (Princeton: Princeton University Press, 2006). See also Lucie Ryzova, *The Age of the Efendiyya: Passages to Modernity in National-Colonial Egypt* (Oxford: Oxford University Press, 2014).
3 Tarek El-Ariss, ed., *The Arab Renaissance: A Bilingual Anthology of the Nahda* (New York: MLA, 2018).
4 A handful of recent and/or prominent studies in English include: Stephen Sheehi, *Foundations of Modern Arab Identity* (Gainesville: University of Florida Press, 2004); Tarek El-Ariss, *Trials of Arab Modernity: Literary Affects and the New Political* (New York: Fordham University Press, 2013); Abdulrazzak Patel, *The Arab Nahda: The Making of the Intellectual and Humanist Movement* (Edinburgh: Edinburgh University Press, 2013); Jens Hanssen and Max Weiss, eds., *Arabic Thought beyond the Liberal Age: Towards an Intellectual History of the Nahda* (Cambridge: Cambridge University Press, 2016); Michael Allan, *In the Shadow of World Literature: Sites of Reading in Colonial Egypt* (Princeton: Princeton University Press, 2016); Elizabeth M. Holt, *Fictitious Capital: Silk, Cotton, and the Rise of the Arabic Novel* (New York: Fordham University Press, 2017); Marilyn Booth, ed., *Migrating Texts: Circulating Translations Around the Ottoman Mediterranean* (Edinburgh: Edinburgh University Press, 2019); Peter Hill, *Utopia and Civilisation in the Arab Nahda* (Cambridge: Cambridge University Press, 2020); and Nadia Bou Ali, *Psychoanalysis and the Love of Arabic: Hall of Mirrors* (Edinburgh: Edinburgh University Press, 2020).
5 Many sources discuss these developments. For Beirut, see Jens Hanssen, *Fin de Siècle Beirut: The Making of an Ottoman Provincial Capital* (Oxford: Oxford University Press, 2009).
6 Venturing a comprehensive definition of the Nahda is something of a fool's errand. For some more detailed attempts to capture the complexities of the movement and its subsequent influence, see Jens Hanssen and Max Weiss, "Introduction," in *Arabic Thought beyond the Liberal Age: Towards an Intellectual History of the Nahda*, ed. Jens Hanssen and Max Weiss (Cambridge: Cambridge University Press, 2016), 1–37. For an analysis of the use of the word "Nahda," see Hannah Scott Deuchar, "'Nahda': Mapping a Keyword in Cultural Discourse," *Alif: Journal of Comparative Poetics*, no. 37 (2017): 50–84.
7 For one example, see Toufoul Abou-Hodeib, *A Taste for Home: A Modern Middle Class in Ottoman Beirut* (Stanford: Stanford University Press, 2017), 49–82. For public reform and the Nahda, see Dyala Hamzah, *The Making of the Arab Intellectual: Empire, Public Sphere and the Colonial Coordinates of Selfhood* (London: Routledge, 2012).

8   Samah Selim, *Popular Fiction, Translation, and the Nahda in Egypt* (London: Palgrave Macmillan, 2019), 37.
9   Ibid., 5.
10 Zaydan, as cited and discussed in Hanssen, *Fin de Siècle Beirut*, 16.
11 Muhammad al-Muwaylihi, *What Isa Ibn Hisham Told Us or A Period of Time*, ed. and trans. Roger Allen, vol. 2(New York: New York University Press, 2015), 166–9.
12 See Joseph Ben Prestel, *Emotional Cities: Debates on Urban Change in Berlin and Cairo, 1860-1910* (Oxford: Oxford University Press, 2017), especially Chapter 4 "Neighbourhood of Passion: Losing Rationality in Azbakiyya."
13 Till Grallert, "To Whom Belong the Streets? Investment in Public Space and Popular Contentions in Late Ottoman Damascus," *Bulletin d'études orientales* 61 (2012): 237–59. See also Hanssen, *Fin de Siècle Beirut*, 1–10.
14 Khuri-Makdisi, *The Eastern Mediterranean and the Making of Global Radicalism* (Berkeley: University of California Press, 2010), 60–93. See also Adam Mestyan, "Arabic Theater in Early Khedivial Culture, 1868-1872: James Sanua Revisited," *International Journal of Middle East Studies* 46, no. 1 (2014): 117–37.
15 For a discussion of specific licenses acquired by presses, see Ami Ayalon, *The Arabic Print Revolution: Cultural Production and Mass Readership* (Cambridge: Cambridge University Press, 2016).
16 Donald J. Cioeta, "Ottoman Censorship in Lebanon and Syria, 1876-1908," *International Journal of Middle East Studies* 10, no. 2 (1979): 167–86.
17 Palmira Brummett, "Censorship in Late Ottoman Istanbul: The Ordinary, the Extraordinary, the Visual," *Journal of the Ottoman and Turkish Studies Association* 5, no. 2 (2018): 75–98.
18 Cioeta, "Ottoman Censorship." Cioeta downplays the difference between censorship in Egypt and the rest of the Ottoman Empire, at least before 1885. Grallert also explains that press censorship laws were less strict in the Ottoman provinces, particularly cosmopolitan port cities like Beirut, before the 1870s. Grallert, "To Whom Belong the Streets?," 332.
19 Elif Bas, "The Role of Armenians in Establishing Western Theater in the Ottoman Empire," *Asian Theater Journal* 37, no. 2 (2020): 448.
20 Mestyan, "Arabic Theater in Early Khedival Culture, 1868-1872," 121.
21 Ziad Fahmy, *Ordinary Egyptians: Creating the Modern Nation through Popular Culture* (Stanford: Stanford University Press, 2011), 93–4. Fahmy also explores the creative ways people tried to bypass this censorship, including changing the name of the play.
22 Jayson Harsin and Mark Hayward, "Stuart Hall's 'Deconstructing the Popular': Reconsiderations 30 Years Later," *Communication, Culture and Critique* 6, no. 2 (2013): 203.
23 Richard Jacquemond and Frédéric Lagrange, eds., *Culture Pop en Égypte: Entre mainstream commercial et contestation* (Paris: Riveneuve, 2020).
24 Armbrust Walter, *Mass Culture and Modernism in Egypt* (Cambridge: Cambridge University Press, 1996).
25 Fahmy, *Ordinary Egyptians*. More recently, Fahmy has also explored the early proliferation of radio as a forum for state and Arab nationalist propaganda during the populist regime of Gamal Abdel Nasser (in office from 1956 to 1970). See Ziad Fahmy, "Early Egyptian Radio Transitioning from Media-Capitalism to Media-Etatism, 1928-1934," *Middle East Journal of Culture and Communication* 15 (2022): 92–112.

26 Selim, *Popular Fiction*.
27 Christopher Silver, *Recording History: Jews, Muslims and Music across Twentieth Century North Africa* (Stanford: Stanford University Press, 2022).
28 See in particular: Wasif Jawhariyya, *The Storyteller of Jerusalem: The Life and Times of Wasif Jawhariyyeh 1904-1948*, ed. Salim Tamari, Issam Nassar, and Nada Elzeer (Northampton, MA: Olive Branch Press, 2014); Rebecca L. Stein and Ted Swedenburg, eds., *Palestine, Israel, and the Politics of Popular Culture* (Durham: Duke University Press, 2005).
29 For instance, see Dwight Fletcher Reynolds, *Arab Folklore: A Handbook* (Westport: Greenwood Press, 2007).
30 See Blake Atwood, *Underground: The Secret Life of Videocassettes in Iran* (Cambridge, MA: MIT Press, 2021).
31 Andrew Hammond, *Pop Culture in North Africa and the Middle East: Entertainment and Society around the World* (Santa Barbara: ABC-CLIO, 2017); Andrew Hammond, *Popular Culture in the Arab World: Art, Politics, and the Media* (Cairo: AUC Press, 2007).
32 Christiane Gruber and Sune Haugbolle, eds., *Visual Culture in the Modern Middle East: Rhetoric of the Image* (Bloomington: Indiana University Press, 2013). A number of essays consider the question of satirical cartoons.
33 Alanoud Alsharekh and Robert Springborg, eds., *Popular Culture and Political Identity in the Arab Gulf States* (London: Saqi Books, 2008).
34 M. Keith Booker and Isra Daraiseh, *Consumerist Orientalism: The Convergence of Arab and American Popular Culture in the Age of Global Capitalism* (London: I.B. Tauris, 2019); Walter Armbrust, ed., *Mass Mediations: New Approaches to Popular Culture in the Middle East and Beyond* (Berkeley: University of California Press, 2000); Walid El Hamamsy and Mounira Soliman, eds., *Popular Culture in the Middle East and North Africa: A Postcolonial Outlook* (London: Routledge, 2014); Anthony Gorman and Sarah Irving, eds., *Cultural Entanglement in the Pre-Independence Arab World: Arts, Thought and Literature* (New York: Bloomsbury Publishing, 2020); Sherifa Zuhur, ed., *Colors of Enchantment: Theater, Dance, Music, and the Visual Arts of the Middle East* (Cairo: AUC Press, 2001). For a closer look at the modern phenomenon of the global entertainment scene and its power dynamics, see Tanner Mirrlees, *Global Entertainment Media: Between Cultural Imperialism and Cultural Globalization* (New York: Routledge, 2013).
35 Such as the work of Michel Foucault and others informed by his methodology. See Foucault, *Power/Knowledge: Selected Interviews and Other Writings, 1972-1977* (New York: Pantheon Books, 1980); Edward Said, *Culture and Imperialism* (New York: Vintage Books, 1994). For relevant discussions in postcolonial theory and popular culture, see Stuart Hall, "The West and the Rest: Discourse and Power," in *Race and Racialization: Essential Readings*, ed. Tania Das Gupta, et al., (Toronto: Canadian Scholars Press, 2007). See also Juan Llamas-Rodriguez and Viviane Saglier, "Postcolonial Media Theory," *Oxford Research Encyclopedia of Communication*, August 31, 2021, https://doi.org/10.1093/acrefore/9780190228613.013.1065.
36 Eman Elnemr, "Modernism, Licentiousness, Rebellion: Egypt in the First Half of the Twentieth Century," (Lecture, Berliner Seminar, EUME, Forum Transregionale Studien, Berlin, January 19, 2022). For an example of gender-related scandals in Beirut, see John Boonstra, "Scandal in Fin-de-Siècle Beirut: Gender, Morality, and Imperial Prestige Between France and Lebanon," *Journal of World History* 28, no. 3/4 (2017): 371–93.

Chapter 1

1 *Thamarat al-Funun*, 1314, January 7, 1901: 8, brackets in the original.
2 The image was, inter alia, published in *Salname-yi vilayet-i Suriye, ʿarabi 1309*, 24 (Şam-i Şerif, 1892), 247.
3 "Hatt-ı hümayun ve kanun-ı esasi" ([Der-i Saʿadet]: Matbaʿa-yı ʿAmire, 1876; orig. December 23, 1876). On the genealogy of the constitution, see Aylin Koçunyan, *Negotiating the Ottoman Constitution 1839-1876*, Collection Turcica 24 (Paris: Louvain, 2018).
4 See Donald Quataert, "Part IV: The Age of Reforms," in *An Economic and Social History of the Ottoman Empire*, ed. Halil İnalcık and Donald Quataert, 1600-1914, vol. 2 (Cambridge: Cambridge University Press, 1997), 759–943.
5 Ami Ayalon, "Modern Texts and Their Readers in Late Ottoman Palestine," *Middle Eastern Studies* 38, no. 4 (2002): 17–40. Adam Mestyan, Till Grallert, et al., *Jaraʾid: A Chronology of Arabic Periodicals (1800–1929)*, v. 1.0 (Zenodo, December 29, 2020), https://doi.org/10.5281/zenodo.4399240, provide a comprehensive data set on all Arabic periodicals published before 1930.
6 This paper is based on the Damascene newspapers *Suriye* (official gazette, surviving collections: 1882–8, 1899–1902), *al-Muqtabas* (1908–16, Muhammad Kurd ʿAli, repeatedly changing title), and *al-ʿAsr al-Jadid* (1908–12?, Nasif Abu Zayd) and systematic readings of reprints from unavailable issues of the Damascene papers *Suriye*, *al-Sham* (1896–1909), and *Dimashq* (1878–80) as well as reports from Damascus published in the Beiruti newspapers of *al-Bashir* (1875–1914, Jesuits), *Lisan al-Hal* (1877–1914, Khalil Sarkis), and *Thamarat al-Funun* (1875–1908, Jamʿiyyat al-Funun and ʿAbd al-Qadir al-Qabbani). I also make cursory references to the newspapers *Hadiqat al-Akhbar* (1881–8, Khalil al-Khuri), *al-Janna* (1879–84, Salim al-Bustani), *al-Iqbal* (1902–?), *al-Ittihad al-ʿUthmani* (1908–?), and *al-Misbah* (1880–1904) from Beirut and to *al-Quds* (Jerusalem, 1908–14).
7 There is a wealth of scholarship on the Ottoman modernizing project and emerging middle classes. See, for example, Toufoul Abou-Hodeib, *A Taste for Home: The Modern Middle Class in Ottoman Beirut* (Stanford: Stanford University Press, 2017); Cem Emrence, *Remapping the Ottoman Middle East: Modernity, Imperial Bureaucracy, and the Islamic State*, Library of Ottoman Studies 31 (London: I.B. Tauris, 2012); Jens Hanssen, *Fin de Siècle Beirut: The Making of an Ottoman Provincial Capital* (Oxford: Clarendon Press, 2005); Stefan Weber, *Damascus: Ottoman Modernity and Urban Transformation, 1808–1918*, trans. Stephen Cox, vol. I (Aarhus: Aarhus Universitetsforlag, 2009); Nadir Özbek, "'Beggars' and 'Vagrants' in Ottoman State Policy and Public Discourse, 1876–1914," *Middle Eastern Studies* 45, no. 5 (2009): 783–801; Lucie Ryzova, *L'effendiyya ou la modernité contestée*, Collection 15/20 (Cairo: Cedej, 2004). On the mutual dependency of the press and the state, see Till Grallert, "Investigating Ottoman Press Censorship in the Eastern Mediterranean Through Conceptual History: The Peculiar Use of 'Incident' (Haditha)," *Die Welt des Islams*, forthcoming.
8 See Dale Eickelman and Armando Salvatore, "The Public Sphere and Muslim Identities," *European Journal of Sociology* 43, no.1 (2002): 92–115; Nilüfer Göle, "The Gendered Nature of the Public Sphere," *Public Culture* 10, no. 1 (1997): 61–82; Suad Joseph, "The Public/Private: The Imagined Boundary in the Imagined Nation/State/Community: The Lebanese Case," *Feminist Review*, no. 57 (1997): 73–92;

Akram Fouad Khater, "'House' to 'Goddess of the House': Gender, Class, and Silk in 19th-Century Mount Lebanon," *International Journal of Middle East Studies* 28, no. 3 (1996): 325–48; Elizabeth Thompson, "Public and Private in Middle Eastern Women's History," *Journal of Women's History* 15, no. 1 (2003): 52–69; Till Grallert, "To Whom Belong the Streets? Property, Propriety, and Appropriation: The Production of Public Space in Late Ottoman Damascus, 1875-1914" (PhD Thesis, FU Berlin, 2014).

9 See Reinhart Koselleck, "Richtlinien für das 'Lexikon politisch-sozialer Begriffe der Neuzeit,'" *Archiv für Begriffsgeschichte* 11 (1967): 81–99; Alp Eren Topal and Einar Wigen, "Ottoman Conceptual History: Challenges and Prospects," *Contributions to the History of Concepts* 14, no. 1 (2019): 93–114; Florian Zemmin and Henning Sievert, "Conceptual History of the Near East: The Sattelzeit as a Heuristic Tool for Interrogating the Formation of a Multilayered Modernity," *Contributions to the History of Concepts* 16, no. 2 (2021): 1–26.

10 Farha Ghannam, *Remaking the Modern: Space, Relocation, and the Politics of Identity in a Global Cairo* (Berkeley: University of California Press, 2002), 92–3 and Abraham Marcus, "Privacy in Eighteenth-Century Aleppo: The Limits of Cultural Ideals," *International Journal of Middle East Studies* 18 (1986): 167 point to similar difficulties in looking for terms corresponding to "privacy" in local idioms.

11 For a detailed discussion, see Grallert, "To Whom Belong the Streets," ch. 2.

12 *Al-Janna*, 1368, February 4, 1884; *Lisan al-Hal*, 1021, December 29, 1887; *Thamarat al-Funun*, 872, February 11, 1892; *Thamarat al-Funun*, 876, March 14, 1892; *Thamarat al-Funun*, 879, April 5, 1892. See Jens Hanssen, "Public Morality and Marginality in fin-de-siècle Beirut," in *Outside in: On the Margins of the Modern Middle East*, ed. Eugene Rogan (London: I.B. Tauris, 2002), 196; Fruma Zachs and Sharon Halevi, "From Difaʿ Al-Nisaʾ to Masʾalat Al-Nisaʾ in Greater Syria: Readers and Writers Debate Women and Their Rights, 1858–1900," *International Journal of Middle East Studies* 41, no. 4 (2009): 617.

13 See Maurus Reinkowski, *Die Dinge der Ordnung: Eine vergleichende Untersuchung über die osmanische Reformpolitik im 19. Jahrhundert* (München: Oldenbourg, 2005), 233.

14 "Ceza-yi kanunname-yi hümayunu," in *Düstur*, vol. 1, Tertip I (Der-i Saʿadet: Matbaʿa-yi ʿAmire, 1872; orig. July 9, 1858), sec. 1a. The other two were crimes against the state/dynasty (*devlet*) and against individuals (*bir şahs*). For a revisionist discussion, firmly situating the Penal Code in the Ottoman context, see Tobias Heinzelmann, "The Ruler's Monologue: The Rhetoric of the Ottoman Penal Code of 1858," *Die Welt des Islams* 54, no. 3-4 (2014): 292–321.

15 "Matbuʿat nizamnamesi," in *Düstur*, vol. 2, Tertip I (Der-i Saʿadet: Matbaʿa-yi ʿAmire, 1872; orig. December 31, 1864), secs. 13–14. Art. 14 clarified that moral values might be specific to particular communities. "Matbuʿat kanunu," in *Düstur*, vol. 1, Tertip II (Der-i Saʿadet: Matbaʿa-yi ʿOsmaniye, 1913; orig. July 29, 1909), sec. 19.

16 "Hatt-ı hümayun ve kanun-ı esasi," sec. 11.

17 "Ijtimaʿat-i ʿumumiye kanunu," in *Düstur*, vol. 1, Tertip II (Der-i Saʿadet: Matbaʿa-yi ʿOsmaniye, 1913; orig. June 9, 1909), sec. 8, *al-Muqtabas*, 947, April 4, 1912: sec. 2; Hisni ʿAbd al-Hadi, trans., "Qanun al-jamaʿat wa sharah al-mughammad bihi," *al-Muqtabas* 6, no. 10 (September 25, 1911; orig., June 9, 1909), sec. 8, https://openarabicpe.github.io/journal_al-muqtabas/tei/oclc_4770057679-i_69.TEIP5.xml#div_31.d1e3413.

18 The application of the term "ancien régime," as coined by Tocqueville, to the Ottoman context was suggested by Ariel Salzmann, "An Ancien Regime Revisited: 'Privatization' and Political Economy in the Eighteenth-Century Ottoman Empire," *Politics Society* 21, no. 4 (1993): 393–423, https://doi.org/fdtmdt. This corresponds to the "politics of notables," originally suggested by Albert Hourani, "Ottoman Reform and the Politics of Notables," in *The Modern Middle East: A Reader*, ed. Albert Hourani, Philip S. Khoury, and Mary C. Wilson (Berkeley: University of California Press, 1993), 83–109; for Damascus, see Linda Schatkowski Schilcher, *Families in Politics: Damascene Factions and Estates of the 18th and 19th Centuries* (Stuttgart: Steiner, 1985).

19 *Al-Bashir*, 1474, February 4, 1901: 3.

20 *Salname[-yi vilayet-i Suriye], sene 1286*, 2 ([Dimashq]: Suriye Litughrafiyya Matbaʿası, 1869), 43; *Salname-yi vilayet-i Suriye, sene 1300*, 15, 1882, 254a; Nuʿman Qassatli, *al-Rawda al-ghannaʾ fi Dimashq al-fayha* (Beirut, 1879), 109; ʿAbd al-Rahman Bey Sami, *Qawl al-haqq fi Bayrut wa Dimashq aw sifr al-salam fi Bilad al-Sham* (Cairo: Matbaʿat al-Muqtataf, 1896), 77–8.

21 Weber, *Damascus*, 2009, II:11–15, 40–50 provides locations and descriptions of some cafés; *al-Muqtabas*, 327, March 26, 1910: 3; *al-Muqtabas*, 486, September 28, 1910: 3; *Lisan al-Hal*, 1104, October 15, 1888: 2.

22 "Turuk ve ebniye nizamnamesi," in *Düstur*, vol. 2 (Der-i Saʿadet: Matbaʿa-yı ʿAmire, 1863), 393–410, §15–19; "Taʿlimat bi-haqq ʿumum wazaʾif al-dawaʾir al-baladiyya," in *al-Dustur*, vol. 2 (Beirut: al-Matbaʿa al-Adabiyya, 1885; orig. July 25, 1867), 436–8, §6, 14; "Vilayat-i belediye kanunu," in *Düstur*, vol. 4, Tertip I (Istanbul: Matbaʿa-yi ʿAmire, 1879; orig. October 5, 1877), 538–53, §62. For a discussion of municipal and building codes, see Malek Sharif, *Imperial Norms and Local Realities: The Ottoman Municipal Laws and the Municipality of Beirut (1860–1908)* (Würzburg: Ergon, 2014), 51–113; Weber, *Damascus*, 2009, I:83–6; Hanssen, *Fin de Siècle Beirut*, 214–16.

23 *Al-Muqtabas*, 466, September 5, 1910: 4; *Lisan al-Hal*, 86, September 5, 1878: 4; *Lisan al-Hal*, 6425, September 8, 1910: 2.

24 Qassatli, *al-Rawda al-ghannaʾ*, 109–10; *al-Janna*, 1368, February 4, 1884; *Lisan al-Hal*, 272, June 17, 1880.

25 *Thamarat al-Funun*, 47, March 9, 1876: 4; *Thamarat al-Funun*, 48, March 16, 1876: 4.

26 *Thamarat al-Funun*, 380, May 8, 1882: 4.

27 *Al-Muqtabas*, 84, March 28, 1909: 2.

28 *Al-Bashir*, 628, September 21, 1882: 3; 1355, October 17, 1898: 3; 1372, February 13, 1899: 3; *Lisan al-Hal*, 782, August 20, 1885: 3.

29 See "Ajwaba al-ʿulamaʾ ʿan al-tamthil," *al-Haqaʾiq* 2, no. 3 (September 25, 1911): 85–96, https://OpenArabicPE.github.io/journal_al-haqaiq/tei/oclc_644997575-i_15.TEIP5.xml#div_3.d1e562.

30 On his life and the theater, see Regina Karachouli, "Abu Ḥalil Al-Qabbani (1833–1902) - Damaszener Theatergründer und Prinzipal," *Die Welt des Islams* 32, no. 1 (1992): 83–98; ʿAdil Abu Shanab, "Hayat Abi Khalil al-Qabbani," *Mawqif al-adabi* 89 (1978): 102–12.

31 *Lisan al-Hal*, 133, February 17, 1879: 3; *Lisan al-Hal*, 198, October 2, 1879: 1; *Lisan al-Hal*, 217, December 8, 1879: 4; *Thamarat al-Funun*, 212, January 20, 1879: 4.

32 *Lisan al-Hal*, 607, September 20, 1883: 3; *Lisan al-Hal*, 617, October 25, 1883: 1.

33 Adam Mestyan, *Arab Patriotism: The Ideology and Culture of Power in Late Ottoman Egypt* (Princeton: Princeton University Press, 2017), 215, 217. ʿAbd al-Wahhab

al-Sharka, "Aqwal al-'ulama' fi al-tamthil 4: al-Jawab al-thalith 'ashr," *al-Haqa'iq* 2, no. 6 (December 22, 1911): 227, https://OpenArabicPE.github.io/journal_al-haqaiq/tei/oclc_644997575-i_18.TEIP5.xml#div_7.d2e1421 claimed that the theater was shut down and acting banned from all schools by imperial degree. Abu Shanab, "Hayat Abi Khalil al-Qabbani," 102–3 references a similar account of a ban but doubts its veracity.

34 *Lisan al-Hal*, 196, September 25, 1879; *Lisan al-Hal*, 244, March 11, 1880. See Stefan Weber, "Der Marğa-Platz in Damaskus: Die Entstehung eines modernen Stadtzentrums unter den Osmanen als Ausdruck eines strukturellen Wandels (1808–1918)," *Damaszener Mitteilungen* 10 (1998): 327. On the institution of *islahhâne*s in the Ottoman Empire, see Nazan Maksudyan, "Hearing the Voiceless - Seeing the Invisible: Orphans and Destitute Children as Actors of Social, Economic, and Political History in the Late Ottoman Empire," (PhD Thesis, Sabanci University, 2008), 195–293.

35 See Raphael Cormack's chapter in this book.

36 *al-Muqtabas*, 1082, January 6, 1913. Weber, *Damascus*, 2009, II:50 claims that the theater was opened in 1902. Newspapers do not mention *Zahra Dimashq* until 1909 but the theater *"Zahra Suriyya"* in Beirut in the early 1900s. *Lisan al-Hal*, 3884, November 28, 1901; *Lisan al-Hal*, 4162, November 29, 1902; *Lisan al-Hal*, 4195, January 12, 1903.

37 *Al-Muqtabas*, 82, March 25, 1909: 2; *al-Muqtabas*, 140, June 1, 1909: 3; *Lisan al-Hal*, 6069, July 15, 1909: 3.

38 *Al-'Asr al-Jadid*, 175, March 2, 1910: 4; *al-Muqtabas*, 318, March 15, 1910: 4; *al-Muqtabas*, 319, March 16, 1910: 4.

39 *Al-Muqtabas*, 60, February 28, 1909: 3; *al-Muqtabas*, 81, March 24, 1909: 3.

40 *Al-'Asr al-Jadid*, 199, April 2, 1910: 4; *al-Muqtabas*, 17, January 9, 1909: 3.

41 *Al-'Asr al-Jadid*, 91, November 19, 1909: 4. These were not the first film screenings in Damascus. A traveling projectionist performed during the nights of Ramadan, September 1909; *al-Bashir*, 1930, September 27, 1909: 4.

42 *Al-Muqtabas*, 318, March 15, 1910: 4; *al-Muqtabas*, 1433, March 10, 1914: 3.

43 *Al-Muqtabas*, 384, May 31, 1910: 4.

44 Qassatli, *al-Rawda al-ghanna'*, 115–16; see also Gustav Bauernfeind, Journal Entry (Damascus, March 23, 1889).

45 Sami, *Qawl al-haqq*, 73–4, 77–8; *al-Bashir*, 1396, August 5, 1899; *Thamarat al-Funun*, 1313, December 31, 1900; *Thamarat al-Funun*, 1314, January 7, 1901; Muhammad Kurd 'Ali, "'Umran dimashq (5): Mutanazzahatuha," *al-Muqtataf* 26, no. 10 (October 1901): 881.

46 For instance, the teachers of the British Syrian Schools used to take their students to the gardens during the summer months. Similarly, the journal of the British Consul John Dickson is full of entries recounting walks or a ride in the gardens surrounding the city. Helen Butchart, "Cholera at Damascus," *British Syrian Mission Schools and Bible Works*, no. 1 (1892): 12–18; Meta Johnston, "School Work in Damascus," *British Syrian Mission Schools and Bible Works*, no. 1 (1899): 12–14; E. Harrison, "On the Banks of the Barada," *Daughters of Syria*, no. 1 (January 1907): 17–19; MECA, GB165-0086, John Dickson, Journal Entry (Damascus, June 25, 1882, June 20, 1884, May 18, 1888).

47 PRO, FO 195/1480, Damascus 31, John Dickson to Earl of Dufferin, (July 19, 1884); Gustav Bauernfeind, Journal Entry (Damascus, May 12, 1889). See *Thamarat al-Funun*, 684, May 28, 1888.

48 Roman Oberhummer and Heinrich Zimmerer, *Durch Syrien und Kleinasien: Reiseschilderungen u. Studien* (Berlin: Reimer, 1899), 44–5; see *al-Bashir*, 991, December 12, 1889; *Thamarat al-Funun*, 1314, January 7, 1901.
49 Gustav Bauernfeind, Journal Entry (Damascus, May 4, 1889).
50 Bauernfeind, Journal Entry (Damascus, April 23, 1889); *Lisan al-Hal*, 86, September 5, 1878.
51 *Jarid*, a game of throwing sticks on horseback is mentioned by Oberhummer and Zimmerer, *Durch Syrien und Kleinasien*, 69; Alfred von Kremer, *Mittelsyrien und Damascus: Geschichtliche, Ethnografische und Geografische Studien in den Jahren 1849, 1850 u. 1851* (Wien: P.P. Mechitharisten, 1853), 108; Bauernfeind, Journal Entries (Damascus, December 2, 1888, December 21, 1888). Locations mentioned for this game include the Green Meadows west of the town and the plains south of Bawwabat Allah.
52 Hermann Götz, *Eine Orientreise* (Leipzig: Seemann, 1901; orig. March 1897), 194; Sami, *Qawl al-haqq*, 73–4; *al-Muqtabas*, 30, January 24, 1909; *al-Muqtabas*, 486, September 28, 1910; *al-Muqtabas*, 709, June 21, 1911; *Lisan al-Hal*, 1335, May 18, 1891; *Lisan al-Hal*, 5016, February 6, 1906; *Lisan al-Hal*, 5456, July 15, 1907; *Thamarat al-Funun*, 272, March 16, 1880; *Thamarat al-Funun*, 1691, September 21, 1908.
53 After the trade of *hashish* had been banned from the vicinity of Marja Square when it became the center of the modern administration, *hashish* was easily available and consumed in the cafés inside and outside Bab Tuma; *Lisan al-Hal*, 269, June 7, 1880; *Lisan al-Hal*, 272, June 17, 1880; *Lisan al-Hal*, 284, July 29, 1880. See also *al-Bashir*, 1492, June 10, 1901; *al-Muqtabas*, 49, February 15, 1909.
54 Gustav Bauernfeind, Journal Entry (Damascus, May 12, 1889) mentions Christian families drinking 'araq in the gardens at Bab Tuma during Ramadan. PRO, FO 78/2419, Damascus Consular 20, Dickson to Earl of Derby, (December 24, 1875); PRO, FO 195/1113, Damascus 1, Dickson to Elliot (January 6, 1876); *Thamarat al-Funun*, 212, January 20, 1879; *al-Janna*, 1368, February 4, 1884.
55 Mrs. Mackintosh, *Damascus and Its People: Sketches of Modern Life in Syria* (London: Seeley, Jackson, and Halliday, 1883), 46; Muhammad Kurd 'Ali, "'Umran dimashq (5): Mutanazzahatuha."
56 *A Month in Palestine and Syria, April 1891 (With 39 Original Silver Print Photographs Dry Mounted)*, 1891, 34–5, accessed May 2, 2022, https://commons.wikimedia.org/wiki/Category:A_Month_in_Palestine_and_Syria.
57 Unfortunately, no reproduction is currently openly licensed. *Damaskus. Jahrmarkt Karussell*, Postcard (Damascus, 1917), accessed February 27, 2013, https://www.delcampe.net/en_GB/collectables/item/96537990.html; *Damaskus: Belustigung* (Damascus, 1917), accessed August 6, 2021, https://www.delcampe.net/en_GB/collectables/item/1016539471.html; *Damas - Fête Foraine*, 1921, Postcard, 1921, accessed February 26, 2013, https://www.delcampe.net/en_GB/collectables/item/105553178.html; *[Damas - Fête Foraine]*, 1921, Postcard, 1921, accessed February 26, 2013, https://www.delcampe.net/en_GB/collectables/item/105558832.html.
58 James Grehan, "Smoking and 'Early Modern' Sociability: The Great Tobacco Debate in the Ottoman Middle East (Seventeenth to Eighteenth Centuries)," *The American Historical Review* 111, no. 5 (2006): 1356, 1364; Dana Sajdi, "Peripheral Visions: The Worlds and Worldviews of Commoner Chroniclers in the 18th Century Ottoman Levant," (PhD Thesis, Columbia University, 2002), 346–51; Abdul-Karim Rafeq, "Public Morality in the 18th Century Ottoman Damascus," *Revue des Mondes Musulmans et de la Méditerranée* 55/56 (1990): 189.

59 All prices have been normalized to piasters (Ps) and metrical notation.
60 Qassatli, *al-Rawda al-ghanna'*, 109; Sami, *Qawl al-haqq*, 77–8; Gustav Bauernfeind, Journal Entry (Damascus, April 26, 1889); *al-Muqtabas*, 686, May 25, 1911: 4.
61 Gustav Bauernfeind, Journal Entry (Damascus, April 23, 1889).
62 NACP, RG 84 Damascus, vol. 87, Damascus 67, N. Mishaqa to Ravndal (December 28, 1900); *al-Muqtabas*, 8, December 24, 1908; *al-Muqtabas*, 60, February 28, 1909.
63 *Lisan al-Hal*, 5965, March 11, 1909; *Lisan al-Hal*, 6162, November 2, 1909.
64 *Al-Muqtabas*, 384, May 31, 1910: 4; *al-Muqtabas*, 1433, March 10, 1914: 3.
65 *Lisan al-Hal*, 86, September 5, 1878.
66 MECA, GB165-0086, John Dickson, Journal Entry (Damascus, June 21, 1887); PRO, FO 195/1984, Damascus 31, N. Mishaqa to Currie, (June 25, 1897); *Hadiqat al-Akhbar*, 1262, November 2, 1882; *Lisan al-Hal*, 198, October 2, 1879.
67 *Lisan al-Hal*,1344, June 22, 1891; *Lisan al-Hal*, 1345, June 25, 1891.
68 *Al-Bashir*, 1333, May 16, 1898; *al-Bashir*, 1385, May 15, 1899; *Lisan al-Hal*, 5418, May 31, 1907.
69 *Thamarat al-Funun*, 234, June 23, 1879.
70 *Lisan al-Hal*, 2962, November 9, 1898. For the prevailing confusion of calendars and thus the dates of these annual festivities, see Till Grallert, "Catch Me If You Can! Approaching the Arabic Press of the Late Ottoman Eastern Mediterranean Through Digital History," ed. Simone Lässig, *Geschichte Und Gesellschaft* 47, no. 1, Digital History (2021): 66–9, https://doi.org/gkhrjr.
71 MECA, GB165-0086, John Dickson, Journal Entry (Damascus, May 18, 1888); *Lisan al-Hal*, 634, December 24, 1883; *Lisan al-Hal*, 933, February 24, 1887; *Thamarat al-Funun*, 532, May 25, 1885.
72 *Al-Bashir*, 1853, April 13, 1908; *al-Muqtabas*, 416, July 7, 1910.
73 *Lisan al-Hal*, 933, February 24, 1887: 3.
74 *Al-Bashir*, 1329, April 9, 1898; *Suriyya*, 1722, July 27, 1899: 1; *Suriyya*, 1729, September 14, 1899.
75 *Lisan al-Hal*, 4119, September 8, 1902. Weber, Damascus, 2009, II: 253 traced the earliest reference to this garden to 1908, but it is already mentioned in *al-Bashir*, 1439, June 2, 1900.
76 *Al-Bashir*, 1811, June 22, 1907.
77 NACP, RG 84 Damascus, vol. 10, Damascus 103, N. Mishaqa to Ravndal (July 31, 1908); PRO, FO 618/3, Damascus Draft 29, G. P. Devey to Lowther (August 3, 1908); *Lisan al-Hal*, 5780, August 4, 1908; *Thamarat al-Funun*, 1684, August 3, 1908.
78 *Thamarat al-Funun*, 1691, September 21, 1908.
79 *Al-Bashir*, 997, January 22, 1890; *Lisan al-Hal*, 255, April 19, 1880; *Lisan al-Hal*, 1588, February 14, 1894.
80 *Al-Muqtabas*, 20, January 12, 1909; *al-Muqtabas*, 151, June 14, 1909; *Lisan al-Hal*, 6099, August 19, 1909; *Lisan al-Hal*, 6101, August 21, 1909.
81 *Al-Muqtabas*, 416, July 7, 1910.
82 *Al-Bashir*, 997, January 22, 1890; *al-Bashir*, 1853, April 13, 1908; *al-Muqtabas*, 416, July 7, 1910. Habib Abu Khalil Efendi al-Shammas, proprietor of the *Zahra Dimashq* theater is the only traceable one among them.
83 "Vilayat-i belediye kanunu."
84 *Al-Muqtabas*, 1167, April 16, 1913 quoting *Tanin*; *Lisan al-Hal*, 1335, May 18, 1891; *Lisan al-Hal*, 1338, June 1, 1891.
85 *Lisan al-Hal*, 5456, July 15, 1907.

86 *Al-Muqtabas*, 7, December 23, 1908.
87 *Al-Muqtabas*, 540, December 3, 1910.
88 M. Şükrü Hanioğlu, *The Young Turks in Opposition* (New York: Oxford University Press, 1995), 105–7.
89 PRO, FO 195/1984, Damascus 37 confidential, W. S. Richards to Currie (July 20, 1897), PRO, FO 195/1984, Damascus 38 confidential, Richards to Currie (July 23, 1897), PRO, FO 195/1984, Damascus 40 Confidential, Richards to Currie (July 26, 1897).
90 PRO, FO 195/1940, Damascus 37, H. C. A. Eyres to Currie (September 17, 1896).
91 Ibid.
92 Such as *Suriyya*, 1802, March 21, 1901.
93 MECA, GB165-0086, John Dickson, Journal entry (Damascus, May 24, 1887).
94 *Thamarat al-Funun*, 634, June 6, 1887.
95 *Thamarat al-Funun*, 684, May 28, 1888.
96 Ibid., 1 with reference to *Suriye*.
97 See Özbek, "'Beggars' and 'Vagrants'"; Melis Hafez, *Inventing Laziness: The Culture of Productivity in Late Ottoman Society* (Cambridge: Cambridge University Press, 2022); Avner Wishnitzer, "Yawn: Boredom and Powerlessness in the Late Ottoman Empire," *Journal of Social History* 55, no. 2 (2021): 400–25; *Reading Clocks, alla Turca: Time and Society in the Late Ottoman Empire* (Chicago: University of Chicago Press, 2015), 73–4, 116–17.
98 PRO, FO 78/2419, Damascus Consular 20, John Dickson to Earl of Derby (December 24, 1875).
99 *Thamarat al-Funun*, 212, January 20, 1879.
100 *Lisan al-Hal*, 269, June 7, 1880, *Lisan al-Hal*, 272, June 17, 1880, *Lisan al-Hal*, 284, July 29, 1880.
101 *Al-Janna*, 1368, February 4, 1884.
102 *Thamarat al-Funun*, 814, December 22, 1890: 1.
103 *Lisan al-Hal*, 4223, February 14, 1903. The order was renewed in the runoff to the anniversary of the sultan's accession to the throne on September 1, 1903; *Lisan al-Hal*, 4393, September 3, 1903.
104 Such as *Lisan al-Hal*, 586, July 9, 1883: 1; *Lisan al-Hal*, 1607, April 25, 1894: 1; *Lisan al-Hal*, 1613, May 16, 1894: 4.
105 *Al-Bashir*, 1753, May 14, 1906.
106 *Thamarat al-Funun*, 1653, December 23, 1907.
107 *Al-Bashir*, 1841, January 20, 1908.
108 *Thamarat al-Funun*, 1691, September 21, 1908.
109 David Commins, "Religious Reformers and Arabists in Damascus, 1885–1914," *International Journal of Middle East Studies* 18, no. 4 (1986): 405–25, https://doi.org/10/ffd9rv.
110 *Al-Muqtabas*, 30, January 24, 1909.
111 *Al-Muqtabas*, 35, January 30, 1909.
112 *Al-Bashir*, 1937, November 13, 1909; *al-Bashir*, 1938, November 20, 1909; *al-Muqtabas*, 16, January 7, 1909; *al-Muqtabas*, 43, February 8, 1909; *al-Muqtabas*, 930, March 16, 1912.
113 *Al-Muqtabas*, 708, June 20, 1911.
114 *Al-Bashir*, 1020, April 13, 1892.
115 *Thamarat al-Funun*, 1313, December 31, 1900: 5.
116 *Lisan al-Hal*, 1147, March 18, 1889.

117 *Al-Bashir*, 962, March 23, 1889.
118 *Al-Bashir*, 1481, March 23, 1901.
119 Muhammad Saʿid al-Qasimi, *Qamus al-sinaʿat al-shamiyya*, ed. Zafir al-Qasimi, vol. 1 (Paris: Mouton & Co., 1960), 108–9, 155–6; Jamal al-Din al-Qasimi and Khalil al-ʿAzm, *Qamus al-sinaʿat al-shamiyya*, ed. Zafir al-Qasimi, vol. 2 (Paris: Mouton & Co., 1960), 329, 335, 382, 434, 442, 469; Ilyas Qudsi, "Nubdha tarikhiyya fi 'l-hiraf al-dimashqiyya," *Actes du Sixième Congrès International des Orientalistes, tenu en 1883 à Leide* Deuxième Partie, Section 1: Sémitique (1885; orig., August 12, 1882): 16; Sami, *Qawl al-haqq*, 67; see also James A. Reilly, "Women in the Economic Life of Late-Ottoman Damascus," *Arabica* 42, no. 1 (1995): 79–106.
120 See for instance the statistics published in the "Bulletin de l'Alliance Israélite Universelle" (AIU Bulletin) and the British Syrian Schools' periodical "Daughters of Syria."
121 E.g. *Salname-yi vilayet-i Suriye*, 12 (Dimashq: Vilayet matbaʿasi-yi litugrafiya daʾiresi, 1879), 131; *Salname-yi vilayet-i Suriye 15*, 151, 299; *Salname-yi vilayet-i Suriye, 1304 ʿarabi*, 19, 1887, 250; *Salname-yi vilayet-i Suriye, ʿarabi 1311*, 26 (Dimashq: Vilayet matbaʿası, 1894), 105; *Salname-yi vilayet-i Suriye, ʿarabi 1313*, 28 (Suriye: Vilayet matbaʿası, 1896), 90–1; *Salname-yi vilayet-i Suriye, sene 1317*, 31, 1899, 119, 331; *al-Bashir*, 1018, March 30, 1892; *Hadiqat al-Akhbar*, 1266, December 2, 1882; *Thamarat al-Funun*, 220, March 17, 1879; *Thamarat al-Funun*, 869, January 25, 1892.
122 Jamal al-Din al-Qasimi and al-ʿAzm, *Qamus*, 2:260–1, 403, 415.
123 Till Grallert, "Urban Food Riots in Late Ottoman Bilad Al-Sham as a 'Repertoire of Contention,'" in *Crime, Poverty and Survival in the Middle East and North Africa: The "Dangerous Classes" Since 1800*, ed. Stephanie Cronin (London: I.B. Tauris, 2020), 157–76, https://doi.org/10.5040/9781838605902.ch-010.
124 PRO, FO 195/2024, Damascus 53, W. S. Richards to O'Conor (November 2, 1898).
125 For Ottoman clothing laws until 1829, see Donald Quataert, "Clothing Laws, State and Society in the Ottoman Empire, 1720–1829," *International Journal of Middle East Studies* 29 (1997): 403–25.
126 Qassatli, *al-Rawda al-ghannaʾ*, 126; Mackintosh, *Damascus and Its People*, 60; *Month in Palestine and Syria*, 8. On the *mandil* and the trade of the *mandilci*, purveyor of kerchiefs, see Jamal al-Din al-Qasimi and al-ʿAzm, *Qamus*, 2:471.
127 Sami, *Qawl al-haqq*, 70.
128 William Shortland Richards, "Report on the Trade of Damascus for the Year 1898," in *Diplomatic and Consular Reports*, vol. 2306 (London: Harrison and Sons, 1899; orig. June 15, 1899), 4. See also the numerous photographs that attest to the presence of women in public available on the Library of Congress' website.
129 Karl Baedeker and Albert Socin, *Palaestina und Syrien: Handbuch für Reisende*, 1st ed. (Leipzig: Baedeker, 1875), 493.
130 On the Damascene preference for striped cloth and the various patterns and colors, see Gustav Bauernfeind, Journal Entries (Damascus, November 28, 1888, May 7, 1889), who bought *izar*s with red, blue, and green stripes; N. Mishaqa, NACP, RG 84 Damascus, vol. 87, "Report on the Trade of Damascus for This Year 1899," (October 24, 1900); William Shortland Richards, "Report on the Trade of Damascus for the Year 1902," in *Annual Series of Trade Reports)*, vol. 3059 (London: Harrison and Sons, 1903; orig. July 6, 1903), 9; *al-Bashir*, 1098, November 8, 1893; Mackintosh, *Damascus and Its People*, 72–3.
131 *Thamarat al-Funun*, 381, May 15, 1882 reported on groups of young men, Christians as well as Muslims, snatching the *izar* from a girl on Darwishiyya Street in front of

the Mushiriyya. "Indecent acts" (*fi 'l shani '*) were listed in the official crime statistics, which, however, I did not venture to read systematically; for example *al-Bashir*, 1335, May 28, 1898; *al-Bashir*, 1357, October 31, 1898; *al-Muqtabas*, 461, August 30, 1910; *al-Muqtabas*, 539, December 1, 1910; *al-Muqtabas*, 663, April 29, 1911; *al-Muqtabas*, 705, June 17, 1911; *al-Muqtabas*, 816, October 30, 1911; *al-Muqtabas*, 1224, June 22, 1913; see also *Salname-yi vilayet-i Suriye*.

132 *Lisan al-Hal*, 5824, September 24, 1908; PRO, FO 371/560, 44/F.37930/08, Damascus 51, G. P. Devey to Lowther (October 1, 1908). For the competing factions, see Commins, *Islamic Reform*, 129 and Commins, "Religious Reformers," 414, Philip S. Khoury, *Urban Notables and Arab Nationalism: The Politics of Damascus, 1860–1920* (New York: Cambridge University Press, 1983), 56–7. Both refer only to Devey's report, but Khoury fabricates a demonstration. Both scholars missed the correlation with the month of Ramadan.
133 *Al-Muqtabas*, 9, December 25, 1908, *al-Muqtabas*, 13, December 30, 1908.
134 Official statement of the club, published in *al-Muqtabas*, 22, January 14, 1909.
135 *Al-Muqtabas*, 58, February 25, 1909.
136 *Al-Muqtabas*, 461, August 30, 1910.
137 Weber, *Damascus*, 2009, II:13, 43 could not establish the location of either *qahwat al-junayna al-kubra* or *qahwat al-junayna al-sughra*, but he suspects them to be identical to Café Dimitri on the northeastern fringes of Marja Square in Suq al-Khayl.
138 *Al-Muqtabas*, 465, September 4, 1910: 2. This bashing of Aleppo is unusual.
139 *Al-Muqtabas*, 469, September 8, 1910.
140 Stanford J. Shaw, "The Nineteenth-Century Ottoman Tax Reforms and Revenue System," *International Journal of Middle East Studies* 6, no. 4 (1975): 442.
141 *Lisan al-Hal*, 4223, February 14, 1903; *Lisan al-Hal*, 4393, September 3, 1903.
142 *Thamarat al-Funun*, 1661, February 24, 1908.
143 *Al-Muqtabas*, 930, March 16, 1912.
144 Shaw, "Ottoman Tax Reforms," 442–3; for a table of imperial revenues see ibid., 449.
145 Such as Gustav Bauernfeind, Journal entry (Damascus, May 12, 1889); *al-Bashir*, 1011, May 7, 1890; *Lisan al-Hal*, 1338, June 1, 1891; *Thamarat al-Funun*, 1321, March 4, 1901. In December 1890, the State Council in Istanbul issued orders to close all shops and warehouses storing and selling intoxicating substances in the provinces of Beirut, Aleppo, and Syria—but to no avail; *Thamarat al-Funun*, 814, December 22, 1890.
146 PRO, FO 195/2144, Damascus 12, W. S. Richards to O'Conor, (Damascus, February 10, 1903).
147 *Thamarat al-Funun*, 1479, May 9, 1904.

Chapter 2

1 Marshall McLuhan, *Understanding Media: The Extensions of Man* (New York: Signet, 1964), 7.
2 A reference to Chapter 3 titled "al-qalaq al-mumit wa al-qalaq al-muhyi," in Constantin Zureiq, *Ma al-'amal? Hadith ila al-ajyal al-'Arabiya al-tali'a* (Beirut: Markaz Dirasat al-Wihda al-'Arabiya, 1998).
3 Jacques Berque, *L'Égypte: Impérialisme et révolution* (Paris: Gallimard, 1967), 406.
4 Edward Said, *Orientalism* (New York: Patheon Books, 1978), 6 and 188–9.

5   Stavros Karayanni and Frédéric Lagrange insist Kuchuk was *ghazeya*. Flaubert calls her *'alme*. See Gustave Flaubert, *Flaubert in Egypt: A Sensibility on Tour*, trans. Francis Steegmuller (London: Penguin, 1996), 81.
6   Stavros Karayanni, *Dancing Fear & Desire: Race, Sexuality and Imperial Politics in Middle Eastern Dance* (Waterloo: Wilfrid Laurier Press, 2004), 29.
7   Ratiba al-Hifni, *Al-Sultana Munira al-Mahdiya wa al-ghina' fi Misr qablaha wa fi zamaniha* (Cairo: Dar El Shorouk, 2011), 164.
8   If one were to interpret al-Hifni's comments on al-Mahdiya's voice being close to that of *'alme*'s, one would assume the academic saw al-Mahdiya as part of a low-brow culture. Al-Mahdiya's hoarse voice was literally not polished and, therefore, lacked refinement; it was "vulgar" as *'alme*'s dance was often perceived in the twentieth century. It is also overtly sexualized, as *'alme*'s voice and dance were perceived by the middle class, educated elites.
9   al-Hifni, *Al-Sultana Munira al-Mahdiya wa al-ghina' fi Misr qablaha wa fi zamaniha*, 165.
10 Ibid., 155.
11 Perhaps this morally explosive combination of media, sex, and alcohol is best exemplified in Habiba Messika's popular hit of 1918, where in a lascivious voice the singer repeats: "On my sleeping bed/My legitimate partner came/bringing beer and champaign/He drank and entertained me/and spoiled me, on my sleeping bed." Most probably the available version on vinyl is a sanitized one. The word for "my legitimate partner" (*halili*) is too pompous for the context. It was originally in all probability "my lover" (*habibi*).
12 Ahmad Rami, quoted in al-Hifni, *Al-Sultana Munira al-Mahdiya wa al-ghina' fi Misr qablaha wa fi zamaniha*, 164.
13 Frédéric Lagrange, "Musiciens et poètes en Égypte au temps de la nahda," (Thèse de doctorat, Paris VIII, 1994), 259.
14 Ibid.
15 Um Kulthum recorded under the Odeon label "Ana 'ala Kayfak Ma'darsh abadan Akhalfak" (I am at the Mercy of Your Whims) and "El Khala'a w-el Dala'a mazhabi" in 1926.The lyrics of the latter were composed by Yunus al-Qadi, the same poet who wrote Munira al-Mahdiya's "Irkhi El-Sitara." See Walid El Khachab, "Um Kulthum ra'idat al-tahdith wa ayqunat al-turath," *al-Qahira*, February 4, 2020: 7.
16 See Bermalion El-Begmawy's five Facebook posts between September 29 and October 2, 2022, featuring the hashtag #الست_1931 on the launch year in the career of the Star of the East. https://www.facebook.com/Ywamreb.
17 Raphael Cormack, *Midnight in Cairo: The Divas of Egypt's Roaring 20s* (New York: Norton & Co., 2021), 53.
18 Badi' Khayri, *Mudhakkirat Badi' Khayri*, ed. Ibrahim Hilmi (Cairo: Supreme Council for Culture, 1996).
19 See Wendy Buenaventura, *Serpent of the Nile: Women and Dance in the Arab World* (London: Saqi Books, 1989).
20 Ahmad El-Hadari, *Mawsu'at tarikh al-sinima fi Misr*, 2nd edn. (Cairo: al-Hay'ah al-Misriyah al-'Ammah lil-Kitab, 2019), 150.

Chapter 3

1   Ernest Main, *Iraq from Mandate to Independence* (London: G. Allen & Unwin Ltd., 1935), 17.

2 Sahib al-Shahir, "al-Baladiyya: Maqha min ayyam al-zaman al-jamil," *Dhakira 'Iraqiyya* (supplement of *al-Mada* newspaper), November 2, 2009: 6.
3 Raphael Cormack, *Midnight in Cairo: The Divas of Egypt's Roaring 20s* (New York: W. W. Norton & Company, 2021), 5.
4 Khalid Kishtainy, *Ayyam 'Iraqiyya* (London: Dar al-Hikma, 2011), 51–2.
5 Cormack, *Midnight in Cairo*; Hanan Hammad, *Unknown Past: Layla Murad, The Jewish Muslim Star of Egypt* (Palo Alto: Stanford University Press, 2022); Chris Silver, *Recording History: Jews, Muslims, and Music Across Twentieth Century North Africa* (Palo Alto: Stanford University Press, 2022). Karin van Nieuwkerk, *"A Trade Like Any Other": Female Singers and Dancers in Egypt* (Austin: University of Texas Press, 2008); Virginia Danielson, *The Voice of Egypt: Umm Kulthum, Arabic Song, and Egyptian Society in the Twentieth Century* (Chicago: University of Chicago Press, 1997); Daniel-Joseph MacArthur-Seal, "Intoxication and Imperialism: Nightlife in Occupied Istanbul, 1918–23," *Comparative Studies of Asia, Africa and the Middle East* 37 (2017): 299–313; Camilla Pastor de Maria Campos, "Performers or Prostitutes? Artistes during the French Mandate over Syria and Lebanon, 1921–1946," *Journal of Middle East Women's Studies* 13, no. 2 (2017): 287–311; Anthony Shay, *The Dangerous Lives of Public Performers: Dancing, Sex, and Entertainment in the Islamic World* (London: Palgrave Macmillan, 2014); Avner Wishnitzer, "Eyes in the Dark Nightlife and Visual Regimes in Late Ottoman Istanbul," *Comparative Studies of South Asia, Africa and the Middle East* 37, no. 2 (2017): 245–61; Carole Woodall, "'Awakening a Horrible Monster': Negotiating the Jazz Public in 1920s Istanbul," *Comparative Studies of South Asia, Africa and the Middle East* 30, no. 3 (2010): 574–82.
6 Sami Zubaida, "Entertainers in Baghdad, 1900–1950," in *Inside Out: On the Margins of the Modern Middle East*, ed. Eugene Rogan (London: I.B. Tauris, 2002), 212–30.
7 Paul Starkey, "Nahda," in *Encyclopedia of Arab Literature*, ed. Julie Scott Meisami and Paul Starkey (London: Routledge, 1998), v.2, 573–4.
8 'Abd al-Karim al-'Allaf, *Baghdad al-qadima* (Baghdad: Matba'at al-Ma'arif, 1970), 125.
9 A. D. Firdus 'Abd al-Rahman Karim al-Lami, *Al-hayyat al-ijtima'iyya fi Baghdad* (Beirut: al-Dar al-'Arabiyya lil-Mawsu'at, 2017), 356.
10 Yeheskel Kojaman, *The Maqam Music Tradition of Iraq* (London: Self-published, 2001), 107.
11 al-'Allaf, *Baghdad al-qadima*, 122.
12 Kojaman, *The Maqam Music Tradition of Iraq*, 107.
13 'Abbas Baghdadi, *Li-alla nansa Baghdad fi al-'ishrinat* (Beirut: al-Mu'assasa al-'Arabiyya lil-Dirasat wa al-Nashr, 1998), 109–10; Kojaman, *The Maqam Music Tradition of Iraq*, 107–8.
14 Joseph Massad, *Desiring Arabs* (Chicago: University of Chicago Press, 2007), 278.
15 For more on the regulation of sex work in Iraq, including the mandatory medical examinations and health certificates provided by registered physicians, see Sara Farhan, "The Making of Iraqi Doctors: Reproduction in Medical Education in Iraq," (Ph.D. Dissertation, York University, 2021), 160–3.
16 Zubaida, "Entertainers in Baghdad, 1900–1950," 217.
17 al-'Allaf, *Baghdad al-qadima*, 121; 'Abd al-Karim al-'Allaf, *Qiyan Baghdad fi al-'asr al-'Abbasi wa al-'Uthmani al-akhir* (Baghdad: Matba'at Dar al-Tadamun, 1969), 176.
18 al-'Allaf, *Qiyan Baghdad*, 176.
19 Ma'ruf al-Rusafi, *Diwan Ma'ruf al-Rusafi* (Cairo: Hindawi, 2014), 735.
20 Afsaneh Najmabadi, *Women with Moustaches and Men Without Beards* (Berkeley: University of California Press, 2005), 3. See also Dror Ze'evi, *Producing Desire:*

Changing Sexual Discourse in the Ottoman Middle East, 1500–1900 (Berkeley: University of California Press, 2006).
21 Massad, *Desiring Arabs*, 53–7.
22 For more on same-sex practices and homoerotic desire in Iraq in the 1930s, see Pelle Valentin Olsen, "Cruising Baghdad: Desire Between Men in the 1930s Fiction of Dhu al-Nun Ayyub," *Journal of Middle East Women's Studies* 14, no. 1 (2018): 25–44.
23 Wilson Chacko Jacob, *Working out Egypt: Effendi Masculinity and Subject Formation in Colonial Egypt, 1870–1940* (Durham: Duke University Press, 2011), 183–5. See also Cormack, *Midnight in Cairo*, 63–4.
24 al-ʿAllaf, *Baghdad al-qadima*, 123.
25 al-ʿAllaf, *Qiyan Baghdad*, 196.
26 Liat Kozma, "Women's Migration for Prostitution in the Interwar Middle East and North Africa," *Journal of Women's History* 28, no. 3 (2016): 93–113; Pastor de Maria Campos, "Performers or Prostitutes?"; Lucia Carminati, "Afifa's Migration: Syrian Prostitutes and the 'White Slave Trade' in Port Said," *Journal of Middle East Women's Studies* 17, no. 3 (2021): 473–8.
27 al-Lami, *Al-hayyat al-ijtimaʿiyya fi Baghdad*, 357.
28 Kozma, "Women's Migration for Prostitution," 98.
29 Mudiriyyat al-Shurta al-ʿAmma, *Taqrir al-sanawi li-sanat 1929* (Baghdad: Matbaʿat al-Hukuma, 1929), 81; Mudiriyyat al-Shurta al-ʿAmma, *Taqrir al-sanawi li-sanat 1930* (Baghdad: Matbaʿat al-Hukuma, 1930), 66; Mudiriyyat al-Shurta al-ʿAmma, *Taqrir al-sanawi li-sanat 1931* (Baghdad: Matbaʿat al-Hukuma, 1931), 65.
30 *Taqrir al-sanawi li-sanat 1930*, 66.
31 *Taqrir al-sanawi li-sanat 1931*, 89.
32 Baghdadi, *Li-alla nansa Baghdad fi al-ʿishrinat*, 105–6.
33 Yosef Meʾir, *Hitpathut tarbutit Hevratit shel Yehudey ʿIraq meʾaz 1830 veʿad Yemenu* (Tel Aviv: Naharayim, 1989), 439.
34 *Al-Istiqlal*, November 7, 1938: 4.
35 *Sawt al-Shaʿb*, December 24, 1939: 3.
36 Ibid., 4.
37 For a detailed study of the al-Kuwaiti brothers, see Dafna Dori, "The Brothers al-Kuwaity and the Iraqi Song 1930–1950," (Ph.D. Dissertation, University of Uppsala, 2021). See also ʿAli Nasir Kanana, *Falak an-Nass fi al-Ghinaʾ al-ʿIraqi* (Köln: al-Kamel Verlag, 2016); Al-Hajj Hashim Muhammad al-Rajab, *Al-maqam al-ʿIraqi* (Beirut: Dar al-ʿArabiyya Lilmawsuʿat, 2009).
38 Yehezkel Kojaman, *Al-musiqa al-fanniya al-muʿasira fi al-ʿIraq* (Baghdad: Dar Mesopotamia, 2015), 166–7.
39 ʿAli ʿAbd al-Amir, *Raqsat al-fustan al-ahmar al-akhrira: Sabʿ ʿuqud min taʾrikh al-ʿIraq ʿabar al-ghinaʾ wa al-musiqa* (Milano: Manshurat al-Mutawassit, 2017), 258–60.
40 Kojaman, *The Maqam Music Tradition of Iraq*, 41.
41 Cormack, *Midnight in Cairo*, 9; Hammad, *Unknown Past*.
42 al-ʿAllaf, *Qiyan Baghdad*, 196.
43 Orit Bashkin, *The Other Iraq: Pluralism and Culture in Hashemite Iraq* (Palo Alto: Stanford University Press, 2009), 140–1.
44 Bashkin, *The Other Iraq*, 146–8.
45 Orit Bashkin, "'When Muʿawiya Entered the Curriculum'—Some Comments on the Iraqi Education System in the Interwar Period," *Comparative Education Review* 50, no. 3 (2006): 351. See also Peter Wien, *Arab Nationalism: The Politics of History and Culture in the Modern Middle East* (London: Routledge, 2017), 35–47.

46 For similar trends in the North African music and recording industry, see Silver, *Recording History*, ch. 3 and 5.
47 Ziad Fahmy, *Ordinary Egyptians: Creating the Modern Nation Through Popular Culture* (Stanford: Stanford University Press, 2011), 1–3. See also Walter Armbrust, *Mass Culture and Modernism in Egypt* (Cambridge: Cambridge University Press, 1996); Carmen Gitre, *Acting Egyptian: Theatre, Identity, and Popular Culture in Cairo 1869–1930* (Austin: University of Texas Press, 2009); Lucie Ryzova, *The Age of the Efendiyya: Passages to Modernity in National-Colonial Egypt* (Oxford: Oxford University Press, 2014).
48 Cormack, *Midnight in Cairo*, 8.
49 Faʾiq Shakir, *Al-amrad al-zuhariyya* (Baghdad: Matbaʿt al-ʿAhd, 1934), 6–10. I would like to thank Sara Farhan for sharing Shakir's text with me.
50 Fadil Husayn, "Awqat al-faragh: Niʿma wa naqma," *al-Muʿallim al-Jadid* 1, no. 2 (1935): 218.
51 Orit Bashkin, "Representations of Women in the Writings of the Intelligentsia in Hashemite Iraq, 1921–1958," *Journal of Middle East Women's Studies* 4, no. 1 (2008): 59; Zubaida, "Entertainers in Baghdad, 1900–1950," 213.
52 Haytham Bahoora, "The Figure of the Prostitute, *Tajdid*, and Masculinity in Anti-Colonial Literature of Iraq," *Journal of Middle East Women's Studies* 11, no. 1 (2015): 42–3. See also Haytham Bahoora, "Baudelaire in Baghdad: Modernism, The Body, and Husayn Mardan's Poetics of the Self," *International Journal of Middle East Studies* 45, no. 2 (2013): 313–29.
53 Bahoora, "The Figure of the Prostitute," 44.
54 Muhammad Mahdi al-Jawahiri, *Diwan al-Jawahiri* (Beirut: Dar al-ʿAwda, 1982), vol. 2, 42.
55 Mahmud Ahmad al-Sayyid, "Talib Effendi," in *Al-aʿmal al-kamila li Mahmud Ahmad al-Sayyid*, ed. ʿAli Jawad al-Tahir and ʿAbd al-Ilah Ahmad, 519–30 (Baghdad: Dar al-Hurriyya, 1978).
56 Bashkin, *The Other Iraq*, 194.
57 Bashkin, *The Other Iraq*, 195–207; ʿAli Jawad al-Tahir, *Mahmud Ahmad al-Sayyid: Raʾid al-qissa al-haditha fi al-ʿIraq* (Beirut: Dar al-Adab, 1969), 24–5, 148 and ʿAbd al-Ilah Ahmad, *Al-adab al-ʿIraqi mundhu al-harb al-ʿalamiyya al-thaniya* (Damascus: Ittihad al-Kuttab al-ʿArab, 2001), 224–8.
58 ʿAziz al-Hajj, *Abu Huraira al-Mawsuli: Dhu al-Nun Ayyub wa siratuhu* (London: Riad al-Rayyis, 1990), 36.
59 Dhu al-Nun Ayyub, "Hinama Tathur al-ʿAsifa," in *Al-athar al-kamila li-adab Dhi al-Nun Ayyub*. Vol. 1. (Baghdad: Wizarat al-Iʿlam, 1977), 204.
60 Ibid.
61 Ibid.
62 Ibid.
63 Pastor de Maria Campos, "Performers or Prostitutes?," 288.
64 Ibid., 307.
65 Kozma, "Women's Migration for Prostitution," 94–5. See also Liat Kozma, *Global Women, Colonial Ports: Prostitution in the Interwar Middle East* (New York: Syracuse University Press, 2011); Carminati, "Afifa's Migration," 473–8; Lucia Carminati, "'She Will Eat your Shirt': Foreign Migrant Women as Brothel Keepers in Port Said and along the Suez Canal, 1980–1915," *Journal of the History of Sexuality* 30, no. 2 (May 2021): 161–94.
66 ʿAbd al-Amir, *Raqsat al-fustan al-ahmar al-akhira*, 170.

67 al-ʿAllaf, *Qiyan Baghdad*, 222–3, 252.
68 Ibid., 253, 231.
69 Ibid., 217.
70 Kojaman, *Al-musiqa al-fanniyya al-muʿasira fi al-ʿIraq*, 46.
71 al-ʿAllaf, *Qiyan Baghdad*, 221.
72 Eli Amir, *The Dove Flyer*, trans. Hillel Halkin (London: Halban, 1998), 59, 406.
73 Ibid., 109.

Chapter 4

1 "Salat Blanche: Majmuʿa mutanaqida min al-lughat, wal-azyaʾ wal-raqisat [A contradictory mixture of languages, fashion and dances]," *al-ʿAsifa* 65, December 1, 1933.
2 *al-ʿAsifa*, January 1, 1932, no. 1. Blanche had a tough childhood; she was the concubine of the son of the Sultan ʿAbd al-Hamid since she was fourteen. She was forced to leave the palace after seven years, and started dancing in Istanbul cabarets. After several years in Beirut, she was granted the Lebanese nationality.
3 *al-ʿAsifa*, January 1, 1932, no. 1.
4 *al-ʿAsifa*, December 1, 1933, no. 65.
5 On the economic, political and social evolution of Beirut, see May Davie, *Beyrouth et ses faubourgs (1840–1940): une intégration inachevée* (Beirut: CERMOC, 1996); Carla Eddé, *Beyrouth, Naissance d'une capitale (1918–1924)* (Paris: Actes Sud, 2009); Jens Hanssen, *Fin de Siècle Beirut: The Making of an Ottoman Provincial Capital* (Oxford: Oxford University Press, 2005); Samir Kassir, *Histoire de Beyrouth* (Paris: Fayard, 2003); Samir Khalaf, *Heart of Beirut: Reclaiming the Bourj* (London: Saqi, 2006); Nada Sehnaoui, *L'occidentalisation de la vie quotidienne à Beyrouth, 1860–1914* (Beirut: Dar an-Nahar, 2002); Elizabeth Thompson, *Colonial Citizens: Republican Rights, Paternal Privilege, and Gender in French Syria and Lebanon* (New York: Columbia University Press, 2000).
6 Henry Guys, *Beyrouth et le Liban, Relation d'un séjour de plusieurs années dans ce pays* (Paris: Au Comptoir des Imprimeries, 1850), vol. 1, 82.
7 Louis Enault, *La Vierge du Liban* (Paris: L. Hachette, 1858), 302.
8 *Lisan al-Hal*, May 24, 1899, no. 3122.
9 *Lisan al-Hal*, March 31, 1897, no. 2468; *al-Muqattam*, December 19, 1889.
10 The name of Layla, the former star of Sulayman al-Qardahi, was mentioned in the Egyptian press along with Salama Hijazi in *al-Ahram*, April 2 and May 17, 1888, December 5, 1889 (articles mentioned in Adam Mestyan, "A Garden with Mellow Fruits of Refinement: Music Theatres and Cultural Politics in Cairo and Istanbul, 1867–1892," (Ph.D. Diss., Faculties of the Central European University, Budapest, 2011), 281–2.
11 *al-Muqattam*, September 22, 1897 and *al-Muʾayyad*, October 12, 1899.
12 *al-Muʾayyad*, August 25, 1897.
13 Taysir Khalaf, "Omar Wasfi, al-mumathil al-Misri ila Suriyya baḥthan ʿan al-mutriba Malaka Surur," *Al-Arabi al-Jadid*, August 22, 2020.
14 *al-Muqattam*, September 3, 1897; *al-Muʾayyad*, September 4, 1897; *al-Akhbar*, September 21, 1898; *Jaridat Misr*, October 4, 6, and 12, 1897.
15 *al-Bashir*, January 17, 1898.
16 Taysir Khalaf, *Min Dimashq ila Chicago* (Beirut: al-Muʾassasa al-ʿArabiyya lil-Dirasat wal-Nashr, 2018).

17 Khalaf, "Omar Wasfi."
18 Unfortunately, apart from their records and few ads announcing concerts or plays, the life stories, origin, and career of these early female singers remain unknown.
19 On the emergence of record industry in the region, see Ali Jihad Racy, "Musical Change and Commercial Recording in Egypt, 1904–1932," (Ph.D. Diss., Urbana-Champaign: University of Illinois, 1977); Pekka Gronow, "The Record Industry Comes to the Orient," *Ethnomusicology* 25, no. 5 (1981): 251–84; Frédéric Lagrange, "Musiciens et poètes en Égypte au temps de la Nahda," (Ph.D. Diss., Paris VIII University, Paris, 1994); Bernard Moussali and Lambert Jean, "Géostratégie de l'enregistrement commercial," in *Les Premiers Chanteurs des Bilad al-Sham*, eds. Kamal Kassar, Mustafa Sa'îd, and Diana Abbani (Beirut: AMAR Foundation, 2014); Diana Abbani, "Musique et société au temps de la Nahda," (PhD Diss., Paris 4 - Sorbonne University, Paris, 2018).
20 On the commodification of music, see Andy Bennett, "Towards a Cultural Sociology of Popular Music," *Journal of Sociology* 44, no. 4 (2008): 419–32; Roland Gelatt, *The Fabulous Phonograph, 1877–1977* (New York: MacMillan Publishing Company 1977); Mark Katz, *Capturing Sound: How Technology Has Changed Music* (Berkeley: University of California Press, 2004); Timothy Dean Taylor, *Strange Sounds: Music, Technology, and Culture* (New York: Routledge, 2001).
21 On the emergence of the middle class and new ways of consumption in Beirut: Akram Fouad Khater, *Inventing Home: Emigration, Gender, and the Middle Class in Lebanon, 1870–1920.* (Berkeley: University of California Press, 2001); Toufoul Abou-Hodeib, "Taste and class in late Ottoman Beirut," *International Journal of Middle East Studies* 43, no. 3 (2011): 475–92.
22 *Lisan al-Hal*, March 30, 1921, no. 8273; October 20, 1923, no. 8890; December 8, 1923, no. 9087; March 2, 1925, no 9429; June 6, 1925, no. 9509; June 2, 1926, no. 9786; November 15, 1928, no. 10414; April 25, 1929, no. 19531.
23 On the legal status of women artists under the French mandate, see Camilla Pastor de Maria Campos, "Performers or Prostitutes? Artistes during the French Mandate over Syria and Lebanon, 1921–1946," *Journal of Middle East Women's Studies* 13, no. 2 (2017): 287–311.
24 This was not particular to Beirut, as Lagrange demonstrates it in his study on women singers in Egypt: Frédéric Lagrange, "Women in the Singing Business, Women in Songs," *History Compass* 7, no. 1 (2009): 226–50.
25 After a short stay in Egypt in 1931, her father, Georges Daccache advertised her in a sequence of ads published in the press to promote her. He gloated about the Egyptian training she had with "the best musicians and men of honor" (*al-Barq*, January 12, 1931, no. 3389). A few weeks later, he published another letter announcing her return after a tour in several Arab countries, in which they thanked the Palestinian authorities and the people for their hospitality and the celebrations made in her honor. Laure rejoiced at her concerts in Amman, including one under the prince's patronage and another reserved for women under the princess' patronage (*al-Barq*, November 16, 1932, no. 3452).
26 The *muwashahhat* (sing. *muwashah*) are a vocal musical genre based on a poetic form in classical Arabic and entirely composed. Thought to be of medieval Andalusian origin, they are rooted in the modal and rhythmic cycles of Arab music. They form one of the pillars of the traditional musical suit *al-wasla*, like *al-adwar* (sing.dawr), which are also a vocal form (semi-composed semi improvised) that flourished at the end of the nineteenth century in Egypt.

27 *Lisan al-Hal*, March 20, 1907, no. 5360.
28 Hanssen, *Fin de Siècle Beirut*, chapter 4, 115–37.
29 *al-ʿAsifa*, October 29, 1932, no. 23.
30 *al-ʿAsifa*, July 22, 1933, no. 49.
31 Ibid.
32 *al-Idhaʿa*, Year 1, 1938, no. 3.
33 *al-ʿAsifa*, April 30, 1933, no. 37.
34 *al-ʿAsifa*, January 29, 1932, no. 5.
35 Ibid.
36 Ibid.
37 *al-ʿAsifa*, February 12, 1932, no. 7.
38 *al-ʿAsifa*, January 15, 1932, no. 3.
39 Ibid.
40 *al-ʿAsifa*, February 11, 1933, no. 27.
41 Ibid.
42 *al-ʿAsifa*, January 8, 1932, no. 2.
43 *al-Maʿrad*, December 11, 1924, no. 259.
44 Karin van Nieuwkerk, *"A Trade Like Any Other": Female Singers and Dancers in Egypt* (Austin: University of Texas Press, 2008).
45 *al-ʿAsifa*, May 28, 1934, no. 84.
46 *al-ʿAsifa*, April 30, 1933, no. 37.

Chapter 5

1 M. M. Badawi, "Introduction," in *Modern Arabic Literature*, ed. M. M. Badawi (Cambridge: Cambridge University Press, 1993), 23.
2 Olivia C. Harrison, *Transcolonial Maghreb: Imagining Palestine in the Era of Decolonization* (Stanford: Stanford University Press, 2015).
3 The Spanish Protectorate in Morocco (1912–56) occupied a smaller northern zone, with its capital in the historic center of Andalusi culture of Tétouan. Like the French, Spanish authorities took an active interest in Moroccan music and arts, but largely focused on Andalusi heritage in an effort to establish cross-cultural linkages between Morocco and Spain, the historic al-Andalus. This section focuses on French colonial interventions due to France's wider influence throughout the Maghreb region; for more on the Spanish project, see Eric Calderwood, *Colonial al-Andalus: Spain and the Making of Modern Moroccan Culture* (Cambridge, MA: Harvard University Press, 2018); and Samuel Llano, "Empire, Diplomacy, and the Racial Imagination: Spain at the Cairo Congress of Arab Music (1932)," *Journal of North African Studies*, doi:10.1080/13629387.2022.2089123.
4 On associationism, see Raymond Betts, *Assimilation and Association in French Colonial Theory, 1890–1914* (Lincoln: University of Nebraska Press, 2004).
5 On arts and crafts, see James Mokhiber, "'Le protectorat dans la peau,'" in *Revisiting the Colonial Past in Morocco*, ed. Driss Maghraoui (London: Routledge, 2013), 257–84; on Islamic practice, see Edmund Burke III, *The Ethnographic State: France and the Invention of Islam* (Berkeley: University of California Press, 2014); on urban planning and architecture, see Janet L. Abu-Lughod, *Urban Apartheid in Morocco* (Princeton: Princeton University Press, 1980).

6   Elizabeth Matsushita, "Disharmony of Empire: Race and the Making of Modern Musicology in Colonial North Africa," (Ph.D. Diss., University of Illinois at Urbana-Champaign, 2021).
7   Patricia M. E. Lorcin, *Imperial Identities: Stereotyping, Prejudice, and Race in Colonial Algeria* (London: I.B. Tauris, 1995).
8   Jonathan Wyrtzen, "National Resistance, Amazighité, and (Re-)Imagining the Nation in Morocco," in *Revisiting the Colonial Past in Morocco*, ed. Driss Maghraoui (London: Routledge, 2013), 184–204.
9   For example, the Three Days of Moroccan Music concert that was sponsored by the French Protectorate in Rabat in 1928 had its first day programming split into two sections, "Berber music" and "urban music," the latter primarily Andalusi music. Two of the concerts at the 1939 Fez Congress of Moroccan Music were also expressly split into "Berber music" and "Andalusian music" sections.
10 Alexis Chottin, *Corpus de musique marocaine* (Paris: Service des arts indigènes, 1931), and *Tableau de la musique marocaine* (Paris: Librairie Orientaliste Paul Geuthner, 1939).
11 Jonathan Glasser, *The Lost Paradise: Andalusi Music in Urban North Africa* (Chicago: University of Chicago Press, 2016), 177–8.
12 Jonathan Holt Shannon, *Performing al-Andalus: Music and Nostalgia across the Mediterranean* (Bloomington: Indiana University Press, 2015).
13 Calderwood, *Colonial al-Andalus*.
14 Glasser, *The Lost Paradise*, 120–1.
15 Ziad Fahmy, *Ordinary Egyptians: Creating the Modern Nation through Popular Culture* (Stanford: Stanford University Press, 2011).
16 Christopher Silver, "The Sounds of Nationalism: Music, Moroccanism, and the Making of Samy Elmaghribi," *International Journal of Middle East Studies* 52 (2020): 23–47.
17 Glasser, *The Lost Paradise*, 139.
18 ANOM Box ALG GGA 15H/1 "Algerian Press" Box 1.
19 Glasser, *The Lost Paradise*, 139.
20 Archives privées Prosper Ricard 11AP/302 "Caire: Congrès de musique arabe" (Archives du Musée Quai-Branly).
21 1er *Congrès de la musique marocaine* (program) (Casablanca: Imprimeries Réunies, 1939); Patrocinio García Barriuso, *Ecos del Magrib: La Musique Hispano-Musulmane au Maroc* (Tangier: Éditorial Tanger, 1940), 26–33.
22 *La T.S.F. et le Cinéma à l'École: Bulletin Trimestriel* (Rabat: Direction de l'Instruction Publique, des Beaux Arts et des Antiquités Quatrième Année, Avril-Juin 1932).
23 Philip Thornton, *The Voice of Atlas: In Search of Music in Morocco* (London: Alexander Maclehose & Co., 1936), 22–3.
24 *La Radio Marocaine* (Casablanca/Paris), Année 5, No. 35 (July 6, 1934), Année 7, No. 120 (February 21, 1936), Année 7, No. 129 (April 24, 1936), Année 7, No. 142 (July 24, 1936).
25 Jean-Louis Planche, "Notice SAFIR El Boudali," Dictionnaire Algérie (January 9, 2014), accessed May 27, 2022, https://maitron.fr/spip.php?article152168.
26 El Boudali Safir, "La musique arabe en Algérie," in *Documents Algériens* (Service d'Information du Cabinet du Gouverneur Générale de l'Algérie: Série Culturelle No. 36, June 20, 1949), 1.
27 Manoubi Snoussi, "Folklore Tunisien: Musique de Plein Air: L'Orchestra Tabbal et Zakkar," in *Revue des Études Islamiques* (Paris: Paul Geuthner Orientalist Library, 1961), 150.

28 Ibid., 150.
29 Mourad Sakli, "Avant-Propos," in *Initiation à la musique tunisienne, Volume 1: Musique Classique*, eds. Mourad Sakli, Rachid Sellami, and Lassaad Kriaa (Sidi Bou Saïd: Centre des Musiques Arabes et Méditerranénnes, 2004).
30 Omnia El Shakry, *The Great Social Laboratory* (Stanford: Stanford University Press, 2007).
31 Glasser, *The Lost Paradise*, 1.
32 Barriuso, *Ecos del Magrib*, 45–7.
33 Moulay Idris ben Abdelali El Idrissi, *Kashf al-ghita'* (Rabat: Al-Taba'a al-Wataniyya, 1939), 2.
34 Salah El Mahdi, "Préface," in *Patrimoine Musicale Tunisien, 2e Fascicule: Ensemble des Tawchihs et Zajals Tunisiens* (République Tunisienne, Sécretariat d'État aux Affaires Culturelles et l'Information, 1963).
35 Ali Jihad Racy, "Historical Worldviews of Early Ethnomusicologists: An East-West Encounter in Cairo, 1932," in *Ethnomusicology and Modern Music History*, ed. Stephen Blum, Philip Bohlman, and Daniel Neuman (Urbana: University of Illinois Press, 1991), 68–91.
36 Ruth F. Davis, *Ma'luf: Reflections on the Arab Andalusian Music of Tunisia* (Lanham: Scarecrow Press, 2004), 51.
37 Prosper Ricard Archives privées.
38 Mahmoud Guettat, "La Tunisie dans les documents du Congrès du Caire," in *La Musique Arabe: Le Congrès du Caire de 1932*, ed. Philippe Vigreux (Cairo: CEDEJ, 1992).
39 For more on this, see Matthew Machin-Autenrieth, "Spanish Musical Responses to Moroccan Immigration and the Cultural Memory of al-Andalus," *Twentieth-Century Music* 16, no. 2 (June 2019): 259–87.

Chapter 6

1 Tawfiq al-Hakim, *Sijn al-'Umr* (Cairo: Dar El Shorouk, 2003 [1964]), 65.
2 This was almost certainly based on Najib al-Haddad's (d.1899) Arabic translation of the play.
3 Hakim, *Sijn al-'Umr*, 65.
4 (Beirut: Dar Bayrut, 1956).
5 (Reading: Ithaca Press, 1996).
6 (Austin: University of Texas Press, 2021).
7 (Princeton: Princeton University Press, 2018).
8 (Cairo: GEBO, 1998).
9 (Cairo: GEBO, 2003).
10 (Houndmills: Palgrave Macmillan, 2011).
11 (Kuwait: al-Majlis al-Watani li-l-Thaqafa wa-l-Funun wa-l-Adab, 1980).
12 Peter Hill, "The Arabic Adventures of Télémaque: Trajectory of a Global Enlightenment Text in the Nahḍah," *Journal of Arabic Literature* 49, no. 3 (2018): 171–203.
13 *Jaridat Misr*, May 17, 1918, quoted in Lutfi 'Abd-al-Wahhab, *Al-masrah al-Misri: al-Mawsim al-masrahi 1917–1918* (Cairo: Wizarat al-Thaqafah, al-Markaz al-Qawmi lil-Masrah, 2001), 243–4.
14 Rifa'a Rafi' al-Tahtawi, Takhlis al-Ibriz fi Talkhis Bariz (Cairo: Hindawi, 2017 [1834]), 133.

15 'Ali Mubarak, *'Alam al-Din*, vol. 2 (Alexandria: Jaridat al-Mahrusa, 1882), 397 (esp. 402); Muhammad al-Muwaylihi, *What Isa Ibn Hisham Told Us [Hadith 'Isa ibn Hisham], Volume Two* (New York: New York University Press, 2015), 166–7. Translated by Roger Allen.
16 See Amr Zakaria Abd Allah, "The Theory of Theater for Egyptian Nationalists in the First Quarter of the Twentieth Century," *Quaderni di Studi Arabi* 4 (2009): 193–204.
17 Muwaylihi, *What Isa Ibn Hisham Told Us*, vol. 2, 168–9.
18 Ibid., 168–71.
19 For more on this, see Raphael Cormack, "Who's Afraid of Musical Theater?" in *Cultural Entanglement in the Pre-Independence Arab World: Arts, Thought and Literature*, ed. Anthony Gorman and Sarah Irving (London: I.B. Tauris, 2021), 33–50.
20 Like all "firsts," the issue of which was the "first Arabic play" is controversial (and perhaps given too much weight). Philip Sadgrove, *The Egyptian Theater in the Nineteenth Century: 1799–1882* (Reading: Ithaca Press, 1996) noted that two conflicting dates are given for the first performance of *al-Bakhil* (1847 or February 1848). Sadgrove has also proposed that the "first Arabic play" may have been an Algerian text in Philip Sadgrove and Shmuel Moreh, *Jewish Contributions to Nineteenth Century Arabic Theater: Plays from Algeria and Syria: A Study and Texts* (Oxford: Oxford University Press, 1996).
21 Muhammad Yusuf Najm, *al-masrahiyya fi al-adab al-'Arabi al-hadith, 1847–1914* (Beirut: Dar Bayrut, 1956), 107–14.
22 Ilham Khuri-Makdisi, *The Eastern Mediterranean and the Making of Global Radicalism, 1860–1914* (Berkeley: University of California Press, 2010), 92.
23 On 'Antar (and his association with Ahmad 'Urabi), see Mestyan, *Arab Patriotism*, 191–3; on Harun al-Rashid, see 219–25.
24 Ussama Makdisi, *Age of Coexistence: The Ecumenical Frame and the Making of the Modern Arab World* (Oakland: University of California Press, 2019), 90.
25 For a more recent study of the portrayal of the "peasant" in modern Egypt Lila Abu-Lughod, *Dreams of Nationhood: The Politics of Television in Egypt* (Chicago: University of Chicago Press, 2005).
26 Samah Selim, *The Novel and the Rural Imaginary in Egypt 1880–1985* (London: Routledge, 2004), 1–24 (quote at 4–5).
27 See for instance Beth Baron, "Readers and the Women's Press in Egypt," *Poetics Today* 15, no. 2 (1994): 217–40.
28 Taha Husayn, *Al-Ayyam*, vol. 1 (Cairo: Dar al-Ma'arif, 1942), 87–8.
29 Pierre Cachia "Introduction: Translations and Adaptations," in *Modern Arabic Literature* (The Cambridge History of Arabic Literature), ed. M. M. Badawi (Cambridge: Cambridge University Press, 1993), 35.
30 Ami Ayalon, "Arab Booksellers and Bookshops in the Age of Printing, 1850–1914," *British Journal of Middle Eastern Studies* 37, no. 1 (2010): 73–93, esp. 91–2.
31 Najm, *al-Mashrahiyya*, 169–73.
32 C. R. Ashbee, *Fantasia in Egypt*, King's College Cambridge Archives, CRA/3/5, 21–7.
33 Yusuf Wahbi, *'Ishtu alf 'am*, vol. 1 (Cairo: Dar al-Ma'arif, 1973), 16–23. After this performance, Wahbi describes seeing Sheikh Ahmed Shami's troupe perform *Romeo and Juliet*, perhaps the same troupe that al-Hakim had seen around the same time in Disuq).
34 Wahbi, *'Ishtu alf 'am*, vol. 1, 22.

35 *Al-Watan*, July 11, 1912 in Sayyid ʿAli Ismaʿil, *Masirat al-masrah fi Misr, 1900–1935* (Cairo: Hindawi, 2017), 402–3.
36 Wahbi, *ʿIshtu alf ʿam*, vol. 1, 16.
37 Mestyan, *Arab Patriotism*, 191–3.
38 See Ferial Ghazoul, "The Arabization of Othello," *Comparative Literature* 50, no. 1 (1998): 1–31; Sameh F. Hanna, "Decommercializing Shakespeare: Mutran's Translation of 'Othello,'" *Critical Survey* 19, no. 3 (2007): 27–54.
39 As early as 1926, popular magazines in Egypt were idolizing al-Qardahi and other Egyptian dramaturges as the pioneers of Tunisian theater. See, for example, *Kull Shay*, January 4, 1926, 10. See also Khalid Amine and Marvin Carlson, *The Theatres of Morocco, Algeria and Tunisia: Performance Traditions of the Maghreb* (Basingstoke: Palgrave Macmillan, 2012), 71–9.
40 Amine and Carlson, *The Theaters of Morocco, Algeria and Tunisia*, 75–7.
41 To hear these and other recordings by Hijazi, see the CD collection released by AMAR foundation in Beirut 2017 "Salama Higazi: Pioneer of the Arab Musical Theater."
42 Samuel England, "An Ayyubid Renaissance: Saladin, from Knighthood to Nahḍa," *Alif: Journal of Comparative Poetics* 38 (2018): 37–61.
43 Omar Sayfo, "From Kurdish Sultan to Pan-Arab Champion and Muslim Hero: The Evolution of the Saladin Myth in Popular Arab Culture," *Popular Culture* 50, no. 1 (2017): 65–85.
44 Najm, *al-Mashrahiyya*, 111–12. Quote from *al-Ahram*, February 4, 1909 (reproduced by Najm).
45 Or, according to ʿAli al-Raʿi, The Egyptian Tunisian Troupe.
46 For more on Qardahi in Tunisia, see Amine and Carlson, *The Theaters of Morocco, Algeria and Tunisia*, 77.
47 ʿAli Muhammad Hadi Rabiʿi, *al-Firaq al-masrahiyya al-Misriyya fi al-ʿIraq: Vol 1. Firqat Jurj Abyad* (Sharjah: al-Hayʾa al-ʿArabiyya lil-Masrah, 2019), appendix 1, 138–41.
48 Amine and Carlson, *The Theaters of Morocco, Algeria and Tunisia*, 88.
49 Suʿad Abyad, *Jurj Abyad: Al-masrah al-Misri fi miʾat ʿam* (Cairo: Dar al-Maʿarif, 1970), 226–8, quote from 227.
50 Jabir Sulayman, "Nusri al-Jawzi wa-l al-haraka al-masrahiyya fi Filistin: Qiraʾa fi dhakiratihi wa awraqih," *Majallat al-Dirasat al-Filistiniyya* 7, no. 28 (1996): 135–46.
51 Fatima Rushdi, *Kifahi fi-l-Masrah wa-l-Sinima* (Cairo: Dar al-Maʿarif, 1970), 101.
52 "Wataniyyat Fatima Rushdi," *Mirʾat al-Sharq*, May 24, 1930, 3. Yusuf Wahbi was also criticized in Palestine for not boycotting Jewish venues.

Chapter 7

1 "The Lofty Castle at the Anvers Exposition," *al-Mathaf* 16, June 1894: [121].
2 Including: Ami Ayalon, *The Arabic Print Revolution: Cultural Production and Mass Readership* (Oxford: Oxford University Press, 2016); Stephen Sheehi, "Arabic Literary-Scientific Journals Precedence for Globalization and the Creation of Modernity," *Comparative Studies of South Asia, Africa and the Middle East* 25, no. 2 (2005): 439–49; Elizabeth Holt, "Narrating the Nahda: The Syrian Protestant College, *al-Muqtataf*, and the Rise of Jurji Zaydan," in *One Hundred and Fifty*, ed. Nadia El Cheikh, Lina Choueiri, and Bilal Orfali (Beirut: American University of Beirut Press, 2015), 273–80.

3   For Ottoman journals, see Palmira Brummett, *Image and Imperialism in the Ottoman Revolutionary Press, 1908–1911* (Albany: SUNY Press, 2000); Ahmet Ersoy, "Ottomans and the Kodak Galaxy: Archiving Everyday Life and Historical Space in Ottoman Illustrated Journals," *History of Photography* 40, no. 3 (2016): 330–57. For Arabic periodicals, see Hala Auji, "Printed Images in Flux: Examining Scientific Engravings in Nineteenth-Century Arabic Periodicals," in *Visual Design: The Periodical Page as a Designed Surface*, ed. Andreas Beck, Nicola Kaminski, Volker Mergenthaler, and Jens Ruchatz (Hannover: Wehrhahn Verlag, 2019), 119–36; Auji, "Picturing Knowledge: Visual Literacy in Nineteenth-Century Arabic Periodicals," in *Making Modernity in the Islamic Mediterranean*, ed. Margaret S. Graves and Alex Dika Seggerman (Bloomington: Indiana University Press, 2022), 72–93.
4   "The Telephone," *al-Muqtataf* 2, no. 8 (1877): 208.
5   Such as the illustrations seen in the publication *Abu Naddara* (The Bespectacled One; Cairo, 1877–8; Paris, 1878–1910), which published satirical cartoons criticizing the Egyptian Khedives and Ottoman rulers. My discussion does not extend to this publication because it was mostly based in Paris. See Ayalon, *The Press in the Arab Middle East* (Oxford: New York University Press, 1995), 44–5. See also Sarah H. Awad, "Political Caricatures in Colonial Egypt: Visual representations of the people and the nation," in *Cultural Entanglement in the Pre-Independence Arab World: Arts, Thought and Literature*, ed. Anthony Gorman and Sarah Irving (New York: Bloomsbury Publishing, 2020), 163–94.
6   By Butrus al-Bustani (1819–83) and his son Salim al-Bustani (1848–84).
7   Initially *Akhbar Tibbiyya* (1874–76), the journal was founded at the Syrian Protestant College in Beirut in 1874 by Dr. George Post, published at the American Mission Press (AMP). By 1884, the journal was also edited by Ibrahim al-Yaziji (1847–1906) and Bishara Zilzal.
8   First published by Yaʿqub Sarruf (1852–1927) and Faris Nimr (1856–1951) at the AMP in Beirut. Production shifted to Cairo in 1884, when the editors immigrated to Egypt.
9   Established by Syrian émigré Jurji Zaydan (1861–1914).
10 By Yaʿqub Nawfal and his son Constantine Nawfal. Yaʿqub was a sales agent for al-Bustani's *al-Jinan* in Alexandria. "List of Agents," *al-Jinan* 8 (1876–77).
11 Headed by Ibrahim al-Yaziji and Bishara Zilzal, who worked on *al-Tabib* before immigrating to Cairo.
12 Ayalon, *The Arabic Print Revolution*, 123–35; Ayalon, *The Press in the Arab Middle East*, 31.
13 The Hamidian press law required state authorization for periodicals and newspapers; copies were submitted to the state's press bureau (est. 1862), which monitored press (and theater) activity for any offensive or disruptive subject matter. Brummett, *Image and Imperialism*, 5.
14 Ayalon, *The Press in the Arab Middle East*, 53.
15 While they were predominantly men at the time, some journals were edited or owned by women. See Fruma Zachs and Sharon Halevi, *Gendering Culture in Greater Syria: Intellectuals and Ideology in the Late Ottoman Period* (London: I. B. Tauris, 2014); Marilyn Booth, *May Her Likes Be Multiplied Biography and Gender Politics in Egypt* (Berkeley: University of California Press, 2001).
16 Dyala Hamzah, "Introduction," in *The Making of the Arab Intellectual: Empire, Public Sphere, and the Colonial Coordinates of Selfhood*, ed. Dyala Hamzah (London:

Routledge, 2013), 1–2. See also Anne-Laure Dupont, "What is a *katib 'amm*? The Status of Men of Letters and the Conception of Language According to Jurji Zaydan," *Middle Eastern Literatures* 13, no. 2 (2010): 171–81.

17 Hamzah, "Introduction," 1–2.
18 For public benefit, see Toufoul Abou-Hodeib, *Taste for Home: The Modern Middle Class in Ottoman Beirut* (Stanford: Stanford University Press, 2020), 1–28.
19 This notion of the intellectual came before that of the widely discussed *muthaqqaf*, which Dyala Hamzah calls "the alienated figure of the modern intellectual." Hamzah, "Introduction," 1.
20 For instance, according to Ayalon "in Egypt in 1897 the 'over 20,000' who subscribed to newspapers and journals constituted only 5 percent of the literate public." Ayalon, *The Press in the Arab Middle East*, 153.
21 Some notes to readers even tried to shame them into paying by threatening to humiliate them by publishing the full names of subscribers who owed the press money. *Al-Mathaf* 26 (1894): 207.
22 While there are no clear records on literacy rates during the nineteenth century, Ayalon suggests that the number remained in the single digits until at least the First World War. He also posits that illiteracy rates in the Arab World remained at 80–90 percent until at least the mid-twentieth century, and even by then the majority of the population remained illiterate with only minor variations from one country to the other. Ayalon, *The Press in the Arab Middle East*, 140–5.
23 Shirine Hamadeh, "Public Sphere in the Eastern Mediterranean," in *A Companion to Islamic Art and Architecture*, ed. Finbarr Flood and Gülru Necipoğlu (Hoboken: Wiley, 2017), 1103.
24 Adam Mestyan speaks of these spaces, including journals, in which ideologies on patriotism, via the Khedival state, were circulating. See Mestyan, *Arab Patriotism: The Ideology and Culture of Power in Late Ottoman Egypt* (Princeton: Princeton University Press, 2017). For mass culture and public audiences, see Ziad Fahmy, *Ordinary Egypt: Creating the Modern Nation through Popular Culture* (Stanford, CA: Stanford University Press, 2011).
25 See Ersoy, "Ottomans and the Kodak Galaxy," 330–57.
26 Such as Ayalon, *The Press in the Arab Middle East*, 154–6; Sheehi, *The Arab Imago: A Social History of Portrait Photography* (Princeton: Princeton University Press, 2016), 90. For reading rooms and how booksellers and presses publicized their products, see Ayalon, "Arab Booksellers and Bookshops in the Age of Printing, 1850–1914," *British Journal of Middle Eastern Studies* 37, no. 1 (2010): 73–93. However, the claim that publications were read out loud in public squares or cafés may not be easy to prove given Ottoman restrictions on the public sphere at the time. For street life and the Ottoman public sphere, see Till Grallert's contribution in this volume.
27 Despite restrictive Ottoman publishing laws several private and state-sanctioned gazettes managed to obtain the necessary licenses and permissions for publication. See Brummett, *Image and Imperialism*.
28 Sheehi, *The Arab Imago*, 90.
29 As Filip di Tarrazi indicates, these terms were used interchangeably and were often the subject of debate among publishers. See Tarrazi, *Tarikh al-Sahafa al-'Arabiyya*, vol. 3–4 (Beirut: al-Matba'a al-Adabiyya, 1914), 7.
30 Exceptions like the American Missionary weekly journal for Arabic readers, *al-Nashra al-'Usbu'iyya*, which printed numerous images per issue, including some as color tints, made use of engravings readily available at the AMP, which were

also sold there. For more on *al-Nashra al-'Usbu'iyya*, see Deanna Ferree Womack, *Protestants, Gender, and the Arab Renaissance in Late Ottoman Syria* (Edinburgh: Edinburgh University Press, 2019), 85–142.

31 Other journals, like *al-Ahram* (The Pyramids; Cairo), had more paying subscribers (around 6,000) during the late 1800s. Sheehi, "Arabic Literary-Scientific Journals," 442–3.
32 *Al-Manara* (The Lighthouse; Alexandria, 1888) published by Najib Gharghur and Salim Bishara al-Khuri, (erroneously) claims to be the first illustrated journal. The journal is listed in Tarrazi, *Tarikh al-Sahafa*, 65.
33 Thanks to Till Grallert for his insights on this important point.
34 "Announcement," *al-Muqtataf* 7, no. 1 (1882), opening page.
35 See Geoffrey Roper, "The Beginnings of Arabic Printing by the ABCFM, 1822–1841," *Harvard Library Bulletin* 9, no. 1 (1998): 50–68; Dagmar Glaß, "Malta, Beirut, Leipzig and Beirut Again: Eli Smith, the American Syria Mission, and the Spread of Arabic Typography in Nineteenth-Century Lebanon" (Beirut: Orient-Institut Beirut, 1998); Hala Auji, *Printing Arab Modernity: Book Culture and the American Press in Nineteenth-Century Beirut* (Leiden: Brill, 2016). For other challenges facing private publishing at the time, see Kathryn Schwartz, "The Political Economy of Private Printing in Cairo, As Told from a Commissioning Deal Turned Sour, 1871," *International Journal of Middle East Studies* 49, no.1 (2017): 25–45.
36 Auji, *Printing Arab Modernity*.
37 Some presses between the 1850s and 1880s also purchased engraved blocks and typefaces from the American Mission Press in Beirut. Auji, "Printed Images in Flux."
38 For example, *al-Manara*, may have featured drawings by Alberto Fabbi (1858–1906), an Orientalist painter in Bologna, Italy, although it is not clear who made the engraving blocks.
39 *Al-Muqtataf* 4 (1876): 60; "al-Khala'iq al-Hayya fi al-Sayarat (Life in the Solar System)," *al-Tabib*, December 1884: 363; and "al-Khala'iq al-Hayya fi al-Sayarat (Life in the Solar System)," *al-Tabib*, January 1885: 422.
40 The same image, and a similar credit line, appear in an issue of *al-Hilal*. See *al-Hilal* 2, no. 10, January 15, 1894: 289.
41 Before the 1880s, most non-court/state funded artists in Syria and Egypt received either a formal education in Europe, at academies or at studios as apprentices, or an informal one as apprentices of European artists residing in Ottoman cities. However, painting, namely of icons, was long taught in Ottoman provinces at regional monasteries and churches. Artist Daoud Corm (1852–1930), for instance, studied icon painting with the Jesuits in Beirut, while painter Nicolas al-Sayegh (1863–1942) was trained in the Orthodox Church in Jerusalem. In Istanbul, some artists learned the basics of drawing as part of their military education. There were also small schools/workshops that taught painting and drawing before the major art academies were established, like the School of Fine Arts in Istanbul (1883) and Cairo (1908). For more on these artists, see Sarah Rogers, "Daoud Corm, Cosmopolitan Nationalism, and the Origins of Lebanese Modern Art," *The Arab Studies Journal* 18, no. 1 (2010): 46–77; Nisa Ari, "Spiritual Capital and the Copy: Painting, Photography, and the Production of the Image in Early Twentieth-Century Palestine," *The Arab Studies Journal* 25, no. 2 (2017): 60–99. For a discussion of Lebanese artists before the 1940s, and the changing views on *taswir*, see Kirsten Scheid, *Fantasmic Objects: Art and Sociality from Lebanon, 1920–1950* (Bloomington: Indiana University Press, 2022).

42 Beyond the minimal amount of identifying information (rarely included in footnotes in articles), it is difficult to get a good sense of where engravings came from. From images on hand, it is clear that many engravings were either purchased from Euro-American sources or were copied/engraved by local artisans. Auji, "Picturing Knowledge."
43 For instance, Mikhaʾil Farah engraved many images in *al-Jinan*, *al-Muqtataf*, and *al-Tabib* from the 1870s. He may have worked in some capacity for the AMP where these publications were first printed. Other engravers named in inscriptions were Salim Fadil, whose engravings appeared in *al-Bayan* and *al-Diyaʾ* (Illuminations; 1898–1899, Cairo), and Muhammad Hussain, who produced at least one engraving for an issue of *al-Bayan*, see *al-Bayan*, no. 2, April 1897: 60. Similarly informal views on copyright were seen in literary production at this time. For more on copyrights, see Nicole Khayat, "What's in a Name? Perceptions of Authorship and Copyright During the Arabic Nahda," *Nineteenth-Century Contexts* 41, no. 4 (2019): 423–40.
44 Inscriptions typically included the terms *hafr* (engraved), *naqsh* (drawing), or *taswir* (image-making) followed by the engraver's name.
45 By the early 1900s, some artists from the region began using printing methods and publications as part of their practice. The most notable example is Khalil Gibran (1883–1931), who produced drawings and paintings for publication in the New York-based art journal *al-Funun* (The Arts, 1913–16), which he co-edited with fellow Syrian émigrés in New York. See Anneka Lenssen, *Beautiful Agitation: Modern Painting and Politics in Syria* (Oakland: University of California Press, 2020).
46 Zachs and Halevi, *Gendering Culture*.
47 Based on my research into similar engravings across a variety of contemporaneous publications in Europe, Britain, and the United States, one possible (yet overlooked) link is the American journal *The Eclectic Magazine of Foreign Literature, Science, and Art* (New York, 1844–1907). Other journals that served as sources for Arabic publications like *al-Tabib* and *al-Muqtataf* included *The Youth's Companion* (Boston, 1836–1939), *Scientific American* (NY), and *The Popular Science Monthly* (London), among many others (including Italian and French journals popular among readers in Cairo and Alexandria).
48 See Auji, "Picturing Knowledge."
49 Describing similar contemporaneous engravings in American newspapers: "For the newspaper reader, such an image likely recalled an uneasy link between the two forms of electricity—unleashed and tamed, magnificent and mundane—even as residents became more comfortable with the urban infiltration of electric lights." Laura Turner Igoe, "Capturing 'Jove's Autograph': Late Nineteenth-Century Lightning Photography and Electrical Agency," *Panorama* 2, no. 1 (2016), https://doi.org/10.24926/24716839.1535.
50 Auji, "Picturing Knowledge," 85.
51 Another example is an article on the stomach that describes the function of an accompanying diagram, see *Al-Tabib* 1, no. 2 (1884): 28.
52 Walter Benjamin, *The Work of Art in the Age of Its Technological Reproducibility and Other Writings on Media* (Cambridge, MA: Harvard University Press, 2008), 40.
53 Shelly Jarenski, *Immersive Words: Mass Media, Visuality, and American Literature, 1839–1893* (Tuscaloosa: The University of Alabama Press, 2015), 3.
54 Jonathan Crary, *Suspensions of Perception: Attention, Spectacle, and Modern Culture* (Cambridge, MA: MIT Press, 1999), 1.
55 Crary quoted in Jarenski, *Immersive Words*, 4.

56 Crary, *Suspensions of Perception*, 362.
57 One example is an article on "natural/nature's illusions" in *al-Muqtataf* that describes, in very complicated terms, the science behind mirages, or fata morgana. While the editors were clearly trying to lessen the supernatural elements of such a phenomenon, their very description of the mirage of a boat floating in the air, or a caravan walking in the clouds, may have sounded mysterious and magical to most readers. *Al-Muqtataf* 1, no. 8 (1876): 177–80.
58 See Ellen Samuels, "Examining Millie and Christine McKoy: Where Enslavement and Enfreakment Meet," *Signs: Journal of Women in Culture and Society* 37, no. 1 (2011): 53–81.
59 On imperialist racialized desire at the time, see Ann Laura Stoler, *Race and the Education of Desire: Foucault's History of Sexuality and the Colonial Order of Things* (Durham: Duke University Press, 1995).
60 Samuels, "Examining Millie and Christine."
61 See examples in Edhem Eldem, "The Search for a Vernacular Ottoman Photography," in *The Indigenous Lens?: Early Photography in the Near and Middle East*, ed. Markus Ritter and Staci G. Scheiwiller (Berlin and Boston: De Gruyter, 2017), 29–56. See also Nancy Micklewright, "Orientalism and Photography," in *The Poetics and Politics of Place: Ottoman Istanbul and British Orientalism*, ed. Zeynep Inankur, Reina Lewis, and Mary Roberts (Istanbul: Pera Müzesİ, 2011), 99–110.
62 Timothy Mitchell explains that race, as an ethnographic concept, was first understood as "characters." Mitchell, *Colonising Egypt* (Berkeley: University of California Press, 1991), 105. As Ilham Khuri-Makdisi notes, it is important to avoid the pitfalls of an anachronistic discussion of race and ethnicity. Khuri-Makdisi, *The Eastern Mediterranean and the Making of Global Radicalism, 1860–1914* (Berkeley: University of California Press, 2010), 161–4.
63 Marwa Elshakry, *Reading Darwin in Arabic, 1860–1950* (Chicago: Chicago University Press, 2013), 82.
64 As noted by Qasim Amin in an *al-Muqtataf* issue from 1899, Egypt was more "advanced" as a "country with a former civilization, with historical traditions, religions, laws and customs," quoted in Elshakry, *Reading Darwin*, 87.
65 Ibid.
66 See Eldem, "The Search for a Vernacular Ottoman Photography"; Micklewright, "Orientalism and Photography."
67 Mitchell makes a similar argument, via Edward Lane's ethnographic work, as performing this contradictory duality. Timothy Mitchell, *Colonising Egypt* (Berkeley: University of California Press, 1988), 27.
68 Ahmet Ersoy, "Osman Hamdi Bey and the Historiophile Mood: Orientalist Vision and the Romantic Sense of the Past in Late Ottoman Culture," in *The Poetics and Politics of Place*, 145–55.
69 Ahmad Fahmi, "al-Funun al-Jamila," *al-Muqtataf* 11, no. 5 and 6 (1887): 260–5 (part 1); 329–40 (part 2). An excerpt of the article was translated into English by Katharine Halls in Lenssen, Rogers, and Shabout, *Modern Art in the Arab World: Primary Documents* (New York: Museum of Modern Art, 2018), 37–42.
70 Quoted translation by Halls and in Lenssen, Rogers, and Shabout, *Modern Art in the Arab World*, 41.
71 Ibid., 42.
72 "Fann al-Taswir," *al-Mathaf*, October 30, 1894: 325. This first line of the article, as well as several other sentences and sections in this 4-paged entry, seem to be lifted

verbatim from Syrian scholar Butrus al-Bustani's entry on the subject of painting, first published in his encyclopedia around 1882. Butrus al-Bustani, "Taswir, *Peinture*, Painting," *Kitab Da'irat al-Ma'arif*, vol. 6 (Beirut, 1876–1900), 137–45.

73   The article concludes with a discussion of contemporary practices and lauds the drawings of an (Egyptian?) *adib* named Najib Afandi Malik. According to the text, his "imitation of nature" using charcoal is so "perfect" that his services as a portrait artist—using the same medium he "mastered"—are frequently sought by patrons in Egypt and the region. Ibid., 328.

74   See Mary Roberts, *Istanbul Exchanges: Ottomans, Orientalists, and Nineteenth-Century Visual Culture* (Berkeley and Los Angeles: University of California Press, 2015).

75   "Announcement," *al-Mathaf*, August 14, 1894: 183.

Chapter 8

1   Molly Levine, Review of *The Gift of the Nile: Hellenizing Egypt from Aeschylus to Alexander. Classics and Contemporary Thought, 8*, by Phiroze Vasunia, *Bryn Mawr Classical Review*. Accessed April 16, 2020. https://bmcr.brynmawr.edu/2002/2002.08.32

2   Christopher Patridge, "Orientalism and the Occult," in *The Occult World*, ed. by Christopher Patridge (New York: Routledge, 2015), 620.

3   Carter Lupton, "'Mummymania' for the Masses – Is Egyptology Cursed by the Mummy's Curse?" in *Consuming Ancient Egypt*, ed. Sally MacDonald and Michael Rice, 1st edn. (New York: Routledge, 2009), 23.

4   Andrew H. Bellisari, "Raiders of the Lost Past: Nineteenth-Century Archaeology and French Imperialism in the Near East 1798-1914," (MA diss., Rutgers College, New Brunswick, New Jersey, 2010), 29.

5   Edward W. Said, *Orientalism: Western Conceptions of the Orient*, Reprint. with a New Afterword (New York: Penguin Books, 1995), 83.

6   Giovanni Belzoni, *Narrative of the Operations and Recent Discoveries within the Pyramids, Temples, Tombs and Excavations in Egypt and Nubia; And of a Journey to the Coast of the Red Sea, In Search for Old Berenice; And Another to the Oasis of Jupiter Ammon* (London: John Murray, 1820), 25.

7   Lynn Parramore, *Reading the Sphinx: Ancient Egypt in Nineteenth Century Literary Culture* (New York: Palgrave Macmillan, 2008), 28.

8   Deborah Philips, *Fairground Attractions: A Genealogy of the Pleasure Ground* (London: Bloomsbury Academic, 2012), http://dx.doi.org/10.5040/9781849666718.ch-006

9   Jeffrey Cass, "Interrogating Orientalism: Theories and Practices", in *Interrogating Orientalism: Contextual Approaches and Pedagogical Practices*, ed. Diane long Hoeveler and Jeffrey Cass (Columbus: The Ohio State University Press, 2006), 23.

10 In contrast to the "official" interest in ancient Egypt evident in King Pedro I's visit to Egypt in the mid-nineteenth century and his royal order to bring in an Egyptian collection to be housed in the National Museum of Brazil, popular appeal to ancient Egypt did not materialize before the twentieth century, concurrently with the spread of the spiritual Kardecist movement. A hybrid spiritism which combines Hindu and Christian precepts, Kardecists are partially inspired by

the ancient Egyptian Ka/Ba concepts. Ancient Egypt grew even more popular afterwards with plots set in ancient Egypt in modern Brazilian fiction, the most popular book of which is the Spiritist book *The Voice of Ancient Egypt*, republished since 1946. Similarly, in Japan, interest in ancient Egypt translated as the serious study of ancient Egypt or Egyptology began in the first decade of the twentieth century, commemorated in the work of the Japanese pioneering Egyptologists Katsumi Kuroita (1874–1946), Shougorou Tsuboi (1863–1913) and Kosaku Hamada (1881–1938). Conversely, Egyptomania was unheard of in Japan until 1965, when a Tutankhamun exhibition was held in Tokyo. In the aftermath of the massive Egyptian exhibition, ancient Egypt was featured in TV documentary films and other popular culture media. See Pedro Paulo A. Funari and Raquel dos Santos Funari, "Ancient Egypt in Brazil: A Theoretical Approach to Contemporary Uses of the Past," *Archaeologies: Journal of the World Archaeological Congress* 6 (2010): 53; Nozomu Kawai, "Egyptological Landscape in Japan: Past, Present, and Future," *CIPEG Journal* 1 (2017): 51-53, 55.

11 Charlotte Booth, *The Myth of Ancient Egypt* (Stroud: Amberley Publishing, 2011), cxlvii.
12 Kyle Haddad-Fonda, "The Rhetoric of 'Civilization' in Chinese-Egyptian Relations," *Middle East Institute*, August 1, 2017, https://www.mei.edu/publications/rhetoric-civilization-chinese-egyptian-relations#_ednref3
13 José Miguel Parra, "Europe's Morbid 'Mummy Craze' Has Been an Obsession for Centuries," *National Geographic*, December 12, 2019, https://www.nationalgeographic.co.uk/history-and-civilisation/2019/12/europes-morbid-mummy-craze-has-been-obsession-centuries
14 Kevin M. DeLapp, "Ancient Egypt as Europe's 'Intimate Stranger'", in *Negotiating Identities: Constructed Selves and Others*, ed. Helen Vella Bonavita (Amsterdam, the Netherlands: Rodopi, 2011), 173.
15 Mustafa Serdar Palabıyık, "Ottoman Travelers' Perceptions of Africa in the Late Ottoman Empire (1860-1922): A Discussion of Civilization, Colonialism and Race," *New Perspectives on Turkey* 46 (2012): 197-98, 203.
16 Georg G. Iggers, Q. Edward Wang, and Supriya Mukherjee, *A Global History of Modern Historiography*, 1st edn. (London: Pearson Education Limited, 2008), 88.
17 Donald Malcolm Reid, *Whose Pharaohs? Archaeology, Museums, and Egyptian National Identity from Napoleon to World War I* (Berkeley and Los Angeles, CA: University of California Press, 2002), 52-53.
18 See ʿAbd al-Rahman al-Rafiʿi, *Shuʿaraʾ al-wataniyah fi Misr: Tarajimuhum wa-shiʿruhum al-watani wa-al-munasabat allati nazamu fiha qasaʾidahum*, 3rd edn. (Cairo: Dar al-Maʿarif, 1992), 12; Taha Wadi, *Diwan Rifaʿa al-Tahtawi: Jamʿ wa-dirasa*, 4th edn. (Cairo: Dar al-Maʿarif, 1995), 83; and Ahmad Musa al-Khatib, *Al-shiʿr fi al-dawriyat al-Misriya, (1828-1882): Tawthiq wa-dirasa*, 1st edn. (Cairo: Dar al-Maʾmun lil-Tibaʿa wa-al-Nashr, 1987), 110.
19 Al-Tahtawi's poetic references to ancient Egypt are overwhelmingly generic and purposefully cited to support the lines' main theme; as a consequence, if in a poem al-Tahtawi extolled Muhammad ʿAli's "Egyptian" army, ancient Egyptian military power would be cited in such a context. Only in one poem, "Muqaddima Misriya Wataniya" (A Nationalistic Egyptian Preamble), references to ancient Egyptian famous sites are unusually mentioned such as Heliopolis, Memphis, Tennis, and Thebes, see Taha Wadi, *Diwan Rifaʿa al-Tahtawi: Jamʿ wa-dirasa*, 4th edn. (Cairo: Dar al-Maʿarif, 1995), 109-110.

20 Rifaʿa Rafiʿ al-Tahtawi, *Al-murshid al-amin lil-banat wa-al-banin*, 1st edn. (Egypt: Matbaʿat al-Madaris al-Malakiya, 1872), 124.
21 Rifaʿa Rafiʿ al-Tahtawi, *Manahij al-albab al-Misriya fi mabahij al-adab al-ʿasriya* (Cairo: Hindawi Foundation for Education and Culture, 2014), 105.
22 Ahmad Musa al-Khatib, *Al-shiʿr fi al-dawriyat al-Misriya (1828-1882): Tawthiq wa-dirasa*, 1st edn. (Cairo: Dar al-Maʾmun lil-Tibaʿa wa-al-Nashr, 1987), 111.
23 Ibid., 114.
24 Fayza Haikal, "Egypt Past Regenerated by Its Own People", in *Consuming Ancient Egypt*, ed. Sally MacDonald and Michael Rice (London: Routledge, 2016), 127.
25 At this early stage of his literary career, Shawqi was evidently influenced by European (notably French) literary authors. It is thus claimed that his poem "Kibar al-Hawadith fi Wadi al-Nil" was composed with Victor Hugo's collection of historical poems titled *La Légende des siècles* (The Legend of the Ages) (first published in 1859) in mind. See Shawqi Dayf, *Al-adab al-ʿArabi al-muʿasir fi Misr*, 10th edn. (Cairo: Dar al-Maʿarif, 1992), 111.
26 Harley Lietzelman, "Pharaonism: Decolonizing Historical Identity," *Prized Writing 2014-2015, UC Davis*. Accessed October 5, 2020. https://prizedwriting.ucdavis.edu/sites/prizedwriting.ucdavis.edu/files/users/snielson/9%20-%20Litzeilman.pdf
27 Reid, 208.
28 Ahmad Shawqi, *ʿAdhraʾ al-Hind* (Cairo: Hindawi Foundation for Education and Culture, 2017), 10.
29 Ibid.
30 Ibrahim al-Yaziji, 'Athar adabiya', *al-Bayan* 14 (16 December, 1897), reprinted in Editor-in-Chief, "Thaniyan: al-Nathr – maʿraka naqdiya hawl riwayat *ʿAdhraʾ al-Hind*," *Fussul* 2 (March 1983), 303.
31 Ibid.
32 Shakib Arsalan, *Shawqi, aw sadaqat arbaʿin sana* (Cairo: Matbaʿat Mustafa al-Babi al-Halabi, 1936), 61.
33 Ronald H. Fritze, *Egyptomania: A History of Fascination, Obsession and Fantasy* (London: Reaktion Books, 2016), 337.
34 Shawqi was not the only writer who capitalized on the high potential of the Arabic popular fiction business. Some Egyptian writers found this genre appealing; often translating global popular fiction from English (and other European languages) into Arabic for the new, avid Arabic readership. Muhammad Lutfi Jumʿa (1886-1953), for instance, was a writer and a dramatist whose key contributions to Egyptian Egyptomania were translations of popular, (Egyptian-themed) Victorian and Edwardian fiction. Jumʿa chose to translate Guy Boothby's Gothic Egypt bestseller *Pharos, the Egyptian* (1899) as the Arabic novel *al-sahir al-khalid/al-intiqam al-haʾil* in 1906 in the popular serial *Musamarat al-shaʿb* (The People's Entertainments), billed as the "most widely circulating illustrated social fiction weekly in Egypt." Samah Selim, "Pharaoh's Revenge: Translation, Literary History and Colonial Ambivalence", in *The Making of the Arab Intellectual: Empire, Public Sphere and the Colonial Coordinates of Selfhood*, ed. Dyala Hamzah (New York: Routledge, 2013), 25. *Musamarat al-shaʿb* also published non-translated fiction by bestselling writers such as Shawqi, who published his last and non-Pharaonic novelette, *Waraqat al-As: Qissa tarikhiya* (The Myrtle Leaf: A Historical Story) in 1904. See Kamil al-Shinnawi, *Zuʿamaʾ wa fannanun wa udabaʾ* (Cairo: Hindawi Foundation for Education and Culture, 2017), 74.
35 Reuven Snir, *Modern Arabic Literature: A Theoretical Framework* (Edinburgh, UK: Edinburgh University Press, 2017), 114.

36 Ahmed Darwesh, "Wa khayr jalis fi al-zaman riwaya jamila," *Dr. Ahmed Darwesh (Al-zama' lil-ma'rifa)*, March 30, 2017, http://www.drahmeddarwesh.com/?p=853
37 Muhammad Shafiqul Rahman al-Nadawi, "Riwayat 'Adhra' al-Hind li-Ahmad Shawqi: Dirasa tahliliya," *Aqlam al-Hind* 3 (July – September 2018). https://www.aqlamalhind.com/?p=1076
38 Ahmad Shawqi, *'Adhra' al-Hind* (Cairo: Hindawi Foundation for Education and Culture, 2017).
39 Irfan Shahid, "Shawqi wa Misr al-fir'awniya," *Fussul* 2 (March 1983): 322-323.
40 Other endeavors in de-Orientalizing Egyptomania in fin-de-siecle Arabic popular fiction include other writers of the Egyptian Nahda such as Jum'a was faithful to its de-Orientalizing and anti-imperial enterprise. Conscious of *Pharos, the Egyptian*'s imperial fantastical overtones of ancient Egypt, Muhammad Lutfi Jum'a used free translation as a de-colonizing textual strategy that appears like an act of writing back to an Edwardian imperial Egyptomaniac text, where Pharos, the ancient Egyptian villainous priest who is bent to destroy Western civilization in Boothby's novel, turned to be an avenger worthy of the Arabic readers' sympathy in Jum'a's translation. See Samah Selim, *Popular Fiction, Translation and the Nahda in Egypt* (Cham, Switzerland: Palgrave Macmillan, 2019), 158.
41 Shahid, 323-324.
42 Like the work of al-Tahtawi, Shawqi's Pharaonic quartet is replete with references to a "civilized" ancient Egypt, where the rule of law prevailed, an efficient, operative administration apparatus was in effect, and industry and craftsmanship were mastered. See Ahmad Shawqi, *'Adhra' al-Hind aw Tamaddun al-Fara'ina li-amir al-shu'ara' Ahmad Shawqi*, edited and introduced by Ahmad Ibrahim al-Hawari (Cairo: Ain for Human and Social Studies, 2005), 17-18.
43 Matti Moosa, *The Origins of Modern Arabic Fiction*, 2nd edn. (Boulder & London: Lynne Rienner Publishers, 1997), 223.
44 Pierre Cachia, *Ṭāhā Ḥusayn: His Place in the Egyptian Literary Renaissance* (London: Luzac & Company LTD., 1956), 34.
45 Matti, 223.
46 Muhammad Hasan 'Abdallah. *Kliyubatra fi al-adab wa al-tarikh* (Cairo: al-Hay'a al-Misriya al-'Amma lil-Ta'lif wal-Nashr, 1971), 38.
47 Anna Maria Montanari, *Cleopatra in Italian and English Renaissance Drama* (Amsterdam: Amsterdam University Press, 2019), 18.
48 Jonathan Gil Harris, *Shakespeare and Literary Theory* (Oxford: Oxford University Press, 2010), 197. There have been a few poetic representations of Cleopatra which preceded Shawqi's verse play *Masra' Kliyubatra* in 1927. The obscure poet Mahmoud Emad (1891-1965) published a historical narrative poem titled "Markus Antonyus wa Kliyubatra" (Marcus Antonius and Cleopatra) in 1917. See 'Abd al-Latif 'Abd al-Halim Abu Hammam, "Al-tajrib fi al-qasida al-'amudiya," *Nadwat afaq al-tajrib fi al-qasida al-'Arabiya al-mu'asira fi al-rub' al-akhir min al-qarn al-'ishrin: Ma'a ihtifa' khas bi-dhikra Amin Nakhla*, ed. Abd al-Aziz Jum'a, et al., (Kuwait: The Foundation of Abdulaziz Saud Al-Babtain's Prize for Poetic Creativity, 2001), 20, in addition to another poem that features Cleopatra titled "Kliyubatra tuhasib nafsaha fi al-sa'a al-akhira" (Cleopatra Self-Reflects in the Last Hour) by Wali al-Din Yakan (1873-1921), published in *Al-Muqtataf* (March 1924), 249-52.
49 Muhammad al-Barbari, "Hadith lil-Ustaz Muhammad 'Abd al-Wahhab: Al-Mawsim al-Jadid – *Masra' Kliyubatra* – *Majnun Layla*," *al-Sabah* 162 (3 November 1929), 4.

50. "Intaziru riwayat *Masra' Kliyubatra*," *al-Sabah* 173 (19 January 1930).
51. Bayram al-Tunisi, *Bayram al-Tunisi: Al-a'mal al-kamila*, vol. 2 (Cairo: Maktabat Madbuli, 2002), 679.
52. Elyas Sahhab, *Al-musiqa al-'Arabiya fi al-qarn al-'ishrin: Mashahid wa mahattat wa wujuh* (Lebanon: Dar al-Farabi, 2009), 42.
53. Frédéric Lagrange and Mustafa Said, "128 – Munira al-Mahdiyya 5," *Foundation for Arab Music Archiving & Research*. Accessed November 3, 2020. https://www.amar-foundation.org/128-munira-al-mahdiyya-5/
54. Israel Gershoni and James P. Jankowski, *Egypt, Islam, and the Arabs: The Search for Egyptian Nationhood, 1900-1930* (New York: Oxford University Press, 1986), 184.
55. Elliot Colla, *Conflicted Antiquities: Egyptology, Egyptomania, and Egyptian Modernity* (Durham and London: Durham University Press, 2007), 215.
56. G. M. Wickens, trans. "Little Pharaoh, a Short Story by Maḥmüd Taimür," *Journal of Arabic Literature* 10 (1979), 109.
57. Ibid.

Chapter 9

1. The French Mandate to Syria and Lebanon (1923–46), in Algeria (1830–1962), and in Tunisia (1881–1956).
2. From 1517 until 1867, with an interruption during the French occupation of 1798 to 1801.
3. Ella Schochat, "Egypt: Cinema and Revolution," *The African e-Journals Project* 2, no. 4 (1983): 22.
4. The revolution began on July 23, 1952, and was led by Mohamed Naguib and Gamal Abdel Nasser.
5. Taste is the ability to make discriminating judgments about aesthetic and artistic matters, see Michèle Ollivier and Viviana Fridman, "Taste/Taste Culture: International Encyclopedia of the Social and Behavioral Sciences," (n.d.), http://educ.jmu.edu/~brysonbp/symbound/papers2001/Olivier.html#:~:text=K1N%206N5%20Canada,Taste%2FTaste%20Culture,particular%20states%20of%20social%20relations.
6. Critics in public magazines also classified films as Egyptian versus colonial.
7. Haykal is one of the most significant Egyptian nationalists of that era, and his work influenced nationalistic education in Egyptian schools. He came from a family of wealthy landowners in the Delta, attended secular schools in Cairo, got his doctorate from the Sorbonne in Paris in 1912. He worked as a lawyer in Egypt, had a successful political career, and was a prominent journalist and writer. As a result, his interpretations and viewpoints were passed down through generations, see Benjamin Geer, "The Priesthood of Nationalism in Egypt: Duty, Authority, Autonomy," (Ph.D. Diss., School of Oriental and African Studies, University of London, 2011), 189.
8. Haykal intentionally placed the word *Fallah* (Peasant) after *Masri* (Egyptian) because he wanted the character to be Egyptian, and "peasant" to be seen as merely an adjective. I will explain this point later in the chapter.
9. Elliott Colla, "How *Zaynab* Became the First Arabic Novel," *History Compass* 7, no. 1 (2009): 5.
10. Muhammad Y. Gamal, "Foreign Movies in Egypt: Subtitling, Dubbing and Adaptation," in *Foreign Language Movies – Dubbing vs Subtitling*, ed. Angelika Goldstein and Biljana Golubović (Hamburg: Verlag Dr. Kovač 2009), 1.

11 Ibid.
12 Hassan Eid, "Sinima Ramsis: Muharabat al-ajanib li-idaratiha wa-aʿmaliha," *al-Sabah*, January 15, 1932: 15.
13 One of the distinguished Egyptian directors and a leading figure for the neo-realist stream.
14 Salah Abu Sayf, "Al-sinima fi Misr sinaʿa qawmiya yajib himayatuha," *al-Sabah* 294, May 15, 1932.
15 Mahmoud Qasim, *Tarikh al-sinima al-Misriya* (Arab Press Agency, 2018), 6–8.
16 Ibid., 7–8.
17 Ibid., 8.
18 Ibid., 9.
19 "Sharika lil-sinima am madha?! Tanaqud wa taharrub," *al-Masrah*, May 24, 1926: 16.
20 "Sharikat Film Isis: Hadith maʿa Wedad Bek ʿUrfi *Nidaʾ Allah*," *al-Masrah*, March 28, 1927: 7.
21 He is a leading economist, nationalist, thinker, and the founder of Studio Misr, the leading film studio in the country established in Egypt in 1934.
22 "Mahzala fi thawb mashruʿ watani," *Ruz al-Yusuf*, August 18, 1927: 11.
23 "Film *Layla*: ʿAziza Amir baʿd kasb al-maʿraka," *Ruz al-Yusuf*, November 24, 1927: 14.
24 Ibid.
25 Qasim, *Tarikh al-sinima al-Misriya*, 17.
26 "Diʿaya khatira ʾla Misr," *Ruz al-Yusuf*, February 7, 1928: 19.
27 Salma Mubarak, "Iqtibas al-nawʿ fi sardiyyat al-rif: *Zaynab* al-riwaya wa al-film al-samit," in *Al-iqtibas min al-adab ila al-sinima: Mahatat fi tarikh mushtarak*, ed. Salma Mubarak and Walid El Khachab, 1st edn. (Cairo: El-Maraya, 2021), 70–1.
28 Qasim, *Tarikh al-sinima al-Misriya*, 63–4.
29 Ibid., 23–4.
30 Ibid., 60–1.
31 Ibid., 23.
32 Ibid., 32–4.
33 Mahmoud Qasim cited many examples of critical reviews published without names in local newspapers in his *Tarikh al-sinima al-Misriyya*.
34 "Diʿaya khatira ʾla Misr," *Ruz al-Yusuf*, February 7, 1928, 19.
35 Salma Mubarak and Walid El Khachab, "Muqaddima: Al-Iqtibas fi al-sinima al-Misriyya: Mahattat tarikhiyya wa mafaheem taʾsisiya," in *Al-iqtibas min al-adab ila al-sinima: Mahatat fi tarikh mushtarak*, ed. Salma Mubarak and Walid El Khachab, 1st edn. (Cairo: El-Maraya, 2021), 10–11.
36 Colla, "How *Zaynab* Became the First Arabic Novel," 5–6.
37 Ibid., 7.
38 "*Zaynab* ʾla al-shasha al-bayda," *Ruz al-Yusuf* 169, April 22, 1930: 19.
39 The authors also mention the influence of theater on Egyptian cinema and find that during the first few decades of the local film production, films based on novels were more common than those based on plays. 25–8.
40 Mubarak and El Khachab, "Muqaddima: Al-Iqtibas fi al-sinima al-Misriyya," 12–15.
41 Ibid., 28–33.
42 Muhammad H. Haykal, *Zaynab* (Cairo: Hindawi Foundation for Education and Culture, 2012), 10.
43 This was not limited to the film industry, but also prevalent in art making by people like Mahmoud Mokhtar and Mohamed Nagi—which, in turn, were informed by similar novels.

44 Mubarak, "Iqtibas al-naw' fi sardiyyat al-rif," 69.
45 Haykal, *Zaynab*, 10.
46 Mubarak, "Iqtibas al-naw' fi sardiyyat al-rif," 74.
47 Haykal, *Zaynab*, 11.
48 Mubarak, "Iqtibas al-naw' fi sardiyyat al-rif," 75–6.
49 Qasim, *Tarikh al-sinima al-Misriya*, 44.
50 Ibid., 41.
51 Ibid., 46.
52 Mubarak, "Iqtibas al-naw' fi sardiyyat al-rif," 73. The only exception the author made was *Zaynab*, the 1952 version by Karim. This version was a response to critical views and intellectual development.
53 Qasim, *Tarikh al-sinima al-Misriya*, 42.
54 Raja' al-Naqqash, "Udaba'una wa-l sinima: Min *Zaynab* ila *al-Tariq*," *al-Hilal* 10, October 1, 1965: 21.
55 Qasim, *Tarikh al-sinima al-Misriya*, 44.
56 Ibid., 44–5.
57 He is a central figure of the Nahda. He participated as a jurist, Islamic modernist and one of the founders of the Egyptian national movement and Cairo University.
58 Geer, "The Priesthood of Nationalism in Egypt," 191–202.
59 Ibid., 203–21.
60 Ibid., 193.
61 Zaki Cohen, *Zaynab riwaya jadida* (Cairo: Matba'at al-Jarida, 1913), 214, quoted in Geer, "The Priesthood of Nationalism in Egypt."
62 Geer, "The Priesthood of Nationalism in Egypt," 201–10.
63 Qasim, *Tarikh al-sinima al-Misriya*, 8.
64 Ibid., 13. Qasim states that *Qubla Fi al-Sahra'* (Kiss in the Desert) is controversial because it was not produced by an Egyptian producer. Although it was screened six months before *Layla*, the latter was considered the first Egyptian film. The author states that *Kiss in the Desert* is the first film shot in Egypt, not Egyptian. Qasim, *Tarikh al-sinima al-Misriya*, 13–14.
65 Haykal, *Zaynab*, 35.
66 'Ali al-Ra'i, "*Zaynab* bayna al-riwaya wa-l nathr al-fanni," *al-Majalla* 56, September 1, 1961: 6–7.
67 Muhammad Karim, *Mudhakkirat Muhammad Karim* (Cairo: Akadamiyat al-Funun, 2006), 86.
68 Ibid., 7.
69 Ibid., 8.

BIBLIOGRAPHY

1er Congrès de la musique marocaine (program). Casablanca: Imprimeries Réunies, 1939.
Abbani, Diana. "Musique et société au temps de la nahda." Ph.D. diss., Paris 4 - Sorbonne University, Paris, 2018.
ʿAbd al-Amir, ʿAli. *Raqsat al-fustan al-ahmar al-akhrira: Sabʿ ʿuqud min taʾrikh al-ʿIraq ʿabar al-ghinaʾ wa al-musiqa*. Milano: Manshurat al-Mutawassit, 2017.
ʿAbd Allah, Amr Zakaria. "The Theory of Theater for Egyptian Nationalists in the First Quarter of the Twentieth Century." *Quaderni di Studi Arabi* 4 (2009): 193–204.
ʿAbdallah, Muhammad Hasan. *Kliyubatra fi al-adab wa al-tarikh*. Cairo: al-Hayʾa al-Misriya al-ʿAmma lil-Taʾlif wal-Nashr, 1971.
ʿAbd-al-Wahhab, Lutfi. *Al-masrah al-Misri: al-Mawsim al-masrahi 1917–1918*. Cairo: Wizarat al-Thaqafa, al-Markaz al-Qawmi lil-Masrah, 2001.
Abou-Hodeib, Toufoul. *A Taste for Home: The Modern Middle Class in Ottoman Beirut*. Stanford: Stanford University Press, 2017.
Abou-Hodeib, Toufoul. "Taste and Class in late Ottoman Beirut." *International Journal of Middle East Studies* 43, no. 3 (2001): 475–92.
Abu-Lughod, Janet L. *Urban Apartheid in Morocco*. Princeton: Princeton University Press, 1980.
Abu-Lughod, Lila. *Dreams of Nationhood: The Politics of Television in Egypt*. Chicago: University of Chicago Press, 2005.
Abu Sayf, Salah. "Al-sinima fi Misr sinaʿa qawmiya yajib himayatuha." *al-Sabah* 294, May 15, 1932.
Abu Shanab, ʿAdil. "Hayat Abu Khalil al-Qabbani." *Mawqif al-adabi* 89 (1978): 98–112.
Abyad, Suʿad. *Jurj Abyad: Al-masrah al-Misri fi miʿat ʿam*. Cairo: Dar al-Maʿarif, 1970.
Ahmad, ʿAbd al-Ilah. *Al-adab al-ʿIraqi mundhu al-harb al-ʿalamiyya al-thaniya*. Damascus: Ittihad al-Kuttab al-ʿArab, 2001.
al-ʿAllaf, ʿAbd al-Karim. *Baghdad al-qadima*. Baghdad: Matbaʿat al-Maʿarif, 1970.
al-ʿAllaf, ʿAbd al-Karim. *Qiyan Baghdad fi al-ʿasr al-ʿAbbasi wa al-ʿUthmani al-akhir*. Baghdad: Matbaʿat Dar al-Tadamun, 1969.
Allan, Michael. *In the Shadow of World Literature: Sites of Reading in Colonial Egypt*. Princeton: Princeton University Press, 2016.
Alsharekh, Alanoud and Robert Springborg, ed. *Popular Culture and Political Identity in the Arab Gulf States*. London: Saqi Books, 2008.
Amine, Khalid and Marvin Carlson. *The Theatres of Morocco, Algeria and Tunisia: Performance Traditions of the Maghreb*. Basingstoke: Palgrave Macmillan, 2012.
Amir, Eli. *The Dove Flyer*. Translated by Hillel Halkin. London: Halban, 1998.
Ari, Nisa. "Spiritual Capital and the Copy: Painting, Photography, and the Production of the Image in Early Twentieth-Century Palestine." *The Arab Studies Journal* 25, no. 2 (2017): 60–99.
Armbrust, Walter. *Mass Culture and Modernism in Egypt*. Cambridge: Cambridge University Press, 1996.

Armbrust, Walter, ed. *Mass Mediations: New Approaches to Popular Culture in the Middle East and Beyond*. Berkeley: University of California Press, 2000.

El-Ariss, Tarek. ed., *The Arab Renaissance: A Bilingual Anthology of the Nahda*. New York: MLA, 2018.

El-Ariss, Tarek. *Trials of Arab Modernity: Literary Affects and the New Political*. New York: Fordham University Press, 2013.

Arsalan, Shakib. *Shawqi, aw sadaqat arbaʿin sana*. Cairo: Matbaʿat Mustafa al-Babi al-Halabi, 1936.

Ashbee, C.R. *Fantasia in Egypt*. King's College Cambridge Archives, CRA/3/5, 21–7.

Atwood, Blake. *Underground: The Secret Life of Videocassettes in Iran*. Cambridge, MA: MIT Press, 2021.

Auji, Hala. "Picturing Knowledge: Visual Literacy in Nineteenth-Century Arabic Periodicals." In *Making Modernity in the Islamic Mediterranean*, edited by Margaret S. Graves and Alex Dika Seggerman, 72–93. Bloomington: Indiana University Press, 2022.

Auji, Hala. "Printed Images in Flux: Examining Scientific Engravings in Nineteenth-Century Arabic Periodicals." In *Visual Design: The Periodical Page as a Designed Surface*, edited by Andreas Beck, Nicola Kaminski, Volker Mergenthaler, and Jens Ruchatz, 119–36. Hannover: Wehrhahn Verlag, 2019.

Auji, Hala. *Printing Arab Modernity: Book Culture and the American Press in Nineteenth-Century Beirut*. Leiden: Brill, 2016.

Awad, Sarah H. "Political Caricatures in Colonial Egypt: Visual Representations of the People and the Nation." In *Cultural Entanglement in the Pre-Independence Arab World: Arts, Thought and Literature*, edited by Anthony Gorman and Sarah Irving, 163–94. New York: Bloomsbury Publishing, 2020.

Ayalon, Ami. "Arab Booksellers and Bookshops in the Age of Printing, 1850–1914." *British Journal of Middle Eastern Studies* 37, no. 1 (April 2010): 73–93.

Ayalon, Ami. *The Arabic Print Revolution: Cultural Production and Mass Readership*. Cambridge: Cambridge University Press, 2016.

Ayalon, Ami. "Modern Texts and Their Readers in Late Ottoman Palestine." *Middle Eastern Studies* 38, no. 4 (2002): 17–40.

Ayalon, Ami. *The Press in the Arab Middle East*. Oxford: New York University Press, 1995.

Ayyub, Dhu al-Nun. "Hinama Tathur al-ʿAsifa." In *Al-athar al-kamila li-adab Dhi al-Nun Ayyub*. vol. 1, 195–219. Baghdad: Wizarat al-Iʿlam, 1977.

Baedeker, Karl and Albert Socin. *Palaestina und Syrien: Handbuch für Reisende*, 1st ed. Leipzig: Baedeker, 1875.

Badawi, M. M. *Modern Arabic Literature*. Cambridge: Cambridge University Press, 1993.

Baghdadi, ʿAbbas. *Li-alla nansa Baghdad fi al-ʿishrinat*. Beirut: Al-Muʾassasa al-ʿArabiya lil-Dirasat wa al-Nashr, 1998.

Bahoora, Haytham. "Baudelaire in Baghdad: Modernism, The Body, and Husayn Mardan's Poetics of the Self." *International Journal of Middle East Studies* 45, no. 2 (2013): 313–29.

Bahoora, Haytham. "The Figure of the Prostitute, *Tajdid*, and Masculinity in Anti-Colonial Literature of Iraq." *Journal of Middle East Women's Studies* 11, no. 1 (2015): 42–62.

al-Barbari, Muhammad. "Hadith lil-Ustaz Muhammad ʿAbd al-Wahhab: Al-Mawsim al-Jadid – *Masraʿ* Kliyubatra – *Majnun Layla*." *al-Sabah* 162, November 3, 1929.

Baron, Beth. "Readers and the Women's Press in Egypt." *Poetics Today* 15, no. 2 (1994): 217–40.

Barriuso, Patrocinio García. *Ecos del Magrib: La musique Hispano-Musulmane au Maroc.* Tangier: Éditorial Tanger, 1940.

al-Barudi, Fakhri. *Awraq wa Mudhakkirat Fakhri al-Barudi, 1887–1966: Khamsun 'aman min hayat al-watan.* Edited by Da'ad al-Hakim, vol. 1. Dimashq: Manshurat Wazarat al-Thaqafa, 1999.

Bas, Elif. "The Role of Armenians in Establishing Western Theater in the Ottoman Empire." *Asian Theater Journal* 37, no. 2 (2020): 442–63.

Bashkin, Orit. *The Other Iraq: Pluralism and Culture in Hashemite Iraq.* Palo Alto: Stanford University Press, 2009.

Bashkin, Orit. "Representations of Women in the Writings of the Intelligentsia in Hashemite Iraq, 1921–1958." *Journal of Middle East Women's Studies* 4, no. 1 (2008): 53–82.

Bashkin, Orit. "'When Mu'awiya Entered the Curriculum'—Some Comments on the Iraqi Education System in the Interwar Period." *Comparative Education Review* 50, no. 3 (2006): 346–66.

Bellisari, Andrew H. "Raiders of the Lost Past: Nineteenth-Century Archaeology and French Imperialism in the Near East 1798–1914." MA thesis, Rutgers College, New Brunswick, 2010.

Belzoni, Giovanni. *Narrative of the Operations and Recent Discoveries within the Pyramids, Temples, Tombs and Excavations in Egypt and Nubia; And of a Journey to the Coast of the Red Sea, In Search for Old Berenice; And Another to the Oasis of Jupiter Ammon.* London: John Murray, 1820.

Benjamin, Walter. *The Work of Art in the Age of Its Technological Reproducibility and Other Writings on Media.* Cambridge, MA: Harvard University Press, 2008.

Bennett, Andy. "Towards a Cultural Sociology of Popular Music." *Journal of Sociology* 44, no. 4 (2018): 419–32.

Berque, Jacques. *L'Égypte: Impérialisme et révolution.* Paris: Gallimard, 1967.

Betts, Raymond. *Assimilation and Association in French Colonial Theory, 1890–1914.* Lincoln: University of Nebraska Press, 2004.

Booker, M. Keith and Isra Daraiseh. *Consumerist Orientalism: The Convergence of Arab and American Popular Culture in the Age of Global Capitalism.* London: I.B. Tauris, 2019.

Boonstra, John. "Scandal in Fin-de-Siècle Beirut: Gender, Morality, and Imperial Prestige Between France and Lebanon." *Journal of World History* 28, no. 3/4 (2017): 371–93.

Booth, Charlotte. *The Myth of Ancient Egypt.* Stroud: Amberley Publishing, 2011.

Booth, Marilyn. *May Her Likes Be Multiplied Biography and Gender Politics in Egypt.* Berkeley: University of California Press, 2001.

Booth, Marilyn, ed. *Migrating Texts: Circulating Translations Around the Ottoman Mediterranean.* Edinburgh: Edinburgh University Press, 2019.

Bou Ali, Nadia. *Psychoanalysis and the Love of Arabic: Hall of Mirrors.* Edinburgh: Edinburgh University Press, 2020.

Brummett, Palmira. *Image and Imperialism in the Ottoman Revolutionary Press, 1908–1911.* Albany: SUNY Press, 2000.

Buenaventura, Wendy. *Serpent of the Nile: Women and Dance in the Arab World.* London: Saqi Books, 1989.

Burke III, Edmund. *The Ethnographic State: France and the Invention of Islam.* Berkeley: University of California Press, 2014.

Cachia, Pierre. "Introduction: Translations and Adaptations." In *Modern Arabic Literature*, edited by M. M. Badawi, 1–35. Cambridge: Cambridge University Press, 1993.

Cachia, Pierre. *Ṭāhā Ḥusayn: His Place in the Egyptian Literary Renaissance*. London: Luzac & Company LTD, 1956.
Calderwood, Eric. *Colonial al-Andalus: Spain and the Making of Modern Moroccan Culture*. Cambridge, MA: Harvard University Press, 2018.
Carminati, Lucia. "Afifa's Migration. Syrian Prostitutes and the 'White Slave Trade' in Port Said." *Journal of Middle East Women's Studies* 17, no. 3 (2021): 473–8.
Carminati, Lucia. "'She Will Eat Your Shirt': Foreign Migrant Women as Brothel Keepers in Port Said and along the Suez Canal, 1980-1915." *Journal of the History of Sexuality* 30, no. 2 (May 2021): 161–94.
Cass, Jeffrey. "Interrogating Orientalism: Theories and Practices." In *Interrogating Orientalism: Contextual Approaches and Pedagogical Practices*, edited by Diane Long Hoeveler and Jeffrey Cass, 25–45. Columbus: The Ohio State University Press, 2006.
Chottin, Alexis. *Corpus de musique marocaine*. Paris: Service des arts indigènes, 1931.
Chottin, Alexis. Tableau *de la musique marocaine*. Paris: Librairie Orientaliste Paul Geuthner, 1939.
Cioeta, Donald J. "Ottoman Censorship in Lebanon and Syria, 1876–1908." *International Journal of Middle East Studies* 10, no. 2 (1979): 167–86.
Colla, Elliott. *Conflicted Antiquities: Egyptology, Egyptomania, and Egyptian Modernity*. Durham and London: Durham University Press, 2007.
Colla, Elliott. "How *Zaynab* Became the First Arabic Novel." *History Compass* 7, no.1 (2009): 1–12.
Commins, David. *Islamic Reform: Politics and Social Change in Late Ottoman Syria*. Oxford: Oxford University Press, 1990.
Commins, David. "Religious Reformers and Arabists in Damascus, 1885–1914." *International Journal of Middle East Studies* 18, no. 4 (1986): 405–25.
Cormack, Raphael. *Midnight in Cairo. The Divas of Egypt's Roaring 20s*. New York: Norton & Co., 2021.
Cormack, Raphael. "Who's Afraid of Musical Theater?" In *Cultural Entanglement in the Pre-Independence Arab World: Arts, Thought and Literature*, edited by Anthony Gorman and Sarah Irving, 33–50. London: I.B. Tauris, 2021.
Crary, Jonathan. *Suspensions of Perception: Attention, Spectacle, and Modern Culture*. Cambridge, MA: MIT Press, 1999.
Danielson, Virginia. *The Voice of Egypt: Umm Kulthum, Arabic Song, and Egyptian Society in the Twentieth Century*. Chicago: University of Chicago Press, 1997.
Darwesh, Ahmed. "Wa khayr jalis fi al-zaman riwaya jamila." *Dr. Ahmed Darwesh (Al-zama lil-maʿrifa)*, March 30, 2017, http://www.drahmeddarwesh.com/?p=853.
Davie, May. *Beyrouth et ses faubourgs (1840–1940): Une intégration inachevée*. Beirut: CERMOC, 1996.
Davis, Ruth F. *Ma'luf: Reflections on the Arab Andalusian Music of Tunisia*. Lanham: Scarecrow Press, 2004.
Dayf, Shawqi. *Al-adab al-ʿArabi al-muʿasir fi Misr*, 10th ed. Cairo: Dar al-Maʿarif, 1992.
DeLapp, Kevin M. "Ancient Egypt as Europe's "Intimate Stranger.""" In *Negotiating Identities: Constructed Selves and Others*, edited by Helen Vella Bonavita, 171–92. Amsterdam: Rodopi, 2011.
Deuchar, Hannah Scott "'Nahda': Mapping a Keyword in Cultural Discourse." *Alif: Journal of Comparative Poetics* 37 (2017): 50–84.
"Diʿaya khatira 'la Misr." *Ruz al-Yusuf*, February 7, 1928.
Dori, Dafna. "The Brothers al-Kuwaity and the Iraqi Song 1930–1950." Ph.D. diss., University of Uppsala, 2021.

Dupont, Anne-Laure. "What is a katib ʿamm? The Status of Men of Letters and the Conception of Language According to Jurji Zaydan." *Middle Eastern Literatures* 13, no. 2 (2010): 171–81.
Eddé, Carla. *Beyrouth, Naissance d'une capitale (1918-1924)*. Paris: Actes Sud, 2009.
Eickelman, Dale and Armando Salvatore. "The Public Sphere and Muslim Identities." *European Journal of Sociology* 43, no. 1 (2002): 92–115.
Eid, Hassan. "Sinima Ramsis: Muharabat al-ajanib li-idaratiha wa-aʿmaliha." *al-Sabah*, January 15, 1932.
Eldem, Edhem. "The Search for a Vernacular Ottoman Photography." In *The Indigenous Lens?: Early Photography in the Near and Middle East*, edited by Markus Ritter and Staci G. Scheiwiller, 29–56. Berlin and Boston: De Gruyter, 2017.
Elnemr, Eman. "Modernism, Licentiousness, Rebellion: Egypt in the First Half of the Twentieth Century." Lecture, Berliner Seminar, EUME, Forum Transregionale Studien, Berlin, January 19, 2022.
Elshakry, Marwa. *Reading Darwin in Arabic, 1860–1950*. Chicago: Chicago University Press, 2013.
Emrence, Cem. *Remapping the Ottoman Middle East: Modernity, Imperial Bureaucracy, and the Islamic State*. Library of Ottoman Studies 31. London: I.B. Tauris, 2012.
Enault, Louis. *La vierge du Liban*. Paris: L. Hachette, 1858.
England, Samuel. "An Ayyubid Renaissance: Saladin, from Knighthood to Nahḍa." *Alif: Journal of Comparative Poetics* 38 (2018): 37–61.
Ersoy, Ahmet. "Osman Hamdi Bey and the Historiophile Mood: Orientalist Vision and the Romantic Sense of the Past in Late Ottoman Culture." In *The Poetics and Politics of Place: Ottoman Istanbul and British Orientalism*, edited by Zeynep Inankur, Reina Lewis, and Mary Roberts, 145–55. Istanbul: Pera Müzesi, 2011.
Ersoy, Ahmet. "Ottomans and the Kodak Galaxy: Archiving Everyday Life and Historical Space in Ottoman Illustrated Journals." *History of Photography* 40, no. 3 (2016): 330–57.
Fahmy, Ziad. "Early Egyptian Radio Transitioning from Media-Capitalism to Media-Etatism, 1928–1934." *Middle East Journal of Culture and Communication* 15 (2022): 92–112.
Fahmy, Ziad. *Ordinary Egyptians: Creating the Modern Nation Through Popular Culture*. Stanford: Stanford University Press, 2011.
Farhan, Sara. "The Making of Iraqi Doctors: Reproduction in Medical Education in Iraq." Ph.D. diss., York University, 2021.
"Film *Layla*: ʿAziza Amir baʿd kasb al-maʿraka." *Ruz al-Yusuf*, November 24, 1927.
Flaubert, Gustave. *Flaubert in Egypt: A Sensibility on Tour*, trans. Francis Steegmuller. London: Penguin, 1996.
Foucault, Michel. *Power/Knowledge: Selected Interviews and Other Writings, 1972-1977*. Pantheon Books, 1980.
Fritze, Ronald H. *Egyptomania: A History of Fascination, Obsession and Fantasy*. London: Reaktion Books, 2016.
Funari, Pedro Paulo A. and Raquel dos Santos Funari. "Ancient Egypt in Brazil: A Theoretical Approach to Contemporary Uses of the Past." *Archaeologies: Journal of the World Archaeological Congress* 6 (2010): 48–61.
Gamal, Muhammad Y. "Foreign Movies in Egypt: Subtitling, Dubbing and Adaptation." In *Foreign Language Movies- Dubbing vs Subtitling*, edited by Angelika Goldstein, Bilijana Golubovic, 1–16. Hamburg: Verlag Dr. Kovac, 2009.
Geer, Benjamin. "The Priesthood of Nationalism in Egypt: Duty, Authority, Autonomy." Ph.D. diss., School of Oriental and African Studies, University of London. 2011.

Gelatt, Roland. *The Fabulous Phonograph, 1877–1977*. New York: MacMillan Publishing Company, 1977.
Gershoni, Israel and James P. Jankowski. *Egypt, Islam, and the Arabs: The Search for Egyptian Nationhood, 1900–1930*. New York: Oxford University Press, 1986.
Ghannam, Farha. *Remaking the Modern: Space, Relocation, and the Politics of Identity in a Global Cairo*. Berkeley: University of California Press, 2002.
Ghazoul, Ferial. "The Arabization of Othello." *Comparative Literature* 50, no. 1 (Winter 1998): 1–31.
Gitre, Carmen. *Acting Egyptian: Theater, Identity, and Popular Culture in Cairo 1869–1930*. Austin: University of Texas Press, 2009.
Glaß, Dagmar. *Malta, Beirut, Leipzig and Beirut Again: Eli Smith, the American Syria Mission, and the Spread of Arabic Typography in Nineteenth-Century Lebanon*. Beirut: Orient-Institut der Deutschen Morgenländischen Gesellschaft, 1998.
Glasser, Jonathan. *The Lost Paradise: Andalusi Music in Urban North Africa*. Chicago: University of Chicago Press, 2016.
Göle, Nilüfer. "The Gendered Nature of the Public Sphere." *Public Culture* 10, no. 1 (1997): 61–82.
Gorman, Anthony and Sarah Irving, ed. *Cultural Entanglement in the Pre-Independence Arab World: Arts, Thought and Literature*. New York: Bloomsbury Publishing, 2020.
Götz, Hermann. *Eine Orientreise*. Leipzig: Seemann, 1901.
Grallert, Till. "Catch Me If You Can! Approaching the Arabic Press of the Late Ottoman Eastern Mediterranean Through Digital History." *Geschichte und Gesellschaft* 47, no. 1, *Digital History* (2021): 58–89.
Grallert, Till. "Investigating Ottoman Press Censorship in the Eastern Mediterranean Through Conceptual History: The Peculiar Use of "Incident" (Haditha)." *Die Welt des Islams*, forthcoming.
Grallert, Till. "To Whom Belong the Streets? Investment in Public Space and Popular Contentions in Late Ottoman Damascus." *Bulletin d'études orientales* 61 (2012): 237–59.
Grallert, Till. "To Whom Belong the Streets? Property, Propriety, and Appropriation: The Production of Public Space in Late Ottoman Damascus, 1875–1914." Ph.D. Thesis, FU Berlin, 2014.
Grallert, Till. "Urban Food Riots in Late Ottoman Bilad Al-Sham as a 'Repertoire of Contention.'" In *Crime, Poverty and Survival in the Middle East and North Africa: The "Dangerous Classes" Since 1800*, edited by Stephanie Cronin, 157–76. London: I.B. Tauris, 2020.
Grehan, James. "Smoking and "Early Modern" Sociability: The Great Tobacco Debate in the Ottoman Middle East (Seventeenth to Eighteenth Centuries)." *The American Historical Review* 111, no. 5 (2006): 1352–77.
Gronow, Pekka. "The Record Industry Comes to the Orient." *Ethnomusicology* 25, no. 2 (1981): 251–84.
Gruber, Christiane and Sune Haugbolle, ed. *Visual Culture in the Modern Middle East: Rhetoric of the Image*. Bloomington: Indiana University Press, 2013.
Guettat, Mahmoud. "La Tunisie dans les documents du Congrès du Caire." In *La Musique Arabe: Le Congrès du Caire de 1932*, edited by Philippe Vigreux. Cairo: CEDEJ, 1992.
Guys, Henry. *Beyrouth et le Liban, Relation d'un séjour de plusieurs années dans ce pays*. Paris: Au Comptoir des Imprimeries, 1850.
El-Hadari, Ahmad. *Mawsuʻat tarikh al-sinima fi Misr*, 2nd ed. Cairo: Al-Hayʼa al-Misriya al-ʻAmma lil-Kitab, 2019.

Haddad-Fonda, Kyle. "The Rhetoric of "Civilization" in Chinese-Egyptian Relations." *Middle East Institute*, August 1, 2017, https://www.mei.edu/publications/rhetoric-civilization-chinese-egyptian-relations#_ednref3.

Hafez, Melis. *Inventing Laziness: The Culture of Productivity in Late Ottoman Society*. Cambridge: Cambridge University Press, 2022.

Haikal, Fayza. "Egypt's Past Regenerated by Its Own People." In *Consuming Ancient Egypt*, edited by Sally MacDonald and Michael Rice, 123–38. London: Routledge, 2016.

al-Hajj, ʿAziz. *Abu Huraira al-Mawsuli: Dhu al-Nun Ayyub wa siratuhu*. London: Riad al-Rayyis, 1990.

al-Hakim, Tawfiq. *Sijn al-ʿumr*. Cairo: Dar El Shorouk, 2003 [1964].

Hall, Stuart. "The West and the Rest: Discourse and Power." In *Race and Racialization: Essential Readings*, edited by Tania Das Gupta, et al., 56–60. Toronto: Canadian Scholars Press, 2007.

Hamadeh, Shirine. "Public Sphere in the Eastern Mediterranean." In *A Companion to Islamic Art and Architecture*, edited by Finbarr Flood and Gülru Necipoğlu, 1102–21. Hoboken: Wiley, 2017.

El Hamamsy, Walid and Mounira Soliman, ed. *Popular Culture in the Middle East and North Africa: A Postcolonial Outlook*. London: Routledge, 2014.

Hammad, Hanan. *Unknown Past: Layla Murad, The Jewish Muslim Star of Egypt*. Palo Alto: Stanford University Press, 2022.

Hammond, Andrew. *Pop Culture in North Africa and the Middle East: Entertainment and Society Around the World*. Santa Barbara: ABC-CLIO, 2017.

Hammond, Andrew. *Popular Culture in the Arab World: Art, Politics, and the Media*. Cairo: AUC Press, 2007.

Hamzah, Dyala, ed. *The Making of the Arab Intellectual: Empire, Public Sphere and the Colonial Coordinates of Selfhood*. London: Routledge, 2012.

Hanioğlu, M. Şükrü. *The Young Turks in Opposition*. New York: Oxford University Press, 1995.

Hanna, Sameh F. "Decommercializing Shakespeare: Mutran's Translation of 'Othello.'" *Critical Survey* 19, no. 3 (2007): 27–54.

Hanssen, Jens. *Fin de Siècle Beirut: The Making of an Ottoman Provincial Capital*. Oxford: Oxford University Press, 2005.

Hanssen, Jens. "Public Morality and Marginality in Fin-de-Siècle Beirut." In *Outside in: On the Margins of the Modern Middle East*, edited by Eugene Rogan, 183–211. London: I.B. Tauris, 2002.

Hanssen, Jens and Max Weiss, ed. *Arabic Thought Beyond the Liberal Age: Towards an Intellectual History of the Nahda*. Cambridge: Cambridge University Press, 2016.

Harris, Jonathan Gil. *Shakespeare and Literary Theory*. Oxford: Oxford University Press, 2010.

Harrison, Olivia C. *Transcolonial Maghreb: Imagining Palestine in the Era of Decolonization*. Stanford: Stanford University Press, 2015.

Harsin, Jayson and Mark Hayward. "Stuart Hall's 'Deconstructing the Popular': Reconsiderations 30 Years Later." *Communication, Culture and Critique* 6, no. 2 (2013): 201–7.

Haykal, Muhammad H. *Zaynab*. Cairo: Hindawi Foundation for Education and Culture, 2012.

Heinzelmann, Tobias. "The Ruler's Monologue: The Rhetoric of the Ottoman Penal Code of 1858." *Die Welt des Islams* 54, no. 3–4 (2014): 292–321.

Hermann, Rainer. *Kulturkrise und konservative Erneuerung: Muhammad Kurd ʿAli (1876–1953) und das geistige Leben im Damaskus zu Beginn des 20. Jahrhunderts*. Frankfurt am Main: Peter Lang, 1990.

al-Hifni, Ratiba. *Al-Sultana Munira al-Mahdiya wa al-ghina' fi Misr qablaha wa fi zamaniha*. Cairo: Dar El Shorouk, 2011.
Hill, Peter. "The Arabic Adventures of Télémaque: Trajectory of a Global Enlightenment Text in the Nahḍah." *Journal of Arabic Literature* 49, no. 3 (2018): 171–203.
Hill, Peter. *Utopia and Civilisation in the Arab Nahda*. Cambridge: Cambridge University Press, 2020.
Holt, Elizabeth M. *Fictitious Capital: Silk, Cotton, and the Rise of the Arabic Novel*. New York: Fordham University Press, 2017.
Holt, Elizabeth M. "Narrating the Nahda: The Syrian Protestant College, *al-Muqtataf*, and the Rise of Jurji Zaydan." In *One Hundred and Fifty*, edited by Nadia El Cheikh, Lina Choueiri, and Bilal Orfali, 273–80. Beirut: AUB Press, 2015.
Hourani, Albert. "Ottoman Reform and the Politics of Notables." In *The Modern Middle East: A Reader*, edited by Albert Hourani, Philip S. Khoury, and Mary C Wilson, 83–109. Berkeley: University of California Press, 1993 [1968].
Husayn, Fadil. "Awqat al-faragh: Niʿma wa naqma." *al-Muʿallim al-Jadid* 1, no. 2 (1935): 218.
Husayn, Taha. *al-Ayyam*. Cairo: Dar al-Maʿarif, 1942.
Idrissi, Moulay Idris ben Abdelali El. *Kashf al-ghitaʾ*. Rabat: al-Tabaʿa al-Wataniyya, 1939.
Iggers, Georg G., Q. Edward Wang, and Supriya Mukherjee. *A Global History of Modern Historiography*, 1st ed. London: Pearson Education Limited, 2008.
Igoe, Laura Turner. "Capturing 'Jove's Autograph': Late Nineteenth-Century Lightning Photography and Electrical Agency." *Panorama* 2, no. 1 (2016), https://doi.org/10.24926/24716839.1535.
"Intaziru riwayat *Masraʿ Kliyubatra*." *al-Sabah* 173, January 19, 1930.
Ismaʿil, Sayyid ʿAli. *Masirat al-masrah fi Misr, 1900–1935*. Cairo: Hindawi, 2017.
Ismaʿil, Sayyid ʿAli. *Tarikh al-masrah fi Misr fi-l-qarn al-tasiʿ ʿashar*. Cairo: Al-Hayʾa al-Misriya al-ʿAmma lil-Kitab, 1998.
Jacob, Wilson Chacko. *Working out Egypt: Effendi Masculinity and Subject Formation in Colonial Egypt, 1870–1940*. Durham: Duke University Press, 2011.
Jacquemond, Richard and Frédéric Lagrange, ed. *Culture Pop en Égypte: Entre mainstream commercial et contestation*. Paris: Riveneuve, 2020.
Jarenski, Shelly. *Immersive Words: Mass Media, Visuality, and American Literature, 1839–1893*. Tuscaloosa: University of Alabama Press, 2015.
Jawhariyya, Wasif. *The Storyteller of Jerusalem: The Life and Times of Wasif Jawhariyyeh 1904-1948*, edited by Salim Tamari, Issam Nassar, and Nada Elzeer. Northampton, MA: Olive Branch Press, 2014.
Joseph, Suad. "The Public/Private: The Imagined Boundary in the Imagined Nation/State/Community: The Lebanese Case." *Feminist Review* 57 (1997): 73–92.
Kanana, ʿAli Nasir. *Falak an-Nass fi al-ghinaʾ al-ʿIraqi*. Köln: Al-Kamel Verlag, 2016.
Karachouli, Regina. "Abu Ḥalil Al-Qabbani (1833–1902) - Damaszener Theatergründer und Prinzipal." *Die Welt des Islams* 32, no. 1 (1992): 83–98.
Karayanni, Stavros. *Dancing Fear & Desire. Race, Sexuality and Imperial Politics in Middle Eastern Dance*. Waterloo: Wilfrid Laurier Press, 2004.
Karim, Muhammad. *Mudhakkirat Muhammad Karim*. Cairo: Akadamiyat al-Funun, 2006.
Kassir, Samir. *Histoire de Beyrouth*, Paris: Fayard, 2003.
Katz, Mark. *Capturing Sound: How Technology Has Changed Music*. Berkeley: University of California Press, 2004.

Kawai, Nozomu. "Egyptological Landscape in Japan: Past, Present, and Future." *CIPEG Journal* 1 (2017): 51–9.
El Khachab, Walid. "Umm Kulthum ra'idat al-tahdith wa ayqunat al-turath." *al-Qahira*, February 4, 2020.
Khalaf, Samir. *Heart of Beirut: Reclaiming the Bourj*. London: Saqi, 2006.
Khalaf, Taysir. *Min Dimashq ila Chicago*. Beirut: Al-Mu'assasa al-Arabiyya lil-Dirasat wal-Nashr, 2018.
Khalaf, Taysir. "Omar Wasfi, al-mumathil al-Misri ila Suriyya bahthan ʿan al-mutriba Malaka Surur". *Al-Arabi al-Jadid*, August 22, 2020.
Khater, Akram Fouad. "'House' to 'Goddess of the House': Gender, Class, and Silk in 19th-Century Mount Lebanon." *International Journal of Middle East Studies* 28, no. 3 (1996): 325–48.
Khater, Akram Fouad. *Inventing Home: Emigration, Gender, and the Middle Class in Lebanon, 1870–1920*. Berkeley and Los Angeles: University of California Press, 2001.
al-Khatib, Ahmad Musa. *Al-shiʿr fi al-dawriyat al-Misriya (1828–1882): Tawthiq wa-dirasa*, 1st ed. Cairo: Dar al-Maʾmun lil-Tibaʿa wa-al-Nashr, 1987.
Khayat, Nicole. "What's in a Name? Perceptions of Authorship and Copyright During the Arabic Nahda." *Nineteenth-Century Contexts* 41, no. 4 (2019): 423–40.
Khayri, Badiʿ. *Mudhakkirat Badiʿ Khayri*, edited by Ibrahim Hilmi. Cairo: al-Majlis al-ʿAla lil-Thaqafa, 1996.
Khoury, Philip S. *Urban Notables and Arab Nationalism: The Politics of Damascus, 1860–1920*. New York: Cambridge University Press, 1983.
Khuri-Makdisi, Ilham. *The Eastern Mediterranean and the Making of Global Radicalism 1860–1914*. Berkeley: University of California Press, 2010.
Kishtainy, Khalid. *Ayyam ʿIraqiyya*. London: Dar al-Hikma, 2011.
Koçunyan, Aylin. *Negotiating the Ottoman Constitution 1839–1876*. Collection Turcica 24. Paris: Louvain, 2018.
Kojaman, Yeheskel. *Al-musiqa al-fanniyya al-muʿasira fi al-ʿIraq*. Baghdad: Dar Mesopotamia, 2015.
Kojaman, Yeheskel. *The Maqam Music Tradition of Iraq*. London: Self-published, 2001.
Koselleck, Reinhart. "Richtlinien für das 'Lexikon politisch-sozialer Begriffe der Neuzeit." *Archiv für Begriffsgeschichte* 11 (1967): 81–99.
Kozma, Liat. "Women's Migration for Prostitution in the Interwar Middle East and North Africa." *Journal of Women's History* 28, no. 3 (2016): 93–113.
Kremer, Alfred von. *Mittelsyrien und Damascus: Geschichtliche, Ethnografische und Geografische Studien in den Jahren 1849, 1850 u. 1851*. Wien: P.P. Mechitharisten, 1853, https://nbn-resolving.de/urn:nbn:de:gbv:3:5-24187.
Kurd ʿAli, Muhammad. *Khitat al-Sham*, 2nd ed. vol. 4. 6 vols. Bayrut: Dar al-ʿilm, 1969, https://archive.org/details/6_20200926/.
Lagrange, Frédéric. "Musiciens et poètes en Égypte au temps de la nahda." Ph.D. diss., Paris VIII, 1994.
Lagrange, Frédéric. "Women in the Singing Business, Women in Songs." *History Compass* 7, no. 1 (2009): 226–50.
Lagrange, Frédéric and Mustafa Said. "128 – Munira al-Mahdiyya 5." *Foundation for Arab Music Archiving & Research*. Accessed November 3, 2020, https://www.amar-foundation.org/128-munira-al-mahdiyya-5/.
al-Lami, A.D. Firdus ʿAbd al-Rahman Karim. *Al-hayyat al-ijtimaʿiyya fi Baghdad*. Beirut: al-Dar al-ʿArabiyya lil-Mawsuʿat, 2017.

La T.S.F. et le Cinéma à l'École: Bulletin Trimestriel. Rabat: Direction de l'Instruction Publique, des Beaux Arts et des Antiquités, 1929–1941.

Lenssen, Anneka. *Beautiful Agitation: Modern Painting and Politics in Syria*. Berkeley and Los Angeles: University of California Press, 2020.

Lenssen, Anneka, Sarah Rogers, and Nada Shabout, eds. *Modern Art in the Arab World: Primary Documents*. New York: Museum of Modern Art, 2018.

Levine, Molly. Review of *The Gift of the Nile: Hellenizing Egypt from Aeschylus to Alexander. Classics and Contemporary Thought, 8*, by Phiroze Vasunia, Bryn Mawr Classical Review. Accessed April 16, 2020, https://bmcr.brynmawr.edu/2002/2002.08.32.

Lietzelman, Harley. "Pharaonism: Decolonizing Historical Identity." *Prized Writing 2014–2015, UC Davis*. Accessed October 5, 2020, https://prizedwriting.ucdavis.edu/sites/prizedwriting.ucdavis.edu/files/users/snielson/9%20-%20Litzeilman.pdf

Llamas-Rodriguez, Juan and Viviane Saglier. "Postcolonial Media Theory." *Oxford Research Encyclopedia of Communication*, August 31, 2021, https://doi.org/10.1093/acrefore/9780190228613.013.1065.

Llano, Samuel. "Empire, Diplomacy, and the Racial Imagination: Spain at the Cairo Congress of Arab Music (1932)." *Journal of North African Studies* (2022). doi:10.1080/13629387.2022.2089123.

Lorcin, Patricia M. E. *Imperial Identities: Stereotyping, Prejudice, and Race in Colonial Algeria*. London: I.B. Tauris, 1995.

Lupton, Carter. "'Mummymania' for the Masses – Is Egyptology Cursed by the Mummy's Curse?" In *Consuming Ancient Egypt*, 1st ed., edited by Sally MacDonald and Michael Rice, 23–46. New York: Routledge, 2009.

MacArthur-Seal, Daniel-Joseph. "Intoxication and Imperialism: Nightlife in Occupied Istanbul, 1918–23." *Comparative Studies of Asia, Africa and the Middle East* 37 (2017): 299–313.

Machin-Autenrieth, Matthew. "Spanish Musical Responses to Moroccan Immigration and the Cultural Memory of al-Andalus." *Twentieth-Century Music* 16, no. 2 (June 2019): 259–87.

Mackintosh, Mrs. *Damascus and Its People: Sketches of Modern Life in Syria*. London: Seeley, Jackson, and Halliday, 1883.

Mahdi, Salah El. "Préface." In *Patrimoine Musicale Tunisien, 2ème Fascicule: Ensemble des Tawchihs et Zajals Tunisiens*. République Tunisienne, Secrétariat d'État aux Affaires Culturelles et l'Information, 1963.

"Mahzala fi thawb mashru' watani." *Ruz al-Yusuf*, August 18, 1927.

Main, Ernest. *Iraq from Mandate to Independence*. London: G. Allen & Unwin ltd., 1935.

Makdisi, Ussama. *Age of Coexistence: The Ecumenical Frame and the Making of the Modern Arab World*. Oakland: University of California Press, 2019.

Maksudyan, Nazan. "Hearing the Voiceless - Seeing the Invisible: Orphans and Destitute Children as Actors of Social, Economic, and Political History in the Late Ottoman Empire." Ph.D. Thesis, Sabanci University, 2008.

Marcus, Abraham. "Privacy in Eighteenth-Century Aleppo: The Limits of Cultural Ideals." *International Journal of Middle East Studies* 18, no. 1986 (1986): 165–83.

Massad, Joseph. *Desiring Arabs*. Chicago: University of Chicago Press, 2007.

Matsushita, Elizabeth. "Disharmony of Empire: Race and the Making of Modern Musicology in Colonial North Africa." Ph.D. diss., University of Illinois at Urbana-Champaign, 2021.

McLuhan, Marshall. *Understanding Media: The Extensions of Man*. New York: Signet, 1964.

Me'ir, Yosef. *Hitpathut tarbutit Hevratit shel Yehudey 'Iraq me'az 1830 ve 'ad Yemenu*. Tel Aviv: Naharayim, 1989.
Mestyan, Adam. "A Garden with Mellow Fruits of Refinement: Music Theatres and Cultural Politics in Cairo and Istanbul, 1867–1892." Ph.D. diss., Faculties of the Central European University, Budapest, 2011.
Mestyan, Adam. *Arab Patriotism: The Ideology and Culture of Power in Late Ottoman Egypt*. Princeton: Princeton University Press, 2017.
Mestyan, Adam. "Arabic Theater in Early Khedival Culture, 1868–1872: James Sanua Revisited." *International Journal of Middle East Studies* 46, no. 1 (2014): 117–37.
Mestyan, Adam, Till Grallert, et al., "Jara'id: A Chronology of Arabic Periodicals (1800–1929) (v. 1.0)." *Zenodo*, December 29, 2020, https://doi.org/10.5281/zenodo.4399240.
Micklewright, Nancy. "Orientalism and Photography." In *The Poetics and Politics of Place: Ottoman Istanbul and British Orientalism*, edited by Zeynep Inankur, Reina Lewis, and Mary Roberts, 99–110. Istanbul: Pera Müzesi, 2011.
Mirrlees, Tanner. *Global Entertainment Media: Between Cultural Imperialism and Cultural Globalization*. New York: Routledge, 2013.
Mitchell, Timothy. *Colonising Egypt*. Berkeley: University of California Press, 1988.
Mokhiber, James. "Le protectorat dans la peau." In *Revisiting the Colonial Past in Morocco* edited by Driss Maghraoui, 257–84. London: Routledge, 2013.
Montanari, Anna Maria. *Cleopatra in Italian and English Renaissance Drama*. Amsterdam: Amsterdam University Press, 2019.
Moosa, Matti. *The Origins of Modern Arabic Fiction*, 2nd ed. Boulder and London: Lynne Rienner Publishers, 1997.
Moussali, Bernard and Lambert Jean. "Géostratégie de l'enregistrement Commercial." In *Les Premiers Chanteurs des Bilad al-Sham*, edited by Kamal Kassar, Mustafa Sa'id, and Diana Abbani, 214. Beirut: AMAR Foundation., 2014.
Mubarak, Ali. *Alam al-Din*. Alexandria: Jaridat al-Mahrusa, 1882.
Mubarak, Salma. "Iqtibas al-naw' fi sardiyyat al-rif: *Zaynab* al-riwaya wa al-film al-samit." In *Al-iqtibas min al-adab ila al-sinima: Mahatat fi tarikh mushtarak*, edited by Salma Mubarak and Walid El Khachab, 1st edn. Cairo: El-Maraya, 2021.
Mubarak, Salma and Walid El Khachab. "Muqaddima: al-Iqtibas fi al-sinima al-Misriya: Mahattat tarikhiyya wa mafaheem ta'sisiya." In *Al-iqtibas min al-adab ila al-sinima: Mahatat fi tarikh mushtarak*, edited by Salma Mubarak and Walid El Khachab, 1st edn. Cairo: El-Maraya, 2021.
Mudiriyyat al-Shurta al-'Amma. *Taqrir al-sanawi li-sanat 1929*. Baghdad: Matba'at al-Hukuma, 1929.
Mudiriyyat al-Shurta al-'Amma. *Taqrir al-sanawi li-sanat 1930*. Baghdad: Matba'at al-Hukuma, 1930.
Mudiriyyat al-Shurta al-'Amma. *Taqrir al-sanawi li-sanat 1931*. Baghdad: Matba'at al-Hukuma, 1931.
al-Muwaylihi, Muhammad. *What Isa Ibn Hisham Told Us [Hadith 'Isa ibn Hisham], Volume Two*. New York: New York University Press, 2015.
al-Nadawi, Muhammad Shafiqul Rahman. "Riwayat 'Adhra' al-Hind li-Ahmad Shawqi: Dirasa tahliliya." *Aqlam al-Hind* 3, July–September 2018, https://www.aqlamalhind.com/?p=1076.
al-Nadim, 'Abd Allah. *Al-a'dad al-kamila li-majallat al-Ustaz*, vol. II. Cairo: Al-Hay'a al-Misriya al-'Amma lil-Kitab, 1994.
Najm, Muhammad Yusuf. *Al-masrahiya fi al-adab al-'Arabi al-hadith 1847–1914*. Beirut: Dar Bayrut, 1956.

Najmabadi, Afsaneh. *Women with Moustaches and Men Without Beards*. Berkeley: University of California Press, 2005.

al-Naqqash, Raja'. "Udaba'una wa-l sinima: Min *Zaynab* ila *al-Tariq*." *al-Hilal* 10, October 1, 1965.

Nieuwkerk, Karin van. *"A Trade Like Any Other": Female Singers and Dancers in Egypt*. Austin: University of Texas Press, 2008.

Oberhummer, Roman and Heinrich Zimmerer. *Durch Syrien und Kleinasien: Reiseschilderungen u. Studien*. Berlin: Reimer, 1899.

Ollivier, Michèle and Viviana Fridman. *Taste/Taste Culture: International Encyclopedia of the Social and Behavioral Sciences*. Department of Sociology, University of Ottawa. Accessed March 9, 2022, http://educ.jmu.edu/~brysonbp/symbound/papers2001/Olivier.html#:~:text=K1N%206N5%20Canada,Taste%2FTaste%20Culture,particular%20states%20of%20social%20relations.

Olsen, Pelle Valentin. "Cruising Baghdad: Desire Between Men in the 1930s Fiction of Dhu al-Nun Ayyub." *Journal of Middle East Women's Studies* 14, no. 1 (2018): 25–44.

Özbek, Nadir. "'Beggars' and 'Vagrants' in Ottoman State Policy and Public Discourse, 1876-1914." *Middle Eastern Studies* 45, no. 5 (2009): 783–801.

Palabıyık, Mustafa Serdar. "Ottoman Travelers' Perceptions of Africa in the Late Ottoman Empire (1860–1922): A Discussion of Civilization, Colonialism and Race." *New Perspectives on Turkey* 46 (2012): 187–212.

Parra, José Miguel. "Europe's Morbid "Mummy Craze" Has Been an Obsession for Centuries." *National Geographic*, December 12, 2019, https://www.nationalgeographic.co.uk/history-and-civilisation/2019/12/europes-morbid-mummy-craze-has-been-obsession-centuries.

Parramore, Lynn. *Reading the Sphinx: Ancient Egypt in Nineteenth Century Literary Culture*. New York: Palgrave Macmillan, 2008.

Pastor de Maria Campos, Camila. "Performers or Prostitutes? Artistes during the French Mandate over Syria and Lebanon, 1921–1946." *Journal of Middle East Women's Studies* 13, no. 2 (2017): 287–311.

Patel, Abdulrazzak. *The Arab Nahda: The Making of the Intellectual and Humanist Movement*. Edinburgh: Edinburgh University Press, 2013.

Patridge, Christopher. "Orientalism and the Occult." In *The Occult World*, edited by Christopher Patridge, 611–25. New York: Routledge, 2015.

Philips, Deborah. *Fairground Attractions: A Genealogy of the Pleasure Ground*. London: Bloomsbury Academic, 2012.

Planche, Jean-Louis. "Notice Safir El Boudali." *Dictionnaire Algérie*, January 9, 2014. Accessed May 27, 2022, https://maitron.fr/spip.php?article152168.

Prestel, Joseph Ben. *Emotional Cities: Debates on Urban Change in Berlin and Cairo, 1860–1910*. Oxford: Oxford University Press, 2017.

Qasim, Mahmoud. *Tarikh al-sinima al-Misriya*. Giza, Egypt: Arab Press Agency, 2018.

al-Qasimi, Jamal al-Din and Khalil al-'Azm. *Qamus al-sina'at al-shamiyya*. Edited by Zafir al-Qasimi. Vol. 2. Paris: Mouton & Co., 1960.

al-Qasimi, Muhammad Sa'id. *Qamus al-sina'at al-shamiyya*, vol. 1. Edited by Zafir al-Qasimi. Paris: Mouton & Co., 1960.

Qassatli, Nu'man. *al-Rawda al-ghanna' fi Dimashq al-fayha'*. Bayrut, 1879, https://hdl.handle.net/2027/njp.32101007765322.

Quataert, Donald. "Clothing Laws, State and Society in the Ottoman Empire, 1720–1829." *International Journal of Middle East Studies* 29 (1997): 403–25.

Quataert, Donald. "Part IV: The Age of Reforms." In *An Economic and Social History of the Ottoman Empire, 1300-1914*, edited by Halil İnalcık and Donald Quataert, 759–943. Cambridge: Cambridge University Press, 1997.

Qudsi, Ilyas. "Nubdha tarikhiyya fi 'l-hiraf al-dimashqiyya." *Actes du Sixième Congrès International des Orientalistes, tenu en 1883 à Leide*, Deuxième Partie, Section 1: Sémitique (1885): 1–34.

Rabi'i, 'Ali Muhammad Hadi. *al-Firaq al-masrahiyya al-Misriyya fi al-'Iraq: Vol. 1. Firqat Jurj Abyad*. Sharjah: al-Hay'a al-'Arabiyya lil-Masrah, 2019.

Racy, Ali Jihad. "Historical Worldviews of Early Ethnomusicologists: An East-West Encounter in Cairo, 1932." In *Ethnomusicology and Modern Music History*, edited by Stephen Blum, Philip Bohlman, and Daniel Neuman, 68–91. Urbana: University of Illinois Press, 1991.

Racy, Ali Jihad. "Musical Change and Commercial Recording in Egypt, 1904–1932." Ph.D. diss., Urbana-Champaign: University of Illinois, 1977.

Rafeq, Abdul-Karim. "Public Morality in the 18th Century Ottoman Damascus." *Revue Des Mondes Musulmans Et de La Méditerranée* 55/56 (1990): 180–96.

al-Rafi'i, 'Abd al-Rahman. *Shu'ara' al-wataniya fi Misr: Tarajimuhum wa-shi'ruhum al-watani wa-al-munasabat allati nazamu fiha qasa'idahum*, 3rd ed. Cairo: Dar al-Ma'arif, 1992.

al-Ra'i, 'Ali. "*Zaynab* bayna al-riwaya wa-l nathr al-fanni." *al-Majalla* 56, September 1, 1961.

al-Rajab, al-Hajj Hashim Muhammad. *Al-maqam al-'Iraqi*. Beirut: Dar al-'Arabiyya lil-Mawsu'at, 2009.

Reid, Donald Malcolm. *Whose Pharaohs? Archaeology, Museums, and Egyptian National Identity from Napoleon to World War I*. Berkeley and Los Angeles: University of California Press, 2002.

Reilly, James A. "Women in the Economic Life of Late-Ottoman Damascus." *Arabica* 42, no. 1 (1995): 79–106.

Reinkowski, Maurus. *Die Dinge der Ordnung: Eine vergleichende Untersuchung über die osmanische Reformpolitik im 19. Jahrhundert*. München: Oldenbourg, 2005.

Reynolds, Dwight Fletcher. *Arab Folklore: A Handbook*. Westport: Greenwood Press, 2007.

Richards, William Shortland. "Report on the Trade of Damascus for the Year 1898." In *Diplomatic and Consular Reports*, vol. 2306. London: Harrison and Sons, 1899; orig. June 15, 1899.

Richards, William Shortland. "Report on the Trade of Damascus for the Year 1902." In *Annual Series of Trade Reports)*, vol. 3059. London: Harrison and Sons, 1903; orig. July 6, 1903.

Roberts, Mary. *Istanbul Exchanges: Ottomans, Orientalists, and Nineteenth-Century Visual Culture*. Oakland: University of California Press, 2015.

Rogers, Sarah. "Daoud Corm, Cosmopolitan Nationalism, and the Origins of Lebanese Modern Art." *The Arab Studies Journal* 18, no. 1 (2010): 46–77.

Roper, Geoffrey. "The Beginnings of Arabic Printing by the ABCFM, 1822–1841." *Harvard Library Bulletin* 9, no.1 (1998): 50–68.

Rose, Richard B. "The Ottoman Fiscal Calendar." *Middle East Studies Association Bulletin* 25, no. 2 (1991): 157–67.

Rushdi, Fatima. *Kifahi fi-l-masrah wa-l-sinima*. Cairo: Dar al-Ma'arif, 1970.

Ryzova, Lucie. *The Age of the Efendiyya: Passages to Modernity in National-Colonial Egypt*. Oxford: Oxford University Press, 2014.

Ryzova, Lucie. *L'effendiyya ou la modernité contestée*. Collection 15/20. Cairo: Cedej, 2004.

Sadgrove, Philip. *The Egyptian Theater in the Nineteenth Century: 1799–1882*. Reading: Ithaca Press, 1996.

Sadgrove, Philip and Shmuel Moreh. *Jewish Contributions to Nineteenth Century Arabic Theater: Plays from Algeria and Syria: A Study and Texts*. Oxford: Oxford University Press, 1996.

Safir, El Boudali. "La musique arabe en Algérie." In *Documents Algériens*. Service d'Information du Cabinet du Gouverneur Générale de l'Algérie: Série Culturelle No. 36, June 20, 1949.

Sahhab, Elyas. *Al-musiqa al-ʿArabiya fi al-qarn al-ʿishrin: Mashahid wa mahattat wa wujuh*. Lebanon: Dar al-Farabi, 2009.

Said, Edward. *Culture and Imperialism*. New York: Vintage Books, 1994.

Said, Edward. *Orientalism*. New York: Pantheon Books. 1978.

Said, Edward. *Orientalism: Western Conceptions of the Orient*. Reprinted with a New Afterword. New York: Penguin Books, 1995.

Sajdi, Dana. "Peripheral Visions: The Worlds and Worldviews of Commoner Chroniclers in the 18th Century Ottoman Levant." Ph.D. Thesis, Columbia University, 2002.

Sakli, Mourad. "Avant-Propos." In *Initiation à la musique tunisienne, Volume 1: Musique Classique*, edited by Rashid Sellami, Lassad Kria, and Mourad Sakli, 7–10. Sidi Bou Saïd: Centre des Musiques Arabes et Méditerranénnes, 2004.

Salzmann, Ariel. "An Ancien Regime Revisited: "Privatization" and Political Economy in the Eighteenth-Century Ottoman Empire." *Politics Society* 21, no. 4 (1993): 393–423.

Sami, ʿAbd al-Rahman Bey. *Qawl al-haqq fi Bayrut wa Dimashq aw sifr al-salam fi Bilad al-Sham*. Misr: Matbaʿat al-Muqtataf, 1896.

Samuels, Ellen. "Examining Millie and Christine McKoy: Where Enslavement and Enfreakment Meet." *Signs: Journal of Women in Culture and Society* 37, no. 1 (2011): 53–81.

Sayfo, Omar. "From Kurdish Sultan to Pan-Arab Champion and Muslim Hero: The Evolution of the Saladin Myth in Popular Arab Culture." *Popular Culture* 50, no. 1 (2017): 65–85.

al-Sayyid, Mahmud Ahmad. "Talib Effendi." In *Al-aʿmal al-kamila li Mahmud Ahmad al-Sayyid*, edited by ʿAli Jawad al-Tahir and ʿAbd al-Ilah Ahmad, 519–30. Baghdad: Dar al-Hurriyya, 1978.

Schatkowski Schilcher, Linda. *Families in Politics: Damascene Factions and Estates of the 18th and 19th Centuries*. Stuttgart: Steiner, 1985.

Scheid, Kirsten. *Fantasmic Objects: Art and Sociality from Lebanon, 1920–1950*. Bloomington: Indiana University Press, 2022.

Schochat, Ella. "Egypt: Cinema and Revolution." *The African e-Journals Project* 2, no. 4 (1983): 22–32.

Schwartz, Kathryn. "The Political Economy of Private Printing in Cairo, As Told from a Commissioning Deal Turned Sour, 1871." *International Journal of Middle East Studies* 49, no.1 (2017): 25–45.

Sehnaoui, Nada. *L'occidentalisation de la vie quotidienne à Beyrouth, 1860–1914*. Beirut: Dar an-Nahar, 2002.

Selim, Samah. *The Novel and the Rural Imaginary in Egypt 1880–1985*. London: Routledge, 2004.

Selim, Samah. "Pharaoh's Revenge: Translation, Literary History and Colonial Ambivalence". In *The Making of the Arab Intellectual: Empire, Public Sphere and the Colonial Coordinates of Selfhood*, edited by Dyala Hamzah, 20–39. New York: Routledge, 2013.

Selim, Samah. *Popular Fiction, Translation and the Nahda in Egypt*, Cham: Palgrave Macmillan, 2019.

Shahid, Irfan. "Shawqi wa Misr al-firʿawniya." *Fussul* 2 (1983): 322–8.

al-Shahir, Sahib. "al-Baladiyya: Maqha min ayyam al-zaman al-jamil." *Dhakira ʾIraqiyya* (supplement of *al-Mada* newspaper), November 2, 2009.

Shakir, Faʾiq. *Al-amrad al-zuhariyya*. Baghdad: Matbaʿt al-ʿAhd, 1934.

Shakry, Omnia El. *The Great Social Laboratory*. Stanford: Stanford University Press, 2007.

Shannon, Jonathan Holt. *Performing al-Andalus: Music and Nostalgia Across the Mediterranean*. Bloomington: Indiana University Press, 2015.

Sharif, Malek. *Imperial Norms and Local Realities: The Ottoman Municipal Laws and the Municipality of Beirut (1860–1908)*. Würzburg: Ergon, 2014.

"Sharika lil-sinima am madha?! Tanaqud wa taharrub." *al-Masrah*, May 24, 1926.

"Sharikat film Isis: Hadith maʿa Wedad Bek ʿUrfi *Nidaʾ Allah*." *al-Masrah*, March 28, 1927.

Shaw, Stanford J. "The Nineteenth-Century Ottoman Tax Reforms and Revenue System." *International Journal of Middle East Studies* 6, no. 4 (1975): 421–59.

Shawqi, Ahmad. *ʿAdhraʾ al-Hind*. Cairo: Hindawi Foundation for Education and Culture, 2017.

Shawqi, Ahmad. *ʿAdhraʾ al-Hind aw Tamaddun al-Faraʿina li-amir al-shuʿaraʾ Ahmad Shawqi*, edited and introduced by Ahmad Ibrahim al-Hawari. Cairo: Ain for Human and Social Studies, 2005.

Shay, Anthony. *The Dangerous Lives of Public Performers: Dancing, Sex, and Entertainment in the Islamic World*. London: Palgrave Macmillan, 2014.

Sheehi, Stephen. *The Arab Imago: A Social History of Portrait Photography*. Princeton: Princeton University Press, 2016.

Sheehi, Stephen. "Arabic Literary-Scientific Journals Precedence for Globalization and the Creation of Modernity." *Comparative Studies of South Asia, Africa and the Middle East* 25, no. 2 (2005): 439–49.

Sheehi, Stephen. *Foundations of Modern Arab Identity*. Gainesville: University of Florida Press, 2004.

al-Shinnawi, Kamil. *Zuʿamaʾ wa fannanun wa udabaʾ*. Cairo: Hindawi Foundation for Education and Culture, 2017.

Silver, Christopher. *Recording History: Jews, Muslims and Music Across Twentieth Century North Africa*. Stanford: Stanford University Press, 2022.

Silver, Christopher. "The Sounds of Nationalism: Music, Moroccanism, and the Making of Samy Elmaghribi." *International Journal of Middle East Studies* 52 (2020): 23–47.

Snir, Reuven. *Modern Arabic Literature: A Theoretical Framework*. Edinburgh: Edinburgh University Press, 2017.

Snoussi, Manoubi. "Folklore Tunisien: Musique de Plein Air: L'Orchestra Tabbal et Zakkar." In *Revue des Études Islamiques*, 143–157. Paris: Paul Geuthner Orientalist Library, 1961.

Starkey, Paul. "Nahda." In *Encyclopedia of Arab Literature*, edited by Julie Scott Meisami and Paul Starkey, 573–, vol. 2. London: Routledge, 1998.

Stein, Rebecca L. and Ted Swedenburg, ed. *Palestine, Israel, and the Politics of Popular Culture*. Durham: Duke University Press, 2005.

Stoler, Ann Laura. *Race and the Education of Desire: Foucault's History of Sexuality and the Colonial Order of Things*. Durham: Duke University Press, 1995.

Südenhorst, Julius Zwiedinek von. *Syrien und seine Bedeutung für den Welthandel.* Wien: A. Hölder, 1873, https://hdl.handle.net/2027/wu.89097051411.
Sulayman, Jabir. "Nusri al-Jawzi wa-l al-haraka al-masrahiyya fi Filistin: Qira'a fi dhakiratihi wa awraqih," *Majallat al-Dirasat al-Filistiniyya* 7, no. 28 (1996): 135–46.
al-Tahir ʿAli Jawad. *Mahmud Ahmad al-Sayyid: Raʾid al-qissa al-haditha fi al-ʿIraq.* Beirut: Dar al-Adab, 1969.
al-Tahtawi, Rifaʿa Rafiʿ. *Al-murshid al-amin lil-banat wa-al-banin,* 1st ed. Egypt: Matbaʿat al-Madaris al-Malakiya, 1872.
al-Tahtawi, Rifaʿa Rafiʿ. *Manahij al-albab al-Misriya fi mabahij al-adab al-ʿasriya.* Cairo: Hindawi Foundation for Education and Culture, 2014.
al-Tahtawi, Rifaʿa Rafiʿ. *Takhlis al-ibriz fi talkhis Bariz.* Cairo: Hindawi, 2017 [1834].
Tarrazi, Filip di. *Tarikh al-Sahafa al-ʿArabiyya,* vols. 3–4. Beirut: Al-Matbaʿa al-Adabiyya, 1914.
Taylor, Timothy Dean. *Strange Sounds: Music, Technology, and Culture.* New York: Routledge, 2001.
Thompson, Elizabeth. *Colonial Citizens: Republican Rights, Paternal Privilege, and Gender in French Syria and Lebanon.* New York: Columbia University Press, 2000.
Thompson, Elizabeth. "Public and Private in Middle Eastern Women's History." *Journal of Women's History* 15, no. 1 (2003): 52–69.
Thornton, Philip. *The Voice of Atlas: In Search of Music in Morocco.* London: Alexander Maclehose & Co., 1936.
Topal, Alp Eren and Einar Wigen. "Ottoman Conceptual History: Challenges and Prospects." *Contributions to the History of Concepts* 14, no. 1 (2019): 93–114.
al-Tunisi, Bayram. *Bayram al-Tunisi: Al-aʿmal al-kamila,* vol. 2. Cairo: Maktabat Madbuli, 2002.
Wadi, Taha. *Diwan Rifaʿa al-Tahtawi: Jamʿ wa-dirasa,* 4th ed. Cairo: Dar al-Maʿarif, 1995.
Wahbi, Yusuf. *ʾIshtu alf ʿam.* Cairo: Dar al-Maʿarif, 1973.
Watenpaugh, Keith. *Being Modern in the Middle East: Revolution, Nationalism, Colonialism, and the Arab Middle Class.* Princeton: Princeton University Press, 2006.
Weber, Stefan. *Damascus: Ottoman Modernity and Urban Transformation, 1808–1918.* Translated by Stephen Cox, 2 vols. Aarhus: Aarhus Universitetsforlag, 2009.
Weber, Stefan. "Der Marğa-Platz in Damaskus: Die Entstehung eines modernen Stadtzentrums unter den Osmanen als Ausdruck eines strukturellen Wandels (1808–1918)." *Damaszener Mitteilungen* 10 (1998): 291–344 (Tafel 77–88).
Wickens, G. M., trans. "Little Pharaoh, a Short Story by Maḥmüd Taimür." *Journal of Arabic Literature* 10 (1979): 109–16.
Wien, Peter. *Arab Nationalism: The Politics of History and Culture in the Modern Middle East.* London: Routledge, 2017.
Wishnitzer, Avner. "Eyes in the Dark: Nightlife and Visual Regimes in Late Ottoman Istanbul." *Comparative Studies of South Asia, Africa and the Middle East* 37, no. 2 (2017): 245–61.
Wishnitzer, Avner. *Reading Clocks, Alla Turca: Time and Society in the Late Ottoman Empire.* Chicago: University of Chicago Press, 2015.
Wishnitzer, Avner. "Yawn: Boredom and Powerlessness in the Late Ottoman Empire." *Journal of Social History* 55, no. 2 (2021): 400–25.
Womack, Deanna Ferree. *Protestants, Gender, and the Arab Renaissance in Late Ottoman Syria.* Edinburgh: Edinburgh University Press, 2019.

Woodall, Carole. "'Awakening a Horrible Monster': Negotiating the Jazz Public in 1920s Istanbul." *Comparative Studies of South Asia, Africa and the Middle East* 30, no. 3 (2010): 574–82.
Wyrtzen, Jonathan. "National Resistance, Amazighité, and (Re-)Imagining the Nation in Morocco." In *Revisiting the Colonial Past in Morocco*, edited by Driss Maghraoui, 184–204. London: Routledge, 2013.
al-Yaziji, Ibrahim. "Athar adabiya." *al-Bayan* 14, December 16, 1897, reprinted in Editor-in-Chief, "Thaniyan: Al-Nathr – maʿraka naqdiya hawl riwayat ʿAdhraʾ al-Hind." *Fussul* 2, (March 1983): 303–9.
Zachs, Fruma and Sharon Halevi. "From Difaʿ Al-Nisaʾ to Masʾalat Al-Nisaʾ in Greater Syria: Readers and Writers Debate Women and Their Rights, 1858–1900." *International Journal of Middle East Studies* 41, no. 4 (2009): 615–33.
Zachs, Fruma and Sharon Halevi. *Gendering Culture in Greater Syria: Intellectuals and Ideology in the Late Ottoman Period*. London: I.B. Tauris, 2014.
"Zaynab ʿla al-shasha al-bayda." *Ruz al Yusuf* 169, April 22, 1930.
Ze'evi, Dror. *Producing Desire: Changing Sexual Discourse in the Ottoman Middle East, 1500–1900*. Berkeley: University of California Press, 2006.
Zemmin, Florian and Henning Sievert. "Conceptual History of the Near East: The Sattelzeit as a Heuristic Tool for Interrogating the Formation of a Multilayered Modernity." *Contributions to the History of Concepts* 16, no. 2 (2021): 1–26.
Zubaida, Sami. "Entertainers in Baghdad, 1900–1950." In *Inside Out: On the Margins of the Modern Middle East*, edited by Eugene Rogan, 212–30. London: I.B. Tauris, 2002.
Zuhur, Sherifa, ed. *Colors of Enchantment: Theater, Dance, Music, and the Visual Arts of the Middle East*. Cairo: AUC Press, 2001.
Zureiq, Constantin. *Ma al-ʿamal? Hadith ila al-ajyal al-ʿArabiya al-taliʿa*. Beirut: Markaz Dirasat al-Wihda al-ʿArabiya, 1998.

Arabic Periodicals

al-Akhbar (Beirut)
al-ʿAsifa (Beirut)
al-ʿAsr al-Jadid (Damascus)
al-Barq (Beirut)
al-Bashir (Beirut)
al-Bayan (Beirut)
Dimashq (Damascus)
al-Diyaʾ (Cairo)
Hadiqat al-Akhbar (Beirut)
al-Iqbal (Beirut)
al-Ittihad al-ʿUthmani (Beirut)
al-Janna (Beirut)
Jaridat Misr (Cairo)
al-Jinan (Beirut)
Lisan al-Hal (Beirut)
al-Masrah (Cairo)
al-Mathaf (Alexandria)
Mirʾat al-Sharq (Jerusalem)

al-Muʾayyad (Cairo)
al-Muqattam (Cairo)
al-Misbah (Beirut)
al-Muqtabas (Damascus)
al-Muqtataf (Beirut; Cairo)
al-Quds (Jerusalem)
Ruz al-Yusuf (Cairo)
al-Sabah (Cairo)
al-Sham (Damascus)
Suriye (Damsascus)
al-Tabib (Beirut)
Thamarat al-Funun (Beirut)
al-Watan (Cairo)

INDEX

'Abbas Hilmi II (king, khedive)   152
Abbasid   61
Abbas Pasha   43
Abdul Hamid II (Sultan)   6, 19, 25, 28, 121
Aboura, Mostefa   94, 95
Abullu (Apollo, journal)   153, 155
Abu Sayf, Salah   160
    "Al-sinima fi Misr sina'a qawmiya yajib himayatuha" (cinema in Egypt is a national industry that must be protected)   160
Abu Shadi, Ahmad Zaki   154, 155
Abyad, George   110, 111
adab   147
al-adab al-asri (contemporaneous literature)   151
al-adab al-'umumiyya   19, 37
adwar   72, 74
Agoub, Joseph   148
    "Dithyrambe sur l'Égypte" (poem)   148
al-Ahali (The People, newspaper)   64
Ahmad, Ratiba   73
Ahmed, Hussam   39
    Last Nahdawi: Taha Hussein and Institution Building in Egypt, The   39
Al-Ahram (newspaper)   150
Aida (Verdi, opera)   104, 109
aïta   86, 96
al-Akoudi, Sheikh Ibrahim   112
'Ala Hayakil Baalbek (The Ruins of Baalbek, 1936)   77
Alamphone   47
alcohol ban   17, 19, 28–30, 38
alcohol consumption   19, 23, 37
"Al Eih Helef Ma Yekalemnish" ("Really! He's Sworn not to Talk to Me," song)   47
Aleppo   57

Alexandria   120, 121
Alf Layla wa Layla (the Arabian Nights)   152
Algeria   83, 85, 87, 88
al-'Allaf, 'Abd al-Karim   65
Alliance Israelite Universelle   28
'alma   71
al-Siyasa al-Usbu'iyya (journal)   165
'Amara Café   30
amateur musical associations   87–90, 95
Amazigh (Berber) music   84, 85
Amin, Mostafa   45, 46
Amin, Nadira   73
Amin, Qasim   171
Amine, Khalid   102
Amir, Aziza   50, 158, 159, 161, 162
Amir, Bahiyya   78, 80
Amir, Eli   65, 66
    Mafriach Hayonim (The Dove Flyer)   65–6
al-'amma   4
ancient Egypt   144, 145, 155
    imagining in Nahda modern Egypt   145–9
ancient Greece   92, 144
ancient Rome   144
Andalusi
    culture   85
    identity   87
    revival movement   88, 92, 94
al-Andalusi, Zuhayr   22
Andalusi music in North Africa   82–99
    Arabic Nahda (renaissance)   82–4
    in colonial era   84–8
    knowledge   93–8
    performance   88–93
Anglican Protestants   28
angoisse (anguish)   40
anti-colonialism   164
Antony and Cleopatra (Shakespeare)   153
Antun, Farah   102, 103, 110

Salah al-Din and the Kingdom of Jerusalem (play)   110, 111
Arab-Berber racial myth   85
Arab(ic)
   cinema   157
   culture   82, 84, 88, 93, 112, 113
   drama   101, 104, 111, 112
   history   61
   identity   4, 40, 82, 83, 86, 99, 108
   illiteracy rates in   204 n.22
   intelligentsia   4
   literature   83, 148
   music   86, 88, 91–3, 96, 97
   musical renaissance   82
   musicology   93–7
   nationalism   83
   periodical press   120, 122, 124
   publishing industry   117
"Arab music in Algeria" (Safir)   92
El-Ariss, Tarek   3
Armbrust, Walter   7
Arslan, Shakib   150, 151
art music   72–4
Ashbee, C. R.   106, 107
al-ʿAsifa (The Storm, newspaper)   69, 70, 76–80
Asma (al-Bustani)   126
al-ʿAsr al-Hadith (The New Era, magazine)   64
ʿAtallah, Amin   112
ʿAtish, Badiʿa   63
al-ʿAttar, Shaykh Hasan   147
authenticity   84, 90, 95, 157–9, 175
Ayalon, Ami   105, 121, 204 n.22
Ayyub, Dhu al-Nun   64, 65
   "Hinama Tathur al-ʿAsifa" (When the Storm Blows)   64, 65
Azbakiyya (Ezbakieh)   5

Bachetarzi, Mahieddine   89–90
Badawi, M. M.   83
Baghdadi nightclubs. *See malahi*
Bahoora, Haytham   63
Bakathir, ʿAli Ahmad   154
baladi
   attire   49
   dance   50, 51
ballet   50
ballroom dancing   59

banat al-qahwa/ banat al-alhan/ banat al-musiqa (Women of the Café/ Women of melodies/Women of music)   71, 74
Barada at al-Sufaniyya   22, 23
al-Bashir (newspaper)   72
Bashkin, Orit   61
Bauernfeind, Gustav   24
al-Bayan ("The Bulletin," journal)   117, 126, 128, 135
BBC   90
El-Begmawy, Bermalion   47
Beirut   2–4, 6, 18, 21, 34, 55, 83, 120
Belzoni, Giovanni   145, 155
Ben Smaïl, Mohamed   94
"Berber *dahir*" (decree of 1930)   85
Berque, Jacques   40
Bey, Asʿad   29
Bey, Osman Hamdi   137
Beyk, Muhammad Duri   124
Biladi Biladi (poem)   52
Bourguiba, Mohammed   112
boys in women's clothing   56
Brihi, Mohamed   90
British colonialism   53, 55, 154
British Museum, The   145
brothels   42, 51, 56, 59, 62
Brummett, Palmira   6
Buenaventura, Wendy   50
Bullock, William   145
al-Burayk, Mikhaʾil   23
al-Bustani, Butrus   203 n.6, 208 n.72
Bustani, Saadallah   102
al-Bustani, Salim   126
Buthayna   79
Butrus IV   31
buyut ʿumumiyya   19

cabarets   3, 5, 9, 11, 41, 47–50, 69, 70, 78. *See also malahi*
Cachia, Pierre   7, 106
Café al-Darwishiyya   30
Café al-Hammam   30
Café Bab Tuma   30
café-chantants   71, 72
Café Dimitri Faʿsi   30
cafés   5, 8–10, 17–21, 24, 26–30, 35, 36, 55, 58, 66
Cairo   2–5, 43, 54, 55, 57, 77, 83, 120, 121

Cairo Congress of Arab Music
     (1932)   90, 97
Cairo Opera House   108
Calderwood, Eric   87
     Colonial al-Andalus   87
Caliphate of Córdoba   86
Campos, Camilla Pastor de Maria   64
capitalism   3, 168
Carioca, Taheya   50
Carlson, Marvin   102
     *Theaters of Morocco, Algeria
          and Tunisia: Performance
          Traditions of the Maghreb,
          The*   102
Carter, Howard   146, 153
Casino Baghdad   59
casinos (*kazinat*)   20, 25, 50, 59, 62
censorship laws   6, 121
Champollion   144
Charfeddine, Moncef   101
Chicago World's Fair (1893)   73
Chottin, Alexis   86, 94, 98
     Corpus of Moroccan Music   86, 94
     Tableau of Moroccan Music   86
Christian Reconquista   86
Christians   31
Cinema and Acting Company   162
cinemas   7, 8, 10–13, 21–2, 24, 41, 43, 49,
     50, 59, 61, 62, 157
Cioet, Donald   6
classical music   82, 84, 87, 88, 91, 93
Cleopatra (Haggard)   151
Cleopatra VII (queen)   152–3
Cohen, David   59
Colla, Elliott   165
colonial encounter   147
colonial gaze   42, 150
colonialism   40
Committee of Union and Progress
     (CUP)   29, 34
commodification   49
Condor Film   158, 162
Conservatory of Algiers   88
Conservatory of Moroccan Music   91
Constitution of 1876   19, 28
Constitution of 1908   19
Coquette, The (al-Ghandura, 1935)   49
Corm, Daoud   126, 205 n.41
Cormack, Raphael   40, 48, 54, 60, 62

*Midnight in Cairo: The Divas of Egypt's
     Roaring 20s*   40
cosmopolitanism   70
Coup d'État Attempt in Syria (1897)   27
Crary, Jonathan   132
culture(al)
     capitalism   145, 154
     memory   82, 85
     nationalism   40
     production   11, 12, 40, 43, 44, 55, 154
     products   39, 41, 43, 52
     revival   55
     turn   8
curfew   21

Daccache, Georges   197 n.25
Daccache, Laure (Lur Dakkash)   74, 76,
     197 n.25
al-Damanhuri, Shaykh Ahmad Abu'l
     Faraj   1
Damascus   3, 4, 25, 27, 29, 31, 34, 57
Darwish, Sayed   41, 48
Darwishiyya Street   23
David, Jacques Louis   140
Dawud al-Maskubi   29
de Lanoye, Ferdinand   150
     *Ramses le Grand, ou l'Egypte il y a trois
          mille trois cents ans* (*Ramses the
          Great, or, the Egypt of 3300 Years
          Ago*)   150
Deleuze, Gille   41
Denon, Vivant   145
     *Voyage dans la Basse et la Haute
          Égypte pendant les campagnes de
          générale Bonaparte*   145
d'Erlanger, Rodolphe   92–3, 98
     La Musique Arabe   92–3
de Sacy, Silvestre   148
Description de l'Égypte   144, 145
dévergondage. *See khala'a*
Dietrich, Marlene   47
Dijla, Sabiha   60
Dijla, Salima   60–2
Dinshaway (Mar'i, play)   6
Diodorus Siculus   144
divas   41, 44–8, 50, 51, 54, 57–62
divine laws (*hudud*)   29
Documents algériens (periodical)   91
Dom Pedro I (king)   146

Dumu' al-Hubb (*Love Tears*, 1936) 169
Driss, M. M. 101–2
"Drop Those Curtains" (record) 44, 47
Dumas, Alexandre 49
　Lady of the Camellias, The 49

early Egyptian film industry 157–75
　British and French companies
　　in 157–8
　critical practices 163–7
　critiques 169–71
　film practices and intellectual
　　reality 159–63
　film shot in Egyptian desert and Nile
　　Valley 158–9
　Haykal's nationalism 171–2
　rural narrative 167–9
　Zaynab (1930) and national
　　identity 171–2
Ebers, Gerge 151
　Eine Ägyptische Königstochter 151
Edrei, Elie 51
education reform 3
Efendi, As'ad 30
Efendi, 'Aziz 30
Egypt(ian) 1–5, 6, 40, 42–5, 51, 57,
　　100–12, 118, 121
　antiquities 145, 147, 155
　art 155
　civilization 155
　craze 145, 146
　culture 62, 167
　exhibitions 145
　film industry 50
　identity 62, 164, 167, 173
　literature 165, 172
　mummies 146, 147, 156
　nationalism 148, 171–2, 175
　westernization of 144
"Egyptian Hall" (1821) 145
Egyptian Revolution (1919) 7, 44, 157
Egyptology 145, 146, 150, 151
Egyptomania 144, 145, 146, 209 n.10
　imagining ancient Egypt in modern
　　Egypt 145–9
　as Orientalist construct 144–5
　Shawqi and 149–53
　Tutankhamun's tomb and modern
　　Egyptomaniac Egyptians 153–5

　in western/globalized popular
　　entertainment industries 145
Egyptosophy 144
Eid, Hassan 160
"El Khala'a wel-Dala'a mazhabi"
　　(Libertinage and Coquetterie
　　Are My Doctrine, song) 41,
　　48, 52
Elmaghribi, Samy 89
El Moutribia 89, 90
Elnemr, Eman 9
England, Samuel 110
engravings in illustrated Arabic
　　journals 117–43
　advertisements 123
　challenges to procuring
　　illustrations 124
　diagrams and unseen images 127–32
　engravers and 125–6
　everyday audiences 120–2
　novelty, spectacle, and
　　exoticism 133–8
　photo engraving and
　　lithography 124–5
　as popular entertainment 126–7
　subscribers 122–3
　taswir (picture-making) 138–42
　as visual compendiums of
　　encyclopedic knowledge
　　and imaginative pictorial
　　entertainment 123–4
ethno-racial hierarchy 94, 98
Europe(an) 42
　colonialism 57, 83, 99, 173
　enlightenment 39
　films 159
　musicology 93, 95
European Renaissance 144, 145
Exposition International d'Anvers
　　(1894) 117
extramarital sexuality 17, 28

Fahmi, Ahmad 139, 140, 142
　"The Fine Arts" (al-Funun
　　al-Jamila) 139
Fahmi, Aziz Ahmad 155
　"Wahi Nefertiti" (Nefertiti's
　　Revelation) 155
Fahmi, Hikmat 80

Fahmy, Ziad 7, 62, 89
  Ordinary Egyptians: Creating the Modern Nation through Popular Culture 7, 89
Faisal I (king) 53
"Fann al-Taswir" (Art of Image-making) 141–2
Farah, Iskandar 104
Farah, Mikhaʾil 206 n.43
Farhan, Sara 56
Fathiyya 73
female performers in Beirut 69–81
  female artists depiction in press 74–5
  fin-de-siècle women singers 71–2
  proud of their profession 76–7
  rise of female scene 72–4
  sad life story 78–9
  stigmatized 79–81
  women stories 75–6
femininity 79–81
Fez Congress of Moroccan Music (1939) 85, 90, 91, 94–6, 98
Fi Bilad Tut Ankh Amon (*In Tutankhamen's Country*, film, 1923) 158, 161, 172
"Fik ʿAsharet Kutshina fi-l Balkuna" ("Come and Play a Game of Cards in the Balcony," song) 48
films. *See* cinemas
fine art 140, 142
Fitzmaurice, George 162
Flaubert, Gustave 42, 43
Flower of Damascus (*Zahra Dimashq*) 22
foreign cinema 160
fortunas 44
France, Anatole 151
  Taïs 151
freedom of speech 19
Free Officers Revolution (1952) 100
French
  colonialism 84
  mandate 64, 70, 73, 74, 76
  musicology 93, 94
French Catholic 28
French Expedition (1798) 147
Furat, Salima 62

Gamal, Samia 50
gambling 17, 18, 28–30, 37
García Barriuso, Patrocinio 94, 95, 98
gardens 22–4
Gardens of the Provincial Treasurer (*junaynat al-defterdar*) 25
gay sex 43
Geer, Benjamin 171
gender 11, 17, 19, 33, 54, 80
George, Zakiyya 54, 60
German Protestants 28
Ghadat al-Sahara (*Belle of the Desert*, 1929) 159, 163
Ghanem, Mohamed 97
al-Ghazali, Nazim 60
Gibb, Hamilton 165
Gibran, Khalil 206 n.45
Gitre, Carmen 101
  Acting Egyptian: Theater, Identity, and Political Culture in Cairo 1869-1930 101
Glasser, Jonathan 86–8, 94
  Lost Paradise, The 86
Global South 146
Goeine, Yvonne 162
Grallert, Till 5
Great Britain 44
Green Meadows 22, 23
Guettat, Mahmoud 97, 98

Hac Yolunda (On the Way to the Pilgrimage) 147
El-Hadari, Ahmad 50, 157, 161
  Tarikh al-sinima fi Misr (*The History of Cinema in Egypt*) 161
al-Haddad, Najib 102, 105, 109, 110
  Salah al-din al-Ayyubi 105, 109, 110
Haggard, H. Rider 151
el-Haj, Muhafiz 37
al-Hakim, Tawfiq 100, 101, 103, 106, 107, 111, 154
  ʿAwdat al-Ruh (Return of the Spirit) 154
  Bird from the East, A (ʿ*Usfur min al-Sharq*) 100
  Prison of Life, The (*Sijn al-ʿUmr*) 100
  Return of the Spirit (ʿ*Awdat al-Ruh*) 100
al-Hakim, Tira 58, 72

al-Halabiyya, Fayruz   74, 76, 80
Hall, Asaph   132
al-Hallaq, Ahmad al-Budayri   23
Hamadeh, Shirine   121
Hamama, Fatin   60
Hamidian Gardens   26
Hamidian period (1876–1909)   6
Hamidian publishing laws   122
Hammad, Hanan   60
Hammond, Andrew   8
al-Haqaʾiq (journal)   22
Harb, Talʿat   162
"Harrag ʿAlaya Baba Maruhsh El-Sinima" (My Father Forbade Me to Go to the Cinema, song)   41
Harrison, Olivia   83
  Transcolonial Maghreb   83
Hashemite monarchy   53, 61
Haykal, Muhammad Hussein   105, 159, 165, 167, 170–2, 174, 212 n.7
  Fi Awqat al-Faragh (*During Free Time*)   171
  "National Literature" (Haykal)   171
  Zaynab (novel)   105, 166, 168, 169, 173
El-Hefny, Mahmoud Ahmed   97
Herodotus   144
heterosexual practices   43
hidâ   96
al-Hifni, Ratiba   44, 45
Ḥijazi, Salama   100, 102–4, 109, 111
al-Hilal ("The Crescent," journal)   117, 126, 135
Hill, Peter   102
His Master's Voice   47
al-Hoda, Nur   74
homoeroticism   57
Hugo, Victor   107
  Mary Tudor (play)   107
Hull, Edith Maude   162, 165, 172
human equality   33
Husain, Zuhur   60
Husayn Nazim Pasha   30
Husni, Daud   49, 77
Hussein, Taha   39, 105, 106, 159
al-Huzuz, Munira   54, 60

Ibrahim, Hafiz   154, 155
Al-Idhaʿa (magazine)   77

El Idrissi, Idris ben Abdelali   91, 96
  Uncovering the Secrets of Music   96
iftar   23
imaginary   12, 74, 82, 87, 144, 147, 148, 158, 168
immorality   26, 31, 42, 75, 80
improvisation   47, 72, 77
indecent acts (*fiʿl shaniʿ/fiʿl munkar*)   33
industrialization   42
Industrial Revolution   42
"Initiation to Tunisian Music" (radio program)   93
Institute of Oriental Music   77
International Congress of Orientalists (1894)   149, 151
Iraq
  culture   54, 55, 60–2
  female performers in   57–62, 65, 66
  foreign performers in   58
  modernity and development   53–5, 60, 62, 65
  national identity   62
  nocturnal practices   54, 55, 57–9, 61, 65, 66
  revolt (1920)   58, 65
Iraqi Children's Welfare Society   62
Iraqi Jews   59, 66
Iraqi Ministry of Education   62
al-ʿIraqiyya, Salima   60–2
Iraq revolution (1958)   53, 56
Iraq Times, The (newspaper)   53
"Irkhi El-Sitara illi fi rihna" (Drop Those Curtains, song)   41, 52
Isis Film Corporation   161
Iskandar, ʿAfifa   54, 59, 60
islahhâne/dar al-islah   22
Islam(ic)
  customs (ʿadat)   34
  history   61
  morals   19, 28, 31
Islamic Revolution (1979)   8
Islamophobia   99
Ismaʿil, Sayyid ʿAli   101, 107
  Masirat al-Masrah fi Misr: 1900-1930 (*The March of Theater in Egypt: 1900-1930*)   101
  Tarikh al-Masrah fi Misr fi-l-Qarn al-Tasiʿ ʿAshar (*The History*

*of Theater in Egypt in the 19th
    Century*) 101
al-Istambuliyya, Stella 78, 79
Istanbul 37, 120
Istiqlal Party 85

Jabal Qasiyun 22, 23
Jacob, Wilson 57
Jamal, Malaka 79
Jamal Pasha 112
Jamati, Habib 169
Jarenski, Shelly 132
al-Jawahiri, Muhammad Mahdi 63
Jawhara Café 59
Jawqat al-Ḥisan (The Beautiful Women's
  ensemble) 73
al-Jawzi, Nusri 112
Jews 31. *See also* Iraqi Jews
al-Jinan ("The Gardens," journal) 117,
  126, 127, 135
Jomard, Edmond-François 148
Jubran, Marie 74, 76, 77
Jumʿa, Muhammad Lutfi 210 n.34,
  211 n.40
al-junayna al-ʿumumiyya 25
junaynat al-defterdar 26

Ka/Ba concepts 209 n.10
Kabyle Berbers 85
Kaiser Wilhelm II 25, 32
al-Kallachiyya 56
Kamil, ʿAdil 154
Kanj Pasha, Shahin 1–2
karagöz performance 24, 37
Karam, Karam Melhem 76
Kardecist movement 208 n.10
Karim, Muhammad 159, 168, 169, 172,
  174
Karr, Jean-Baptiste Alphonse 169
Kashar, Bamba 44, 50, 51
Katsumi Kuroita 209 n.10
Kawkab al-Parisiana (The Star of the
  Parisiana). *See* Khayyat, Nina
Kawkab al-Sharq 70
Kawthar al-Arab (The Nectar of the
  Arabs). *See* Khayyat, Nina
El Khachab, Walid 166
khalaʿa 11, 36, 41–6, 48, 50, 52
Khalil, Abu 71

al-Kharrab Café 30
al-Khashshab, ʿAli 149
  rubaʿiya 149
khawal 57
Khayri, Badiʿ 49, 52
Khayyat, Nina 77
Khuri-Makdisi, Ilham 5, 104
  *Eastern Mediterranean and the making
    of global radicalism, The* 104
King Tutankhamun's tomb 146, 147,
  153–6
Kit Kat cabaret 50
Kosaku Hamada 209 n.10
Kozma, Liat 64
Kuchuk Hanum 42, 43
al-Kuwaiti, Dawud 59, 60
al-Kuwaiti, Salih 59, 60

Lagrange, Frédéric 46, 154
Lama, Badr 158, 162
Lama, Ibrahim 158, 159, 162
L'Andaloussia 94–5
Layla 71, 72
Layla (1927) 50, 159, 161, 172
League of Nations 53
leisure 17, 22, 27, 36, 53, 54, 57–9, 61,
  62, 65, 66
Levant 71, 72, 77
liberal/conservative divide 40–1
Liberal Constitutionalist party 159
libertinage. *See khalaʿa*
"Libertinage (or Debauchery) and
  Coquetterie are my Doctrine"
  (song) 47
liberty 33–6
Liberty Gardens (*hadiqat al-hurriyya*) 26
Lisan al-Hal (newspaper) 70, 75
literary-scientific journals 127
literature 5, 10, 12, 13, 55, 61, 83, 147,
  148, 165
lithography 124
Lord Carnarvon 153
Lumière, Auguste 160
Lumière, Louise 160
Lutfi Efendi 27
Lyautey, Hubert 85

McKoy, Christine 135
McKoy, Millie 135

McLuhan, Marshall 40
Madame Blanche 69, 70
Maghreb(i) 82, 83, 85, 87, 89, 97–9
  culture 88
  music 86, 95, 97
mahallat 19
mahallat ʿumumiyya 29
El Mahdi, Salah 93, 96, 99
  al-turath al-musiqi al-tunisi (*Tunisian Musical Heritage*) 96
al-Mahdiya, Munira 41, 44–9, 52, 73, 106, 107, 110, 111, 154, 192 n.8
Mahfouz, Naguib 154–6
  "Yaqazat al-Mumya" (The Awakening of the Mummy) 155, 156
Main, Ernest 53
  Iraq from Mandate to Independence 53
al-Majalla (The Magazine, magazine) 64
al-Majalla al-Musiqiya (magazine) 45
Majdi, Salih 148
Makdisi, Ussama 105
malahi 53–9
  dancing, singing, and sex work in 62–6
  female performers and divas in 57–62
  maqam, shaʿar performances and 55–7
  male dancers 55–6
maʾluf 92, 93, 96, 97
al-manafiʿ al-ʿumumiyya 19
Manetho 144
al-Manfaluti, Mustafa Lutfi 169
  Magdoline (*Under the Shadows of the Linden Tree*) 169
maqahi (Baghdadi cafés) 54–7
maqamat 93
maqam performances 55–6
al-Maʿrad (magazine) 70, 75
Marʿi, Hassan 6
Marie *al-Jamila* (The Beautiful). *See* Jubran, Marie
Marja Square 20, 22, 23, 25, 29
Marrakech 90
al-marsah al-ʿumumi 22
Martyrs Square. *See* Sahat al-Burj
Masabni, Badiʿa 73, 76, 77, 106

Mashriq 83, 88, 99
al-Masrah (magazine) 161
Massad, Joseph 57
mass media 7, 132
materiality 39, 41
materialization 39
al-Mathaf ("The Museum," journal) 117, 123, 127, 141, 142
Al-Mawsuʿat (journal) 150
Mestyan, Adam 6, 101, 104–5, 108
  Arab Patriotism: The Ideology and Culture of Power in Late Ottoman Egypt 101, 104
Middle East 8, 10, 54, 55, 57
Midhat Pasha 22, 25
military music 25
Ministry of Interior 29, 31, 37
Ministry of Public Education 27
Min Layali Bayrut (Of Beirut's Nightlife) 76
al-Misriya, Naʿima 73, 154
al-Misriyya, Tira. *See* al-Hakim, Tira
mission civilisatrice 28
Mitchell, Timothy 135
modernity/modernization/modernizing 2, 3, 5, 9, 10, 25, 39–41, 43, 46, 49, 50, 57, 60, 62, 65, 70, 74, 75, 82, 84, 92, 99, 121
  ideology 18
  Iraq 53–5
  material 42
  moral effects of 42
modern media. *See* Nahda media
Mohammad, Mohammad ʿAwadh 155
  "al-Maqama al-Haramiya" (The Pyramidic *Maqama*) 155
Mohammed Ali 43
moral anxiety 11, 40–4, 49–52
moral corruption (*fasad*) 17, 21, 62, 65
morality 10, 19, 41, 51, 54
  of aesthetics 44–7, 49
  political 48
  pre-Victorian and Victorian 43
Moroccan French Protectorate 84, 87, 95, 97
Morocco/Moroccan 83, 85, 96, 99
  culture 84
  music 86
Moshe, Hasiba 72

movie theaters 41, 43, 49, 52
M'tiri, Faqih 90, 97
al-Muʿallim al-Jadid (The New Teacher, journal) 62
Mubarak, Ali Pasha 102, 124
   ʿAlam al-Din (*The Sign of Religion*) 102
Mubarak, Salma 166, 167, 169
mughanniyyat/mutribat (professional singers) 74
mumisat. *See* sex work/sex workers
mummymania 156
mummies, trade in 146
municipal gardens 25
municipality (*baladiyya*) 20, 25, 35, 36
al-Muqtabas (newspaper) 27, 30, 35
al-Muqtataf ("The Selections," journal) 117, 123, 124, 126, 127, 132, 135, 139, 140, 154, 155
Murad, Regina 60, 65
Murad, Salima 54, 59–60, 66
musical conferences 97–8
musical genres 73
   Arab classical 82
   Egyptian 77
al-Musiqa (journal) 49
al-musiqa al-sharqiyya (*Mashriqi* music) 97
Muslims 17, 31, 37
Mutran, Khalil 108, 154, 155
   "Isis aw al-Husn al-Khalid" (Isis, Or Immortal Beauty) 155
   "Nashid Tut ʿAnkh Amun" (Tutankhamun's Anthem) 154
   ʿUtayl (play) 108
   "Waqfa fi Zil Timthal li-Raʿmsis al-Kabir" (Standing in the Shadow of the Statue of Great Ramses) 155
muwashahhat 74, 197 n.26
al-Muwaylihi, Muhammad 5, 102, 103
   Hadith ʿIsa Ibn Hisham 5, 102, 103

al-Nadim, ʿAbd Allah 1–2, 52, 105, 148
Nahda 8, 55. *See also individual entries*
   and everyday entertainment 3–7
   Iraqi 61
   modernizing work 41
   movement 39, 40

popular histories of 9–14
   in rural areas 105
   on stage and on celluloid 49–51
   studies 39, 40
   and theater 101–4
Nahda media 40, 45, 49–52
   moralities of 41–4
Nahdawi intellectuals 2–5, 8, 9, 119, 143
Naji, Ibrahim 154, 159
Najm, Muhammad Yusuf 101, 106
   al-Masrahiyya fi-l-Adab al-ʿArabi al-Hadith 101, 106
Najmabadi, Afsaneh 57
Napoleon 43
Napoleon's Campaign 146
al-Naqqash, Marun 104
   al-Bakhil (*The Miser*, play) 104
al-Naqqash, Rajaʾ 169
al-Naqqash, Salim 104
Nasr, Shaykh ʿAli Abu'l 1
national bourgeoisie 10, 11, 18, 43–5, 50, 51
National Gardens (*hadiqat al-umma*) 26
national identity 55, 62, 99, 157–9, 162, 164, 167, 171–2, 174, 175
nationalism 7, 40, 52, 83, 148, 171–2
nationalist state-building 83, 84
National Museum, Brazil 146
Naʿim 56
nightlife 10–12, 40, 53–5, 57, 59, 62–6
non-Arab identity 82
non-Muslims 17, 28
North African musicology 93
Novel and the Rural Imaginary in Egypt, 1880-1985, The (Selim) 105
nuba 91–5
nuba oshshak 94
Nuwas, Abu 62
"Nuzhat al-Nufus" ("The Pleasant Promenade of the Souls," cabaret) 44

occult 144, 151
Odeon Records 47, 109
opera comique 49
orgies 43
Orientalism 42, 145, 146, 152
Orientalist discourse 75
Orientalist images 119, 136

Orientalist photographs   135
Oriental Music Club   77
Ottoman Empire   4, 5, 17, 34, 54, 55, 120, 121, 137, 147, 157
   publishing in   6
Ottoman provinces, British occupation of   53
Ottoman Tanzimat (reorderings)   3

Palestine   112, 113
pan-African identity   99
pan-Arabic
   culture   111
   identity   82
pan-Arabism   4, 61, 82, 83, 89, 99
Paris Colonial Exposition (1931)   95
al-Parisiana   70
Pathé   47
Pedro I (king)   208 n.10
Penal Code (1858)   19
Pharaonism   149, 154, 155
phonograph   72, 73, 88
photo-engraved plates   125
photo engraving   124
pop culture   40
popular behavior
   regulating and criminalizing   27–8
popular culture   6–10, 40, 46, 53–5, 59, 61, 62, 66, 74, 89, 145
popular entertainment   4, 5, 7–9, 18, 19, 41, 50
   Egyptomania in   145
   engravings as   126–7
   in Iraq   54, 55, 66
popular entertainment in late Ottoman Damascus (1875–1914)   17–38
   cafés and taverns   19–21
   forms   23–4
   gardens   22–3
   liberty after 1908   33–6
   Ottoman practicality and quotidian practices   36–8
   popular practices and proper fun   24–33
   theaters and cinemas   21–2
popular music   73
press codes   19
press laws   6
printed portraits   123, 142
print media   39, 122
private space   18, 43, 52
proper public gardens   24–6
prostitutes/prostitution   43, 64, 75
public, concept of   19
public assemblies   19
public benefit (*manfa'a 'amma/maslaha 'amma*)   4, 103, 121, 127
public morality (*adab 'umumiyya/akhlaq 'umumiyya*)   17, 28, 31, 37
public order (*al-raha al-'umumiyya/asayiş-i 'umumi*)   19, 21, 36, 51
public parks   25
public spaces   11, 18, 43, 52, 57, 63, 65, 76, 80, 121–2
public venues (*al-mahallat al-'umumiyya*)   11, 37

al-Qabbani, Abu Khalil   22, 71, 72, 104
al-Qadi, Mohammad Yunus   52, 154, 155
qalaq   40
al-Qardaḥi, Sulayman and traveling theatrical troupes   102
   in 1920s and 1930s   111–13
   Othello performance in Sohag   105–9
   as pan-Arab dramaturge   104–5
   performance as Saladin in Tunis   109–11
   theater and Nahda   101–4
qasa'id   72
Qasim, Mahmoud   157, 159–63, 169, 170, 172
   Dalil al-aflam fi al-qarn al-'ishrin fi Misr wa al-'alam al-'Arabi (*Twentieth Century Films' Guide of Egypt and the Arab World*)   160
   Mawsu'at al-sinima al-'Arabiyya (*Encyclopedia of the Arab Cinema*)   159–61
Qassatli, Nu'man   22, 24, 32
Qubla Fi al-Sahra' (*Kiss in the Desert*, 1927)   159, 161, 162, 164, 165, 172
Qutb, Sayyid   105

racialization   135

racial sciences   135
Racy, A. J.   97
radio   7, 11, 41, 43, 52, 59, 61, 88, 90–3
Radio-Alger   91
radio al-Sharq (Radio-Orient)   77
Radio-Rabat   90, 91, 96
Radio Tunis   93
Rahlu   57
al-Raʿi, ʿAli   173, 174
Ramadan (ʿeid al-fitr)   17, 18, 23, 28, 31, 36, 37
Rami, Ahmad   46
Ramses Cinema   160
Ramses Company for Cinema Production   159
Ramses II (king)   151, 152
raqs sharqi (belly dancing)   42, 43, 50, 51
al-Rashid, Harun   61
Rashidiyya Institute   93, 97
Rashid Rida affair   30
al-Razek, ʿAli ʿAbd   47
   al-Islam wa Usul al-Hukm (Islam and the Foundations of Government)   47
al-Raʿi, Ali   102
   Al-Masrah fi-l-Watan al-ʿArabi (Theater in the Arab World)   102
record industry   72–3
red-light districts   50, 52, 56
Reinaud, Joseph   148
religious norms   28
"Repertoire of Arab and Moorish Music" (Yafil)   89
Revue musicale de l'Afrique du Nord   87–8
Ricard, Prosper   90
Rifaʿa, ʿAli Fahmi   148, 149
   "ʿArus al-afrah" (Bride of the Jubilees, poem)   149
Er Rihala (newspaper)   90
al-Rihani, Najib   111, 112
Rosito, Victor   161
Rosti, Estafan   161
Rouanet, Jules   89
al-Rusafi, Maʿruf   56
   "Wajhu Naʿim" (Naʿim's Face, poem)   56
   "al-Yatim al-Makhduʿ" (The Defrauded Orphan, poem)   56

Rushdi, Fatima   44, 51, 73, 111–13, 153
Russian Imperial Palestine Society   28
Ruz al-Yusuf (magazine)   162, 165

al-Sabah (magazine)   160
Sabiʿ café   55–7
Sabra, Wadia   77, 97
Sabry, Randa   39
   "Passion des bibliothèques et quête du livre chez les voyageurs égyptiens partis en Europe au temps de la Nahda," ("Bibliophilia and the Quest for Books among Egyptian Travellers in Europe during Nahda,")   39
Sadgrove, Philip   101
   Egyptian Theatre in the Nineteenth Century, 1799-1882, The   101
Safir, El Boudali   88, 91, 92, 95
Sahat al-Burj   70
Said, Edward   42, 145
"Saʿit al-Haz Ma Titʿawwadshi" (A Happy Hour Cannot be Missed, song)   41
Sakli, Mourad   93
salat Blanche (performance hall)   69, 70
sales tax   37
Salt, Henry (Mr.)   145
same-sex practices   56, 57
Sanuʿa, Yaʿqub   105
Sarina   73
Sarruf, Yaʿqub   110
satirical songs   74
Sattelzeit   18
Sawsan   70, 79
al-Sayegh, Nicolas   205 n.41
al-Sayyid, Mahmud Ahmad   63–5
   "Talib Effendi"   63–5
al-Sayyid al-Badawi, *mawlid* of   1
Saʿada, Badriyya   72
Saʿdun Park Casino   59
Saʿid, Nuri   60
Schochat, Ella   158
Scott, Walter   109, 110
   Talisman   109
Second Constitutional period (1908–20)   6
Şehabettin, Cenap   147

Selim, Samah 4, 7, 105
  Popular Fiction, Translation, and the Nahda in Egypt 7
Service of Native Arts 90
sexuality 10, 44, 49, 50, 54, 56, 57, 80
sexualization 135
sexual violence (*ghasabiyyat*) 33
sex work/sex workers 36, 37, 54–8, 65
  female 62–4
  male 56
Shakir, Fa'iq 62
El Shakry, Omnia 93
Shalfun, Iskandar 98
Shambir, Camille 77
al-Shami, Ahmad 106, 107
al-Shammas, Habib Efendi 22
Shannon, Jonathan Holt 87
Shata, Sayed 41
Al-Shatt café 58
Shawqi, Ahmad 155, 210 n.34
  'Adhra' al-Hind aw Tamaddun al-Fara'ina (The Maid of India/The Civilization of the Pharaohs) 150–2
  and Cleopatra 152–3
  Dal wa Tayman aw Akhir al-Fara'ina (*Dal and Tayman or the Last Pharaohs*) 150, 151
  Egyptomania and 149–52
  "Jazirat al-'Adhara" ('The Virgins' Island) 151
  "Kibar al-Hawadith fi Wadi al-Nil" (Major Events in the Nile Valley) 149–51, 153
  Ladiyas 152
  Ladiyas, Dal wa Tayman 152
  Ladiyas aw Akhir al-Fara'ina (*Ladiyas or the Last of the Pharaohs*) 150
  "Mafakhir al-fara'ina" (Feats of the Pharaohs, poem) 154
  Masra' Kliyubatra (*Death of Cleopatra*) 153
  Shaytan Binta'ur (The Satan/Demon of Pentawer) 152
  "Tut 'Ankh Amun wa-hadarat 'asrih" (Tutankhamun and the Civilization of His Time, poem) 154

al-Shawwa, Sami 77
Shaykh Arslan tomb 23
sha'ar performances 56, 57
She (Haggard) 151
Sheehi, Stephen 122
Sheik, The (Hull) 172
Shihab al-Din, Muhammad 148, 149
Shougorou Tsuboi 209 n.10
Shukri Pasha 30
Silver, Chris 89
Silver, Christopher 7
  Recording History: Jews, Muslims and Music across Twentieth Century North Africa 7
Sirri, Fatma 73
al-Siyasa al-Usbu'iyya (newspaper) 159, 165
Snoussi, Manoubi 92, 93, 98
social capital 19
social change 42, 52, 76
social norms 33, 81
social reform (*islah*) 3, 4, 119, 121
sociopolitical songs 74
socio-satirical monologue 73
Son of the Sheik, The (Hull) 162, 165, 172
Sous les Tilleuls (Karr) 169
State Council 29
Strabo 144
street culture 10
Su'ad al-Ghajariya (*Su'ad The Gypsy*, 1928) 163
al-Sufaniyya 25
Suq al-Khayl 20, 23, 29
Suq 'Ali Pasha 29
Surur, Malaka 72–3, 79
Syria 109–11, 118, 121

el-Tabei, Mohamad 46
al-Tabib ("The Physician," journal) 117, 124, 126, 127, 135
al-Tahtawi, Rifa'a Rafi' 13, 39, 102, 147, 148
  Manahij al-albab al-Misriya fi mabahij al-adab al-'asriya (*The Paths of Egyptian Minds in the Joys of Modern Arts*) 148
  al-murshid al-amin lil-banat wa-al-banin (*The Reliable Guide for Girls and Boys*) 148

Takhlis al-Ibriz fi Talkhis Bariz (*Extracting Pure Gold in the Overview of Paris*) 13, 39, 102
tamaddun al-watan (civilizing the nation) 148
al-Tamari, Salim 7
taqatiq/qudud (popular light women songs) 72, 74, 154
Tarnan, Khemais 97
taswir (picture-making) 138–42
tavern girls (*bint al-hana*) 21
taverns 19–21
Taymur, Mahmud 155
  "Fir'awn al-Saghir" (Taymur) 155
El Tazi, Hadj Othman 90
télégraphie sans filr (TSF, wireless) 90
Telemaque (Fenelon) 102, 104
textual space 122
Thamarat al-Funun (periodical) 28
theater(s) 5–6, 21–2, 24, 36, 49
  Arabic 104, 107, 111
  Khedivial 6
  and Nahda 101–4
  performances in 22
  rules and regulations 6
Thornton, Philip 90–1
Three days of Moroccan music concert series (1928) 85, 95
transgressions 28, 29, 31, 33, 35–7, 65, 81
transnationalism 55
traveling theater performances 101, 103
al-Tunisi, Bayram 52, 154, 155
Tunisia 83, 96, 97, 109–12
"Tunisian Folklore" (Snoussi) 92
Tunisian music 92, 96
turuq 'umumiyya 19

udabatiyya (minstrels) 2
'ulama' 22, 34
Um Kulthum 41, 44–8, 52, 192 n.15
Under Egypt's Sky (Taht Sama' Misr, 1928) 51
'Urabi Revolt (1881–2) 2
urbanization 42, 92
urban society 18, 168, 170
Urfi, Wedad 51, 161
al-Ustaz (The Master, journal) 1, 2

value systems 39, 40, 42
van Nieuwkerk, Karin 80
venereal diseases 62
Vienna Exposition (1873) 137
vinyl discs 11, 41, 43, 45–9
visual culture 3, 8, 10
Volpi, Mario 49

al-Wafi, Ahmad 98
Wahbi, Yusuf 106–8, 111, 158–60
al-Wahhab, Muhammad 'Abd 48, 60
Wasfi, Omar 72
Western
  civilization 168
  culture 163, 164
  education 159, 163
  fashion 32
  films 172
  intellectual trends 160
  literature 172
  modernism 159
  music 58, 59
  Orientalism 144
  practices 42
westernization (*tafarnuj*) 73, 74, 81, 144
women
  attire reform 34
  as audiences 75
  bodies 32, 33, 49–51, 63, 75, 80
  non-Muslim 32
  performers, singers and dancers 35–7, 53–5, 57–66, 135 (*see also* female performers in Beirut)
  presence in public places 18, 19, 28, 30–3, 63, 80
  prohibit wearing make-up 34
  propriety 34
  role in entertainment 10, 35, 75
  sex workers 57, 62–4
  voices 70, 75–7, 79, 80
World War I 5, 46, 58, 70, 71, 73, 111, 157
World War II 44, 73
Wyrtzen, Jonathan 85

Yafil, Edmond 88, 89
Yakan, Wali al-Din 154
Yaldız, Jamila 78

al-Yaziji, Ibrahim   150
al-Yaziji, Nasif   183 n.6
Young Turk Revolution (1908)   27, 29, 33
YouTube   48
al-Yusuf, 'Abd al-Rahman Bey   30
al-Yusuf, 'Abd al-Rahman Pasha   37
Yusuf, Sultana 54, 60

Zaghloul, Saad   44

zajal (event)   1, 2, 154
Zaydan, Jurji   4, 110, 151
   Salah al-Din al-Ayyubi   110
Zaynab (1930, film)   159, 164–72
al-Zayyat, Ahmad Hasan   159
Zubaida, Sami   56, 65
Zulfikar, Ibrahim   162
Zureiq, Constantin   40
el-Z'enni, Omar   73

www.ingramcontent.com/pod-product-compliance
Lightning Source LLC
Chambersburg PA
CBHW071824300426
44116CB00009B/1421